A Robinson-Patman Primer

A
ROBINSON-PATMAN
PRIMER

A Businessman's Guide
to the Law Against
Price Discrimination

EARL W. KINTNER

The Macmillan Company

Collier-Macmillan Limited, London

Prologue

Why Read This Book?

In our free enterprise system the allocation of goods and services is not achieved through the dictates of big government, nor do we tolerate such vital decision-making to reside in the hands of private monopoly. Centralized decision-making in either form must necessarily result in the three classical evils described by Adam Smith: high prices, a limitation on production, and a deterioration in the quality of the goods produced. For this reason, we have sought another means of regulating our economic order. Economic decision-making is decentralized. The allocation of goods and services is a function of consumer choice. And the vehicle for making the system work is the concept of free entry into free competitive markets.

If competition is the vehicle, one of its most crucial ingredients is price. In a competitive market, various businesses compete for the consumer's dollar. Competition takes many forms, but a lower price is certainly a powerful inducement to purchase. Companies that overprice go out of existence. The quantity of production becomes a function of consumer demand. The deterioration in quality of products and services attendant to monopoly disappears, with consumer choices being channeled to the products of lower-priced, efficient, and high-quality producers. For these reasons, determinations of price are among the most important and difficult decisions that constantly beleaguer the American businessman. A mistake can mean business failure.

Because pricing is so important under our system, it was inevitable that pricing abuses would occur. The abuses took three basic forms. By *fixing* prices among competitors or imposing prices on one's distributors, price competition, and thus lower prices, could be avoided. By unfair or *discriminatory* pricing, such as below-cost pricing in one market by a

v

company with a monopoly in another market, where prices could be raised to subsidize the below-cost prices, competitors could be driven out of business. By *deceptive* pricing, such as offering an item at "below list price," where in fact the item had never been offered at list, trade could be diverted from legitimate competitors because of the belief of the consumer that he was getting a bargain.

To prevent such abuses, our antitrust and trade regulation laws were devised. Implicit in these laws is a recognition that government has a role to play in the allocation of goods and services. But that role is not assumption of the pricing function. Rather, it is to provide the ground rules to assure that competition is both free and fair. Violation of these laws can subject the price fixer, discriminator, or deceiver to heavy penalties. For this reason, the difficulties of the pricing decision to the American businessman become compounded. Not only must he be careful not to price himself out of the market, he must be wary of the laws confining or restricting his pricing decision.

Of the three basic areas of the law governing pricing, undoubtedly the one most difficult for the businessman to comprehend is that governing price discrimination. He is able to understand the reason for, and what is involved in, the prohibition against price fixing. Deceptive pricing is a gimmick, and he knows it. But to tell him that he is required to compete in price, and then to say that, in certain circumstances, he cannot undersell a competitor, may seem somewhat inconsistent and irrational. That he may not be able to give a lower per unit price or an advertising allowance or service to a large customer may seem patently unreasonable. That he may have no defense, even though his competitors are engaged in the same practice, may seem completely unintelligible. Add to this the intricacies and refinements of the price discrimination law, and even the honest businessman may be inclined to throw up his hands in dismay.

And yet, a price discrimination law is necessary both to the nation as a whole and to the survival of the very businessman who criticizes its apparent inconsistencies and confusing requirements. Man both damns and fears what he does not understand.

My experience with businessmen over many years, both with the Federal Trade Commission (FTC) and in the private practice of law, has convinced me that the overwhelming majority of businessmen will make every effort to comply with the law *if they understand it.* Enlightened self-interest requires no less. It is with the honest belief that honest businessmen both desire and need to acquire a close degree of familiarity with this most important body of law that I have undertaken to write this book.

Succeeding chapters will relate why the laws were enacted, the policy behind them, what they provide, who enforces them, and how they are enforced. This book is not, however, a comprehensive treatise of every phase of price discrimination law. A library of many volumes would be necessary for that task. Rather, my intention is to provide a primer for the aware business executive. If the general practitioner who counsels businessmen similarly finds the primer helpful, as I hope he will, I shall be content with my effort. Every effort has been made to state every major premise of the price discrimination law and to provide meaningful examples of the application of the law to business practices. The scholarly propensity for footnotes has been ruthlessly suppressed here.

This book is not designed to teach businessmen how to be their own Robinson-Patman lawyers. The very idea is folly, because these laws are infinitely subtle and appear in an infinite variety of guises. But the businessman's awareness of these laws can be heightened, and if he is sufficiently aware to consult a specialist *before* the consequences of a contemplated course of action descend on him, a precious gain has been won.

Acknowledgment

Any book of this character is the product of many minds. I must gratefully acknowledge the assistance of two of my colleagues, Stephen S. Mayne and Jack L. Lahr, who made substantial research and editorial contributions to this book. Other colleagues, Thomas Meehan, Joseph E. Casson, Martin Schneiderman, James F. Mauze, James P. Mercurio, and Salvatore A. Romano, also contributed valuable research. My colleague Mark Joelson assisted in the final review of the text.

Bernie R. Burrus, Professor of Law at the Georgetown Law Center and my colleague in private practice, rendered invaluable research and editorial assistance as we together laboriously hammered out the shape and substance of this book during the past two years.

Finally, I must thank my wife, Pat, my son, Christopher, and my law partners for their patience and understanding during the long and trying period of this book's gestation.

E. W. K.

Contents

A Robinson-Patman Primer

Free Enterprise and the Role of Government Regulation

A belief in the constructive value of free enterprise is the lifeblood of the American economic way of life. Those who hold to this belief would protect the freedom of individuals and freely established corporate enterprises to borrow and save, to invent and produce, and to profit or fail. Free markets are looked to as the basic regulator of most of our economy.

The present wealth of our country may be fairly attributed to the freedom our people have enjoyed to develop themselves through education and hard work. Our great national resources and the accumulation of capital and human talent in large impersonal organizations have, to be sure, permitted dramatic technological developments in the twentieth century; but without the spur of competition among businesses large and small, no monolithic organization, however wealthy and well organized, could have produced the material prosperity and cultural opportunities that America now enjoys. American history justifies the faith of the great part of our business community in free enterprise.

1

Committed as we are to a system of democratic self-government, the shape of our economy can justify itself only as it contributes to the general welfare. Popular acceptance depends on a continued demonstration by the business community of the benefits that a free economic system can supply. Continued acceptance of the basic belief in the value of free enterprise by the business community itself is essential to broader acceptance by an ever more sophisticated public. To every captain of industry today, whether he commands a rowboat or an ocean liner, is presented a crucial challenge to assume responsibility for demonstrating by his words and his action his belief in the importance of free enterprise. He must assume this responsibility in his business life just as in his private life; he must assume the responsibility of a free citizen who wishes to remain free.

The problem is how to preserve the meaning of free enterprise. How can we maintain competitive free enterprise and all the benefits that free enterprise brings?

Even a nation dedicated to freedom must impose some restraints on the conduct of its citizens. At first we were content with an absolute minimum of restraint in the economic sphere as well as in the political sphere. But as the industrial revolution gained impetus and as our society became more complex, the need for more sophisticated restraints became painfully evident. In the heyday of our industrial development, a few used their individual freedom without regard to the many. Tolstoy described nineteenth-century Czarist Russia in terms that describe any nation in the midst of industrial revolution. "If the arrangement of society is bad and a small number of people have power over the majority and oppress it, every victory over nature will inevitably serve only to increase that power and that oppression. That is what is actually happening."

Restraints on rampant individualism were necessary in America, and restraints were imposed. But the *nature* of the restraint devised has a peculiarly American cast.

Americans hold centralization of power to be an absolute evil, regardless of whether that power is political or economic. Just as we reject the unchecked exercise of the power of decision by the state, so also do we reject the concentration of power in a few private hands. The cartelization of a nation's economy may well lead to the cartelization of its polity. A brief reference to the status of guilds in early mercantile economies is enough to establish the point.

Americans have always been activists. We are not disposed to apathy in the face of a threat to our vision of the good society. It became clear early in our history that some means would have to be devised to shake off the spread of private economic autocracy. The answer forged by our democratic processes was uniquely American. Think for a moment of the intellectual picture at the moment of decision. By that time a large number of Continental theorists had grappled with the problem. Saint Simon and the other academic socialists had long since published their answers to concentration of economic power in private hands. Karl Marx had completed his labors at the British Museum. The authors of the Paris Commune had furnished a brief augury of things to come. These theorists all held that the answer to undue concentration of economic power in a few private hands was concentration of economic power in the state. In America people wedded to the dispersion of power would not easily accept statism as a reply to monopolization. The instrument we devised to snip the tentacles of monopoly was the Sherman Antitrust Act of 1890. By the terms of that act, contracts, combinations, and conspiracies in restraint of trade, and monopolization, attempts to monopolize, and conspiracies to monopolize were declared to be illegal.

Instead of transferring economic power from one monolith to another, we invented a device to promote dispersal of power among private entrepreneurs. The major premise of antitrust is an unshakable belief in the efficacy of a competitive, free enterprise economy. The ideal to be realized is unlimited opportunity for entry into the market place, unlimited opportunity for self-development, and the resolution of economic issues by the unthwarted exercise of free market forces. In the process of taking power from monopolists only a minimum of power was transferred to the state. The sole reason for that transfer was to provide a governmental device for the dispersion of monopolistic power and the prohibition of harmful economic aggrandizement.

The basic principle embodied in our antitrust and trade regulation laws is conservative. These laws are based on a belief that the best method for reaching economic decisions is the unhampered interplay of free market forces. These laws were designed to preserve competition, not to eradicate it. These laws attack those forces that would restrict the right to compete. These instruments of national economic policy afford a means for avoiding the concentration of power, whether that concentration is in private hands, as in a monopoly, or in the hands of the government, as in a statist regime. They are a monument to the ingenuity of free men determined to preserve economic individualism. The existence of these instruments has meant that the American nation could reap the benefits of an expanding technology unhampered by cartels or controls.

This American ingenuity in the development of pragmatic solutions to national needs has extended to the enforcement of the antitrust and trade regulation laws as well as to the origination of those laws. By 1912 there was a universal recognition that a flexible instrument for the enforcement of laws insuring free and fair competition was needed. In that year, the platforms of the three political parties contained a plank to create an administrative agency to implement these vitally important laws. In 1914, that agency, the Federal Trade Commission (FTC), was created by the passage of the Federal Trade Commission Act. Modeled on the Interstate Commerce Commission (ICC), which was created in 1887 to regulate the nation's transportation system, the FTC was given a combination of judicial, legislative, and executive powers. This combination of powers has enabled the commission to devise and employ a wide variety of techniques to enforce the antitrust and trade regulation laws and to educate the community in the meaning of those laws. The history of the commission furnishes another example of the use of the principles of flexibility, moderation, and pragmatism by the American people to preserve their precious economic freedom.

The year 1914 also saw passage of the third of our triad of antitrust laws, the Clayton Act. Whereas the Sherman Act was a general statute, proscribing restraints of trade in general terms, the Clayton Act was directed at specific practices considered to be particularly inimical to competition. Included were certain types of price discriminations, exclusive arrangements, mergers, and interlocking directorates. Section 2 of that act, which contained the price discrimination prohibition, was the precursor of the Robinson-Patman Act of 1936.

The American answer to the problem of monopoly has been a good one. There has been no attempt to convert unlimited private power into unlimited governmental control. Instead, the single thrust of our political effort has been to guarantee individual freedom by limited governmental regulation. There has been no departure from the ideals of a plural, decentralized, permissive society dedicated to individualism.

The preservation of the ideal of a free enterprise economy from the threat engendered by the rise of the trust was a signal accomplishment. The governmental devices designed to preserve economic individualism have, on the whole, been very successful. However, new challenges threaten this ideal and new responses are continually needed. The pace of change is startling. The velocity and intensity of economic evolution approaches a state of constant revolution. New ways of accomplishing economic tasks proliferate. In space technology, for instance, we are seeing the onset of what may be a significant trend in economic organization. The rise of the government-sponsored nonprofit corporation and the university-sponsored nonprofit corporation and the development of ever more sophisticated relationships between prime contractors and subcontractors may have unforeseen consequences in the allocation of industrial power. This is not to suggest that there is anything sinister in these new developments, but they are indications of the constant need to assess the impact of organizational innovation on our traditional ideals. Another massive challenge facing the American pattern of economic organization is the gargantuan needs of underdeveloped nations faced with the task of expanding a narrow industrial base to meet the ever-rising expectations of increasing populations. A factor now shaping the future is the prolonged and unremitting struggle to integrate minority groups, in a meaningful way, into our economic and political order.

This is not an exhaustive list of identifiable factors impinging on the future of our competitive free enterprise economy; undoubtedly, trends not yet identified are already shaping the future. The purpose here is only to suggest the enormity of the task of preserving the ideal of individualism in a world where the shape of things changes with each tick of the clock.

At the present time a number of thoughtful citizens are actively debating the question of whether an economy dedicated to individualism and the profit motive can adequately satisfy great public needs for education, research, resource development, foreign aid, and defense.

However, a clear look at the shape and pace of change does not reveal either that our ideal must be abandoned or that the instruments that we have devised to effectuate that ideal have become obsolete. Our ideal, if vigorously defended, and our institutions, if imaginatively and effectively used, can deliver us from the perils that beset us. The best way to answer challenge is to set imaginative and daring men free. Mankind is best served in a society where the power of decision is dispersed and where an educated and responsible citizenry devises wise and effective solutions to national problems. Therefore, economic individualism must be defended. Antitrust and trade regulation laws will continue to be the most effective weapon in the conduct of that defense. So long as we insure that entry to the market place and the opportunity to compete in the market place exist and are not threatened by coercion or unlawful combination or stifling monopoly, then the creative and talented individual—our ultimate, last, and only hope—will have the opportunity to exercise his talents. So long as the free play of competition guarantees that the wages of obsolescence is failure, we need not fear change. Compliance with the antitrust laws by responsible businessmen and vigorous enforcement of the antitrust laws by responsible government agencies, therefore, become primary duties of those immediately charged with the defense of the national belief in free enterprise.

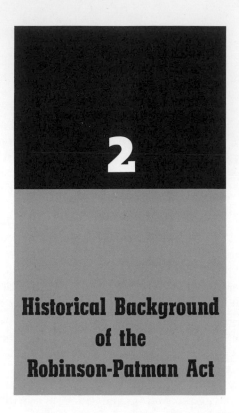

2

Historical Background of the Robinson-Patman Act

SECTION 2 OF THE CLAYTON ACT

The idea that discriminations in price could be a form of destructive competition that should be regulated by Congress developed shortly after the turn of the twentieth century. At that time, the antitrust activities of the federal government were largely directed toward breaking up the large monopolistic combinations that had developed in major industries. The government soon realized, however, that many of the anticompetitive practices would not cease merely because a trust was busted. It would be necessary to regulate the activities of some of our larger industrial concerns to prevent further monopolies.

The first specific congressional attempt to regulate price discrimination was embodied in Section 2 of the Clayton Act of 1914, and was directed at the territorial price discriminations practiced by the large monopolists of the day. These discriminations were largely in the form of localized price cutting to force out competitors. The expense of the price cut was usually offset by a corresponding raising of prices in some other part of the country where the seller had a monopoly, or it was offset by coerced rebates from the railroads or other shippers. The price discriminations were aimed largely at injuring competing sellers or manufacturers within a particular market. In order for these price discriminations to be effective there had to be a somewhat structured economic system. The seller would have to know that his competitor would be forced to use the same distribution system and could not make up the price cut in any other way.

The response of Congress to these evils was Section 2 of the Clayton Act (reprinted in its entirety in Appendix II), which made it unlawful for any person "either directly or indirectly to discriminate in price between different purchasers of commodities . . . where the effect of such discrimination may be to substantially lessen competition or tend to create a monopoly in any line of commerce." The language of this section contemplated continuance of the traditional manufacturer-wholesaler-retailer method of doing business and sought only to prevent discrimination at one of those levels of competition. Because the seller discriminating in price was, himself, relying on this distribution system to carry his price cutting to the market, this section could effectively restrict the direct price discriminations so commonly associated with cutthroat competition.

At the time of the passage of this section, it was not anticipated that there would be any serious alteration in the traditional tripartite marketing system. Nor was it considered necessary to extend the coverage of the section beyond a single "line of competition"—because it was not anticipated that there would be any opportunity for discrimination across competitive lines. The section proved relatively effective in eliminating the direct types of discrimination that prompted its passage. But the act was passed when the American economic community was on the threshold of drastically altering its merchandising practices. Shortly after the passage of the act, the chain store would develop into a major factor in the consumer market. It would do so by short-cutting many of the traditional distribution methods in favor of direct dealings on a volume basis with manufacturers. In other words, the chain stores would cut across the competitive lines that Congress, in passing Section 2 of Clayton, anticipated would remain unaltered. Under such circumstances, what was needed most was a flexible judicial approach to the language of Section 2. Unfortunately, the language of this section was strictly construed by the courts, and in 1923 the United States Second Circuit Court of Appeals so interpreted "line of commerce" as to limit the section's application to a lessening of competition between sellers. Buyer-level injury was not considered to be covered by the section. It was not

until six years later that the Supreme Court finally corrected this interpretation in *Van Camp & Sons* v. *American Can Co.* To do so the Court
had to ignore much of the legislative history of the act, and rely on the
"clear language" of the section to apply its restrictions to buyers.

The *Van Camp* decision, however, fell far short of remedying the
deficiencies of the section. Courts still gave such a narrow reading to the
"substantially lessen competition" clause that it was extremely doubtful
whether one local merchant engaged in resale of the seller's goods could
ever sustain sufficient injury to meet the requirement of substantiality.
Thus, only a large retailer, such as a chain buyer, could effectively rely on
the section, even after *Van Camp,* and these were the very ones inducing
the price discriminations from the sellers.

The section was also seriously crippled by two provisos added to the
bill before passage. The most damaging of these was the exception from
the act for quantity discounts. Anticipating only seller-level discrimination, Congress saw no compelling reason to prohibit volume discounts or
discriminations for variances in quantity because all sellers could sup-
posedly realize similar savings on such dealings. That not all buyers could
demand such discounts was not a discrimination contemplated by Section
2. The net effect of this exception was to exempt completely the chain
store practice of demanding large discounts for their volume purchases
without reference to the seller's actual saving under this method. Thus, a
small variation in quantity could support a large difference in price.

The section also excepted all price discriminations made to meet
competition, thus granting immunity to all pricing retaliation. So serious
a loophole was created by this exception, that Congressman Wright
Patman has described the meeting competition clause as "one of the main
reasons" that the law against price discrimination broke down. The few
independent retailers who could surmount the hurdles of "line of commerce" and "substantially lessen competition" would quickly find that
the manufacturer could readily point to a competitor engaging in similar
discounting and, thereby, avoid the section's application.

GROWTH OF CHAIN STORES

But it was not the exemptions or strict judicial interpretations that
caused the eventual amendment of Section 2. Rather, the section simply
was not geared to deal with the newly developed distribution methods
and the subtle coercions of the big-volume direct buyers. A major chain
store did not employ the traditional middleman considered so vital to
the operation of the manufacturer-wholesaler-retailer system. Instead,
the chain store bought directly from the manufacturer. The chain store

would, nonetheless, demand the standard brokerage commission in the form of a price reduction, and, because the manufacturer would otherwise pay it when dealing with wholesalers, it would be given at no additional cost by the manufacturer in order to placate a large-volume buyer. This "price reduction" would be passed on to the consumer as a lower retail price or used in advertising the retailer's goods. The independent retailer, forced to use the old brokerage route, could not obtain such savings and meet either the lower price or the increased advertising.

In other instances, the chain buyer might deal in such large volumes that the sheer size of his order gave him extraordinary leverage over the manufacturer. Discounts could be obtained far in excess of the cost savings for such quantity purchases. Or the buyer might wish some promotional service or facility as an additional return on his order. This might take the form of inclusion in the manufacturer's advertising campaigns or simply a special packaging for display purposes.

All of these practices represented new and different forms of price discrimination largely nonexistent when Section 2 of the Clayton Act was passed. Furthermore, they were discriminations that crossed competitive lines; that is, they were given to large-volume, direct-purchase retailers and denied to wholesalers—an arrangement that is really a buyer-level injury *totally* outside anything contemplated by Section 2, the *Van Camp* decision notwithstanding.

The cumulative effect of all these various exceptions, loopholes, and novel discriminatory arrangements was a total circumvention of the application of Section 2 by the chain store industry. Later, congressional hearings would reveal that the A & P Tea Co. had received discriminations and allowances of over $8 million in one year alone—all without fear of prosecution under the Clayton Act. Little of this enormous discount could ever be traced to ultimate consumer benefit in the form of lower prices. Left in this unbridled economic position, the chain stores were reshaping the economic face of the American retail market. The share of the retail market enjoyed by chain stores increased from 9 per cent in 1926 to 25 per cent in 1933, and the trend showed no sign of abating.

This trend toward mass marketing carried with it certain other traditionally unattractive side effects, not the least of which was absentee ownership. Because the large chains operated through local outlets controlled by the parent corporation, they were slowly eliminating the independent retailer. This was especially evident in the retail grocery market where much concern was expressed for the increasing disappearance of the local "corner grocer."

Being the group most seriously threatened by the growth of chain stores, retail and wholesale grocers were among the first to initiate activity to halt the burgeoning discriminations of the chain grocery stores. The first reaction was to form associations, primarily to increase bargaining strength with manufacturers, but also to increase their lobbying position with the government. The grocery associations attempted to arouse public interest by emphasizing the absentee ownership issue in the hope of stimulating some federal reaction.

The initial reaction to this growing concern over the chain store practices came from one of the recently created federal agencies of the New Deal. Codes of Fair Competition were promulgated under the National Industrial Recovery Act of 1933 to serve as industry guidelines for the regulation of discriminatory practices. Although they promised to stem the ever increasing power of the chain stores, the codes were short-lived. Bogged down in verbal confusion, they were eventually invalidated by the *Schechter* decision in 1935 as an unconstitutional delegation of legislative power to private groups. This meant that, short of legislative reform, there could be no additional relief expected from the government. This predicament led the retail and wholesale grocers to devote all their efforts toward the introduction of legislation in Congress. It was at the 1935 meeting of the United States Wholesale Grocers Association that the first model statute proposing comprehensive price discrimination legislation was suggested. Drafted by H. B. Teegarden, the proposal was introduced into the House of Representatives later that same year by Representative Wright Patman.

Even though the Grocers Association can be credited with formulating the original proposal, it was not alone responsible for the tremendous public outcry then being heard concerning the chain stores. In 1928, the Senate directed the FTC to conduct an investigation into the chain store industry. The focus of the investigation was to be the area of discriminatory pricing and the effectiveness of the Clayton Act in regulating it. The final report of that investigation was published as a Senate document in 1935. The information contained therein confirmed many of the worst suspicions about discriminatory practices in the chain store industry. The report disclosed a disturbing array of discriminations ranging from "dummy" brokerage to secret promotional allowances. It explored at great length the numerous subterfuges employed by chain stores to coerce discounts from buyers. The practices revealed by this report would serve as the factual backdrop for the formulation of the Robinson-Patman Act. So great was the impact of this exposé on the chain store industry that Representative Wright Patman later remarked that "one certain big concern had really caused the passage of this Act, the A & P Tea Company."

The FTC report served to focus the attention of the legislature on reform of the practices revealed and finally laid to rest any notions that existing price discriminations could be effectively controlled by minor amendments to Section 2 of the Clayton Act. Congress quickly realized that comprehensive legislation was the only solution, and a number of bills directed toward this result were introduced in both houses. The Patman Bill, which eventually was enacted without major alteration, was intended to counteract the discriminatory practices enumerated in the FTC Chain Store Report. The bill singled out certain of the practices for individual prohibition in addition to the general restriction placed on price discriminations. This accurately reflects the belief prevalent at that time that some of the discriminations were more pernicious than others— especially in those cases where the discount was disguised as something else, such as a brokerage fee.

LEGISLATIVE HISTORY

The legislative history of each section of the Robinson-Patman Act will be considered in detail in the respective chapters concerning such sections. We will now consider the legislative history of the act as a whole.

The Patman Bill was introduced in the House on June 11, 1935 and remained in committee until, in amended form, it was reported out on March 4, 1936. During the period that the bill was in committee it became apparent to the chain store industry, as well as to other sectors of industry, that the Patman Bill posed the most serious threat to existing merchandising practices. Consequently, a tremendous amount of pressure was brought to bear in an effort to tone down the bill before it was reported to the floor. Certain factors of the proposal also greatly disturbed the heavy-industry sector. During the hearings, a proposal was introduced to define *price* as the amount received minus freight costs defrayed by the seller. This base-point pricing method would have had the effect of confining price to f.o.b. arrangements and thus precluded the "delivered price" practices then in use. The base-point price definition was eventually dropped in what many commentators have described as a concession to heavy industry. There is some evidence in the record that the existence of independent legislation, already under consideration at that time, which focused directly on base-point pricing, was equally responsible for the deletion of the controversial definition of price. Whatever the reason, the event would prove fortuitous in that it served to isolate the chain stores in their opposition to the bill and would eventually provide the Patman forces with a strong bargaining position in the conference committee.

It was also during the House hearings that the farm cooperatives expressed their concern over the brokerage provisions in the bill. They feared that their practice of charging brokerage fees to large sellers and then distributing the profits from their operation to their various members would be precluded. It was believed that under the original language of the bill this would constitute a seller's payment of brokerage to an agent of the buyer and would be prohibited. The cooperatives, therefore, proposed that the bill be amended to include an exception for services actually rendered, as well as a clause permitting the distribution of profits to association members. Because the cooperatives maintained that they did perform actual brokerage services, the "for services rendered" proviso was thought to provide an exemption for their activities. This would seem the most logical construction of congressional intent in this area, because the farm cooperatives were largely a reaction to the competitive disadvantage created by the chain buyers and the bill was admittedly aimed at restricting the power of the chain stores. The amendment was added to the bill, although, as will be seen in the chapter on brokerage, it provided scant protection to the cooperatives.

Opposition to the Patman proposal during the time it was in committee became so intense that Representative Patman was led to complain that "a powerful lobby has gone into action against our bill. Much money is being spent to hire people with influence in an effort to try to persuade Members of Congress in both the House and the Senate to vote against this bill." This lobby proved largely ineffective in its opposition to the Patman Bill during the House committee hearings; the bill reported out of that committee, although somewhat amended, largely resembled the original Patman proposal so far as regulation of the chain store industry was concerned.

The House activity on the Patman Bill had been stimulated by the introduction of the companion measure, the Robinson Bill, in the Senate. Until then, the Patman Bill had remained unexplainably dormant in the House committee. By the time the Senate began hearings, the chain store industry had mobilized its opposition and the Senate considerations offered an interesting alternative not available during the House hearings. About the same time that the Robinson Bill was introduced in the Senate, another proposal, the Borah-Van Nuys Bill, was also placed before that body for consideration. Modeled on the Canadian Price Discrimination Act, the measure provided criminal penalties but also excluded quantity discounts and was otherwise difficult to apply. Seeing this as the weaker bill, and recognizing that the mood of Congress was such that some price discrimination legislation was bound to pass, the chain store industry adopted the strategy of supporting the Borah-Van Nuys Bill during the Senate hearings. With the announced purpose of supporting the Borah-Van Nuys measure, twenty-seven witnesses attacked the provisions of the Robinson Bill. This approach proved eminently successful in dampening Senate enthusiasm for the Robinson Bill, and that measure was the subject of a number of damaging amendments while in committee and later on the floor of the Senate during debate.

These amendments to the Robinson Bill took the form of exemptions for special industries, for example, an exemption for raw materials and for component parts used in further manufacture. Far more damaging than any of the limited exemptions was the addition of a restatement of the "meeting competition" defense that was part of the original Clayton Act. It had been the availability of this defense that had so completely emasculated the original law and prompted the Federal Trade Commission to propose the amendment of the Clayton Act. In fact, the initial FTC proposal had simply suggested elimination of this defense as the solution to the major roadblock to effective application of the act.

The last major alteration of the Robinson Bill constituted a major reversal for the chain store interests. Influenced by the support given to the Borah-Van Nuys Bill, the Senate appended that measure to the Robinson Bill, as Section 3. Thus, instead of having the Robinson Bill replaced by the more difficult to enforce criminal measure, the Robinson Bill was expanded to include possible criminal penalties for certain activities. Although this quite clearly represented a backfiring of the opposition's strategy, the over-all effect of the opposition to the Robinson Bill was moderately successful in the Senate. Many of the bill's stronger provisions were excised through exemptions, and the "meeting competition" defense offered a broad escape for many others.

Similar efforts to weaken the Patman Bill were attempted when that measure reached the floor of the House. In addition to the special industries exemptions added in committee, two amendments were offered during the course of the floor debates that would have narrowed greatly the intended scope of the bill. The first amendment was an attempt to restore the "meeting competition" clause—an effort that was successful in the Senate. Fearing that this would simply reestablish the confusion current under the existing Clayton Act provisions, Representative Patman mounted a strenuous and effective opposition to the amendment. A similar fate met an attempt to insert the clause "purchased under like conditions" after the requirement that the goods involved be of like grade and quality. The thrust of this amendment would have been to greatly expand the possible facts that could remove a particular sale from the coverage of the act. For example, the credit arrangements for a given sale could be considered a "condition" capable of exempting the transaction. Such an amendment would have been very similar to the quantity discount loophole already in the Clayton Act, because it would enable a seller to accomplish discriminatory pricing merely by varying the terms of sale to two different customers. Congressman Patman vigorously opposed the amendment and succeeded in having it rebuffed by the House. Having survived this flurry of floor amendments, the bill was approved by an overwhelming majority of 290 to 16.

The House measure was then sent to the Senate, where it suffered a major setback. The Senate amended everything after the enabling clause with the Senate version of the Robinson Bill. Normally this would not be a serious impediment to the eventual adoption of a strong act; however, in this case the Robinson Bill had been the subject of a successful assault by the chain store opposition, and, therefore, already contained numerous debilitating amendments. Following this Senate amendment, the two bills were submitted to the Joint Conference Committee for the formulation of a compromise solution. It was believed that this would result in an extensive weakening of the Patman Bill which, until now, had escaped relatively unscathed. In a somewhat surprising turn of events, the House measure prevailed on almost every controversial issue and the major enforcement provisions of the Patman Bill were preserved largely intact. The Senate Conferees proved willing to recede on almost every pertinent point, even to deleting the overly broad "meeting competition" defense amended to the Robinson Bill in favor of the narrower "meeting competition" defense of the Patman Bill. The areas in which the Senate bill was successful were largely in those provisions that strengthened the bill, including having the penal sections of the Borah-Van Nuys Bill added to the Robinson-Patman Bill as Section 3 of that measure. This compromise bill was approved by both houses of Congress and was finally signed into law on June 19, 1936.

The Robinson-Patman Act, although largely the original proposal of Representative Patman, nonetheless represents extensive legislative compromise both in the House committee and in the Joint Conference Committee. As a result, the end product is not the hallmark of clarity. It has been variously described as unworkable, hopelessly obscure, and the "Typhoid Mary" of antitrust. Much of this consternation results from the confusing language that was settled on in the joint conference. In protecting major provisions, the House conferees often sacrificed structural precision. Not all of the blame can be attributed to legislative compromise, however, because much of the confusion existing today stems from clauses unaffected by the congressional maneuverings. The statute employs a confusing combination of interrelated sections to regulate a method of doing business—mass merchandising—that was only vaguely understood at the time the bill was enacted.

This confusion surrounding the meaning of various sections of the act has made resort to legislative history essential in any examination of the act's provisions. But even the legislative history must be selectively considered. The fact that the Patman Bill managed to remain relatively unaltered through the deliberations in the House, and also prevailed in large part in the joint conference, indicates that the House reports and debates will provide the most pertinent reflection of congressional intent. Conversely, the extensive amending of the Senate measure and its subsequent undoing in joint conference render the Senate deliberations of questionable value in assessing the purposes behind the resulting act.

What is perhaps the most curious aspect of the Robinson-Patman Act is not discussed in either the committee reports or the floor debates. That is the fact that the act is directed against sellers who discriminate despite the fact that it was the activities of the large chain buyers that initially prompted the legislation. It has been suggested that this was largely the result of the belief, current at that time, that a measure regulating buyers would be considered unconstitutional by the Supreme Court. This position was somewhat supported by two earlier Supreme Court cases involving buyer and seller controls. In 1912, the Court had sustained state-imposed restrictions on seller activity in *Central Lumber Co.* v. *South Dakota*. Fifteen years later, the Court overturned state regulations on buyers in *Fairmont Creamery Co.* v. *Minnesota*. Congress is alleged to have interpreted these two decisions as indicating a constitutional distinction between buyer and seller restrictions. Consequently, determined to regulate the area, Congress chose the safest method of so doing. If this interpretation is correct, and the actual circumstances of the two cases would cast considerable doubt on that fact, then it appears that the entire approach of the Robinson-Patman Act was fashioned by a misreading of these somewhat obscure cases. The *Fairmont* decision declared unconstitutional a state statute that criminally penalized *any* discriminations in price—except shipping costs—without regard to competitive conditions or relative market conditions. Furthermore, the statute was allegedly directed at monopolistic activities, although Fairmont Creamery was a small producer in a highly competitive market. The Court based its ultimate conclusion on interference with freedom of contract, a theory that would seem to apply with equal force to seller or buyer. Lastly, the decision is an assessment of the state police power in an area where there was federal activity. It would seem, therefore, that there was little real ground for congressional uneasiness over restrictions on buyers, and the circuitous approach of Robinson-Patman was unnecessary.

To further obscure the question, the only consideration given to the constitutionality of the act during congressional debate concerned a rather short reflection on the congressional power to protect interstate commerce from destructive practices that injure competition. No mention is made of any concern over buyer abuses; in fact, the prohibition against buyer inducement of discriminations was included in the Robinson-Patman Act as a matter of apparent afterthought, and exists as the only section that would constitute a direct restriction on chain buyers. Congressional attention to the discriminatory practices of Standard Oil and the railroads may well provide an alternative theory for explaining the seller orientation of Robinson-Patman. The original Section 2 was definitely a seller-oriented control and was devised to handle the traditional forms of seller discrimination—thus, its inadequacy in a mass-merchandising market is apparent. The original proposals for reform merely contemplated amendment of the existing section by deletion of the more obvious loopholes. This, in turn, developed into a full-blown replacement of the existing section with a far more detailed regulatory scheme, but the mold had already been set in the shape of a continuation of the approach of the old Section 2. This would certainly explain congressional attention to the earlier evils prompting original Clayton 2 and would also explain congressional silence on what would otherwise seem the obvious alternative of buyer controls.

3

A Bird's-Eye View
of the
Robinson-Patman Act

As we have seen, Section 2 of the Robinson-Patman Act is an amendment to Section 2 of the Clayton Act and is divided into six parts. Section 2 of the Robinson-Patman Act imposes civil prohibitions, whereas Section 3 contains criminal prohibitions.

Section 2(a) is the heart of the act. It prohibits sellers from discriminating in price. The section also provides a defense when an otherwise unlawful price discrimination can be cost justified by the seller, and other limited defenses and exceptions.

Section 2(b) is related to 2(a) and sets forth burdens of proof in defending a violation. Section 2(b) also provides that a price discrimination is not unlawful if it is made in good faith to meet the equally low price of a competitor. That a lower price was made to meet lawful competition is a complete defense to a Section 2(a) violation.

Section 2(c) is a self-contained section prohibiting the seller from paying any brokerage fee, commission, or an equivalent to a buyer or the buyer's agent. Section 2(c) also prohibits a buyer from accepting any such brokerage fee or commission.

Sections 2(d) and 2(e) are closely related and prohibit a seller from granting discriminatory allowances [2(d)] and services and facilities [2(e)] to a buyer unless such assistance is made available to other competing buyers on proportionally equal terms.

Section 2(f) is the section of the act dealing with buyers who knowingly receive price discriminations declared unlawful in Section 2(a). Remembering again the congressional concern over the purchasing power wielded by large buyers to exact price discriminations, Section 2(f) is designed to deal directly with such buyers.

Section 3 declares it unlawful for a seller to provide certain secret allowances to the buyer. It also forbids territorial price reductions or sales at unreasonably low prices where the seller's purpose is to destroy competition or to eliminate a competitor.

PRICE DISCRIMINATION PRACTICES BY THE SELLER: SECTION 2(A)

We will first consider the "jurisdictional elements"—those conditions that will invoke the power of the Federal Trade Commission or the courts to consider the lawfulness of the pricing transactions. In this connection we will consider which sellers are within the reach of Section 2(a), and will then consider the competitive effects necessary to give rise to a completed violation of Section 2(a) by a seller.

Which Sellers Can Be Reached Under 2(a)?

Turning first to the *commerce requirement,* Section 2(a) begins, "That it shall be unlawful for any person engaged in commerce, in the course of such commerce . . . ." If a seller, such as a corporation, is engaged in purely local commerce within one state, the prohibitions of the act do not apply. It should be mentioned, however, that many states have comparable acts that can regulate local pricing activities. Also, by contrast, the scope of control is more limited here than in the Sherman Act, under which intrastate activities affecting interstate commerce can be reached. If a local seller in Illinois unlawfully discriminates between his two Chicago buyers, for example, the act does not apply. But if this seller discriminates between a Chicago buyer and a competing St. Louis buyer, the commerce requirement of the act is satisfied—that is, a state line has been crossed in the transaction.

In a famous case involving Standard Oil, the Supreme Court had to interpret this commerce requirement. Gasoline was shipped from Whiting, Indiana, to bulk storage tanks near Detroit, Michigan. The government charged that certain unlawful discriminatory practices took place in the distribution of the gasoline from these storage tanks to local Detroit buyers. The defendant sellers in this suit said, in effect, "You cannot charge any Section 2(a) violation because these Detroit practices are not in commerce—every act charged as unlawful took place entirely in Michigan." The Supreme Court rejected this argument and concluded that the practices all took place in the flow of commerce from Whiting, Indiana, to the Detroit area buyers. The interstate character of the acts was not lost by storing the gasoline in Detroit.

Price discrimination by a United States seller in foreign commerce is not covered by the act; thus, if a seller in the United States discriminates unlawfully between foreign buyers, the transaction cannot be reached. The act is, however, applicable to transactions in the import trade. If a foreign seller discriminates between competing American purchasers, it may be difficult as a practical matter to reach the seller because he cannot be served abroad with service of process. But if he is "found" within the United States through the presence of a domestic agent or controlled subsidiary, service of process and federal jurisdiction may be effected on the foreign seller for purposes of enforcing the statute.

Next, there is the requirement that the *same seller make at least two sales to different purchasers, reasonably close in point of time.* A sale to one buyer and an outright refusal to sell to another cannot come under Section 2(a). Similarly, a sale to one buyer and a consignment to another cannot normally be reached under Section 2(a).

The requirement for *reasonably contemporaneous sales* affords protection to the seller and prevents any "freezing" of pricing practices over long periods of time. Without this requirement, a seller simply could not change his prices at any time without fear of violating the act. Of course, individual situations in particular industries will determine what are contemporaneous sales under the law. A two-month difference between two sales might not be reached under Section 2(a) in one industry, whereas an even longer period between sales might be reached in another industry. Inventory turnover, fluctuation of prices in the market place, and other factors are considered in determining if this time requirement has been satisfied; no rule of thumb exists.

The requirement that the *same seller* make these sales raises interesting questions when a parent corporation makes one of the sales while a wholly owned subsidiary makes the other. Under these circumstances the courts appraise the degree of control exercised by the parent corporation over its subsidiary to determine if the latter is but an instrument of the former. If the subsidiary acts independently and without direction by its parent, it may be considered a separate seller, and differing prices for the same commodity between parent and subsidiary would not be illegal price discriminations.

Another legal invention—the doctrine of the "indirect purchaser"—has been developed over the years to determine who are the actual purchasers to whom the sales are made. Suppose Manufacturer M sells to Wholesaler W, who in turn sells to Retailers R_1 and R_2. Suppose, furthermore, that Manufacturer M, not Wholesaler W, really controls sales to R_1 and R_2. Such control might occur by having M's salesman call on R_1 and R_2, take the order, and then refer it to W. Although it would appear that M has made only one sale—that being to W—a court might hold that R_1 and R_2 were indirect purchasers from M because of M's activity in obtaining these retailers as customers. If different prices were charged R_1 and R_2, an illegal price discrimination might be involved.

Now we turn to the requirement that the sales be of *commodities*. This means goods, not services. For example, the act would not reach a consulting engineering firm that charged different rates for engineering services to different companies. Such a contract would be for the sale of services, not for the sale of goods. Radio or TV broadcasting time is another example of a service to which the act would not apply under current case law. Only tangible goods in the conventional sense are embraced by the term *commodities*. Service discriminations may, however, be illegal as "unfair methods of competition" under Section 5 of the Federal Trade Commission Act.

The commodities involved must be of *like grade and quality*. When identical goods are sold, these requisites are, of course, satisfied. But how much difference between similar commodities will allow an "escape hatch" from a Section 2(a) charge of price discrimination? It has been held that a price discrimination in the sale of identical goods between those sold under a private brand label and those sold under a prominent trademark is embraced by Section 2(a). On the other hand, minute physical differences, strangely enough, have caused some courts to rule the transaction beyond the reach of Section 2(a). The better view seems to be, however, that such small differences will not prevent goods from being of "like grade and quality." For instance, in one case, sales of cans 3 and 14/16 inches and 3 and 12/16 inches high were reached under Section 2(a). The Attorney General's Committee to Study the Antitrust Laws aptly summarized the current rule in these terms: "Actual or genuine physical differentiations between two different products adapted to the several buyers' uses, and not merely a decorative or fanciful feature, probably remove differential pricing of the two from the reach of the Robinson-Patman Act."

Judicial refusal to recognize brand names and trademark differences in considering like grade and quality, is not completely consistent with marketing realities. Marketing executives well appreciate that two identical products standing side by side on a shelf will not sell alike where only one is a widely advertised, national brand. Hypothetically, Coca-Cola will sell better than Sparkle Cola in the market place, even if they are of identical composition. Following this hypothesis a little further, if Coca-Cola and Sparkle Cola are sold *in different bottle designs* by the same bottling distributor to different competing purchasers at different prices, it will be understandably difficult to convince a sophisticated businessman that this is an unlawful price discrimination under Section 2(a).

Some relief from the harsh consequences of the judicial rulings on like grade and quality may be provided, however, by a recent decision in which a court of appeals gave recognition to the marketing realities by taking into consideration the higher consumer demand for nationally advertised products over the physically identical private label products in assessing whether the requisite injury to competition under Section 2(a) had been occasioned by the price differential. The court held that if the price differential does no more than reflect the greater consumer demand for a product sold under a popular trademark, then no competitive injury can occur.

What Are the Competitive Effects Necessary to Show a Completed Section 2(a) Violation?

Sections 2(a)'s concluding proviso reads:

> That it shall be unlawful . . . to discriminate in price . . . where the effect of such discrimination [1] may be substantially to lessen competition or [2] tend to create a monopoly in any line of commerce, [3] or to injure, destroy or prevent competition with any person who either [a] grants [b] or knowingly receives the benefit of such discrimination, [c] or to customers of either of them.

Basically, Congress sought to distinguish price discrimination practices having no real anticompetitive effect on commerce from pricing situations that have anticompetitive consequences. Only those discriminations having one of the listed adverse effects on competition are illegal. The nature of the competitive effect necessary to finding a violation of Section 2(a) varies both with the standard of illegality relied upon and the level of competition affected.

It should be noted that there are three distinct tests of illegality under Section 2(a) [(1), (2), or (3) above]. The first two, which are carryovers from the original Section 2 of the Clayton Act, require an adverse competitive impact in the total relevant market, whereas the inquiry under the third test—that portion added by the Robinson-Patman amendments to the original Section 2—focuses more narrowly upon the probability of an adverse impact on the competitive relationship between the discriminating seller and his competitors (primary-line injury), between the favored and disfavored purchasers (secondary-line injury), and between the customers of either of them (third-line injury). The Robinson-Patman amendments had the desired effect of easing the burden of demonstrating the illegality of a price discrimination by eliminating the necessity for an exhaustive market analysis. For this reason the original Section 2 tests of illegality contained in the present Section 2(a) generally have not been relied upon to establish a violation of the act. Let us now consider the contexts in which competitive injury under the Robinson-Patman amendments ([3] above) can be found.

Primary-Line Injury at the Seller's Level

Consider the situation in which two sellers, S_1 and S_2 are competing in the market place for the sale of goods. S_1 and S_2 are competing in Pennsylvania, and S_1 is also selling in other states, but not in competition with S_2. Suppose S_1 ruthlessly sets out to drive S_2 out of business. Suppose, furthermore, that in order to accomplish this purpose, S_1 slashes his long-established prices by 25 per cent in Pennsylvania. S_1 sells below cost in Pennsylvania but is able to do this because he has raised his prices in the area where S_2 does not compete. Here is a clear case of primary-line or seller's-level injury. The purpose and effect of S_1's price reduction is to destroy S_2 in Pennsylvania. In addition to creating liability under Section 2(a) of the Robinson-Patman Act, this practice may also amount to an attempt to monopolize, prohibited by Section 2 of the Sherman Act, or to a violation of Section 3 of the Robinson-Patman Act. Of course, if S_1 did not have the economic power to work competitive injury on S_2, no violation would have occurred.

Secondary-Line Injury at the Buyer's Level

Consider the situation in which a hypothetical manufacturer-supplier, M, sells to two buyers, B_1 and B_2, who are in direct competition with each other. Now, suppose that M lowers his price to B_1 but not to B_2. The requisite effect on competition will be present if B_2 is significantly less able to compete with B_1 because of the price discrimination.

Let us now vary the situation and consider buyer-level injury again. Suppose that B_1 is a "split distributor," competing with B_2 for the same customers and also selling to a retailer, R_1, who sells to these customers. The fact that B_1 is not in competition with B_2 on sales to R_1 does not prevent any price differential granted in favor of B_1 from wreaking the necessary competitive injury with respect to the competition that does exist between B_1 and B_2.

A more difficult problem is raised by the following facts: M sells to two wholesalers, B_1 and B_2; B_1 sells to a retailer, R_1; and B_2 sells to another retailer, R_2; R_1 and R_2 are in direct competition with one another for the same consumers; B_1 and B_2 do not directly compete with each other since each retailer, R_1 and R_2 has an exclusive dealing contract with his wholesaler. In other words, B_1 cannot sell to R_2, and B_2 cannot sell to R_1. Thus, B_1 and B_2 buy from the same supplier, each wholesales the product in the same market, and the retailers supplied by each compete for the patronage of the same consumers. While not falling within the traditional notion of competition, it would seem that B_1 and B_2 are competitors in practical effect since a wholesaler's success will depend in large part upon the success of the retailers to which it sells. If a lower price to one of the wholesalers, B_1, results in a lower price to his customer R_1, enabling R_1 to underprice R_2, and if R_2's business declines and causes as a result a decline in B_2's sales to R_2, then B_2 would appear to be injured in his competition with B_1, the favored wholesaler-purchaser. B_2 should be permitted to sue M for the competitive injury suffered by him at the secondary level. The disfavored retailer R_2, of course, may also have a cause of action against M for the resulting injury at the third level in his competition with R_1.

An entirely different situation arises where B_1 and B_2 do not compete for the same customers, either directly or indirectly. Suppose that M is a refiner-supplier of gasoline, that B_1 runs a fleet of taxicabs, and that B_2 is a retail gasoline dealer. Because B_1 purchases gasoline for use in his taxicabs and not for resale, he is not in competition with B_2. M can, therefore, quote B_1 a lower gasoline price without fear of working any injury to competition.

Another common situation in which no buyer-level injury is present occurs where B_1 and B_2 do not actually compete in a geographic market. Suppose M, our gasoline supplier, sells to B_1 in Alaska and to B_2 in Florida. B_1 and B_2 obviously do not compete for the same business, so there is no buyer-level competitive injury if B_2 receives a lower price than B_1. There is a more difficult situation when the geographic areas are close to one another. If B_1 sells to customers in downtown Chicago and B_2 sells to customers in the suburbs of Chicago, it may well be that B_1 and B_2 would be considered as competitors for the same customers. Any price discrimination between B_1 and B_2 could, therefore, have the requisite buyer-level injury.

Even in those situations in which there is a discrimination in price between two buyers who compete for the same business, there must be an adverse effect on competition *as a result* of this price discrimination. If the "injured" buyer loses business in the market place not as a direct result of a price cut given to his competitor, but because of poor management, a bad location, or his own pricing policies, it cannot be said that there is an injury to competition as a result of the price differential.

Third-Line Injury

This type of injury is suffered by a disfavored customer in his competition with customers of the supplier's favored buyer, three steps down the distribution chain. Suppose our gasoline supplier, M, who may be a refiner, sells his gasoline both to an integrated jobber-retailer, JR_1, and to an independent jobber, J_2, who in turn sells to a retail gasoline station, R_2, who competes with JR_1 for the same retail business. M sells at a lower price to J_2 than JR_1 even though JR_1, in his capacity as a jobber, performs the same functional activities as J_2. If the lower price to J_2 results in a lower price to R_2, enabling R_2 to underprice JR_1 at the retail level, then JR_1 may be injured in his competition with R_2, who in this instance operates at the third level in the favored distribution system.

A more controversial example of third-line injury arises out of the following factual context: Suppose our gasoline supplier, M, sells his gasoline both to a retailer gasoline station, R_1, and to an independent jobber, J, who in turn sells to another retail gasoline station, R_2. R_1 and R_2 both compete for the same retail business. M sells at a lower price to J than to R_1. If the lower price to J results in a lower price to R_2, enabling R_2 to underprice R_1, the necessary competitive injury may have occurred at the retail level.

A situation of this type arose in a FTC case involving Standard Oil. The refiner defended on the ground that resale price fixing (a violation of the Sherman Act) would be necessary if his pricing policy were to be condemned as a violation of the Robinson-Patman Act. Standard argued that the only way it could be certain that its jobber customer did not pass the lower price on to the jobber's retailer customers would be to control the jobber's resale prices, a result which would put it in the strange position of having to violate the Sherman Act by engaging in resale price maintenance in order to avoid violating the Robinson-Patman Act by causing competitive injury among the customers of its buyer. A federal court of appeals rejected this argument and affirmed the FTC's finding of Robinson-Patman Act liability.

Fourth-Line Injury

Although the tests of illegality under the original Clayton Act which were carried forward into the present Section 2(a) [tests (1) and (2), page 21] appear to contain no limitation upon the level of distribution at which competitive injury must occur in order to make a price discrimination actionable under the act, the Robinson-Patman amendments contained in Section 2(a) (test [3], p. 21) have generally been regarded as limited, in terms, to third-line injury. In other words, injury to competition occuring at the fourth level or beyond has not been regarded as creating liability under that standard. The Supreme Court rejected this contention in *Perkins* v. *Standard Oil of California*. Perkins, an integrated wholesaler-retailer, paid a higher price for Standard gasoline than another wholesaler operating in the same market area. The favored wholesaler resold its gasoline to a trucker who in turn resold to retail outlets which were in competition with retail outlets operated by and supplied by Perkins. The retail outlets, to whom the benefits of the price discrimination were passed, operated at the fourth level of distribution: supplier (1), favored wholesaler (2), trucker (3), and retailer (4). It was held that the competitive injury suffered by Perkins in his competition with the favored retailer, a customer of a customer of the favored wholesaler purchaser, was cognizable under Section 2(a). The Court noted, however, that before an injured party can recover damages under the act, "he must . . . be able to show a causal connection between the price discrimination in violation of the Act and the injury suffered. This is true regardless of the 'level' in the chain of distribution on which the injury occurs."

Let us now assume that a Section 2(a) charge has been proved; that is, (1) two or more consummated sales, (2) reasonably close in point of time, (3) of commodities, (4) of like grade and quality, (5) with a difference in price, (6) by the same seller, (7) to two or more different purchasers, (8) for use, consumption, or resale within the United States or any territory thereof, (9) that may result in competitive injury, and (10) the commerce requirement has been satisfied. We will now consider the defenses available to the seller to avoid liability under Section 2(a).

THE SELLER'S POSSIBLE DEFENSES TO A SECTION 2(A) VIOLATION

Even if a prima facie case of a violation of Section 2(a) is established, a seller may have a complete defense to that charge in the two following situations: (1) The price differentials "make only due allowance for differences in the cost, other than brokerage, of manufacture, sale, or delivery resulting from the differing methods or quantities in which such commodities are to such purchasers sold or delivered;" or (2) The price differentials were "made in good faith to meet an equally low price of a competitor, or the services or facilities furnished by a competitor."

Cost Justification

The cost justification defense stems from the economic premise that a seller should not be compelled by law to charge an artificially high price to a particular buyer if the seller can show by facts and figures that it costs less to sell to this particular buyer than to other buyers. If the seller actually makes more money selling to buyer A than to buyer B when the price is the same to both, the act allows the seller to reduce the price to A to the extent that this reduction in price is based on the actual lower cost of selling to A. Such cost savings might result from A's purchasing practices, savings in shipping costs, reduced sales expense, or a host of other factors.

Knowledgeable executives, however, will appreciate that distributive cost accounting is far from an exact science; indeed, in most cases a seller has no idea at all as to the exact cost of selling a certain quantity of goods to a certain customer. Several accounting techniques are customarily used to determine the approximate cost of different parts of the manufacturing and distribution process. But the inexact nature of these cost figures, together with the traditionally strict requirements of the Federal Trade Commission in proving cost justification, has made this defense a difficult and expensive one to prove. Guidelines for making use of the cost justification defense are few, and the hazards are many.

There are recent indications that a more flexible approach will be taken toward this defense in the future. For example, in the *Sylvania Electric Products* case, Sylvania was charged with a violation of Section 2(a) in granting unlawful price differences in sales of about 600 variously priced types of replacement vacuum tubes. These tubes were sold both through the Philco Corporation and through Sylvania's own distributors. Sylvania accounting executives and lawyers undoubtedly appreciated the practical impossibility of cost justifying *exactly* every difference in the sale of each of these 600 items. Time and expense militated against such a formidable task, and even if successful on paper, the results would not have had the mathematical certainty of the engineers' calculations that went into the design of these vacuum tubes. Nevertheless, Sylvania was successful in cost justifying the price difference to the satisfaction of the FTC. Sylvania employed a "weighted-average" method to demonstrate that aggregate price differences in distributing the vacuum tubes through the two outlets justified charging a higher price to Sylvania's own distributors than to Philco. The FTC thus accepted the distribution-pricing policy of Sylvania for its entire product line of 600 vacuum tubes, and on this basis the price difference between individual vacuum tubes was not considered to be of competitive significance. One tube was not designed to be competitive against another tube, so the study reflected the realities of electronic tube distribution.

A few generalizations are appropriate in evaluating cost justification. Suppose manufacturer M sells to three buyers—B_1, B_2, and B_3—and discriminates in favor of B_1. In seeking to cost justify his price to B_1, M contends that the total purchases by B_1 make M's total volume great enough that certain cost economies are possible in M's over-all production process. This is not permissible. M cannot say that the goods sold to B_1 reflect the entire savings in the unit cost of manufacturing. Because the extra volume necessary to the cost economies would vanish if B_2 and B_3 withdrew their business, B_2 and B_3 have just as much right to a price reduction as B_1 on this basis. On the other hand, if M, as a service to his buyers, maintains warehouse facilities for goods after they are sold, and B_1 agrees to take over the warehousing of the goods he buys, or if B_1

accepts less expensive crating, M can pass these cost savings on to B_1 in the form of a price concession.

It is difficult, if not impossible, to cost justify special treatment to new customers or discounts based on the cumulative volume of business per year that have no relationship to the size of individual shipments. A new customer normally is as expensive to serve as an old customer. Annual volume bears no necessary relationship to shipping costs. Similarly, quantity discount schedules must be developed with care if they are to be protected by the cost justification defense. Only if these schedules accurately reflect cost differences will the defense be available. In this connection it is important to note that cost justification must be substantially complete. If a seller can only justify part of the price difference, the defense will not prevail.

The seller whose first efforts to cost justify an otherwise unlawful price discrimination occur *after* a charge under Section 2(a) is made necessarily labors under a disadvantage in the ensuing legal proceedings. The prudent businessman should make some realistic cost justification appraisals to support the price concession *before* the concession is given to a particular buyer. "Good faith" efforts to comply with Section 2(a) before the pricing practices are challenged put a seller in a much better position.

Defense of Meeting Competition

Lowering prices in a good faith attempt to meet an equally low and lawful price of a competitor is a complete defense to an alleged violation of Section 2(a). This defense, however, has always been strictly limited by the Federal Trade Commission, and legislation has even been proposed to abolish it entirely. Thus, although the defense is generally available, strict rules have been developed for designating certain situations in which it may not be employed.

One of the recent issues before the courts is whether the defense of meeting competition is available to a seller who uses Section 2(a) price discrimination aggressively to gain new customers by offering such potential customers a price as low as that of a competitor. The FTC ruled that the defense is available only when a lower price was granted in order to retain an old customer and not when motivated by a desire to obtain new customers. But in the *Sunshine Biscuits* case, a federal court of appeals reversed this ruling and held that price discriminations otherwise prohibited by Section 2(a) can be defended by showing that in striving for new business the price discrimination in favor of a new customer was made in good faith to meet the equally low price of a competitor.

There are a number of restrictions on the use of the defense of meeting competition. First, the seller cannot claim this defense if he knows or should have known that the competitor's price he met was itself unlawful under the Robinson-Patman Act. Secondly, the seller's price discrimination must be a temporary measure to meet competition and not part of a permanent price schedule whereby some customers are systematically charged higher prices than others. Thirdly, an equally low price of a competitor "means an equally low price for a given quantity." Fourthly, it is the view of the FTC that the seller's price discrimination must be limited to meeting a specific individual competitor's price to specific individual customers. Finally, the seller must meet, not beat, his competitor's price to the particular customer.

We can now see that the defense of meeting competition is not an easy "out" for a seller who is alleged to have violated Section 2(a). This defense is severely limited but still absolute when proved.

Other Defenses and Exemptions

Certain transactions are exempted from the provisions of Section 2(a). For example, price changes made in response to changing conditions affecting the market for or the marketability of the goods concerned may not be illegal. This category embraces actual or imminent deterioration of perishable goods, obsolescence of seasonal goods, distress sales under court process, or sales in good faith in the course of discontinuing business in the goods concerned. Section 4 of the act provides that profits legally obtained by a cooperative association may be distributed to members of the association without violation of the act. And, supplementary legislation was passed in 1938 that declares the act not applicable "to purchases of their supplies for their own use by schools, colleges, universities, public libraries, churches, hospitals, and charitable institutions not operated for profit." Sales to the federal government are exempt, and state and municipal bodies probably enjoy this exemption as well. The nature and extent of these exemptions is largely unexplored, however.

PROHIBITIONS AGAINST THE BUYER: SECTION 2(F)

Section 2(f) declares it unlawful for a buyer knowingly to induce or receive a price discrimination that is in violation of Section 2(a).

Like Section 2(a), Section 2(f) relates solely to *price* discrimination. A literal reading of the section would apparently preclude a buyer from being reached for knowing receipt of discriminatory grants of allowances or services and facilities. This apparent legislative omission has been remedied in part by attacking the practice as an unfair method of competition in violation of Section 5 of the Federal Trade Commission Act.

It is a difficult task to prove that a buyer has violated Section 2(f). The Supreme Court has taken the position that there must be some evidence that the buyer knew of the illegality of the price discrimination, and there must also be some evidence of the buyer's knowledge that the concession was not saved from illegality by the defenses of cost justification or meeting competition. It follows that a buyer can avoid a Section 2(f) violation by showing that the seller did not violate Section 2(a) in the first place, that the prices were justified by available defenses, or that the buyer had no knowledge of the seller's violation of Section 2(a).

UNLAWFUL BROKERAGE PAYMENTS: SECTION 2(C)

Section 2(c) is a self-contained legislative enactment, having no relationship to the other sections of the Robinson-Patman Act. Violation of this section is in the nature of a per se wrong, without regard to a showing of competitive injury. By the terms of Section 2(c) it is unlawful: (1) to pay or grant, (2) or to receive or accept, (3) anything of value as a commission, brokerage, or other compensation, or any allowance or discount in lieu thereof, except for services rendered, (4) in connection with the sale or purchase of goods, wares, or merchandise, (5) either to the other party to such transaction or to an agent, representative, or other intermediary therein, (6) where such intermediary is acting in fact for or in behalf, or is subject to the direct or indirect control, of any party to such transaction other than the person by whom such compensation is so granted or paid.

If a seller pays a buyer's broker a sales brokerage commission, Section 2(c) is violated. In effect, it is only the *seller's* broker who can lawfully receive a brokerage fee. And, it makes no difference that the buyer's broker is performing some valuable function, such as warehousing or breaking bulk. The "except for services rendered" clause has been emasculated by cases that say that a buyer's broker does not render services to the seller.

This section is aimed at reaching dummy brokerage payments that are in reality "under the table" price concessions eventually falling into the hands of the buyer. Section 2(c), being self-contained, does not permit a defense of meeting competition or cost justification. Also, unlike Section 2(a), only one transaction—one payment by a seller to a buyer's broker—comprises a Section 2(c) violation, and a specific effect on competition need not be shown. For these reasons it is a far simpler task to prove a Section 2(c) violation than a Section 2(a) violation.

In *Federal Trade Commission* v. *Henry Broch & Company,* a seller's broker accepted a lower commission to clinch a sale, the seller passing on the reduction in the broker's commission as a lower price to the buyer. The Supreme Court held that Section 2(c) had been violated by this transaction. The Court perceived no economic difference between such a transaction and one in which the seller's broker split his brokerage commission with the buyer. The direct relationship between the brokerage fee and the lower price to the buyer was an important consideration in determining that Section 2(c) had been violated. *Broch* would appear to dictate that any adjustment of a broker's fees should be made with reference to all future sales to avoid the fee-splitting hazard on specific sales that was condemned by the Supreme Court.

MERCHANDISING ALLOWANCES AND SERVICES: SECTIONS 2(D) AND 2(E)

If the Robinson-Patman Act prohibited price discriminations alone, many opportunities for evasion and contravention of the basic purpose of the law would be available. Experienced marketing executives know there are many ways in which a supplier can favor one customer over other customers beyond the grant of a concession in price. Think for a moment of all the various types of merchandising assistance that suppliers customarily offer to retailers: advertising and promotional allowances, handbills and signs, window and floor displays and other point-of-purchase display materials, demonstrators and demonstrations, display and storage cabinets, "push money" for sales clerks, special packaging or package sizes, warehouse facilities, return privileges—the list is virtually endless.

When the Robinson-Patman Act was passed, Congress was well aware of the economic importance of advertising and promotional allowances and of merchandising services and facilities furnished by suppliers to customers. The act contains provisions to deal with discriminations by suppliers in these critical areas. Section 2(d) of the act relates to payments or allowances by the seller to the buyer for promotional services and requires such payments to be made available on proportionally equal terms to all competing customers. Section 2(e) deals with services furnished by the seller to the buyer, requiring such services to be made available to all competing customers on proportionally equal terms. Note that these prohibitions are directed only against sellers. The Robinson-Patman Act contains no prohibition against the inducement and receipt of discriminatory advertising and promotional allowances or services and facilities by powerful buyers. As noted above, however, the FTC has moved to remedy this omission. The commission has held that the knowing inducement and receipt of discriminatory advertising and promotional allowances by large buyers is an unfair method of competition, prohibited by the Federal Trade Commission Act.

Essentially, Sections 2(d) and 2(e) provide that if a seller offers advertising allowances or merchandising payments or services to one customer, he must make his offer (1) available (2) to all competing customers (3) on proportionally equal terms. Let us examine each of these three requirements.

The requirement of availability imposes an affirmative duty on a supplier who offers promotional assistance to any of his customers. Suppose that a supplier goes to his largest customer with an offer of an advertising allowance of $1 per case on all goods purchased. In order to comply with the law, the seller must then take action to inform all of his customers who compete with the large customer that the allowance is available to them as well. It is no defense for the seller to say later that the competing customers would have received the allowance had they asked for it if the competing customers were never informed of the availability of the allowance. Preferably, the seller should use the same media to announce the availability of a particular form of merchandising assistance to all competing customers. Thus, if one customer is notified of the availability of an allowance or service by first-class mail, all competing customers should also be notified by first-class mail.

The second requirement is that any promotional plan developed by a supplier must cover all customers who compete with one another. Coverage of all competing customers must be tested in two ways. The first test is essentially geographical: What stores actually compete for the same business? A supplier is required to offer promotional assistance only to those customers who compete in the distribution of the promoted product with any customer who is participating in the promotion. Suppose that a manufacturer sells to ten retail stores in New York City and ten retail stores in San Francisco. The manufacturer can lawfully develop a program of promotional assistance that includes only the New York City retail stores, because they do not compete with the San Francisco retail stores. Caution must be used in defining the area of effective competition, however. Suppose that a manufacturer sells to ten retail stores in Manhattan, ten retail stores in Brooklyn, and ten retail stores in the Bronx. A promotional assistance program limited to the Manhattan customers would be illegal if the Brooklyn and Bronx retail stores compete with the Manhattan retail stores for the same business. The second test of coverage of all competing customers is related to the needs of particular customers. The law prohibits a supplier from so tailoring his promotional assistance plan that it is impossible as a practical matter for some competing customers to participate. It may be that in a particular instance a supplier must develop alternative promotional assistance plans to insure that each competing customer can participate in some manner. In other words, the supplier must offer something that each of his customers, no matter how small, can use effectively.

The law's requirement that promotional allowances or services must be made available to competing customers on "proportionally equal terms" is of cardinal importance. Proportional equality means, basically, to each according to his worth as a retailer. The Robinson-Patman Act does not spell out any single way in which to achieve proportional equality. One method is to compute the amount of payments made or services furnished as a specified percentage of the dollar volume of goods sold or the quantity of goods purchased during a specified time. A seller who offers his customers an advertising allowance of $1 per case on all purchases has made a proportionally equal offer. Offers based on a sliding scale are suspect. For example, an offer of an advertising allowance of 2 per cent on annual purchases up to $1,000, 3 per cent on purchases up to $5,000, and 5 per cent on purchases over $5,000 is not a proportionally equal offer if only a few large customers are able to purchase in sufficient quantities to receive the maximum allowance.

The supplier has the additional duty of checking to insure that every customer participating in a promotional allowance or service program is using the benefits he receives for the intended purpose. If, for instance, a customer is allowed to pocket an advertising allowance without supplying any advertising, both the supplier and the customer may be in difficulty. The FTC might construe such a payment to be a price concession and proceed against the supplier under Section 2(a) of the Robinson-Patman Act and against the customer under Section 2(f).

A few examples will illustrate the application of the principles just described. Suppose that the National Soap Company markets its toilet soap through supermarket chains, drug chains, and independent drug stores. An executive of National Soap Company proposes a program of television advertising allowances. Under the program National Soap would reimburse its customers for one half the cost of any television spot announcements featuring National Soap up to a maximum of 7½ per cent of the customer's annual purchases. The offer would be announced to all customers by means of a form letter. Superficially, this program appears to meet the requirements of Section 2(d) of the Robinson-Patman Act. The offer would be made available to all competing customers on a proportionally equal formula. As a practical matter, however, this program would fail the test of availability to all competing customers. If National Soap knows that only the large supermarket chains and drug chains can afford television advertising, then the offer would not be available in any meaningful sense to its independent drug store customers. In order to meet the test of practical availability, National Soap would have to expand its allowance program to include alternative advertising media. Suppose that the program is enlarged to include radio and newspaper advertising on the same basis. The program still may not be available to all competing customers. If some small stores cannot afford television, radio, or newspaper advertising, National Soap should allow its customers to use the advertising allowance for handbills or in-store displays as well. Its customers would then have a meaningful choice, and every customer would be able to use at least one advertising medium.

Suppose that the Association Cosmetics Company distributes its line through the Colossal Department Store and ten independent drug stores in Middletown. The Colossal Department Store is the largest customer by a wide margin. Association Cosmetics employs a traveling demonstrator, and the Colossal Department Store has asked for an all-day demonstration in its store. If Association Cosmetics accedes to the request of the Colossal Department Store, it must make a proportionally equal offer to the independent drug stores in Middletown who distribute its line in competition with the Colossal Department Store. The offer to the drug stores need not be the same as the offer to the Colossal Department Store. Association Cosmetics complies with the Robinson-Patman Act if its offer is proportionally equal. Suppose that Colossal Department Store has an annual volume of $10,000 in Association Cosmetics products and that the value of the all-day demonstration is $100. The Tom Thumb Drug Store across the street has an annual volume of $1,000 in Association Cosmetics products. Association Cosmetics satisfies the requirements of the Robinson-Patman Act if it offers the Tom Thumb Drug Store promotional services worth $10. Here the offer to the independent drug store might take the form of a short personnel-training program or the furnishing of a demonstration kit.

Retail Greeting Cards, Inc., desperately wants the Colossal Department Store to take on its line. The salesman calling on the store buyer states that if Colossal will take on the line, Retail Greeting Cards will ship to Colossal a complete set of display fixtures and storage cabinets, free of charge. Retail Greeting Cards also sells to a number of small stores who compete with Colossal for the greeting card business. No offer is made to these smaller stores. On these facts, Retail Greeting Cards is clearly guilty of violating Section 2(e) of the Robinson-Patman Act.

The Triple A Cigar Company plans to offer its customers the use of a humidified, self-service display cabinet. The cabinet to be offered will occupy 12 linear feet of store space. Triple A Cigar Company plans to make its offer known to all customers. As a practical matter, however, only very large stores will be able to accommodate a cabinet of this size. On these facts, Triple A Cigar Company is vulnerable to attack under the Robinson-Patman Act, unless it develops alternative offers that can be utilized by smaller stores.

Unlike a Section 2(a) charge, there need be no proof of a competitive injury to show a Section 2(d) or 2(e) violation. Moreover, the seller has no defense of cost justification. The defense of meeting competition, however, is available.

Buyers have duties as well as rights with respect to supplier promotional plans. The reader will recall that although the Robinson-Patman Act does not make it illegal for customers knowingly to induce and receive discriminatory promotional payments or services from suppliers, the FTC has held that the knowing inducement and receipt of discriminatory promotional payments by retailers is a violation of the Federal Trade Commission Act. The commission has recently taken the same position with respect to the inducement or receipt of discriminatory services or facilities from suppliers.

CRIMINAL PROHIBITIONS: SECTION 3

Section 3 of the Robinson-Patman Act is a criminal statute aimed at three specific practices. First, Section 3 declares it a crime for any person who meets the commerce test "to be a party to, or assist in any transaction of sale, or contract to sell, which discriminates against competitors of the purchaser, in that any discount, rebate, allowance or advertising service charge is granted to the purchaser over and above any discount, rebate, allowance, or advertising service charge available at the time of such transaction to said competitors in respect of a sale of goods of like grade, quality, and quantity." This part of Section 3 is designed to reach secret price concessions of a fraudulent nature. It has been little used, both because of the difficulty of proving fraud and because courts have strictly construed its provisions. Where a concession is given on a purchase of 1,000 cases and not on a purchase of 999 cases, some courts have found no violation because a sale of a "like quantity" of goods was not involved.

Secondly, it is a crime for any person "to sell or contract to sell, goods in any part of the United States at prices lower than those exacted by said person elsewhere in the United States for the purpose of destroying competition, or eliminating a competitor in such part of the United States." Within the reach of this part of Section 3 is a seller who makes a geographic price cut with the predatory purpose of destroying competition or eliminating a competitor. In one case, a bakery company with multi-state operations cut its bread price substantially in one city in which it operated, thereby destroying the competition afforded by a local baker. This practice was held to be a violation of Section 3.

Finally, it is a crime for any person "to sell, or contract to sell, goods at unreasonably low prices for the purpose of destroying competition or eliminating a competitor." This provision is also aimed at predatory pricing. What is forbidden would appear to be a sudden drop in prices without economic justification and with the intent to eliminate a competitor.

Section 3 of the Robinson-Patman Act is not a popular enactment. Its language has been criticized as being too vague to give any ascertainable standard of prohibited conduct. This argument was used in the recent *National Dairy Products* case in the hope that the Supreme Court would hold the last part of Section 3 to be unconstitutionally vague. The argument failed. The Supreme Court has also held that Section 3 is not an "antitrust statute," and, therefore, does not provide a cause of action for private litigants seeking treble damages.

4

Jurisdictional Requirements of Section 2(a)

Section 2(a), which prohibits sellers from discriminating in price, is the heart of the Robinson-Patman Act. In this chapter we will consider the problem of precisely which sellers are within the reach of Section 2(a). In order to bring the substantive portions of the act into play, there must be (1) two or more consummated sales, (2) reasonably close in point of time, (3) of commodities, (4) of like grade and quality, (5) with a difference in price, (6) by the same seller, (7) to two or more different purchasers, (8) for use, consumption, or resale within the United States or any territory thereof, (9) which may result in competitive injury. Furthermore, (10) the "commerce" requirement must be satisfied. All ten of these jurisdictional elements must be met in order to invoke the power of the Federal Trade Commission or the courts to consider the lawfulness of pricing transactions.

TWO OR MORE CONSUMMATED SALES

The price discrimination must arise from consummated sales. Two major issues have arisen from this requirement: (1) whether refusals to deal can be attacked as a form of price discrimination, and (2) whether consignments, leases,· and other nonsale property transactions can be treated as sales for the purposes of the act. It can be said generally that a sale to one buyer and an outright refusal to sell to another cannot be attacked under Section 2(a). Similarly, a sale to one buyer and a consignment to another cannot be reached. Generally, the courts insist that only executed transactions are within the purview of the act. We shall proceed with an examination of these two basic propositions.

Refusals to Deal

By way of background, the Supreme Court held in the landmark case of *United States* v. *Colgate & Co.* that a seller has the freedom to select the persons with whom he will deal or continue to deal. This right of customer selection has not been explicitly impaired by any antitrust statute. However, a refusal to deal may be illegal under Section 1 of the Sherman Act or Section 5 of the Federal Trade Commission Act when carried out in concert with others. Also, an individual refusal to deal may be tainted when it is motivated by a desire to further a program of resale price maintenance. Although the seller may state in advance the circumstances under which he will sell, he may not go beyond this mere policy announcement and the simple refusal to deal. Furthermore, if one has a significant degree of monopoly power that he is trying to protect or extend by refusals to deal, Section 2 of the Sherman Act may be violated. The refusal to continue dealing if the purchaser also distributes competing products, or the refusal to sell unless the buyer agrees to take other or "tied" products from the seller, may result in a violation of Section 1 of the Sherman Act or Section 3 of the Clayton Act. Thus, it can be seen that the mere refusal to deal is a legitimate business practice; the presence of some "plus" element is required in order to make it illegal. Once demonstrated to be ancillary to the achievement of an unlawful marketing objective, however, the seller's customer-selection process becomes susceptible to attack.

Because of the difficulties in attempting to demonstrate the existence of an unlawful business purpose and to satisfy thereby the requirement that there be some "plus" element in addition to the mere refusal to deal, attempts were made to attack the practice under the Robinson-Patman Act. But, attacks on refusals to sell as a form of price discrimination have not met with success. Section 2(a) specifically provides that "nothing herein contained shall prevent persons engaged in selling goods, wares, or merchandise in commerce from selecting their own customers in bona fide transactions and not in restraint of trade." This language has been cited in many decisions dismissing Robinson-Patman charges; but, practically speaking, it adds little to the existing case law. As the Supreme Court observed in *Simplicity Pattern,* it merely "codifies the rule of *United States* v. *Colgate."*

The FTC recognized the inapplicability of Section 2(a) to refusals to deal as far back as 1937 when it observed in its *Bird* decision that: "[the seller] may discriminate in the choice of customers." This posture was quickly adopted by the courts, as evidenced by the case of *Shaw's, Inc.* v. *Wilson-Jones Co.,* where the defendant refused to quote a price to the plaintiff while selling its products to the plaintiff's competitor. The United States Third Circuit Court of Appeals explained:

> The phrase "to discriminate in price," employed in Section 2(a) considered by itself and entirely out of its context, might be deemed to include a refusal to offer a price to a customer upon goods which the latter desired to offer for resale. Such a conclusion is insupportable, however, after consideration of other language of the section. *The discrimination in price referred to must be practiced "between different purchasers." Therefore at least two purchases must have taken place.* The term purchaser means simply one who purchases, a buyer, a vendee. It does not mean one who seeks to purchase, a person who goes into the market place for the purpose of purchasing. *In other words, it does not mean a prospective purchaser, or one who wishes to purchase, as the appellant contends.* . . . Past purchases or conversations in respect to possible future purchases are insufficient. [Emphasis supplied.]

The belief has been expressed that an executory contract to sell cannot be relied on to establish price discrimination because it is not a completed sale. In part, this contention is based on the *Goodman & Sons* case, where the plaintiff had entered into a contract with the defendant supplier in which he agreed to purchase 18,000 gallons of lacquer at $1.85 per gallon. The contract was expressly conditioned on the plaintiff's being the successful bidder in the sale of 18,000 gallons of paint to the State of New Hampshire. Unknown to the plaintiff, the defendant submitted a bid on the same proposal at a price of $1.75 per gallon, and the state subsequently awarded the contract to the defendant at that price. The plaintiff contended without success that these facts amounted to an act of discrimination falling within the ban of Section 2(a). The court said that it was not enough that the plantiff would have had to pay a higher price if it had bought the paint; there must be actual sales to two different buyers.

Although the court appeared to be unequivocal in its demand for actual sales, the contingent nature of the plaintiff's contract with the defendant cannot be overlooked. The express condition precedent to the vesting of the defendant's obligation to sell to the plaintiff never occurred, and consequently, there was no enforceable contract between Goodman and the defendant. The acceptance of the plaintiff's bid by the State of New Hampshire was necessary to make the writing operative as an enforceable contract. Thus, the plaintiff was attempting to base his claim on an unenforceable contract, a factor that mitigates to some extent the precedential value of the case.

In at least one decision, however, an executory contract of sale was treated as the equivalent of an actual sale. In *Aluminum Co. of America* v. *Tandet,* the court noted that on execution of a contract, the parties were no longer in the categories of offeror and offeree; they became the seller and the buyer. In the court's view, the incidence of delivery and payment would affect only the type and kind of remedies an aggrieved party would have in the event of a breach of contract, but in no other way was their legal status as seller and buyer diluted. Thus, Tandet qualified as a purchaser within the meaning of the act because there had been a sale, albeit an unexecuted one. And because there had been a sale there was no longer a question of a mere refusal to sell by Alcoa. The situation had advanced beyond that point. The court did recognize the possibility that the result in *Goodman* might appear to be inconsistent with its own holding. That case was distinguished, however, on the ground that no enforceable executory contract had been formed because the essential condition precedent to the vesting of the parties' obligations —the acceptance of Goodman's bid by the State of New Hampshire—had not occurred. The court made no mention of the possible conflict of its decision with the statutory language of the act.

Recently, an attempt was made to base a price discrimination case solely on price list quotations. Plaintiffs argued that the defendant's published price lists showed that the defendant was offering goods to the trade at prices different from those being extended to the plaintiffs. However, the *inference* that discriminatory sales were *likely* to have been made to other purchasers was determined to be insufficient. It was essential to show that the seller actually charged one purchaser a higher price than the price charged one or more of the purchaser's competitors. Similarly, in a different case, a mere allegatiion that a manufacturer quoted different prices to different retailers in the same area did not constitute an adequate statement of a violation of Section 2(a) of the Robinson-Patman Act.

One notable exception has been carved out of the body of case law upholding a supplier's right of refusal to deal where the refusal was only partial, not absolute. In *Bruce's Juices, Inc.* v. *American Can Co.,* the world's largest can manufacturer refused to sell a certain type of can to the plaintiff, a citrus fruit canner, with the freight costs equalized to the canner's Florida plant. However, in accord with its long-established freight-pricing policy, the defendant sold the same type of can to a Texas competitor of Bruce's Juices at a freight-equalized price. Notwithstanding the plantiff's refusal to purchase the cans at the higher, nonequalized price, the court found that American Can had engaged in unlawful price discrimination. It was not necessary for the disgruntled customer to go through with the formality of purchasing the goods at the higher price. In the court's opinion, "the mere fact that the supplier continued to tender the goods at the higher price did not obligate the plaintiff to buy them in order to attain the status of a competing purchaser under the act, as its failure to do so was directly attributable to defendant's own discriminatory practice."

Despite the seemingly broad language in this decision, it is clear that it does not authorize any prospective buyer or recipient of a price list in the open market to be a beneficiary under the act. A review of the situation involving these two parties reveals that they had had a long-established contractual relationship prior to the dispute in this case. In fact, it has been suggested that the case turned on the existence of "oral agreements between the companies that evolved from a course of dealings over a period of years." But even if this case is strictly confined to the factual context in which it arose, it still represents an inroad onto the earlier line of cases to the extent that where the offers are being circulated among present customers, Robinson-Patman liability might attach. And, as a result, if a company intends to cease dealing with one of its customers, care should be taken to see that price lists containing prices higher than those offered to the customer's competitors are not inadvertently sent him. Otherwise, under the *American Can* decision, a supplier could find himself defending a treble-damage action brought by a past customer who had not actually been sold goods at discriminatory prices and who the supplier had decided to cut off completely.

With this exception, then, refusals to deal are not actionable under the price discrimination law. This insistence by the courts on two or more executed transactions has been criticzed as an "empty requirement." It has been argued that since refusals to sell are practically and logically extensions of discrimination in price, discriminatory refusals, like discriminatory sales, should be subjected to the criteria of that section. But although the terms of Section 2(a) are not considered applicable, they, like other specific antitrust prohibitions, determine in part the scope of unfair methods of competition within the prohibition of Section 5 of the Federal Trade Commission Act. Thus, the commission has relied on Section 5 to attack a discriminatory transaction in which the required sale has not been present.

In *House of Materials* v. *Simplicity Pattern Co.*, several retail stores, relying on a previous victory by the commission over the defendant, sought treble-damage relief on the ground that Simplicity had violated Section 2(e) by furnishing discriminatory services and facilities to some of its larger customers. After institution of the suit, Simplicity terminated its agreements with the various plaintiffs. The district court found that Simplicity's sole motive for terminating the contracts with all those who elected to assert their legal rights was to deter these suits through the exercise of economic coercion. In order to further a congressional intent to encourage antitrust enforcement by private suit, the lower court enjoined the refusal to deal as contrary to this public policy. The United States Court of Appeals, however, reversed the lower court's action as having no basis in law or equity, because Simplicity had not violated any antitrust law by refusing to deal.

Seven months after the *Simplicity Pattern* decision, the United States Circuit Court of Appeals for the Second Circuit reached a contrary result, in a case in which a drug company had terminated its account with a wholesaler of drug supplies who had filed a complaint, alleging violations of both Section 2 of the Sherman Act and the Robinson-Patman Act. Even though it was somewhat similar, this case differed from *Simplicity* in that the refusal to deal was allegedly being used to further the defendant's monopoly power. An injunction was issued to prevent behavior that was in and of itself a violation of the antitrust laws. Thus, it can be said that the law still requires that a supplier's refusal to sell be used in the furtherance of some unlawful business objective such as obtaining monopoly power or maintaining resale prices before it becomes actionable.

Consignments, Leases, and Other Nonsale Transfers of Property

As the result of a consent decree in which it agreed to terminate its resale-price-maintenance arrangements with independent distributors and retailers, the General Electric Company undertook a thorough restructuring of its distribution system in the early 1920s. Relying on basic commercial law, General Electric transformed the independent distributors and retailers into agents of General Electric with a responsibility to keep a stock of General Electric products on consignment and to sell them at terms specified by the manufacturer. In 1926, the Supreme Court ruled that the creation of bona fide agents at the retail selling level gave General Electric the right to fix the price at which its goods would be sold directly to the consumer. Immunity from the reach of the antitrust laws thus created, the consignment method of distribution burgeoned in most sectors of the American economy. In its *Ace Book* decision, the commission described well the legal incidences of a consignment when it observed:

In addition to retention of title by the consignor, a *bona fide* consignment relationship will normally contain several of the following elements—deferral of payment on the part of the consignee until after the products have been sold, the privilege of return of all unsold products, receipt of a commission by the consignee for his efforts in selling the products, insurance coverage by the consignor of the goods while on the premises of the consignee, payment by the consignor of property taxes levied on the goods while in the hands of the consignee, periodic accounting by the consignee for sales and inventory on hand, liability of the consignor for the consignee's misrepresentation and negligence in selling the products to consumers, and the segregation of the consignor's products from those of other manufacturers or suppliers. In the normal consignment relationship, title is retained by the consignor until the goods are sold by the consignee. Where such is the case it appears that title is transferred directly from the consignor to the purchaser acquiring possession from the consignee and never vests in the consignee.

Several decades passed before the basic thrust of the *General Electric* decision was extended into the Robinson-Patman area by the courts. In the *Student Book* case, the defendant, majority-owned by the West Publishing Company, and the exclusive distributor in Washington, D. C., of West and some other publications, was the source of between 80 and 90 per cent of the books purchased by law students in the area. Before the fall of 1947, it supplied books to the plaintiff at a 20 per cent discount off of the list price and allowed the return of all unsold books for full credit. In 1947, the seller cut the discount to 6 per cent and discontinued its policy of full credit for returns. However, the defendant continued to deal with the campus book stores of various Washington law schools on the original, more favorable, terms. Subsequently, the contracts with the campus stores were revised in such a way as to transform them into agency agreements under which the books were sold for the defendant on a commission basis. The plaintiff then brought suit charging that the more favorable terms enjoyed by the campus stores constituted price discrimination in violation of Section 2(a). The court, however, held that consignments were not to be treated as "sales" for the purposes of the act. Thus, the plaintiff could not demonstrate that there had been at least two contemporaneous sales at different prices as Section 2(a) requires.

Results similar to that in the *Student Book* decision have prevailed in a number of cases involving other types of nonsale transactions. For example, it has been held that neither the issuance of a loan nor the making of a gift is a "sale" for purposes of antitrust law. And, in at least two decisions, it has been held that the Robinson-Patman Act does not apply to discriminatory leases. Thus, it is clear that Robinson-Patman Act jurisdiction extends only over those transactions involving actual sales.

The usefulness of nonsale transfers to sellers wishing to avoid the proscriptions of the act should not be underestimated, particularly because the availability of certain forms of doing business with a supplier is not a "service" or "facility" that must be made available to all competing customers on proportionally equal terms in conformity with the directives of Section 2(e). Consignment arrangements, for example, not only provide a seller with greater flexibility in his pricing practices, but they permit him to finance the inventories of selected consignees in times of tight credit. Also, they permit small businessmen long on ambition but short on capital the opportunity to establish their own distributorships.

The usefulness of the consignment device, however, has been restricted to some extent by the results that have prevailed in a number of recent decisions by both the commission and the courts. First, in the commission's *Ace Book* decision, a supplier's reliance on the consignment device created Robinson-Patman liability instead of leading to an avoidance of its pitfalls. The respondent, a publisher of paperback books, was charged with discrimination between competing customers by paying disproportionate allowances to large retailers in high-traffic areas. The respondents contended without success that the retailers were not their customers because they purchased the Ace books from wholesalers. The commission said:

> The wording of the wholesaler contracts and the surrounding circumstances indicates that title does not vest in the wholesalers at any time. *A Fortiori,* the title passes directly from respondents to the retailers. . . . Although the record fails to show that the retailers negotiated directly with the respondents, they negotiated directly with the wholesalers, respondents' consignees.

Thus, the retailers—both favored and unfavored—acquiring distribution of respondent's books and magazines through wholesalers were customers of Ace books for purposes of Section 2(d). It is in this manner that consignment arrangements might increase, instead of diminish, a supplier's exposure to Robinson-Patman liability.

Secondly, the efficacy of the consignment device has been impaired by a number of recent decisions that have curtailed, in part, the broad antitrust immunity for consignment transactions created by the *General Electric* case. The Supreme Court's decision in *Simpson* v. *Union Oil Co.,* made it clear that consignment devices that constitute unreasonable restraints of trade in violation of the Sherman Act are no longer automatically legitimized.

It is difficult to estimate the impact that these decisions will have on the Robinson-Patman Act's "sale" requirement. It is likely that attempts will be made to interpret consignment arrangements as sales for price discrimination purposes. The success or failure of such attempts will not, of course, significantly affect the scope of the commission's regulatory authority over this type of activity, because the commission could challenge a discriminatory consignment arrangement as an unfair method of competition proscribed by Section 5 of the Federal Trade Commission Act. In contrast, however, the suppliers' exposure to private treble-damage liability would be expanded considerably by a determination that a consignment is the equivalent of a sale as that term is used in the Robinson-Patman Act, since Section 5 is not an antitrust statute for purposes of Sections 4 and 5 of the Clayton Act.

CONTEMPORANEOUS SALES

The prohibitions of the act can come into play only if the sales are reasonably close in time, because, by definition, a discrimination means that the disparity in price or promotional payments must arise out of similar transactions under comparable circumstances. The courts have held that unlawful discrimination can exist only where the seller's different prices are reasonably close in time and involve delivery of the products sold, also reasonably close in time. The case law is in harmony with the legislative history on this point. To reinforce the exclusion of noncontemporaneous price differentials from the reach of the act, Congress added the following provision to Section 2(a):

> Nothing herein contained shall prevent price changes from time to time where in response to changing conditions affecting the market for or the marketability of the goods concerned, such as but not limited to actual imminent deterioration of perishable goods, obsolescence of seasonal goods, distress sales under court process, or sales in good faith in discontinuance of business in the goods concerned.

The Supreme Court has never passed on the issue of just how close in time the pertinent sales must be in order to be characterized as discriminatory. The nearest it came to discussing the problem was in the case of *Bruce's Juices, Inc.* v. *American Can Co.* The Court said:

> At least two transactions must take place in order to constitute a discrimination. Thus, a contract may be made today which has no legal defect under the Robinson-Patman Act. A week later, another sale may be made at a different price or at a different discount, and the latter taken into consideration with the former may establish a discrimination. Whether a sale would be rendered void only because of simultaneous discrimination or preexisting ones, or whether a contract valid when made becomes void by reason of later transactions, and if so, how much later, are questions we need not decide now.

Undoubtedly, the most pertinent case in this area is *Atalanta Trading Corp.* v. *FTC,* where the respondent was challenged by the commission for granting promotional allowances to Giant Food, a chain store in Washington, D.C., in connection with the sale of canned hams. It was alleged that substantially identical products had been sold to a competitor of Giant five months after the sale to Giant without any provision for allowances, resulting in a violation of the act. In setting aside the commission's cease and desist order the court stated:

> . . . [T]he flaw in the Commission's decision is that the terms of an initial sale in a given territory would freeze the supplier into an immutable position. While it is true that the sale on which the allowance was not made occurred after the July 1954 promotional allowance rather than preceding it, it does not follow that without any time limitation whatsoever the supplier was irrevocably committed upon making the first sale to hold open the same promotional allowance to all other prospective purchasers or to refuse to deal with them. The Commission considered it immaterial whether the subsequent sale followed the promotional allowance by a matter of weeks or months. However, the time interval is a determining factor.

The court also criticized the commission's finding of a violation with respect to an advertising allowance given to Giant six months *after* a sale to a competitor in which no allowance was provided. According to the court:

> The Commission apparently assumed without discussion that if a supplier wishes to grant promotional allowances in a given territory, he must elect to do so upon the first sale made. Under the Commission's rationale any prior sale without an allowance would make a subsequent sale with an allowance unlawful. By the same token any allowance given on the first sale could never be adjusted to meet competition. Such a rigid application of Section 2(d) would stifle rather than encourage competition and have the practical effect of outlawing all promotional allowances. Had Congress so desired, Section 2(d) would have read far differently than it does.

In its recent *Fred Meyer* decision, the United States Court of Appeals for the Ninth Circuit regarded a substantial time interval as indicating only that different prices *might have been* caused by different market conditions, rather than by an accomplished intent to discriminate. In finding a time interval of several months insufficient to defeat the contemporaneous sales requirement, the court observed that the sales were of a single, standardized item widely and frequently sold in the area during the years involved. It was noted that the commission had, in the past, found sales to two competitors three and a half months apart sufficiently comparable on "a showing of continuous sales of regularly promoted items." Furthermore, Meyer's reliance on the *Atalanta* decision was dismissed by the court on the ground that there the sales had been isolated and nonrecurring.

The *Atalanta* decision was found applicable, however, in a subsequent case, where it was held that automobile sales six months apart were not sufficiently contemporaneous. Studebaker-Packard had been left with a large factory inventory of over 400 unsold 1960 model cars several months after the 1961 model had been introduced. These cars were sold at the end of December to Ranchero Motors, a competitor of the plaintiff, Valley Plymouth, at prices at least 25 per cent below those paid by the plaintiff at the time of his last purchase, July 11, 1960. The plaintiff had eleven of the 1960 models on hand and unsold at the time of Ranchero's purchase. The plaintiff's main argument was that the sales in question had been contemporaneous because he was a competitor of Ranchero at the time of the December transaction. The court relied on two factors in rejecting this contention: (1) the elapsed time between the sales and (2) the change in market conditions. It pointed out that the statute expressly protects price changes made in response to changing market conditions such as the obsolescence of seasonal goods. According to the court, a normal change in car models, made in good faith, would come within this proviso. Thus, the six-month time lapse plus a change in market conditions precluded a finding of contemporaneous sales, and the single sale to Ranchero was not actionable.

It has been said that "the purpose of the Act would be defeated, however, if it were given so strict a construction as to require two actual purchases at precisely the same time." Thus, in the *Hartley* v. *Parker* case, a liquor distributor was permitted to sue for treble damages allegedly arising from discriminatory prices, even though the supplier's *last* sale to the plaintiff distributor occurred *before* the favored competing customer had made *any* purchases from the defendant. The plaintiff distributor's allegation that it had a substantial stock of the supplier's products on hand following the termination of the agreement between them, and that the plaintiff was selling these products in competition with the favored distributor, was sufficient to support the price discrimination complaint. Unfortunately, the court set forth no guides by which to determine whether a supplier has allowed enough time to a cut-off distributor to dispose of the supplier's products before a competing distributor can be allowed to purchase the same goods at a lower price. Once again, reference must be made to the distributor's remaining supply and market conditions in determining the point in time beyond which the second sale will cease to be "contemporaneous."

From the preceding it would seem that the question of whether two sales are sufficiently separated to be nondiscriminatory can be answered only by reference to the particular facts and circumstances in each case. If the products are expensive, such as hydroelectric generators, which are sold relatively infrequently, then a time differential of a year or more between the sales may be necessary in order to avoid a violation of the act, the *Atalanta* decision notwithstanding. On the other hand, sales of items whose price structures are more susceptible to the vicissitudes of supply and demand—those that trade in high volume, are perishable or periodically modified, or are subject to technical obsolescence—must be relatively close together in order to be regarded as contemporaneous.

So far, no mention has been made of the problems created by *book* and *future* sales. A sale for future delivery can freely differ in price from a sale for immediate delivery (often referred to as a *spot* sale), either at the time the contract of sale was entered into or at the time of delivery, without creating Robinson-Patman liability. This proposition was explained by Mr. Teegarden, the draftsman of the original Patman Bill, to the House Judiciary Committee as follows:

> On the question of futures, the question is whether a purchaser of futures, let us say, in May, at one price, for delivery in December, when the price of the market in December for spot purchases would be different, would be prohibited under the bill. . . . My answer is it would not; because the conditions affecting the two transactions would be the result of market conditions which obviously would be different. But if a manufacturer said to chain A, "I will give you a December future at $2 a case," and said to independent B at the same time, comparable, "you are going to have to pay $2.50 a case for December futures," that would be a discrimination.

Book pricing can be described as follows: Ordinarily, when suppliers announce an advance in the price of their products, they allow their customers a period of five days, for example, in which to secure options, that is, book orders, to purchase the goods, and a period generally of thirty days in which to take delivery on the options. Subsequent sales at the higher price are not considered to be contemporaneous with the lower-priced option sales. However, the "booking" arrangements must be offered on equal terms to all customers in order to avoid the proscriptions of the act. Unlawful discrimination in price through preferential operation of the booking system has most often occurred through the use of practices under which large buyers with unused balances booked by them at the older price were permitted an extension of delivery time beyond the fixed period applicable to other purchasers. Such practices were condemned in the *Corn Products* case.

COMMODITIES

Section 2(a) of the Robinson-Patman Act states that the sales must be of commodities. It is clear from both the legislative history of the act and subsequent congressional studies, that Section 2(a) was intended to encompass tangible articles of commerce, not intangibles such as services, contract rights, or privileges. In fact, in recognition of this limited application of the term *commodities,* an unsuccessful attempt was made in

1957 to amend the act to define that word as including "services rendered by independent contractors." In the words of the act's author, "commodities" is to be used in the ordinary, "commercial sense to designate any movable or tangible thing that is produced or used as the subject of barter.'"

For the most part, the sparse judicial interpretations of commodities have been consistent with the legislative history. For example, it has been held that the price discrimination laws do not apply to transportation-rate differentials or real estate leases and sales. In the words of the court, in *Gaylord Shops, Inc.* v. *Pittsburgh Miracle Mile:*

> . . . [I]t seems clear from a reading of the Act that where the agreement is not for the transfer of chattels, or the sale of personal property, the defendants cannot be guilty of a violation of the Robinson-Patman Act.

Problems have arisen, however, when tangibles and intangibles are sold in combination with one another for a single price. To the extent any generalization is possible, the rule is that price discrimination cannot be attacked under Section 2(a) when the intangible factors constitute a dominant portion of a contract price. In other words, where the supplying of goods is incidental to a contract for services, the contract cannot be treated as one involving the sale of commodities. For example, in the *General Shale Products* case, a builder was alleged to have sold bricks at a discriminatory price in connection with his contract with a municipal housing authority to construct public housing facilities. The cost of the bricks had been segregated in the contract bid submitted to the authority, and the total sum of the main bid was dependent on the cost of the bricks. Although the bricks for the facilities were supplied by the defendant at a loss to himself, the court found that the contract was an indivisible construction contract, not one for the transfer of chattels. The brick transaction, it said, was woven into a general agreement entitling the company to receive a fixed sum for furnishing the labor and materials required to complete the building operation.

A recent case involved a contract for the sale of news information services, in which a radio station, Tri-State, alleged that the news service had charged it discriminatory rates. Although the right to use the service's written reports was part of the contract, it was held that the dominant purpose of the transaction was to grant the privilege of broadcasting news, an intangible to which Section 2(a) did not apply. The court stated:

> Virtually no transfer of an intangible in the nature of a service, right, or privilege can be accomplished without the incidental involvement of tangibles, and we conclude that in such circumstances the dominant nature of the transaction must control in determining whether it falls within the provisions of the Act.

Somewhat related to the question of contracts for services is the problem of whether or not advertising is a commodity within the meaning of the act. As to radio and television commercials, there has been little doubt that they were not subject to the provisions of Section 2(a), because the physical elements involved in the conveyance of the messages are merely incidental to the predominantly intangible nature of the entire broadcasting process. In 1961, a federal court finally removed any lingering doubts as to the resolution of this issue. Discriminatory rates for sale of network TV advertising time by a national network were held not within Section 2(a), in the *Amana* decision. The case involved a suit by Columbia Broadcasting System for monies due on a contract under which CBS had agreed to produce and broadcast a television show under Amana's sponsorship. In defense of the claim, Amana filed a counterclaim asserting that CBS had granted greater discounts in price to other sponsors than it had to Amana. In affirming the district court's dismissal of Amana's counterclaim, a federal circuit court reasoned:

> . . . [W]e are of the opinion that the reasonable inferences to be drawn from the allegations concerning the written agreements do not admit of the transaction being accurately characterized as a "sale" of television "time" as it is labeled by Amana nor merely as a "services" contract as argued by CBS. Although both services and time are involved we conclude that in its essence the contract alleged is a purchase by Amana of the *privilege* of having itself identified as sponsor of the program broadcast and making use of the permissible portion thereof for advertising its products. [Emphasis added.]

Having established that a privilege was involved, the court proceeded to evaluate the word *commodity* in the context in which it appeared. It was of the opinion that the scope of the word commodity in the Robinson-Patman Act was coextensive with the breadth of that term as it was used in Section 3 of the Clayton Act. In its judgment, the phrase "goods, wares, merchandise, machinery, supplies, and other commodities" did not embrace "the contractual right or privilege of sponsorship identification with the broadcast of a television program and the use of a portion of the broadcast time for products advertising."

The *Amana* decision has been criticized on the ground that the court's "emphasis on verbal niceties . . . subordinates the more important consideration of congressional antitrust policy." Furthermore, it has been suggested that commodities be broadly defined "to exclude only those business dealings which do not lend themselves to uniform pricing." Although it is arguable that such a result is both desirable and in tune with current congressional thinking, it is doubtful that such an interpretation was contemplated by Congress at the time the act was passed. Moreover, it must be remembered that although television commercials are not commodities covered by the Robinson-Patman Act, Section 5 of the Federal Trade Commission Act is available to enforce basic Robinson-Patman policy in the absence of a technical violation of Section 2(a). In fact, this approach was recently suggested with specific reference to television advertising time by the chairman of the FTC during hearings before the Senate Antitrust Subcommittee.

The sale of newspaper advertising space, on the other hand, presents a more open question. The commission made an informal ruling in 1937 that discriminatory rates for advertising space did not involve commodities within the meaning of the act. However, in the same year, the commission successfully challenged a corporation's discriminatory prices for advertising literature that formed part of Christmas Clubs and other savings systems sold to commercial banks. The commission relied on the existence of such tangibles as passbooks and account books as a basis upon which to make a finding that these "systems" were "commodities" within the meaning of the act.

Unfortunately, there has been a dearth of judicial comment on newspaper advertising as a commodity, in part because the courts have not been inclined to decide the issue when the opportunity has arisen. But, even though no court has squarely faced the newspaper advertising problem, there can be little doubt that the basic principles set forth in *Amana* and *Tri-State Broadcasting* should be followed. What is being sold is in the nature of a service, the circulation of ideas to the newspaper's readers. The printed paper is merely a tangible vehicle for the conveyance of these ideas. It is only incidental to the dominant intangible nature of the transaction.

Two recent cases indicate the continuing restrictive reading being given by courts to the commodities requirement of Section 2(a). In *La-Salle Street Press, Inc.* v. *McCormick and Henderson, Inc.*, a federal district court held that discriminatory licensing of a patented proofreading process is not within the ambit of Section 2 (a) since "the sale of a patent license is the sale of the right or privilege of using a particular method or process. . . . As such, it does not fall within that substantial, but decidedly limited, family of tangible and movable chattels which is covered by the term 'commodity.' "

Similarly, the United States Court of Appeals for the Seventh Circuit, in *Baum and Shulman* v. *Investors Diversified Services, Inc.*, applied a restrictive reading of the term *commodities,* in holding that cumulative quantity discount practices in the sale of mutual fund shares could not be attacked as illegal price discrimination. Citing cases denying the applicability of Section 2(a) to news information services, bus tickets and the loan of money, the court said that the word *commodity* is restricted to "products, merchandise or other tangible goods."

LIKE GRADE AND QUALITY

Before discrimination in the sale of commodities becomes actionable under Section 2(a), it must be demonstrated that the products involved in the alleged price differentiation are of like grade and quality. At the outset, it should be noted that this requirement relates solely to the products being sold by the offending supplier. Thus, a competitor need not sell products of a grade and quality identical to those of a discriminating seller as a prerequisite to bringing a private treble-damage action for a primary-line injury. Functional equivalence is all that is normally required in such a case.

Because Congress failed to define the dimensions of the like grade and quality concept in either the hearings or floor debates, primary reliance must be placed on the relatively few adjudications in which that term has been interpreted. Both the commentators and the cases have focused on two fundamental questions: the effect of *minor physical variations* in otherwise identical products and the effect of using *different labels or brand names* on the same products. The ensuing discussion is dichotomized accordingly.

Physical Differences

It should be noted that the act does not speak in terms of *identical* grade and quality. The test is *like* grade, a term that suggests an intent to encompass goods with slight physical or chemical variations. It is clear, however, that commodities made of cheaper materials are not deemed to be of like grade and quality with better items of the same design. Thus, a manufactuer of standard quality gloves may be able to introduce a new line of gloves similar in construction to those of standard quality, but poorly made from inferior material, into the territory of a competitor at a reduced price for the purpose of carrying out some predatory design without running afoul of the price discrimination law. But the presence of nominal physical differences may not exempt price differentials from the proscriptions of the act where the functional utility of the visually different items is not affected. For example, in the *Bruce's Juices* case, the United States Court of Appeals for the Fifth Circuit affirmed a lower court decision in which juice containers different in size by $\frac{1}{8}$-inch were found to be of like grade and quality because they "gave substantially identical performance."

Although it is true that slightly differing goods may be of like grade and quality for purposes of the act, the commission clearly exceeded the outer limits of this requirement in its *Atalanta Trading Corp.* decision.

That case involved an alleged violation of Section 2(d) in connection with sales to selected distributors of specially packaged meat products. In issue was the question of whether or not substantially identical products had been sold to competitors of the favored distributor. All of the meats in question were pork products, namely, hams of varying sizes, pork shoulder "picnics," loin roll, and Canadian bacon. With apparently one exception, they were all sold under the trade name *Unox*. The commission held Section 2(d) to be applicable in this case because "in the general field of pork products, [these different goods] were in competition with each other." In essence, the commission adopted the view of the hearing examiner who stated:

> All of these products were pork . . . and ham is ham, regardless of whether sold in 2 or 5 lbs., or whether wrapped in grocery paper or gift box. These "differences" amount to no more than the distinction between sizes of the same shoe or the same dress. . . . This is a distinction without a difference, more fanciful than real.

The United States Court of Appeals for the Second Circuit rejected the commission's attempt to disregard substantial physical variations in applying the like grade and quality test. The court said:

> The test of products of like grade and quality was evolved to prevent emasculation of the section by a supplier's making artificial distinctions in his product, but this does not mean that all distinctions are to be disregarded. Such a holding would lead to the conclusion that all articles of food are competitive, each with the other—an obvious absurdity. Merely because various articles of food are derived from a common source (in this case, the pig) should not force the vendor of a broad line of such products to market or promote all simultaneously and in an identical fashion. The dietetic habits of the consuming public are not to be controlled by judicial fiat.

Two recent rulings by the Federal Trade Commission indicate that its thinking in this area has changed significantly since the "ham is a ham" attitude displayed in the *Atalanta* decision. In the *Universal-Rundle* decision, the hearing examiner found that the raw materials and manufacturing processes used in making plumbing fixtures with the Universal label were the same as those used in the fixtures made under private labels for purchasers such as Sears Roebuck. Despite these similarities, substantial physical differences in design that had no functional import, but that were found to have created a preference among consumers, were held by the commission to permit the conclusion that the Universal brand fixtures and those with private labels were not of like grade and quality.

Only a short time prior to its *Universal-Rundle* decision, however, the commission reached a different result in the *Kaplan* case, where the products in question also differed in design but not in function. In *Kaplan*, the respondent segregated a particular pattern in its line of shower curtains and decided that one out of a number of purchasers in a particular area would receive an allowance for advertising that particular pattern. The availability of the particular pattern to which the advertising allowance was appended was not made known to the disfavored customers. Because the curtains were found to be the same in every respect, except for the difference in patterns, the respondent was held to have discriminated between purchasers of goods of like grade and quality in violation of Section 2(d). The *Atalanta* decision, on which the respondent relied heavily, was distinguished on the ground that, unlike the present case, it did not involve a unified line of goods, all of which had been used for the same purpose and promoted as a single line.

It has been said that the results in *Universal-Rundle* and *Kaplan* are difficult to reconcile. However, after a close examination of the facts it can be seen that the results in each case stand on firm footing and are clearly consistent with each other. In *Kaplan*, the various designs were merely incidental aspects of the over-all product, for which there had been no evidence of consumer preference. In *Universal-Rundle*, on the other hand, the evidence established a proclivity on the part of the public toward one design over the other. Therefore, it can be said that the existence of a demonstrable customer preference for a particular nonfunctional difference in design will transform a product with a slight physical variation into an item of unique grade and quality for the purposes of the act.

The second case demonstrating a change in the commission's thinking in this area since *Atalanta* is the *Quaker Oats* decision. There, the commission dismissed a complaint that would have resulted in a finding of like grade and quality for various blends of oat flour made according to different specifications and possessing different physical qualities and performance characteristics. It was established that if flour made for one customer were used by another, production problems would result, thereby precluding interchangeability. Despite this fact, the hearing examiner, relying particularly on the fact that the various grades of flour were produced at no difference in cost from the same grade of oats, ruled that they were of like grade and quality. Furthermore, the examiner stressed that it was not enough that the difference in flours be recognized by the seller and the favored buyer alone. Rather, it must be recognized throughout the industry. Relying on the *Universal-Rundle* decision, a majority of the commissioners, however, stated that where there are "substantial physical differences in products which affect consumer preference or marketability . . . such products are not of like grade and quality regardless of whether manufacturing costs are the same or whether objective standards have been established by government or business." The record indicated that the physical differences in the blends had created consumer preferences on the basis of an absence of any interchangeability.

Implicit in the commission's decisions in *Universal-Rundle* and *Quaker Oats* is the notion that the like grade and quality test should be equated with the concept of commercial fungibility, the type of measurement that most clearly reflects current marketing realities. Such a test looks to the purchaser's willingness to pay the same price for either one of the products in question; if he is willing to pay a higher price for one of the products, the two are not of like grade and quality. Although the Supreme Court recently rejected the applicability of this concept to a situation involving goods differing solely as to their brand names, it is still viable in cases where slight physical differences exist. This is not to suggest, however, that the test is one of product "interchangeability" or "cross-elasticity" of demand. To do so would expand the act into a device to regulate the entire business of a supplier; a manufacturer of cellophane and other similar flexible wrapping materials costing the same to produce would have to sell both products at the same price. The test of commercial fungibility comes into play only in those situations in which there are slight physical variations among the goods with the same generic designation.

This approach was first adopted in a Robinson-Patman context by the United States Court of Appeals for the Seventh Circuit in its *Amana Refrigeration* decision. Although it was unnecessary for the court to decide the like grade and quality issue in that case, the comment was made that:

> Although no two [television] programs present the same artistic, educational, or entertainment value to all persons it may well be that so-called prime time programs which have demonstrated comparable audience drawing power would be of like grade and quality from a commercial standpoint to prospective sponsor-advertisers.

Recognition was given to the commercial-fungibility approach in three recent cases. In the *Fred Meyer* decision, a federal court rejected the petitioner's argument that the grade and quality of the peaches in question varied according to where, when, and by whom the peaches were grown and packed. The court found that the various peaches were identically described on the sales invoices. This fact was held to have sufficiently established "commercial fungibility, which is all the Robinson-Patman Act demands." In the *Perma Life Mufflers* case, a federal district judge, "while fully aware of the recent holding of the . . . Supreme Court [in the *Borden* case] . . . that a difference in grade and quality cannot be established 'by a label . . . and its consumer appeal,' " held that the inclusion of a lifetime guarantee in the purchase price of a more expensive line of mufflers, in addition to the existence of "undisputed physical differences" between the two types of mufflers in question, disproved the like grade and quality of these two commodities. In the court's opinion "such a guarantee . . . clearly justified a differential in price, and with equal clarity, constituted a dissimilarity in grade and quality." It is noteworthy that the court apparently relied on the physical variation solely as an excuse to avoid the holding in *Borden* and not as a basis for its finding of dissimilar grade and quality. Once it had been established that *Borden* did not apply, the court proceeded to examine the products in terms of their consumer appeal and found that the guarantee prevented them from being treated as commercially fungible.

On appeal, the United States Seventh Circuit Court of Appeals reversed the district court. Finding evidence that there was no physical difference between the products sold under the different brand names, the court held that, on the basis of the rationale employed in *Borden,* the goods were of like grade and quality, notwithstanding the fact that the product with the lifetime "guarantee may have had more customer appeal and have commanded a higher price in the market place." It should be noted that the reversal was grounded on a factual error and, thus, in no way should it be construed as a rejection of the lower court's suggestion that the consumer-preference test is appropriate in cases involving commodities with slight physical variations.

In *Checker Motors Corp.* v. *Chrysler Corp.,* it was held that the question of whether the defendant's taxicabs and passenger automobiles were of like grade and quality for 2(a) purposes could not be properly resolved on a motion for summary judgment despite differences in paint, exterior trim, seat covers, and various mechanical devices. Checker's theory was that Chrysler's taxicabs are in every respect either equal or superior in quality to its passenger cars, and that, therefore, in the context of price discrimination in favor of taxicab purchasers, the two vehicles should be regarded as possessing like grade and quality. The court responded:

> . . . [C]ross-elasticity of demand, substitutionability, physical appearance, and identity of performance are factors to be considered. . . . Although it seems clear that denominating one vehicle a "taxicab" and an identical one a "passenger car" will not preclude a finding of "like grade and quality" . . . if there are substantial physical differences in products affecting consumer use, preference, or marketability, such products are not of "like grade and quality," regardless of manufacturing costs.

The consumer-preference commercial fungibility test has much to recommend it. It is likely that it will gain the favor of the courts as the only way in which to apply the like grade and quality requirement in a manner consistent with economic reality.

It is important to note that a differential in price between a supplier's sale of a single product and his sale of that product in combination with another item does not constitute a discrimination between purchasers of goods of like grade and quality. Thus, in the *Package Closure Corp.* case, the plaintiff, a supplier of hoods for milk bottles, charged a competing manufacturer with selling hoods in combination with bottle caps at an unconscionably low price in relation to the price charged for hoods alone. The court held that the discount on a combination sale was not unlawful, even though the price charged for the combination discriminated against those who purchased hoods or caps only.

More recently, both the courts and the Federal Trade Commission have recognized that slight variations in products made to order may absolve a supplier from Robinson-Patman Act liability. Thus, in the *Central Ice Cream Co.* case, where a defendant was sued in a private treble-damage action for selling a high-grade ice cream made to a purchaser's special formula at a price different from that charged to its other customers for regular ice cream, a court found the two types of ice cream to be of a different grade and quality. Similarly, the commission advised a manufacturer of iron castings that those goods produced in accordance with individual customer specifications and not shipped off the shelf are not of like grade and quality within the meaning of the price discrimination laws.

We do not mean to suggest, however, that this result will prevail in every case in which slight variations are made in accordance with customer specifications. In the *Fred Meyer* decision of the United States Court of Appeals for the Ninth Circuit, which involved alleged 2(f) violations, the petitioner asserted, without success, that its submittal of additional specifications on its purchase orders for socks from Burlington Industries compelled the conclusion that a grade and quality different from that of the supplier's regular socks resulted. In rejecting this contention, the court noted the absence of any evidence tending to show that these changes produced any difference in marketability, appearance, durability, cost or manner of manufacture, or other indicia of the grade and quality of the goods. Furthermore, the court pointed out, in Burlington's invoices to different customers, the hose were identified by a style number identical to those in the invoices to Fred Meyer. In the court's opinion, this evidence was sufficient to permit the inference that the goods, themselves, were identical.

In summary, as to the impact that physical variations have on the like grade and quality issue, it can be said that actual and genuine physical differences between two different products adapted to the several buyers' uses, and not merely decorative or fanciful features having no demonstrable impact on consumer demand, probably are necessary to remove differential pricing of the two from the reach of the Robinson-Patman Act.

Brand Name Distinctions

The Federal Trade Commission's treatment of brand name distinctions has not been entirely consistent. On the one hand, the commission has, in some instances, regarded brand identity as proving the like grade and quality of physically different products, while on the other hand it has refused to accept brand name distinctions as disproving like grade and quality goods with identical physical characteristics.

The commission's rejection of brand name distinction as tending to disprove the like grade and quality of otherwise identical products occurred as far back as 1938 in the *Hansen Inoculator* decision, a case involving price differentials in the sale of identical pharmaceuticals with different inscriptions on the labels of the containers. Shortly thereafter, the commission refused to accept brand differentiation as a factor in determining whether or not the tires made by U.S. Rubber Co. for private brand distribution were of the same grade and quality as those sold by the supplier's own distributors under the U. S. Royal name. Several years later, the commission had occasion to reaffirm its position on brand name distinctions. In a second *U.S. Rubber Co.* decision, the respondent was prohibited from selling its canvas footwear at prices that differed on the basis of the particular trademark attached to the product. The advertised brands had been sold at higher prices. In another case, a respondent's rubber and canvas footwear were held to be of like grade and quality, regardless of the brand name under which they were sold. Similarly, in the commission's *Page Dairy* decision, a milk supplier was not able to avoid a finding of like grade and quality with the argument that the higher priced milk (one cent per quart more) had a special Vitamin D Homogenized label not present on the other cartons. Finally, a manufacturer of automotive replacement cable products was held to have violated Section 2(a) by selling identical products at different prices to various purchasers of private label brands, in the *Whitaker Cable Corp.* case.

Although this line of cases made it unquestionably clear that there can be no blanket exemption from Section 2(a) for private brand selling, there has been some debate as to whether these cases were of precedential value with respect to a situation in which there existed a demonstrable public demand for a product sold under a particular label. In other words, there was some question as to whether these cases established a consistently settled interpretation by the commission that physical identity is the *sole* touchstone of like grade and quality. That a controversy existed in this area was clearly evident in the 1955 Report of the Attorney General's National Committee to Study the Antitrust Laws. Although the committee majority recommended that "the economic factors inherent in brand names and national advertising should not be considered in the jurisdictional inquiry under the statutory 'like grade and quality' test," the minority was of the view that "business actualities may often contradict the Federal Trade Commission's policy of ignoring brands and trade names in determining what are 'goods of like grade and quality' under the Act."

This debate culminated in the landmark *Borden* case. The Supreme Court reversed the court below and resolved the issue in favor of the commission, stating that a pronounced public preference for a particular brand, which results in the customer's willingness to pay a higher price, does not alter the grade and quality of that product.

The Borden Company had been challenged by the commission for selling chemically identical quantities of brand name and private label evaporated milk at different prices. The record clearly established that the Borden brand milk, along with two others—Pet and Carnation—was a "premium" product that commanded a substantially higher price at all levels of distribution than other less well-known brands. For example, one retail grocer testified as follows:

> A.   Some people say they want [Borden's] Silver Cow milk. In other words, for maybe a coupon on the side of the can or because they have been educated to want that brand. Some of them won't have anything except Carnation, and some of them won't want anything except Pet.
> Q.   They don't care what price . . . .
> A.   If the Doctor tells the woman to put the baby on Pet milk, that is all she wants, you couldn't interest her in something else.

Borden contended that the grade and quality of commodities may vary because of an intense public demand for one product as compared to another.

The United States Court of Appeals for the Fifth Circuit set aside the commission order on the ground that the commission had ignored these clearly demonstrable consumer preferences. Furthermore, the court was disturbed by an apparent inconsistency in the commission's decisions with respect to the meeting competition defense under Section 2(b), where full recognition had been given to the significance of the higher prices commanded by premium products. Briefly, these cases have held that a seller who reduces the price of his premium product to the level of his nonpremium competitors is not merely meeting competition, but undercutting it. Thus, with respect to Section 2(b), the commission had decided that public acceptance, rather than chemical analysis, was the important factor. The Court of Appeals held that this approach was equally applicable to the determination of like grade and quality under Section 2(a). It stated, "We cannot approve of the Commission's construing the act inconsistently from one case to the next, as appears most advantageous to its position in a particular case."

The Supreme Court reversed the judgment of the Court of Appeals and remanded the case for further proceedings. The Court rejected the contention that the commission's previous decisions in the brand name area were applicable to a situation in which the premium label product commanded a higher price in the market place from a substantial segment of the public. It stated that these long-standing interpretations by the agency were entitled to judicial respect. The Court also examined the legislative history of the like grade and quality requirement and concluded that the commission's views best represented the intent of the Congress. During the 1936 hearings on the proposed amendments to Section 2 of the Clayton Act, it was suggested that the proscriptions of Section 2(a) be applied only to goods of like grade and quality and *brand*. Following a vigorous denunciation of the proposal by H. B. Teegarden, the drafter of the bill, as a "specious suggestion that would destroy entirely the efficacy of the bill against large buyers," the amendment was rejected. The Court treated this rejection as a blanket denial of all brand name distinctions. In denying that its holding ignored the realities of the market place, the Court claimed that by prohibiting the consideration of the economic factors inherent in brand names and national advertising in the jurisidictional like grade and quality context it was merely *delaying* the point at which these factors would be considered. Agreeing with the position taken by the Attorney General's National Committee to Study the Antitrust Laws, the Court stated that it would be more appropriate to consider the impact of tangible consumer preferences as between branded and unbranded commodities under the more flexible injury and cost justification provisions of the statute. Finally, the Court chose not to resolve the apparent inconsistency between the commission's *Borden* decision and its 2(b) cases, stating only that it agreed with the commission's holding in *Borden,* and that the Section 2(b) cases were not before the Court at that time.

In a vigorous dissent, Justice Stewart, joined by Justice Harlan, dismissed the sparse legislative history referred to in the majority opinion as indicating no more than a congressional desire not to allow mere differences in brand or design, unaccompanied by any genuine physical, chemical, or market distinction, to negate a finding of like grade and quality. Furthermore, in noting what he considered the serious inconsistency between the *Borden* decision and that line of Section 2(b) cases in which the "meeting competition" defense was held unavailable to a seller who reduced the price of his premium product to the level of his competitors' nonpremium products, Justice Stewart said:

> Could the Commission under §2(b) now prevent Borden from reducing the price of its premium milk to the level of private label milk? I can see no way that it could, short of maintaining a manifestly unstable equilibrium between §2(a) and §2(b). By adopting a keyhole approach to §2(a), the Court manages to escape resolution of the question, but it does so at the cost of casting grave doubt on what I had regarded as an important bulwark of §2(b) against a recognized competitive evil.

It remains for the commission and the courts to come to grips with this apparent anomaly in the commission's position. Until this question is resolved, suppliers of both premium and private brand products anxious to avoid the pitfalls of Section 2(a) will have a difficult course to steer. Assuming that a supplier reduces to the correct level the price of his premium product in those areas in which he also sells private brand goods, and assuming he maintains his original price level for premium products in other noncompeting areas where he does not sell private label goods, the supplier may find himself defending against either a commission complaint or a private treble-damage action brought by a private brand manufacturer who competes with the defendant's private label products. In either case, the defending supplier would face the task of avoiding the beating competition line of Section 2(b) cases mentioned previously. The prospect of a suit is obviously not a happy one, and the more timid suppliers, recognizing the danger of being charged with predatory price cutting on a territorial basis, on the one hand, and, on the other, not wishing to reduce the prices on the lucrative premium label products on a nationwide basis, may end up taking the safest course by *raising* the prices of the private label commodities to the level of their premium products. Such an action would, of course, leave those who manufacture solely private label products with an enormous competitive advantage in this lower-priced, off-brand sector of the market place.

It is difficult to assay with any precision the impact that the *Borden* case will have on private brand production practices. It has been suggested that the caprice of the commission's distinction invites suppliers to develop slight but apparent variations in their private label products in order to satisfy the commission's concern with market preferences. Although such a result is possible, there are some practical considerations that will hinder its pursuit. First, it is the rare case in which a consumer preference for a particular design, the requisite to legitimate differential pricing of only slightly dissimilar products, can be created within a few short months. Thus, more often than not, a supplier would be faced with the prospect of having to wait for a substantial period of time until it could be demonstrated that a customer preference for a particular design existed to the extent that a differential in price was justified. Secondly, the introduction of slight physical variations into the private label line would frustrate to some extent the efficiency and labor-saving methods of today's mass-production techniques. This less economical use of plant machinery would, of course, cut into profits. And, thirdly, the customer who asks the manufacturer for the same product under the customer's private label as that sold under the manufacturer's own label does not wish a product less saleable because of differences occasioned by alteration of the original design for private label purposes.

Even though the decision in the *Borden* case is generally regarded as a blow to that company's competitive flexibility, it has been suggested that, in fact, the decision could be a boon to Borden and other companies whose profits have steadily declined as the retailers' demand for private labels has increased. The retailer has limited space. If he cannot sell a private brand at a substantially lower price against the seller's brands, except for those that are cost justified or developed to meet competition, the retailer may rely more on the seller's brand. The seller has, in effect, leverage to combat his customer's demands for lower prices through private brands. Although these arguments have merit, they presuppose the absence of purely private label suppliers who could meet the price demands and production requirements of the large retailer-purchaser. Such suppliers may not be big enough to fulfill these needs at present. However, there can be little doubt that these small private label producers would eventually expand to meet these demands.

Finally, most of the dispute over the comparative merits and practical implications of the *Borden* decision may have been mooted by the United States Court of Appeals for the Fifth Circuit's recent decision in the *Borden* case following the remand to the commission by the Supreme Court. That court once again approved of Borden's price differential between its private label and brand name evaporated milk, this time on the ground that there was no competitive injury. It stated:

> We are of the firm view that where a price differential between a premium and nonpremium brand reflects no more than a consumer preference for the premium brand, the price difference creates no competitive advantage to the recipient of the cheaper private brand product on which injury could be predicated. . . . The record discloses no evidence tending to show that Borden's price differential exceeds the recognized consumer appeal of the Borden label.

Thus, the Fifth Circuit did as the Supreme Court suggested—it considered the impact of tangible consumer preferences under the more flexible injury to competition provision of the statute.

A PRICE DIFFERENCE

The Supreme Court has said that a discrimination in price is just a difference in price; the other parts of the act determine whether a given price difference is lawful or not. It follows that no violation of Section 2(a) is present if there is no difference in price to competing buyers. If the seller has one sales price, and sells f.o.b. factory to all customers, he is shielded from problems under Section 2(a).

A direct price discrimination is obvious on its face: a seller charges different prices to different buyers. An indirect price discrimination, on the other hand, occurs when differing terms or conditions of sale result in a lower price to certain buyers. We shall see that some indirect price discriminations have also been held illegal under Section 2(d) criteria.

Pricing Systems

A brief description of the various pricing systems might be helpful at this juncture. First of all, *mill-net* refers to the amount received by a seller after excluding the transportation charges that he pays. A *delivered price* is that figure quoted for the commodity as delivered to the buyer at the seller's expense. Thus, a businessman selling the product at a delivered price will receive a mill-net from each sale which will vary according to the freight cost he absorbs.

There are, of course, a number of different types of pricing systems that contain at least some aspect of delivered pricing. For example, under the *single basing-point system,* a supplier first picks a place other than his plant location that he designates as a basing point. His selection will often coincide with the location of his largest competitor's plant site, which explains why many sellers choose the same basing point. The seller determines the price of his product delivered at the basing point, and then adds the transportation costs from that point to the buyer's place of delivery in computing his price to the buyer, even though the commodities are actually shipped straight to the buyer from the seller's factory. As a variation on this theme, some suppliers use a *multiple basing-point system* in which they select two or more basing points. The price to the buyer at the point of delivery is derived by adding to the base price the transportation charges from the basing point nearest the buyer. Under either the single or multiple basing-point method, the buyer generally pays the total cost of transportation from the factory. But then the supplier will reduce the invoice price in the amount necessary to make the buyer's price reflect only the shipping charges from the appropriate basing point.

Under such a system it can be seen that, as with other types of delivered pricing systems, the seller's mill-net return will vary with each sale. In some instances the actual transportation costs from the point of shipment to the point of delivery will be less than the actual freight charges from the basing point to the delivery point that are paid by the purchaser. This difference is referred to as *phantom freight*. For example, if a seller in Pittsburgh uses Chicago as a basing point and sells to a customer in New York, the customer will pay the supplier a delivered price that reflects the freight rate between Chicago and New York even though the supplier shipped directly from its Pittsburgh plant, and, thereby, incurred a smaller shipping cost. On the other hand, when the actual transportation charge from the shipping point to the delivery point is more than the freight rate from the basing point to the point of delivery, as would be the case if the buyer in the preceding example were located in San Francisco, the difference in cost is referred to as *freight absorption,* because the seller pays more for freight than he receives from the purchaser for transportation costs.

A *freight-equalization* formula is a variation on the basing-point theme. Under this system, the supplier adds to his f.o.b. factory price only the amount it would cost him to ship the commodity from the plant site of the competing seller located nearest to the buyer. Such a practice is similar to a *multiple basing-point* system in that it produces the same price to the buyer as if all the seller's competitors were located at basing points.

Multiple-zone pricing is another type of delivered pricing, under which the supplier's mill-net rate will vary with each sale. Instead of charging all customers the same price no matter where delivery is made, as in a universal delivered-price system, the supplier divides the country into a number of geographic zones and charges prices that are uniform within each zone but vary between zones. Thus, the supplier's net profit will differ according to the amount of actual freight costs incurred in each sale.

For a number of years, the commission compared not the delivered prices the buyers paid, but the differing net proceeds received by a supplier who used a basing point, zone, or other delivered-price formula. For example, if a New York supplier sells goods in California at a delivered price identical to the one he charges customers in Connecticut, the seller is receiving a different mill-net from each sale because the freight costs to these two states are substantially different. The commission would then use these different mill-net returns as a basis for a price discrimination action. The view that all delivered pricing, particularly the basing-point system, might be vulnerable to attack under Section 2(a) reached its apex when the *Cement Institute* case came before the Supreme Court in 1948. In issue was the legality of a multiple basing-point system that had been collusively adopted by cement suppliers on an industrywide basis. In addition to condemning this scheme as a systematic price discrimination in violation of Section 2(a), Justice Black's majority opinion contained dicta approving the commission's analysis of price in terms of mill-net receipts. The prevalent tendency has been, however, to regard this dicta as pertaining only to the particular facts of that case, facts that did not raise the question of an individual supplier's use of a basing-point system. Thus, no rule of law has ever prevented the individual supplier from using single or multiple basing points in the course of distributing his product.

In the early 1950s, the commission abandoned its artificial use of the price discrimination law as a sanction against collusive price fixing and ceased its reliance on mill-net receipts as the price to be used in determining whether or not a violation of Section 2(a) had occurred. Rather, it began to focus on the prices actually paid by the buyers. The rejection of the mill-net concept brought the commission's viewpoint into harmony with the clear legislative intent on this point. At the time the Robinson-Patman measure was being considered, Congress rejected an amendment to the original bill that would have prohibited the use of delivered-price systems by directing that price be construed to mean the amount received by the vendor, less any transportation costs. This decision to cease treating delivered prices as per se discriminatory, the net effect of which would be to compel f.o.b. factory pricing, was reiterated by the commission's Advisory Committee on Cost Justification in 1956. It stated in its report:

> In all instances of "geographic" or "delivered" pricing the intent of the parties must be considered—what they mean the price to be. If the arrangement is for the buyer to transport the goods, or pay for the transport, the price obviously does not include freight charges (e.g., $1 per dozen f.o.b. seller's factory, no freight allowed). On the other hand, if it is understood that the seller will transport the goods to the buyer or pay for transport, price includes transport (e.g., $1 per dozen f.o.b. buyer's plant, or $1 per dozen f.o.b. seller's plant, full carload freight allowed) the price is $1 per dozen, i.e., there is no price differential. In finding price it is reality that counts, not form; it is, for example, of no consequence that in one case the seller pays the freight and in another the buyer pays it and deducts the amount on payment of the invoice; either way freight is seller's cost.

The Attorney General's National Committee to Study the Antitrust Laws agreed that the most sensible definition of price was the buyer's actual cost. According to its 1955 report:

> Since the paramount legal inquiry of the Robinson-Patman Act centers on the "injurious" handicaps imposed by discriminations on "disfavored" customers, it is this "actual price" paid by buyers which determines their competitive standing vis-à-vis each other, and hence must be the significant index of legality.

The Meaning of Price Discrimination

Having established a definition for price, the concept of *price discrimination* remains to be examined. It will be remembered that Section 2(a) makes it unlawful "to discriminate in price. . . ." For a number of years there was a dispute as to whether or not the term *discrimination* encompassed more than a mere price difference. The legislative history of the act tended to indicate that this term denoted something of a competitively inimical character. For example, Congressman Utterback, manager of the bill in the House, explained the meaning of price discrimination as follows:

> In its meaning as simple English, a discrimination is more than a mere difference. Underlying the meaning of the word is the idea that some relationship exists between the parties to the discrimination which entitles them to equal treatment, whereby the difference granted to one casts some burden or disadvantage upon the other. If the two are competing in the resale of the goods concerned, that relationship exists. Where, also, the price to one is so low as to involve a sacrifice of some part of the seller's necessary costs and profit as applied to that business, it leaves that deficit inevitably to be made up in higher prices to his other customers; and there, too, a relationship may exist upon which to base the charge of discrimination. But where no such relationship exists, where the goods are sold in different markets and the conditions affecting those markets set different price levels for them, the sale to different customers at those different prices would not constitute a discrimination within the meaning of this bill.

The issue was eventually settled by the 1960 Supreme Court decision in *Anheuser-Busch,* where a unanimous Court said:

> We are convinced that . . . there are no overtones of business buccaneering in the §2(a) phrase "discriminate in price." Rather, a price discrimination within the meaning of that provision is merely a price difference.

> [T]he statute itself spells out the conditions which make a price difference illegal or legal, and we would derange this integrated statutory scheme were we to read other conditions into the law by means of the nondirective phrase "discriminate in price."

In dismissing the conflicting comment by Congressman Utterback, Chief Justice Warren stated that:

> . . . [T]he primary function of statutory construction is to effectuate the intent of Congress, and that function cannot properly be discharged by reliance upon a statement of a single Congressman, in the face of the weighty countervailing considerations which are present in this case.

The Court did not mean to suggest, however, that evidence of predatory intent, unreasonably low local price cuts, or other indicia of business buccaneering would not be relevant in a price discrimination case. Rather, "the existence of predatory intent bears upon the likelihood of injury to competition, and . . . a price reduction below cost tends to establish such an intent." Thus, the Court concluded, "our decision does not raise the specter of a flat prohibition of price differentials, inasmuch as price differences constitute but one element of a Section 2(a) violation."

Furthermore, because price discrimination is synonymous with price differentiation, price equality cannot be unlawful. The act sanctions uniform prices among all customers, regardless of their functional classification. Thus, a supplier may sell to wholesalers, retailers, and consumers at the same price. A wholesaler has no legal right to a price lower than that received by a buyer operating at a lower functional level, such as a retailer. In fact, a supplier is free to charge a wholesaler more than a favored retailer unless the former's retailer customers compete with the direct-buying retailer.

Indirect Price Discrimination Under 2(a)

It is well established that indirect as well as direct price discrimination is within the prohibitions of the act. In addition to the allowances and rebates that are deducted from the seller's price quotation in order to determine the buyer's out-of-pocket cost or net price, there are a variety of collateral contract terms that affect how much the buyer really receives for the contract price. Differences in these terms could be unlawful under Section 2(a) if they amount to an indirect discrimination in price. For example, in its *Corn Products* decision, the Supreme Court held that booking practices by a supplier of glucose, which permitted some favored customers to purchase thirty-day options for glucose at existing prices in a rising market, were unlawful *indirect* discriminations in price. The Court concluded that discriminatory terms of sale were included within the ambit of Section 2(a). A variety of other commercial arrangements incidental to sales contracts—delivery terms, free goods or bonus merchandise, sales return privileges, guarantees against price decline, discounts for cash payments, and warehousing services—that favor some customers over others have been subjected to the proscriptions of Section 2(a). Moreover, differences in freight-equalization terms have been held unlawful. One United States Court of Appeals went so far as to suggest that merely placing former retail customers of a rival distributor on a favorable consignment basis (thereby guaranteeing their sales) in order to induce such customers to transfer their business to the defendant constituted a "prima facie case of indirect price discrimination." Even though the holding in this case is susceptible to attack on jurisdictional grounds, because a consignment is not a sale as Section 2(a) requires, it demonstrates that any discrimination supporting a finding of a resulting reduction in prices to some competitors over others will constitute an indirect discrimination. The test is the result, not the appearance.

On the other hand, bona fide, separate, independent business agreements between a supplier and its customers that have no connection with the sales contracts do not give rise to indirect price discrimination under Section 2(a). For example, in one decision, the commission declined to find that "liberal" payments by a supplier to some of its customers who had performed storage and delivery services for the supplier constituted indirect price discrimination, because "in the absence of some showing that they are grossly in excess of the cost or value of the services rendered, it cannot be found that they constitute any sort of a rebate or price reduction on other merchandise bought by the [customer] from respondent for resale."

Indirect Price Discrimination Under 2(d) and 2(e)

The great practical significance of the distinction between practices constituting indirect price discrimination under Section 2(a), on the one hand, and discriminatory promotional payments or "services and facilities connected with the processing, handling, sale, or offering for sale of [the supplier's] commodity" covered by Sections 2(d) and 2(e), on the other, should not be underestimated. The significance is found in the fact that the adverse competitive-effects requirement of Section 2(a) is not found in either 2(d) or 2(e). Furthermore, the defense of cost justification is not available under the latter two provisions. Thus, disproportionate payments of services and facilities under Section 2(d) and 2(e) are virtually illegal per se, resulting in the unfortunate consequence of hinging the legality of a supplier's activities on the picayune aspects of each particular transaction. Reference was made to this situation in the 1955 Report of the Attorney General's National Committee to Study the Antitrust Laws where it was observed that:

> Virtually identical trade practices have been deemed "allowances" in one case and "indirect discriminations" in another. . . . The decisions, moreover, reveal no guide for distinguishing a justifiable "indirect" discrimination from a flat per se offense. Such legal incongruities, we believe, frustrate equally the Commission's legitimate enforcement objectives and businessmen's good faith attempts to comply.

Attempts have been made by the commission to resolve the dilemma created by the apparent overlap between 2(a) and 2(d)–2(e). The tendency has been to apply 2(d) and 2(e) only where the payments, or services and facilities, have been provided by the supplier to its customers in reference to *subsequent resales* by the latter, and not in connection with the original sale between them. Otherwise, the more stringent standards of 2(d) and 2(e) would frustrate normal price adjustments, which properly should be judged under the more relaxed standards of 2(a).

Availability

Certainly one of the more murky aspects of price discrimination is the concept of availability. In simplest terms, if a supplier's lowest net price is practically available to all of his customers, it is generally agreed that no violation of the price discrimination law has occurred. Thus, if a private label product is available in a meaningful sense to all customers at a price lower than that charged for a brand name product of like grade and quality, then the mere fact that the two products were sold at different prices to competing customers does not result in a violation of the law. The same result should prevail where a schedule of noncost-justified quantity discounts is offered to all customers, the highest bracket (in terms of volume) of which is within the buying capacity of each purchaser. Because there is no inequality of treatment, there is, therefore, no discrimination. Similarly, a noncost-justified price difference resulting from cash discounts or other favorable terms offered to purchasers paying their bills within a specified time should not be unlawful if made available to all customers.

Although there is general accord as to the propriety of the availability concept, there is some dispute as to when in a legal proceeding it should be introduced. At first blush it would appear that the absence of availability should be pleaded and proved by the plaintiff in order to establish a prima facie case of price discrimination. Section 2(a) requires that the seller "discriminate in price." Implicit in such a requirement is that the allegedly disfavored buyers were unable to obtain the same goods at the same low price as their competitors. The Supreme Court has held, however, in the *Anheuser-Busch* case, that price discrimination means nothing more than a "price difference." If this definition is literally applied under all circumstances, then a plaintiff need not negate the possibility that the lower price was available to all customers. Such a rigid application of the Court's holding in *Anheuser-Busch* offends the dictates of common sense. The basic thrust of the act is directed against inequality of treatment. Clearly, this intent would best be effectuated by defining price discrimination as a price difference *plus* unavailability, because inequality of treatment implies lack of availability of the lower price to purchasers paying the higher price. However, accepting for the moment the view that a price difference is the legal equivalent of price discrimination, the burden of alleging and proving availability falls on the defendant.

Accepting availability as one of the supplier's defenses, the question still remains as to whether it would be more appropriate to regard it as a threshold defense raised to defeat the showing of a prima facie case of price discrimination, or whether it would be more appropriately employed as a method to destroy the requisite nexus between price discrimination and competitive injury. At least it is clear that the significance of the availability safety valve cannot be underestimated in light of the frequently insurmountable difficulties attendant to the cost justification defense.

"SAME SELLER" REQUIREMENT

The Robinson-Patman Act speaks in terms of discriminatory prices, allowances, services, and facilities granted by a "person." In order to have a violation of these provisions the offending transactions with the two or more purchasers must stem from the same seller. As uncomplicated as this requirement appears to be, it has caused a good deal of confusion both among businessmen and the courts. The knotty problems arise when parent corporations sell their products through independent subsidiaries or distributors. In a few cases the basic proposition has been made that unless a parent's sales subsidiary is controlled by the parent in its pricing policies, it is a separate legal person, whose prices cannot be measured against those of the supplier in determining whether discrimination has occurred. The separate prices charged by each are not those of the same seller. The issue of whether or not a parent has sufficiently supplanted the corporate autonomy of a subsidiary corporation so as to make the prices charged by one measurable against the prices charged by the other, is primarily a factual one with only general guidelines to be drawn from litigated cases.

There is a large amount of judicial precedent in antitrust and other proceedings that deal with the general problem of parent-subsidiary autonomy. However, limitations of space require that we restrict our examination of these precedents to three cases, two of which have been the most frequently relied on in determining whether the "same seller" corporate relationship exists between a parent and its subsidiary. The fountainhead of the independent subsidiary doctrine is the opinion of the United States Court of Appeals for the Seventh Circuit in the *National Lead* case. In that case, Anaconda Copper Mining Co. and two of its wholly owned subsidiaries were charged with unlawful price discrimination. In ordering the dismissal of the Federal Trade Commission cease and desist order as against the parent corporation, the court stated that:

Though the record shows that International, Anaconda Lead and Anaconda Sales were wholly owned subsidiaries of petitioner and in September 1947, at a date after International had withdrawn from the field, Anaconda, Anaconda Sales and International were controlled by interlocking boards of directors and officers, there is no evidence which militates against the existence and activity of these subsidiaries as separate entities at any time pertinent to this inquiry. Thus, though the evidence tends to prove the incidents of a parent-subsidiary relationship, a fact which has never been in dispute, the closely correlated operation of International and Anaconda Sales reflects no sinister connotation of domination by their common parent, keeping in mind that the only function for which Anaconda Sales was organized was to sell products produced by International in certain western states in which the latter was not licensed to do business.

. . . These sparse gleamings from the record fail to support the Commission's finding of substantial identity. To come within the applicable rule, there must be evidence of such complete control of the subsidiary by the parent as to render the former a mere tool of the latter, and to compel the conclusion that the corporate identity of the subsidiary is a mere fiction.

It should be noted that the court's finding of subsidiary autonomy did not result in a dismissal of the complaint. After finding violations of Section 2(a) by the subsidiaries, the court merely refused to hold the parent responsible for the violations absent an actual exercise of control by the latter over the former. It is conceivable that a different set of standards might have applied had the issue been whether a seller can immunize price discriminations from the proscriptions of Section 2(a) through the utilization of subsidiaries which it has the power to control. It has been suggested that the applicability of *National Lead's* requirement of an actual exercise of control must be limited to the assigning of responsibility for violations of the law and should not be employed in determining whether a violation has, in fact, occurred. A review of the cases subsequent to the *National Lead* decision reveals that it has not been so limited.

Baim & Blank, Inc. v. *Philco Corp.* is the leading case in which immunity from the Robinson-Patman Act was established through the use of a sales subsidiary. A private treble-damage action was brought against Philco and its wholly owned distributor, Philco Distributors, Inc. (P.D.I.), for damages arising out of discrimination in prices and promotional allowances. The plaintiff operated a single retail store in Brooklyn and made all of its purchases from the subsidiary, but never from Philco (the parent) directly. It was alleged that Philco sold its products *directly* to Davega, a twenty-eight-store retail chain located in the greater New York City area, at prices lower than those offered to the plaintiff, and, therefore, violated the act. Baim & Blank attempted to hurdle the parent-subsidiary problem, and, thereby, satisfy the same seller requirement by contending that "in actual fact" the two defendants were a single entity, because, for the most part, they had common officers. The court rejected this common seller argument because there was no evidence that the prices established by P.D.I. were determined by the parent Philco. Furthermore, it was noted that the parent and subsidiary had separate chief sales executives.

The conclusion reached in *Philco,* that the presence of common ownership and common directors does not require a finding that two corporations are the same seller, was recently followed by a federal district court in Connecticut. In the *Southern New England Distributing Corp.* case, the court granted the defendant's motion to dismiss that portion of a complaint in which the plaintiff had asked the court to "pierce the corporate veil" and find that the four defendant corporations were in fact one entity. It was held that the plaintiff had failed to introduce evidence of an "alter-ego" relationship between Admiral Sales Corporation and any of its subsidiaries sufficient to warrant litigating the issue of whether the parent and its subsidiaries were the same seller within the meaning of Section 2(a).

The FTC has demonstrated a willingness to accept a separate entity notion with respect to both parent-subsidiary and brother-sister corporations. For example, in the *Warren Petroleum* decision, the commission declined to hold a parent responsible for the predatory pricing of its 51 per cent owned subsidiary, even though the parent's president consulted with his counterpart in the subsidiary on certain major issues. In its words:

> The law seems to be well settled that mere ownership by one corporation of stock in another corporation, even though such ownership extend to more than 50% of the latter's stock, does not of itself make the owning corporation responsible for the activities of the subsidiary corporation unless the owning corporation shall have asserted control over its subsidiary to the extent of directing and determining its policies and practices, thus making the subsidiary corporation an instrumentality of the owning corporation.

There is confusion as to precisely what degree of control will be tolerated before a unity of identity is created so as to satisfy the same seller requirement. For example, in the commission's *Kay Windsor Frocks* opinion, the sharing of joint showrooms, expenditures, and a common manager resulted in the treatment of two dress manufacturers, a parent and its 50 per cent owned subsidiary, as a single entity for the purpose of finding a 2(d) violation. This result prevailed despite the existence of separate presidents, separate factories, and separate principal places of business.

The absence of hard and fast rules by which a corporation can determine whether its subsidiary possesses sufficient indicia of legal autonomy to be a different seller reduces the value of the independent subsidiary doctrine as a guide by which to chart a corporation's future course of conduct. It must be recognized that the applicability of the *separate seller* concept depends on a factual determination in each case of whether the parent company and its subsidiary or affiliate are independent entities insofar as distribution policies are concerned. This is not to say that the doctrine cannot furnish a considerable measure of immunity from the act; but the danger of an adverse decision by the commission or the courts is such that ultimate reliance on this doctrine as a method by which to achieve greater pricing flexibility should not be counseled.

Even if the legal autonomy of a subsidiary can be established in court, liability might be imposed on the parent through the *indirect purchaser* doctrine. This concept will be discussed at length in connection with the Robinson-Patman Act's two-or-more purchasers requirement. Suffice it to say here that the commission has developed this doctrine for application in those cases where the direct dealings between a manufacturer and retailer have become so extensive that the distributor's autonomy has been supplanted by these activities. The distributor's accounts are viewed in the eyes of the law as the supplier's own customers. Thus, the customers of the distributor may become the supplier's indirect purchasers.

Finally, an important caveat must be noted. If the legal autonomy of a subsidiary is established, the parent must be careful to quote prices to it that are comparable to the parent's quotations to other distributors. Otherwise, the parent may be attacked for activities cognizable under the Robinson-Patman Act. This so-called bathtub theory of discrimination will be discussed in the following section.

TWO OR MORE PURCHASERS OR CUSTOMERS

Not only must there be two or more sales by the same seller in order to bring the Robinson-Patman Act into play, but the offending transactions must be with two or more purchasers. This basically straightforward condition is somewhat complicated by the existence of the previously mentioned indirect purchaser doctrine. Instead of selling directly to retailers, it is a common practice among producers to utilize a distribution system in which goods are sold to wholesalers—generally either autonomous subsidiaries or independent distributors—who, in turn, resell the products at varying prices to the retailers. As we have seen, such a system can immunize a manufacturer from the proscriptions of the act. However, this immunity has been lost in some cases where the direct dealings between the supplier and customers of the wholesalers are so extensive that, in contemplation of law, these customers are treated as the producer's indirect purchasers. In other words, under this principle, customers of a supplier's distributors are regarded as indirect purchasers when the supplier exercises such a degree of control over the sales by the distributors to the retailers that such sales are in all essential respects sales by the supplier. Thus, a supplier may be exposed to Section 2(a) liability when he sells to direct buying retailers at prices different from those paid to the wholesaler-distributors by the supplier's indirect purchaser retailers. The question of whether responsibility for price or promotional allowance differentials attaches to the manufacturer is one of fact in which a decision must be made on a case-by-case basis with a careful scrutiny of the differing circumstances presented in each instance. An examination of the significant cases reveals that the most important factor to be considered is the degree of control exercised by the manufacturer over the prices and other terms of the sale between the intermediary and the retailer or indirect purchaser, who could also be a consumer. It may be remembered that this factor is similar to that used in determining whether a subsidiary is legally autonomous from its parent, but the tests of applicability for the two concepts are different. Although a subsidiary may possess sufficient indicia of autonomy to be legally independent, it is entirely possible that the parent may still have enough contact with the subsidiary's customers to create an indirect purchaser relationship between the two.

The indirect purchaser doctrine first appeared in the commission's *Kraft-Phenix Cheese Corp.* decision, where a cheese producer was found to have solicited orders from the retailers, issued suggested price lists to which the wholesalers usually adhered, and directly exchanged fresh cheese for the retailer's stale cheese. The commission stated: "A retailer is nonetheless a purchaser because he buys indirectly if, as here, the manufacturer deals with him directly in promoting the sale of his products and exercises control over the terms on which he buys." A few years thereafter, in the *Luxor* decision, a supplier's direct solicitation of retailers and its intimate supervision over their pricing policies through Fair Trade contracts resulted in a commission finding that these retailers were the "purchasers" under Section 2(e) even though they obtained the goods from independent jobbers.

Although many commission decisions in which the indirect purchaser concept was relied on reached the courts, the latter were not required to pass on the doctrine's legality because it went unchallenged on appeal. However, in *Klein* v. *The Lionel Corp.*, the plaintiff contended that Lionel's fixing of the minimum retail price of its products, as it was authorized to do by the state's Fair Trade statute, constituted sufficient control over the resale to make Klein a purchaser within the meaning of the act. The United States Court of Appeals for the Third Circuit repudiated the applicability of the concept in private treble-damage actions, at least in cases where the control was exercised through state Fair Trade contracts. Without commenting on the FTC's repeated use of the doctrine, the court rejected the plaintiff's claim on the basis of a long line of cases in which it had been held that an individual can have no cause of action under the act unless he is an actual purchaser from the person charged with the discrimination. The court argued that it would violate the policy of the Fair Trade statute to so construe it as to expose a manufacturer-seller to greater liability when its purpose was to benefit him.

The United States Court of Appeals for the Second Circuit upheld the indirect purchaser doctrine in its *American News Co.* decision. It stated that the requisite "customer" relationship exists if there is direct dealing between the manufacturer and the retailer and if the former controls the terms at which the latter buys. However, this time it was applied against a buyer who had allegedly violated Section 2(f) of the act. In all of the previous indirect purchaser cases, the finding that the seller-customer relation existed was based solely on the conduct of the seller in proceedings brought against the seller. The petitioner, a newsstand chain, charged with inducing and receiving promotional rebates, contended it was an error for the commission to wish the sins of the seller on the buyer, suggesting that the function of the "control" requirement was to punish *sellers* for illegal price control activity. The court did not agree that the doctrine was so grounded. Rather, it felt that it stemmed from a fundamental aim of the act to protect buyers' competitors from the evil effects of direct and indirect price discrimination. The court then stated:

> The method chosen to reach this goal was to forbid *sellers* to make direct or indirect discriminations in price between one purchaser or customer and another, save in certain limited situations. The "customer" or "purchaser" requirement marks one of the outer limits of the seller's responsibility not to discriminate. As long as he exercises control over the terms of a transaction he is held to this duty; otherwise the requirement of the statute could be easily avoided by use of a "dummy" wholesaler. If there is no control the duty naturally ends, for the manufacturer has no power to protect the buyer's competitors.
> . . . Since the requirement is imposed not to punish sellers for their conduct, but to effectuate the purpose of giving protection to buyers' competitors, the "indirect customer" doctrine should apply whether the proceeding is brought against buyer or seller.

Certainly, one of the most controversial applications of the indirect purchaser doctrine has arisen in the automotive replacement parts industry, where the use of *group buying* techniques has resulted in a number of suppliers and purchasers being found to be in violation of the Robinson-Patman Act. Generally, group buying is a system by which several businesses operating at the same level of competition join together to create a purchasing agent who operates at the next highest functional level of competition. The use of such a group buyer secures to the members of the group lower prices from the supplier and may also effect operational savings. Prior to this group buyer line of cases, the indirect purchaser doctrine had been used to compare prices paid by purchasers at the same level of distribution who presumably performed the same functions. However, as the *Purolator Products* decision demonstrates, the commission has expanded the doctrine in order to subject price differentials at different functional levels of distribution to the requirements of Section 2(a). Purolator manufactured automotive replacement filters and sold them nationwide through independent warehouse distributors (WD's), who resold mostly to jobbers but sometimes also to fleets and to dealers. Some of the WD's were affiliated with (that is, own or control or were owned by or controlled by) some or all of the jobbers to whom they sold. Although all of Purolator's WD's received the same base discount plus a 15 per cent "external redistribution discount" for resales to independent jobbers, an additional 4 per cent discount was given to WD's with affiliated jobbers when they provided "internal redistribution"— the double handling of filters successively through the WD's central warehouse and the warehouse of the affiliated jobber—in reselling. As a result of this system, jobbers affiliated with favored distributors received greater discounts than competing independent jobbers.

The commission attacked the difference in price on sales by WD's to independent jobbers for resale to dealers (40 cents, as suggested by Purolator) and the prices charged *by Purolator* itself to integrated and independent WD's for resale by those entities direct to dealers (36.4 and 38 cents, respectively). That is, even though the prices compared (warehouses to jobbers; supplier to warehouses) involved different levels of distribution, the commission felt it could upgrade the jobbers as indirect purchasers from Purolator. Thus, the alleged competitive injury at the jobber level was cognizable under Section 2(a). The commission used the following standard in arriving at its conclusion that the jobbers were purchasers of Purolator:

> Where the prices to be charged the indirect purchaser are effectively established by the manufacturer, and where virtually all of the conditions and terms upon which the sale is to be consummated are fixed by the manufacturer or are subject to its approval, the predicate for a finding that the indirect purchaser is a purchaser from the manufacturer has been constructed. Other factors to be considered in arriving at the conclusion are instances of direct contact between the indirect purchaser and the manufacturer, such as direct negotiation of franchise agreements, direct solicitation of orders by the manufacturer's salesmen even though the orders are filled by the intermediary and

the manufacturer looks to the intermediary for payment, direct negotiations for changes in price, direct policing of the indirect purchaser's resale prices, direct provision of advertising materials, and inspection by the manufacturer to insure that the indirect purchaser is fulfilling the terms of its agreement with the manufacturer's distributor or wholesaler.

The commission's decision was affirmed by the United States Seventh Circuit Court of Appeals, which, for the first time, passed on the legality of the indirect purchaser doctrine. In finding that the commission's doctrine had a reasonable basis in law, the court made the following observation:

> To ensure fair competition among purchasers from the same seller, the Robinson-Patman Act amendments to the Clayton Act forbade sellers to make price discriminations between purchasers except when justified by economies to the seller. If a seller can control the terms upon which a buyer once removed may purchase the seller's product from the seller's immediate buyer, the buyer once removed is for all practical, economic purposes dealing directly with the seller. If the seller controls the sale, he is responsible for the discrimination in the sale price, if there is such discrimination. If the seller cannot in some manner control the sale between his immediate buyer and a buyer once removed, then he has no power by his own action to prevent an injury to competition.

Purolator asserted, however, that even if the commission's concept was sound, it nevertheless had not shown that Purolator exercised the amount of control over sales to jobbers required to apply the concept. Even though it did not pass on the degree of seller control required to turn a buyer once or twice removed into a purchaser within the meaning of the act, the court found that the following stipulated facts constituted sufficient evidence to support the commission's finding of control: Purolator had stipulated that it had *reserved to itself the legal right to control sales* to jobbers and that it had written and supplied the warehouse distributor with jobber agreements, as well as suggested resale price lists. Furthermore, the petitioner had solicited jobbers and urged them to maintain prices, which for the most part had been done.

By way of contrast, reference should be made to two cases in which the supplier did *not* exercise such a degree of control over the transaction as to make subsequent sales by intermediaries to retailers attributable to him. Hopefully, they will provide a better grasp of the quantity and quality of contracts between the parties, which is required before the requisite seller-purchaser relationship can be found.

In the commission's *Whitaker Cable* decision, a manufacturer of automotive replacement products was charged with a 2(a) violation. One of the issues presented was whether the contractual relationship between the manufacturer and the Willard Storage Battery Company was such to constitute Willard's customers as purchasers of Whitaker. Under the arrangement between them, the manufacturer shipped products bearing the Willard brand directly to Willard's customers, but invoices covering the shipments were sent directly to Willard who then paid for these goods. There was no evidence that Whitaker in any way participated in the selection of customers who purchased the Willard line, nor was there any evidence of its control over the sales to them. Willard's customers were found not to be the manufacturer's indirect purchasers.

A few years later in the *Liggett & Myers* decision, the commission sanctioned the supplier's use of "missionary men" to contact its subsidiaries' retailer customers. This was the respondent's only form of contact with the 873,750 retail outlets. These missionary men called on the retailers three or four times a year to build good will, to encourage them to stock and handle adequate quantities of the respondent's cigarettes, and generally to make them more alert in the sale thereof. Whenever possible these contact men arranged store displays and other advertising materials. Also, the Liggett & Myers representatives *directly* replenished a retailer's supply of products when it appeared that the retailer's then present inventory would not last until his wholesaler supplier could make his next delivery. The prices at which the missionary men sold the cigarettes to the retailers were established by the wholesaler. If the retailer did not wish to pay cash for this merchandise, the account was handled by his own wholesaler, to whom the transaction was reported, and by whom the retailer was billed. Such transactions were infrequent and involved only small quantities of cigarettes. The respondent had not exercised the degree of control over these transactions necessary to invoke the indirect purchaser doctrine.

A similar result obtained in *Hiram Walker, Inc.* v. *A & S Tropical, Inc.,* where the court concluded that the quantity and quality of contacts between Hiram Walker and the complaining retailers who purchased their products from independent wholesalers was not sufficient to bring the "indirect purchaser" doctrine into play. The manufacturers' activities with respect to the retailers were found to be limited to promotional work by "missionary" men who provided the retailers with advertising materials and generally acted to supplement Hiram Walker's national advertising efforts. These "missionary" men were not salesmen and did not take orders for products. The manufacturer did not attempt to control the price or terms of resale.

Needless to say, the safest approach would be to have no contact between a manufacturer and its wholesaler's customers and no control over the prices at which these retailers purchase or resell its products. The unsure protection offered by the *Whitaker Cable* and *Liggett & Myers* decisions from the indirect purchaser doctrine should not be relied on without a strong necessity for this type of retailer contact. Furthermore, with respect to parent-independent subsidiary operations, although the activities described here may be insufficient to invoke the indirect purchaser doctrine with respect to the parent and the subsidiary's customers, they may provide sufficient evidence of parent control to destroy subsidiary autonomy.

The indirect purchaser issue is not the only problem of substance that falls within the ambit of the two-or-more-purchasers requirement. It will be remembered that at the close of the discussion of the same seller requirement, brief reference was made to the Robinson-Patman problems created by the existence of a legally autonomous subsidiary that purchases its parent's products. As a result of the so-called bathtub theory of discrimination, a parent corporation must be careful to quote prices to its subsidiary that are comparable to the prices offered other competing distributors. The bathtub theory first appeared in cases under the Sherman Act in which sales subsidiaries were viewed as separate legal persons capable of entering into unlawful conspiracies either with their parent or other corporate affiliates. It was applied to a Robinson-Patman situation in *Danko* v. *Shell Oil Co.* There the court denied a motion to dismiss a complaint alleging that Shell had discriminated in price in favor of its wholly owned service stations to the disadvantage of an independent Shell dealer. The theory advanced in *Danko* was that for antitrust purposes the definitions of purchaser, customer, and distributor are a matter of competitive substance and competitive function and not of form.

The most recent appearance of the bathtub theory was in the *Reines Distributors* case. There, the plaintiff made a motion for a separate trial of the issue of whether the defendant, Admiral Corporation's subsidiary located in Newark, New Jersey (herein called Newark), was a purchaser from the defendant within the meaning of Sections 2(a) and 2(e) and a customer of defendant within the meaning of Section 2(d). If the plaintiff failed to prove that Newark was an independent distributor, then it would have to prove its claim against Admiral by reason of the preferences allegedly given to the defendant's other seventy-nine distributors, a more lengthy and costly method of satisfying the act's two-or-more-purchasers requirement. In granting the motion, the court found that the plaintiff's allegations, if proved, could warrant a conclusion that Admiral's subsidiary was sufficiently autonomous to be a purchaser-customer. It was alleged that Newark had the right to engage and discharge its own personnel, to select its own merchandise and buy only what it chose, to fix prices on resale, to accept or reject factory promotions, to maintain separate books of account and bank accounts, to negotiate advertising and promotional deals with its own customers, and to contract for its own special services. As further evidence that Newark was, in effect, an independent purchaser-customer, the plaintiff planned to offer proof that the subsidiary competed with it for the business of dealers in the plaintiff's territory. The court noted, however, that the mere fact that Newark competed with Reines was only slight evidence of Newark's independence.

SALE FOR USE, CONSUMPTION, OR RESALE WITHIN THE UNITED STATES OR ANY TERRITORY THEREOF

This requirement precludes the application of Section 2(a) to sales made for use, consumption, or resale in a foreign country. It should be noted, however, that this language does not exempt discriminatory sales for import into the United States. Furthermore, the same limitation does not appear in Section 2(c), (d), and (e) of the act. Thus, the brokerage provisions of 2(c) have been applied to export sales in which a discriminatory rebate to the buyer was involved.

The special problems raised with respect to purchases by nonprofit institutions and government agencies for use, consumption, or resale within the United States will be discussed in Chapter 9.

COMPETITIVE INJURY

What are the competitive effects necessary to show a completed Section 2(a) violation? The answer to this question is among the most complicated in the Robinson-Patman area. Section 2(a)'s concluding proviso reads:

> That it shall be unlawful . . . to discriminate in price . . . where the effect of such discrimination [1] may be substantially to lessen competition or [2] tend to create a monopoly in any line of commerce, [3] or to injure, destroy, or prevent competition with any person who either [a] grants [b] or knowingly receives the benefit of such discrimination, [c] or to customers of either of them.

At the outset it must be remembered that the Robinson-Patman Act is designed to reach price discriminations in their *incipiency,* before the harm to competition is effected. It is enough to demonstrate that they "may" have the proscribed effect. But although actual harm to competition need not be proved under Section 2(a), actual injury to a competitor is evidentiary support thereof. A private plaintiff, however, must of course be able to prove that he suffered actual injury to his business or property as the result of the defendant's unlawful activities in order to recover treble damages under Section 4 of the Clayton Act. A probability of harm will not suffice in this instance.

In adding this proviso Congress sought to distinguish price discrimination practices having no real anti-competitive effect on commerce from pricing situations that are of legitimate public concern. Only those discriminations having one of the listed effects on competition are illegal. The nature of the competitive effect necessary to finding a violation of Section 2(a) varies with the standard of illegality relied upon and the level of competition affected.

There are three distinct tests of illegality under Section 2(a) ([1], [2], or [3] above). The first two, which are carryovers from the original Section 2 of the Clayton Act, require an adverse competitive impact in the total relevant market, whereas the inquiry under the third test—that portion added by the Robinson-Patman Amendments to the original Section 2 —focuses more narrowly upon the probability of an adverse impact on the person discriminated against. The Robinson-Patman Amendments had the desired effect of easing the burden of demonstrating the illegality of a price discrimination by eliminating the necessity for an exhaustive market analysis. For this reason, the original Section 2 tests of illegality contained in the present Section 2(a) generally have not been relied upon to establish a violation of the act.

Traditionally, there have been three contexts in which competitive injury has been found by the courts under the Robinson-Patman portion of Section 2(a) (test [3] above). The first is the primary-line injury in which a seller suffers economic injury as a result of regional price cutting by a competitor; this is occasioned by a large seller cutting his prices in one trade area in order to destroy a local competitor who operates in that area. Secondary-line injury is that which occurs at the buyer's level. It results from a discrimination in prices between two buyers who compete for the same business. Finally, there is a third-line injury, which is that suffered by disfavored customers of the supplier in their competition with customers of the favored purchaser, three steps down the distribution chain. This more controversial and less commonly used means for measuring competitive effect will be discussed along with primary and secondary-line injuries in Chapters 5 and 6. At that point, we will also consider the Supreme Court's recent *Perkins* decision, which rejected this traditional limitation upon the levels of cognizable competitive injury and applied the act to fourth-line competitive injury—that suffered by a disfavored buyer in his competition with a customer of a customer of a customer of the discriminating supplier.

THE COMMERCE REQUIREMENT

In general, in determining the commerce coverage of the Robinson-Patman Act, Congress declined to extend its regulatory power to the extent it had in the Sherman Act, where the proscriptions against restrictive and monopolistic practices come into play if the transactions complained of are shown to have *affected* interstate commerce. Although the jurisdictional reach is clearly shorter, its precise limitations are unclear. The "commerce" requirement is not uniformly stated in each section of the act. The interstate commerce requirements of Sections 2(c) and 2(d), and Section 2(e) by implication, are two-fold. Their application is restricted to discriminatory practices by persons "engaged in [interstate] commerce" in the "course of such [interstate] commerce." However, Section 2(a) refers to this jurisdictional requirement in three phrases by adding the condition that "either or any" of the purchases must be "in [interstate] commerce." And, because to have a violation of Section 2(f), a violation of 2(a) must also have occurred, the narrower language of 2(a) must apparently be read into 2(f) as well.

Sales Across State Lines

Some authorities have maintained that the same interstate commerce requirements apply to all sections: 2(a), (c), (d), (e), and (f). Accepting this premise, there would be no need to distinguish between the various sections of the act in any discussion of this jurisdictional requisite. However, an important commission decision in 1962 and subsequent developments create some question as to the accuracy of the premise. It appears that the textual divergence is significant. The absence of Section 2(a)'s third phrase from the act's other provisions appears to have resulted in giving a much broader application to the latter. This conclusion is based mainly on the results that prevailed in the commission's *J. H. Filbert* decision, in the *Shreveport Macaroni* case, both of which dealt with 2(d) and 2(e), in *Rangen, Inc.*, which dealt with Section 2(c), and in *Clausen & Sons, Inc.* v. *Theo Hamm Brewing Co.*, which compared and contrasted the commerce requirement in Sections 2(c), (d), (e) and 3 of the Robinson-Patman Act with that found in Section 2(a).

The effect of these decisions is to eliminate, with respect to 2(c), 2(d), 2(e), and, apparently, Section 3 of the Robinson-Patman Act, the implied requirement that the sale to either the favored or the competing disfavored customer must cross a state boundary. For the purposes of these four sections, the interstate character of a company's business, or that of its buyers, without more, may provide a sufficient commerce nexus to bring its intrastate activities within the ambit of the act. In *Shreveport,* it was the court's view that a discriminatory allowance is "in the course of commerce" within the meaning of 2(d) if it is made or used in interstate commerce and paid by a manufacturer engaged in interstate commerce to customers also engaged in interstate commerce, even if the allowance is made in connection with products sold only within a given state. As we shall see, the results that have prevailed in the Section 2(a) cases do not admit of such a broad application.

As a general proposition, it can be said that a firm is not engaged in commerce if it sells its goods solely in its own state. However, if the goods being resold were purchased from outside the state, then the seller's totally intrastate activities may come within the ambit of 2(a) because of the flow of commerce doctrine, a judicial concept that will be elaborated on later. But, whether a business is engaged in commerce is not really important, because Section 2(a) will apply only if "either or any" of the discriminatory sales are "in commerce." Similarly, the course of commerce language is immaterial, for if a sale is in commerce, then it was necessarily made by a seller in the course of commerce. In order to satisfy the in commerce test, it is the general rule that at least one of the two allegedly discriminatory sales must cross a state line. It was not until the early 1950s, however, that the Supreme Court finally established, in *Moore* v. *Mead's Fine Bread Company,* that it is immaterial whether the higher-priced or lower-priced discriminatory sale moved across a state line.

The plaintiff in *Moore* was engaged in an intrastate bakery business in New Mexico. The defendant was a corporation engaged in the baking business in Clovis, New Mexico. Significantly, it was one of several corporations having interlocking ownership and management. These corporations maintained plants in both Texas and New Mexico and sold all their bread under the name *Mead's Fine Bread.* Besides promoting the product through a common advertising program, these corporations purchased their flour and bread wrappers as a unit. In addition to this close interrelationship with companies located in other states, it was found that the defendant sold bread in Farwell, Texas, a town it served with a bread truck operating out of its New Mexico plant. Moore alleged that the defendant had unlawfully cut the wholesale price of its bread to purchasers in Santa Rosa but had not cut prices in any other town or state, with the result that the plaintiff was forced to close its business.

The United States Court of Appeals for the Fifth Circuit reversed the jury verdict in favor of the plaintiff on the ground that the injury resulting from the price cutting was to a purely local competitor whose business was in no way related to interstate commerce.

The Supreme Court, however, found a violation of Section 2(a). It said:

> We have here an interstate industry increasing its domain through outlawed competitive practices. The victim, to be sure, is only a local merchant; and no interstate transactions are used to destroy him. But the beneficiary is an interstate business; the treasury used to finance the warfare is drawn from interstate, as well as local, sources which include not only respondent but also a group of interlocked companies engaged in the same line of business; and the prices on the interstate sales, both by respondent and by the other Mead companies, are kept high while the local prices are lowered. If this method of competition were approved, the pattern for growth of monopoly would be simple. As long as the price warfare was strictly intrastate, interstate business could grow and expand with impunity at the expense of local merchants.

In support of its conclusion, the Court noted a statement by Congressman Utterback, Manager of the Bill in the House who said: "Where . . . a manufacturer sells to customers both within the state and beyond the state, he may not favor either to the disadvantage of the other; he may not use the privilege of interstate commerce to the injury of his local trade, nor may he favor his local trade to the injury of his interstate trade."

Decisions subsequent to *Moore* have given a restrictive reading to the expansive interpretation of the commerce requirement found in that decision. For example, in *Food Basket, Inc.* v. *Albertsons, Inc.*, Section 2(a) was held to be inapplicable to an interstate supermarket chain which discriminated in price by selling selected food products in one of its stores at prices lower than those charged for identical items in its other stores in the same county. The plaintiff, who competed with the defendant's lower-priced store, contended that under the broad dictum of the *Moore* case, purely local discriminatory sales by a seller engaged in interstate commerce came within the purview of Section 2(a)'s commerce requirement if interstate profits were used to subsidize the local discriminatory sales. Significantly, all of Albertson's stores in the county in question purchased their food requirements from two local wholesale companies who bought for their own account from suppliers and took title to the goods, and the Albertson's stores across a nearby state line, which also sold at higher prices, similarly purchased their goods from independent wholesalers located in that state. The United States Court of Appeals for the Tenth Circuit said that while the Supreme Court in *Moore* did use broad language susceptible to the construction urged by the plaintiff, it rejected the contention that the existence of interstate profits does, by itself, transform local discrimination into a Section 2(a) violation. In *Moore* the interstate sales were used to "underwrite the losses of the local price-cutting campaigns"; the discriminatory sales used to finance the local price-cutting were in interstate commerce. In the instant case, however, the court ruled that none of the discriminatory sales complained of had crossed a state line. The sales of Albertson's in the neighboring state did not provide the requisite interstate nexus since those sales involved goods purchased from local wholesalers. According to the court, "two purely local discriminatory sales in different states do not make out a case of 'in commerce' within the meaning of 2(a)."

By far the most important interstate commerce decision since *Moore* involving Section 2(a) is the *Willard Dairy* case. It is quite possible that this decision has created an additional and restrictive dimension to the jursdictional requirements of 2(a). The defendant was a large interstate enterprise who allegedly engaged in predatory price cutting around Willard, Ohio. This market area was supplied by its Ohio processing plant whose products were also sold elsewhere in the same state at higher prices. The court sustained dismissal of the local competitor's action for damages because of his failure to demonstrate that the sale complained of was one occurring in interstate commerce. In its view, the "fact that the defendant also made interstate shipments from *other than* its Shelby, Ohio, plant to areas in which the plaintiff did not engage in business is immaterial to the issue in the case."

Surprisingly, no real attempt was made by the United States Court of Appeals to distinguish the facts in *Willard* from those in *Moore* v. *Mead's Fine Bread Company.* In *Moore,* it will be remembered, the defendant was both directly engaged in interstate commerce—albeit to a limited extent—and was a member of a group of several corporations, some of which were located in other states, having interlocking ownership and management in addition to a unified purchasing program. In *Willard,* although the local plant charged with the Section 2(a) violation did not directly engage in any interstate activity, it was part of a large interstate enterprise. Therefore, the Sixth Circuit must have concluded either that the *Moore* case turned on the presence of the defendant's interstate truck route into Texas, or that, unlike the Mead's Fine Bread Company, the local dairy in Willard, Ohio, was a highly autonomous intrastate unit of an interstate corporation.

The Supreme Court denied *certiorari,* an action that evoked a rare dissent from Justice Black, who felt the result was contrary to that in the *Moore* case. He stated, "The present case presents an important question of price cutting by interstate business with local plants, each of which services largely a local area but all of which draw on the economic power of the national operation." In his view, judgments such as the one in this case "allow the economic resources and staying power of an interstate company to be used with impunity to destroy local competition, precisely the sort of thing the Robinson-Patman Act was designed to prevent."

The restrictive dimension that has apparently been added to Section

2(a) by the circuit court in this case is similar to the doctrine that has allowed sellers to use *independent sales subsidiaries* to defeat the requirement that the sales in question be in commerce. Although there is scant authority for this intrastate immunity concept, its viability must be assumed in light of the *Willard* case, which provided even broader protection than that supplied by the independent-subsidiary doctrine. For in *Willard,* sanctuary was found in the form of independent local plants. There was "no question but that the defendant was engaged in commerce." But the mere fact that the allegedly discriminatory sales were made from a processing plant that engaged in purely intrastate transactions was sufficient to avoid 2(a)'s condition that the sales be in commerce.

The decision in *Willard* raises the question of just how hospitable the Supreme Court is to the holding in the *Shreveport* case, where *certiorari* was denied, also. There, the United States Court of Appeals for the Fifth Circuit held that a discriminatory allowance is in the course of commerce within the meaning of Section 2(d) if it is made or used in interstate commerce and paid by a manufacturer engaged in interstate commerce to customers also engaged in interstate commerce, even if the allowance is made in connection with products sold only in intrastate competition. The court stated:

> We do not read the statute [Section 2(d)] to qualify payment in the "course of . . . commerce," once that appears, by a further requirement that the payment be in connection with goods sold in interstate commerce, resold in interstate commerce, or that the competition between the competing customers be in interstate commerce where there is ample nexus to interstate commerce in the whole transaction as here. There is no warrant in the law for any such fragmentation.

Certainly, it can be argued that the decisions in these two cases simply represent a disagreement between two United States Circuit Courts of Appeal that the Supreme Court declined to resolve. However, because the holding in *Willard* is so antithetical both in philosophy and result to *Shreveport,* a more plausible explanation of the Court's denial of *certiorari* would be that it has recognized a significant difference between the interstate commerce facets of Section 2(a)'s jurisdictional requirements and those of 2(c), 2(d), and 2(e). Unlike Section 2(d) as interpreted by *Shreveport,* Section 2(a) clearly requires that one of the sales out of which a competitive injury arises must actually cross a state line.

Recognition of a distinction between the commerce requirement of Section 2(a) and the other sections of the Robinson-Patman Act can be found also in *Rangen, Inc.* v. *Sterling Nelson & Sons* and the *Clausen* case. In *Rangen,* both parties were interstate manufacturers of fish food. The plaintiff, a Utah-based producer, sued the defendant, an Idaho-based producer, for bribing a state official of Idaho to prefer the defendant's product. The fish food sales by the defendant to the State of Idaho occurred entirely within intrastate commerce. The Ninth Circuit held that the commercial bribery had occurred "in the course of such commerce" within the meaning of Section 2(c), notwithstanding the fact that no interstate sales were involved and the bribery payments did not pass through interstate commerce, because the bribery "created influences intrastate which injured the free competitive interstate commerce in fish food." Unlike Section 2(a), Section2(c) does not require that the illegal brokerage itself be "in commerce." *Clausen* involved a suit by an independent wholesale distributor of Hamm's products in the Minneapolis-St. Paul area who alleged that the defendant, an interstate beer producer, sold its Minnesota made products to other competing Minneapolis-St. Paul distributors at lower prices and on better credit terms than those charged Clausen. In dismissing the complaint, the court noted that while the alleged violations occurred "in the course of . . . such [interstate] commerce" as Sections 2(a), (d), and (e) require, they did not involve discriminatory sales "in commerce" as Section 2(a) additionally, specifically requires. "That section expressly applies only when either or any of the purchases involved in such discrimination are in [interstate] commerce." The court rejected the applicability of the broad language in *Moore* on the ground that some of the purchases involved in the discrimination therein were, in fact, in interstate commerce. But while rejecting the Section 2(a) claim, the court refused to dismiss the allegations based upon Sections 2 (d) and (e) since the facts alleged satisfied the more lenient commerce requirement contained in those sections.

It would be in the commission's interest to have the expansive approach of the *Shreveport* and *Rangen* decisions applied to all sections of the act, including 2(a); and there are indications that it is attempting to do just that. Evidence of its disposition to disregard the sale in commerce condition in Section 2(a), once a general interstate nexus has been established, can be found in a decision involving the Borden Company, a large interstate producer of dairy products. That decision, however, was reversed by the United States Court of Appeals for the Seventh Circuit. It cited *Willard* in refusing to sustain the commission order on the ground that the alleged price discrimination had not occurred in commerce, as required by Section 2(a). It was undisputed that the sales in question were negotiated in Ohio; the milk was produced, processed, and delivered in Ohio for resale in Ohio. Furthermore, it was established that, because of the highly localized nature of the milk business, the company's district chairmen, in most cases, delegated broad managerial responsibility to local plant managers, including responsibility for determining prices. The court refused to accept the view of Commissioner Dixon that "since it is impossible to divorce the Borden Company and its products, if the

Borden Company is in commerce so must be all its products." Instead, the court found itself in complete agreement with Commissioner Elman's dissenting opinion. He said:

> Section 2(a) of the Clayton Act, as amended, states the jurisdictional requirement respecting "commerce" in three separate ways, and each of these variants of the commerce requirements must be satisfied. . . . [T]he Commission's burden of establishing jurisdiction cannot be discharged merely by a showing that respondent is an interstate concern or that it makes interstate sales not involved in the challenged discrimination.

Commissioner Elman then pointed out that the alleged discriminatory sales from the Ohio plant seemed clearly local and without sufficient interstate incidents. Thus, Borden prevailed because of the commission's failure to demonstrate that interstate sales were involved in the challenged discrimination. Once again, as in *Willard,* we have a case of judicial recognition of a local plant's independence and the concomitant immunity from Section 2(a). The local manager's control over prices isolated the Borden Company from responsibility for the plant's activities.

In *Cream Crest-Blanding Dairies* v. *National Dairy Products,* the United States Sixth Circuit Court of Appeals had the opportunity to reaffirm its 1962 decision in the *Willard* case. As in *Willard,* the defendant was the National Dairy Products Corp. The alleged price discrimination in Michigan was clearly established. Ultimate control over the Lansing, Michigan plant from which the products were shipped reposed in officers outside the state of Michigan. However, the Lansing operation purchased, processed, and sold milk during the time in question entirely within Michigan. Relying on *Willard* and the Seventh Circuit's decision in *Borden,* the court granted the defendant's motion for a summary judgment on the basis of the plaintiff's failure to demonstrate that the discriminatory sales occurred in interstate, and not intrastate, commerce.

In seeking Supreme Court reinstatement of its treble-damage suit, Cream Crest asserted that the Sixth Circuit's *Williard Dairy* decision erroneously read the Supreme Court's finding of interstate commerce in *Moore* v. *Mead's Fine Bread Company* as turning on the presence of delivery truck routes into Texas from a New Mexico plant, instead of on the existence of an affiliated group of corporations operating in several states. Furthermore, the review petition noted that the Seventh Circuit had relied principally on the *Willard* decision in reversing the Federal Trade Commission on this point in the *Borden* case. But as with *Willard,* the Supreme Court declined the opportunity to review the Sixth Circuit's exemption of autonomous intrastate operations of interstate companies from the Robinson-Patman Act. Thus, the use of local plants selling their products solely intrastate is quickly becoming ensconced in the law as a legitimate method by which to avoid the proscriptions of Section 2(a).

Flow of Commerce Doctrine

Problems often arise where facilities for the temporary storage of interstate shipments are used as the distribution points for local sales. Typically, the interstate enterprise has attempted to assert the absence of federal jurisdiction over these local activities on the ground that these products were not sold in interstate commerce. The flow of commerce doctrine arose in response to these claims and set forth stringent conditions that must be met before products shipped between states lose their interstate character. It was not until the landmark case of *Standard Oil v. FTC* in 1949, that the Supreme Court officially sanctioned this stream-of-commerce approach in a Robinson-Patman Act case. In that case, the gasoline that the commission charged had been sold at unjustified price differentials in Michigan was refined in Indiana. That portion of it sold in the Detroit, Michigan, area was then shipped to the petitioner's marine terminal in Michigan. Enough gasoline was accumulated there during each navigation season so that a winter's supply was available from the terminal. The gasoline remained there, or in nearby bulk storage stations, for varying periods and remained under the continual ownership of Standard. Although it was not brought to the terminal pursuant to orders already taken, it was found by the lower court that the demands of the Michigan territory were fairly constant, thus enabling Standard accurately to estimate its customers' demands. The Supreme Court agreed with the United States Court of Appeals for the Seventh Circuit that the subsequent sales to local dealers within the state were well within the jurisdictional requirements of the act. In the Court's words:

> Any other conclusion would fall short of the recognized purpose of the . . . Act to reach the operations of large interstate businesses in competition with small local concerns. Such *temporary storage* of the gasoline as occurs within the Detroit area does not deprive the gasoline of its interstate character. [Emphasis supplied.]

As we have already seen, some interstate corporations have avoided the flow of commerce doctrine by selling in a particular state only those goods produced by it in that state. In the *Willard Dairy* case, the milk allegedly sold at discriminatory prices was produced, processed, and sold solely intrastate; Section 2(a) was therefore not applicable. However, it may not be necessary for the product in question to originate solely in the state of resale in order for an interstate business to obtain a result similar to that in the *Willard* case. In order to bring to a halt the *continuous flow* of the product brought in from another state, it may suffice if it is substantially altered in the state of resale. This result was suggested in the *Foremost Dairies* case, where an interstate dairy products company was charged, in connection with sales in Albuquerque, New Mexico, with violating Section 2(a). Central to the case was whether the sales in question had been in commerce. The record revealed that about 20 per cent of the milk that Foremost supplied to its Albuquerque customers was produced in Colorado. The raw milk was then sent to the Foremost processing plant in Santa Fe, New Mexico. In general, it was found that the milk was shipped out for distribution within hours after its arrival. The petitioners argued that the milk lost its interstate character because of the standardization and pasteurization that took place in New Mexico, the state of ultimate resale, and because title did not pass until the milk arrived there. The court disagreed and found that the milk was in constant flow from its place of origin until final delivery. The processing was found to be a rather negligible operation that did not interrupt the product's interstate movement. The court implied in a footnote that if the raw materials that had moved in interstate commerce had been materially altered in Santa Fe, or warehoused there for an appreciable amount of time, the stream of commerce would have been interrupted. Thus, Foremost met a fate diametrically opposite to that enjoyed by the defendant in the *Willard* decision. The primary distinction between the two cases lies in the fact that the milk sold by the National Dairy Products Corp., in the latter case, had not only been processed in the state of resale, but had been produced there also.

Left unanswered by these cases are two important questions: The first is whether the flow of commerce doctrine will be extended to bring within the purview of Section 2(a) an intrastate firm that resells, solely on an intrastate basis, products the raw materials for which have been purchased in interstate commerce. The second related question is whether a company that resells, solely within its own state, goods purchased from producers in other states comes within the purview of the act because of the stream of commerce concept. The most typical example of this situation would be an independent, intrastate wholesaler who purchases products for resale from manufacturers located outside the state. The problem becomes particularly acute with respect to those sellers who do not deliver the goods to retailers out of stock but order them from the interstate producers only as they are needed to fill an existing demand. These questions are important as they relate either to small intrastate companies or to independent subsidiaries or divisions of a larger interstate parent. We have already seen that "when the supplier himself does not engage in sales transactions across state lines—by deploying his franchised distributors or bona fide independent subsidiaries so that each satisfies only local [intrastate] market demands—Robinson-Patman liability may be minimized." Thus, unless the flow of commerce doctrine attaches to the goods in which the subsidiary traffics, price differentials arising out of sales by local, independent subsidiaries or divisions may not come within the purview of the act because of their intrastate nature.

As to both questions, the relevant in inquiry is: "Once the interstate movement of goods has been established, what breaks the flow of commerce?" Stated differently: "What causes the products to come to rest in the second state?" The cases indicate that in order to interrupt the interstate "flow" of goods, they must be altered, incorporated into a finished product, or brought to rest or stored in the state of resale.

Pertinent to any inquiry under question number one is the result in the *Central Ice Cream* case where a 2(a) violation was alleged against an intrastate ice cream manufacturer. The interstate commerce requirement was found lacking, even though the defendant had purchased the raw materials for his product from neighboring states, because the interstate flow of these ingredients had been interrupted. In the opinion of the federal district court, it was "clear that when these ingredients reached the defendant's Chicago plant, they [had] come to rest and commerce [had] ceased." Neither the district court nor the United States Court of Appeals expressly relied on the subsequent material alteration of the goods. Thus, the mere arrival of the ingredients at a factory controlled by an intrastate enterprise, without more, apparently sufficed to break the flow. However, the United States Court of Appeals for the Fifth Circuit, in the *Foremost Dairies* decision, distinguished *Central* from its own case on the ground that in *Central* the raw materials had been substantially altered prior to resale intrastate. The commission's view of the *Central Ice Cream* case is similar to that expressed by the court in *Foremost*. It stated: "Where . . . the processing substantially alters the product, or where that product is only one of several ingredients in the finished product, it appears that it comes to rest in the state where the processing occurs and at that point leaves the flow of commerce."

In seeking an answer to the second question, the result in *Food Basket, Inc.* v. *Albertson's, Inc.* may provide some assistance. An interstate supermarket chain was charged with unlawful price discrimination by selling certain products in one store at prices lower than those charged for the identical items in its other stores in the same county in Utah. The plaintiff, who competed with the defendant's lower-priced store, unsuccessfully attempted to bring these transactions within the ambit of 2(a) by alleging that the products sold by Albertson's moved in interstate commerce from their various points of origin across state lines to Utah wholesalers in contemplation of sales to Albertson's, and that under the "practical continuity" or "flow of commerce" doctrine, these discriminatory sales were "in commerce." While conceding that Section 2(a) applies "if goods originating out of state . . . [are] shipped to the wholesalers in anticipation of orders from the retailers, or if a substantial part of the goods were shipped directly out of the state to the retailers as drop shipments," the court found no evidence to support the allegation that merchandise was shipped across state lines to the Utah wholesalers in anticaption of the orders from the retailer. The evidence indicated that the goods were purchased by the wholesalers for "their own account," came to rest in the possession of the wholesaler, and then were shipped to the retailers on order. To the extent drop shipping occurred, the court characterized it as "infinitesimal or *de minimis*" and thus insufficient to invoke the proscriptions of the 2(a).

The commission has consistently applied the flow of commerce doctrine to Robinson-Patman cases. In its view: "Interstate movement of the products sold, both prior to and subsequent to the purchase, affects the character of the purchase." It has indicated further that "where goods are shipped from one state into another and sold in a second state in the original package, the goods [have] not come to a rest and their sale [is] an interstate sale." While employment of the "flow of commerce" doctrine in a Robinson-Patman context is no doubt proper in certain instances, it would be undesirable for the commission to apply the doctrine in its broadest sense. It must be remembered that the doctrine was a child of necessity, conceived at a time in which the proscriptions of the Sherman Act were being expanded to the fullest possible extent. A fully developed flow of commerce doctrine was fully consistent with the congressional intent to extend its regulatory power to cover transactions that *affected* interstate commerce. However, in passing the Robinson-Patman Act, the Congress declined to extend its jurisdictional reach to the extent it had done in the Sherman Act. Therefore, unqualified application of flow of commerce cases reared in a Sherman Act context to a Robinson-Patman situation would be to circumvent legislative limitations. Furthermore, when the introduction of the doctrine into a 2(a) environment was originally sanctioned by the Supreme Court, its clear purpose was to prohibit big interstate operations from using legal loopholes to wield their economic power in violation of the act. Thus, to apply the concept to bring intrastate companies, particularly those with no affiliation whatsoever with an interstate parent or sister corporation, within the ambit of the act would be to distort this purpose.

It is evident that the value of intrastate "independence" in terms of eliminating commerce is substantially mitigated by the uncertainty created by the Damoclesian flow of commerce sword. Application of this doctrine could transform an intrastate sale into one in commerce, notwithstanding the intrastate nature of a seller's business, where the wholesaler was a mere conduit for goods shipped from other states, or possibly where sales were made to interstate retail chains who distributed the goods across state lines. This uncertainty counsels against reliance on the independent subsidiary or division concept to eliminate interstate commerce. However, as we have seen, use of the autonomous affiliate might be of some value in eliminating the same seller requirement.

In conclusion, it must be remembered that we have been discussing the three-phased interstate commerce requirement of Section 2(a) only. The flow of commerce approach is more important vis-à-vis Section 2(a) than the other sections because it provides a method by which to circuit the sale "in commerce" requirement not present in the other sections. Under the less restrictive commerce requirements of Section 2(d) and (e), for example, basically local discriminatory practices may be outlawed because interstate communications were used in disseminating advertising financed by the buyer, or solely because of the interstate nature of the recipient's operation. Seldom would reliance need to be placed on the stream of commerce theory in order to subject these activities to the proscriptions of 2(d) and (e).

The *De Minimis* Principle

Brief mention should be made of the *de minimis* principle under which relatively small or insignificant amounts of interstate transactions have been held not to result in Section 2(a) coverage. Application of this principle is well illustrated by the *Baldwin Hills Building Material Co.* case were a retail building materials dealer sued an interstate manufacturer of gypsum wallboard alleging price discrimination in favor of the plaintiff's competitors. The plaintiff and its competitors were located in Southern California, and all of them received the wallboard from the defendant's plant in the same state, with the exception of a small portion which was delivered from Fibreboard's Colorado facility. The plaintiff attempted without success to establish the requisite commerce nexus by showing that a small quantity of wallboard had been shipped from Colorado to the defendant's California plant for distribution within California. During the period in question, Fibreboard sold $21,732,000 worth of wallboard from the California plant, $22,000 of which was attributable to the Colorado made products. Applying the *de minimis* principle, the court concluded that this inclusion of miniscule quantities of wallboard from out-of-state origins did not warrant bringing the case within the purview of 2(a). The plaintiff also attempted to rely upon the sale at a discount of $1,100 worth of wallboard by the defendant to an Arizona customer, who, in turn, resold it to a builder in Southern California. There was no indication Fibreboard was aware that the wallboard would be sent back into California as part of a sale in competition with the plaintiff. For this reason, and in further appplication of the *de minimis* doctrine, the court refused to conclude that this relatively insignificant, isolated transaction served "to make a federal case out of what basically constitutes a local problem."

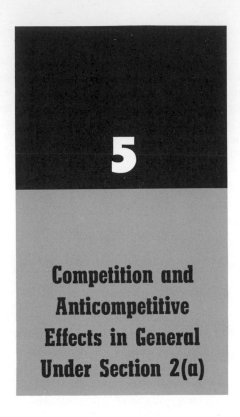

5

Competition and Anticompetitive Effects in General Under Section 2(a)

WHAT KIND OF COMPETITION IS ENCOMPASSED BY THE ACT?

It will be remembered that the adverse competitive effects proviso of Section 2(a) is one of the ten jurisdictional elements that a plaintiff must allege and prove in order to establish a prima facie case of price discrimination. Consequently, the complaining party must carry the burden of proof establishing that the effect of the alleged price discrimination "may be substantially to lessen competition or tend to create a monopoly in any line of commerce, or to injure, destroy, or prevent competition with any person who either grants or knowingly receives the benefit of such discrimination, or with customers of either of them. . . ." The problems attendant to the application of this test have been among the most formidable of those that have arisen during the past decades of Robinson-Patman Act enforcement.

Before one can undertake a meaningful discussion of the competitive injury requirement, it first must be determined what is meant by the term *competition* as it is used in the statute. Competition is defined in

Webster's as: "The efforts of two or more parties acting independently to secure the custom of the third party by the offer of the most favorable terms." In other words, businessmen become competitors by virtue of their attempts to solicit the patronage of the same customers. Competition, of course, exists at every level in a distribution system. Traditionally, the courts have interpreted the Robinson-Patman Act to protect against competitive injury at three functional levels in the distribution chain. They are as follows:

Primary-Line Injury at the Seller's Level

Consider the following hypothetical marketing situation:

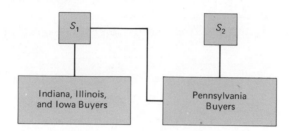

The first seller, S_1, and the second seller, S_2, are competing in the market place for the sale of goods. As the diagram illustrates, S_1 and S_2 are competing in Pennsylvania, and S_1 is also selling in other states, but not in competition with S_2. Suppose S_1 ruthlessly sets out to drive S_2 out of business. Suppose further that in order to accomplish this purpose, S_1 slashes his long-established prices by 25 per cent in Pennsylvania. S_1 sells below cost in Pennsylvania but is able to do this because he has raised his prices in the area where S_2 does not compete. Here is a clear case of primary-line or seller's-level injury. The purpose and effect of S_1's price reduction is to destroy S_2 in Pennsylvania. This practice may also amount to an attempt to monopolize, prohibited by Section 2 of the Sherman Act, or to a violation of Section 3 of the Robinson-Patman Act. Of course, if S_1 did not have the economic power to work competitive injury on S_2, no violation would have occurred. It should be noted that even though most primary-line-injury cases involve geographic or territorial price discrimination, this form of discrimination is by no means the only type under which primary-line injury can arise. Thus, primary-line injury could arise where a supplier cuts his prices to a competitor's customers while selling at higher prices to his own customers in the same market area.

Secondary-Line Injury at the Buyer's Level

Consider the situation in which a hypothetical manufacturer-supplier, M, sells to two buyers, B_1 and B_2, who are in direct competition with each other.

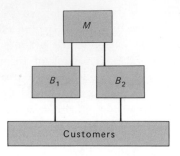

Now, suppose that M lowers his price to B_1 but not to B_2. The requisite effect on competition will be present if B_2 is significantly less able to compete with B_1 because of the price discrimination.

Let us now vary the situation and consider buyer-level injury again.

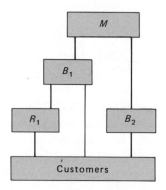

Here B_1 is a *split distributor,* competing with B_2 for the same customers and also selling to a retailer, R_1, who sells to these customers. The fact that B_1 is not in competition with B_2 on sales to R_1 does not prevent any price differential granted in favor of B_1 from wreaking the necessary competitive injury with respect to the competition that does exist between B_1 and B_2.

A more difficult problem is raised in the following situation:

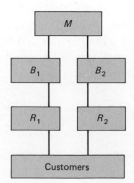

M sells to two wholesalers, B_1 and B_2; B_1 sells to a retailer, R_1; and B_2 sells to another retailer, R_2; R_1 and R_2 are in direct competition with one another for the same consumers; B_1 and B_2 do not directly compete with each other since each retailer, R_1 and R_2, has an exclusive dealing contract with his wholesaler—in other words, B_1 cannot sell to R_2 and B_2 cannot sell to R_1. Thus, B_1 and B_2 buy from the same supplier, each wholesales the product in the same market, and the retailers supplied by each compete for the patronage of the same consumers. While not falling within the traditional notion of competition, it would seem that B_1 and B_2 are competitors in practical effect since a wholesaler's success will depend in large part upon the success of the retailers to which it sells. If a lower price to one of the wholesalers, B_1, results in a lower price to his customer R_1, enabling R_1 to underprice R_2, and if R_2's business declines as a result causing a decline in B_2's sales to R_2, then B_2 would appear to be injured in his competition with B_1, the favored whole-saler-purchaser. B_2 should be permitted to sue M for the competitive injury suffered by him at the secondary level. The disfavored retailer R_2, of course, may also have a cause of action against M for the resulting injury at the third level in his competition with R_1.

An entirely different situation arises where B_1 and B_2 do not compete for the same customers, either directly or indirectly. Suppose that M is a refiner-supplier of gasoline, that B_1 runs a fleet of taxicabs, and that B_2 is a retail gasoline dealer.

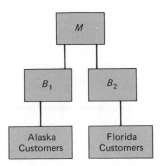

Because B_1 purchases gasoline for use in his taxicabs and not for resale, he is not in competition with B_2. M can, therefore, quote B_1 a lower gasoline price without fear of working any injury to competition.

Another common situation in which no buyer-level injury is present occurs where B_1 and B_2 do not actually compete in a geographic market. Suppose M, our gasoline supplier, sells to B_1 in Alaska and to B_2 in Florida.

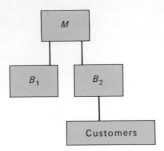

B_1 and B_2 obviously do not compete for the same business, so there is no buyer-level competitive injury if B_2 receives a lower price than B_1. There is a more difficult situation when the geographic areas are close to one another. If B_1 sells to customers in downtown Chicago and B_2 sells to customers in the suburbs of Chicago, it may well be that B_1 and B_2 would be considered as competitors for the same customers. Any price discrimination between B_1 and B_2 could, therefore, have the requisite buyer-level injury.

Third-Line Injury—Customers of Customers

This type of competitive injury, often referred to as tertiary line, is suffered by a disfavored customer in his competition with customers of the supplier's favored buyer, three steps down the distribution chain. Suppose our gasoline supplier, M, who may be a refiner, sells his gasoline both to an integrated jobber-retailer, JR_1, and to an independent jobber, J_2, who in turn sells to a retail gasoline station, R_2, who competes with JR_1 for the same retail business.

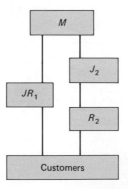

M sells at a lower price to J_2 than JR_1 even though JR_1, in his capacity as a jobber, performs the same functional activities as J_2. If the lower price to J_2 results in a lower price to R_2, enabling R_2 to underprice JR_1 at the retail level, then JR_1 may be injured in his competition with R_2, who, in this instance, operates at the third level in the favored distribution system.

A more controversial example of third-line injury arises out of the following factual context: Suppose our gasoline supplier, M, who may be a refiner, sells his gasoline both to a retail gasoline station, R_1, and to an independent jobber, J, who in turn sells to another retail gasoline station, R_2. R_1 and R_2 both compete for the same retail business. M sells at a lower price to J than to R_1.

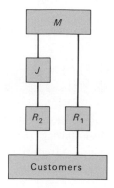

If the lower price to J results in a lower price to R_2, enabling R_2 to underprice R_1, the necessary competitive injury may have occurred at the retail level.

Fourth-Line Injury—Customers of Customers of Customers

This type of injury is suffered by a disfavored customer in his competition with a customer of a customer of the supplier's favored customer. The United States Ninth Circuit Court of Appeals held, in *Standard Oil Co.* v. *Perkins,* that competitive injury below the tertiary level is not cognizable under the Robinson-Patman Act. In its opinion:

> Section 2(a) . . . limits the number of distribution levels on which a supplier's price discrimination will be recognized as potentially injurious to competition. These are: on the level of the supplier-seller in competition with his own customer; on the level of the supplier-seller's customers; and on the level of customers of customers of the supplier-seller.

In *Perkins,* the plaintiff-appellee, an independent gasoline dealer who had both a wholesale and retail business, alleged that Standard's price favoritism to the Signal Oil and Gas Co. had impaired and destroyed competition between Perkins and the Regal Stations Company, both of whom sold Standard's products. The evidence showed that Regal, which persistently undercut the prices of other competing retailers, purchased its gasoline from Western Hyway Oil Company, which in turn had purchased it from Signal, which had originally purchased it from Standard. The following diagram best illustrates this distribution system:

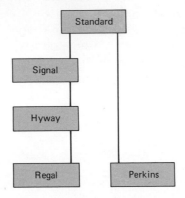

Even granting that the proof demonstrated that Standard uniformly charged Signal substantially less than Perkins, and further granting that Signal similarly passed this price saving on to customers such as Western Hyway, the competition Perkins complained of was not that with Signal or with Signal's customers but rather with Regal, a customer of a customer of a customer of Standard. Thus, the competition between Regal and Perkins existed at the fourth level, which, according to the Ninth Circuit, was beyond the reach of the act. According to the court:

> Section 2(a) . . . does not recognize a causal connection, essential to liability, between a supplier's price discrimination and the trade practices of a customer as far removed on the distributive ladder as Regal was from Standard.

The Supreme Court reversed the court of appeals and reinstated the jury verdict for Perkins. Speaking for the Court, Justice Black said that to view Perkins' "fourth level" injuries as not protected by Section 2(a) is to impose a "wholly . . . artificial" limitation which "is completely unwarranted by the language or purpose of the Act." In reaching its conclusion, the Court relied upon its recent *Fred Meyer* decision in which it was held that any retailer who buys through a wholesaler is a "customer" of the original supplier within the meaning of Section 2(d). It reasoned that to read *customer* more narrowly in Section 2(a) than was done in *Fred Meyer* would allow price discriminators to avoid the sanctions of the act by the simple expedient of adding an additional link to the distribution chain. Thus, the term *customer* appearing in the competitive injury proviso of Section 2(a) includes all persons in the distribution chain who distribute the supplier's product, regardless of the functional level at which they operate and regardless of whether they are direct purchasers of the discriminating supplier. The Supreme

Court has apparently eliminated the third-line limitation heretofore thought to have been contained in Section 2(a). Actionable competitive injury may arise at any level in the distribution scheme, the only limitation being the requirement that there be a causal relationship between the unlawful discrimination and the injury suffered.

CRITERIA FOR COMPETITIVE INJURY

Legislative Background

Although the statute makes no distinction between these various levels of competitive injury in setting forth the criteria that are to be used in determining whether or not the requisite injury to competition has occurred, and although all the courts have attempted to make far-reaching pronouncements on the competitive effects proviso that are intended to be universally applicable to all types of competitive injury, the quantum of proof necessary to establish the substantiality of adverse effects on competition will, as a practical matter, differ depending on the level of injury involved. Doctrinal consistency has not been achieved. Such a distinction has been recognized by the Supreme Court, which, in the *Anheuser-Busch* case, indicated that it would require an explicit demonstration of adverse competitive effects in a primary-line case. And yet, a decade earlier, the Supreme Court stated in its *Morton Salt* opinion, a secondary-line injury case, that the relevant question is whether there exists a "reasonable possibility" that competition may be adversely affected by sales at a price difference to competing customers. In *Anheuser-Busch,* however, the Court maintained that it had not departed from its holding in *Morton* ". . . as to adequacy of proof of tendency to injure competition in cases involving discrimination between purchasers. The instant case . . . involves differences in prices among competing sellers." On the basis of these cases, it can be seen that a more forceful demonstration of an inimical competitive impact may be required in a primary-line case than might be sufficient to satisfy a charge of injurious effect on the customer level. Thus, because the distinctions between these types of levels of competitive injury, however, both the legislative background competitive injury are of practical significance, each of the levels in which Robinson-Patman violations have been found must be separately examined. Before proceeding to an analysis of each of the and the points of general application should be noted.

Turning to the background of the competitive effects provision in the Robinson-Patman Act, it will be remembered that the basic thrust of the price discrimination clause in the original Clayton Act of 1914 was directed against competitive injury at the seller, or primary level. According to the House Report, its purpose was to prevent:

> . . . great and powerful combinations . . . [from lowering the] prices of their commodities, oftentimes below the cost of production in certain communities and sections where they had competition, with the intent to destroy and make unprofitable the business of their competitors, and with the ultimate purpose in view of thereby acquiring a monopoly in the particular locality or section in which the discriminating price is made.

In the furtherance of this purpose, Congress passed Section 2 of the act, which prohibited price discriminations whose effect "may be to substantially lessen competition or tend to create a monopoly in any line of commerce." For a number of years Section 2 was used primarily to combat price discrimination that had a deleterious effect on competition between the seller and his competitors. In 1929, however, the Supreme Court, in its opinion in the *George Van Camp & Sons* case, finally sanctioned the use of Section 2 against price discrimination that adversely affected competition between the supplier's customers. But Congress still was not satisfied, and, in 1936, Robinson and Patman introduced their bills in an attempt to deal more effectively with the problem of competitive injury at the customer level.

The purpose of the 1936 amendments was revealed by the interpretive statements offered by their sponsors during congressional debates. It seems clear from such statements that the sponsors of the bill were aware of the possibility that sellers could destroy rivals through price discrimination or drive out disfavored customers by the same means, all without injury to the consumer. Injured sellers might be replaced by others, and disfavored customers could be replaced by other customers who would enjoy the fruits of discrimination. Competition in the market place might remain strong, but the disfavored victims of discrimination would either be eliminated or have their competitive strength diminished through price discrimination. The bill was designed to protect the competition in the market place afforded by these less fortunate sellers and customers of sellers.

To this end, attention was focused on abolition of the competitive effects requirement and the meeting competition provision of the old Clayton Act, thereby making all price discrimination per se unlawful. During the course of the committee hearings, however, two major flaws were found in this flat prohibition against discriminations in price. First, under the doctrines prevailing at that time, there was some question as to whether or not the federal government could constitutionally regulate pricing conduct that did not adversely affect competition in interstate commerce. Secondly, there was concern over whether or not the bills would cover predatory pricing by sellers bent on destroying their competitors as the original Clayton Act had done. This latter contention was rooted in a fear that the concept of discrimination denoted and thus prohibited only those differentials between competing purchasers, where a price differential would naturally threaten some competitive detriment. In order to remedy these defects, an amended version of the competitive effects clause of the original Clayton Act was restored. To the "substantially lessen competition or tend to create a monopoly in any line of commerce" test of the original Section 2, was added a provision to cover price discriminations that might "injure, destroy, or prevent competition with any person who either grants or knowingly receives the benefit of such discrimination, or with customers of either of them."

The basic thrust of this added provision was to shift the focus of Section 2(a) to the detrimental effect on competition with the individual parties participating in the discriminatory transaction, instead of on the impact of competition in a certain market area or line of commerce as the original Clayton Act had done. The Robinson-Patman amendment dispensed with the necessity for an exhaustive market analysis. It seems clear that the Congress sought thereby to protect competitive relationships between viable *individual* competitors, rather than to confine attention to the previous antitrust standard of protecting competition generally. This concept was new to the law, and presents an easier task for the enforcement agency than occurs when injury to competition as a whole must be proved. Thus, the cases have developed around alleged injury to actual or potential competitors, except that when seller injury is involved, injury to a competitor is not necessarily equated to injury to competition generally.

Meaning of *Substantiality*

Turning now to the points of general application that are relevant to all levels of competitive injury, it should be noted first that the word *substantially,* which was carried over from Section 2 of the original Clayton Act, also limits the words added by the Robinson-Patman Act. Thus, the discrimination involved must not only be a kind the effect of which "may be substantially to lessen competition," it must have a capacity for *substantially* injuring, destroying, or preventing competition. Also, the word *lessen,* which appears in that portion of the competitive injury requirement that was carried over from the original Section 2, and the word *injure,* which was used in the Robinson-Patman amendments, are generally regarded as meaning the same thing.

Although we have noted that the term *substantially* applies not only to the first part of the competitive effects proviso but modifies the subsequent terminology added by the Robinson-Patman Act, the question remaining is, "What does the term *substantially* really mean?" As a practical matter, are substantial competitive effects required or will minimal effects suffice? To a large degree, this question is closely related to the issue of whether Section 2(a) is concerned with detrimental effects on competition or the protection of individual competitors. The more "substantial" the injury that is required under 2(a), the greater the likelihood that competition, not just a competitor, has been injured.

For more than a decade after the passage of the Robinson-Patman Act, both the commission and the courts insisted on the substantiality of the anticompetitive effects. But this application of a *de minimus* approach was sharply curtailed in the 1948 *Morton Salt* decision, a case where discriminations in the price of table salt containers were found to be unlawful. The Supreme Court felt that Congress intended:

> . . . to protect a merchant from competitive injury attributable to discriminatory prices on any or all goods sold in interstate commerce, whether the particular goods constituted a major or minor portion of his stock. Since a grocery store consists of many comparatively small articles, there is no possible way effectively to protect a grocer from discriminatory prices except by applying the prohibitions of the Act to each individual article in the store.

Even though the *Morton Salt* decision has been reiterated in many subsequent decisions, the courts have generally adhered to more exacting criteria for the measurement of competitive adversity. A series of decisions in the United States Court of Appeals for the Seventh Circuit best illustrates this point. For example, in *Whitaker Cable Corp.*, the Seventh Circuit stated that ". . . insignificant 'violations' are not, in fact or in law, violations as defined by the Act. If the amount of the discrimination is inconsequential or if the size of the discrimination is such that it strains credulity to find the requisite adverse effect on competition, the Commission is powerless under the Act to prohibit such discrimination whether first-line or second-line competition be involved."

In *Minneapolis-Honeywell Regulator Co.*, the Seventh Circuit reversed a commission cease and desist order proscribing a quantity discount schedule in the sale of temperature controls. Although it was established that Minneapolis-Honeywell had succeeded in retaining or diverting some business that might otherwise have gone to some of its competitors, the court could not say that the effect of those practices was substantially to injure competition because those competitors were able to enter the field and build a thriving business in spite of M-H's commanding position and alleged wrongful practices. The court took the position that the act requires "substantial, not trivial or sporadic interference with competition to establish a violation of its mandate."

Similarly, in the *American Oil Co.* decision, which will be fully discussed in the material on secondary-line injury, the Seventh Circuit confined the *Morton Salt* doctrine to those violations that did not have a "temporary or transient limited economic impact." The court added, however, that:

> [W]e do not mean to imply that a showing of intended permanency of the price discrimination is necessary to establish a Section 2(a) violation. But there must be something more than an essentially temporary minimal impact on competition.

The court took the same position in the *Borden Co.* case, where one of the alleged 2(a) violations arose out of below-cost sales of a week's duration in a small Indiana town. The respondent's price reduction had been in response to the below-cost prices charged consumers by the town's largest grocery store. In setting aside the cease and desist order, the court rejected the commission's reliance on *Morton Salt,* a secondary-line injury case, as being "wholly inapplicable" in territorial price discrimination cases that allege primary-line injury. Citing its *American Oil* decision, the court concluded that the defendants' course of conduct during the price war, which involved "nothing more than a one-week reduction in a community of 2,500 people made in response to price cutting by the largest grocer, and never repeated, quite clearly indicates that the temporary price reduction during that one week could not have had a substantial adverse effect on competition."

One of the latest Supreme Court pronouncements on this issue was in *FTC* v. *Sun Oil Co.,* where a large step was taken in the direction of restoring the word *substantially* to the position of importance from which it had been taken in the *Morton Salt* case:

> In appraising the effects of any price cut or the corresponding response to it, both the Federal Trade Commission and the courts must make realistic appraisals of relevant competitive facts. Invocation of mechanical word formulas cannot be made to substitute for adequate probative analysis.

Thus, it appears that even where there is injury to competition between individual competitors, there must be some proof of substantial injury, unless such injury is on its face potentially substantial. At the seller or primary level, more proof of competitive effect is necessary.

Even though the term *substantially* means different things at different levels of competitive injury, it can be seen that there is a clear trend away from the position adopted in *Morton Salt,* a trend that is clearly consistent with the basic antitrust objective of fostering effective competition. The application of Section 2(a) to small price variations that have no substantial anticompetitive effect particularly in the context of a primary-line injury case would be tantamount to a legal compulsion of price equality and thus would impede the attainment of antitrust objectives.

Protection of Competitors or Competition

Ever since the 1936 amendments and their focus upon injury to individual competitive relationships (that is, injury to a person in his competition with a discriminating supplier, a favored customer, and so on) instead of upon harm to competition generally (that is, a substantial lessening of competition in any line of commerce), there has been extensive controversy over whether the statutory criteria of Section 2(a) should be employed to avert detrimental effects on competition or whether their thrust should be directed toward the protection of individual competitors. The controversy was precipitated, in large part, by the Supreme Court's *Morton Salt* decision, where a salt supplier's quantity discount schedule was condemned as favoring large chain store buyers of table salt over small independent retailer purchasers. Quoting from the Senate Committee Report, Justice Black, in the majority opinion, concluded that the 1936 Robinson-Patman amendments were "intended to justify a finding of injury to competition by a showing of 'injury to the competitor victimized by the discrimination.'" Thus, he asserted, the Federal Trade Commission need not prove "what would appear to be obvious, that the competitive opportunities of certain merchants were injured when they had to pay respondent substantially more for their goods than their competitors had to pay."

For the most part, Justice Black's suggestion that injury to competitors is the focal point of the competitive effects requirement has been rejected by both the commission and the courts. For example, in its 1954 *Purex* decision, the commission reaffirmed the Robinson-Patman Act's preeminent concern with the vitality of competition rather than the well-being of individual competitors:

> [W]hile Congress intended to insure that the enforcement of the act was not frustrated by the requirement for a generalized showing of injury, it was not its intention . . . to liberalize the test of injury to the extent of making it one of injury to an individual competitor. The language used in the amendment, it may be noted, refers to injury to *"competition"* with the grantor or grantee of the discrimination and not to injury to a *"competitor"* of the grantor or grantee of the discrimination. The fact that a competitor has been injured in a local price-cutting case may tend to show that competition with the grantor has been affected, but it does not follow in every case that because a competitor has been injured, competition has been affected.
>
> .   .   .
>
> The language used in the amendment reflects the then current mood for liberalization of the Act, but yet does not evidence an intent of establishing, as the applicable test, injury to an individual competitor. [Emphasis added.]

This posture was adopted by the Attorney General's National Committee to Study the Antitrust Laws:

> [T]his Committee recommends that analysis of the statutory "injury" center on the vigor of competition in the market rather than hardship to individual businessmen. For the essence of competition is a contest for trade among business rivals in which some must gain while others lose, to the ultimate benefit of a consuming public. Incidental hardships on individual businessmen in the normal course of commercial events can be checked by a price discrimination statute only at the serious risk of stifling the competitive process itself.
> . . . We emphasize that it is not "injury" to *competitors* but adverse effects on "competition *with*" parties privy to discriminations that the statute expressly forbids. Hence we believe that criteria of competitive effects which focus exclusively on individual competitors' sales or profits rather than the health of the competitive process literally go beyond the terms in the law.

More recently, the United States Court of Appeals for the Seventh Circuit, in its 1961 *Anheuser-Busch* decision, summarized these basic considerations as follows:

> The Act is really referring to the effect upon competition and not merely upon competitors. . . . In this respect § 2(a) must be read in conformity with the public policy of preserving competition, but it is not concerned with mere shifts of business between competitors. It is concerned with substantial impairment of the vigor or health of the contest for business, regardless of which competitor wins or loses. The competition which is sought to be protected by this section is a contest between sellers for the buyer's business, because, "competition is, in its very essence, a contest for trade."

And, in the *American Oil Co.* case, a court added, "The protection intended to be afforded by the statute is directed towards the preservation of competition. The statute's concern with the individual competitor is but incidental."

In recent years, however, the commission has given some indication that it no longer rigidly adheres to this injury to competition theory. In a few cases, the position has been taken that the injury to competition requirement is satisfied if it can be demonstrated that the respondent's price cut caused a diversion of business from his competitors. The Federal Trade Commission relied on this approach, for example, in its 1957 *Anheuser-Busch* decision, where it issued a cease and desist order on a finding that the respondent's territorial pricing scheme "resulted in substantial diversion of sales from competitors to itself." The consequences of this position should be self-evident. The substitution of competitors for competition as the focal point of the injury requirement, logically extended, compels the conclusion that a price discrimination is unlawful if it results in a loss by any member of an industry of his market share. Although such a result may have some merit where there are only two competitors in the relevant market area, generally, it will operate to frustrate one of the basic designs of the antitrust laws, namely, price competition. As one federal district court judge stated:

> It is the duty of [the courts] to reconcile the administration of the Robinson-Patman Act with the broader central aim of the antitrust laws: to instill and maintain in the business community active competition among its members. Competition, while it may take many forms, is most meaningful and vigorous when it consists of or includes price rivalry. We must read the Act to encourage price competition wherever possible. Price uniformity is the anti-thesis of competition.

Thus, it is understandable that as a practical matter, the courts have tended to regard the effect on competitors as only one of the indicia of whether or not the proscribed statutory effect on competition has occurred. In other words, the fact that a competitor has been injured may tend to demonstrate the requisite competitive injury, but it does not follow in every case that because a competitor has been injured, competition has been affected. To hold otherwise would be to provide legal support for price stabilization, the anathema of a viable, competitive economy.

In conclusion, it can be said that both the statutory text and the courts have reprehended adverse effects on competitors only in so far as "competition" was also injured. But, although the test requires some injury to competition, injury to a single competitor may, as a practical matter, satisfy this test, particularly if the seller has engaged in predatory pricing, which by its nature has been recognized as necessarily creating a probability of injury to competition as well as to competitors. As the United States Court of Appeals for the Seventh Circuit said, in *Lloyd Fry Roofing Co.* v. *FTC,* although in "most primary line cases . . . a violation cannot be established without a close study of the market, including data as to the discriminator's share of the market, . . . in cases of predatory intent, 'injury to even a single competitor should bring the Act into play.'" Moreover, proof that a discriminatory pricing scheme has led to a diversion of sales away from a supplier's competitors may be sufficient to constitute competitive injury under the Robinson-Patman Act.

Meaning of May

Price discrimination is unlawful where its effect *"may* be substantially to lessen competition." There has been some dispute as to the meaning of the word *may* as it appears in that phrase. Although it is clear that *actual* anticompetitive effects need not be shown in order to establish a violation of Section 2(a), and that it is enough if the discrimination "may" have an adverse effect on competition, there is no universal agreement as to the precise degree to which the Robinson-Patman Act functions as an incipiency statute and reaches potential harm. The debate as to the meaning of *may* was precipitated by the 1945 Supreme Court's *Corn Products* decision. Several decades prior to that decision, the Supreme Court had expressed the view that the word *may* was not used by Congress to prohibit a mere possibility of the anticompetitive consequences described; rather, it was intended to prevent activities that would *probably* have the requisite inimical effect. But in *Corn Products,* the Court created uncertainty as to the meaning of *may* when it said:

> The statute [Section 2(a)] is designed to reach such discriminations "in their incipiency," before the harm to competition is effected. It is enough that they "may" have the prescribed effect. . . . [T]he use of the word "may" was not to prohibit discriminations having "the mere possibility" of those consequences, but to reach those which would *probably* have the defined effect on competition. [Emphasis supplied.]

So far so good, but then the Court added:

> . . . [T]he statute does not require that the discriminations must in fact have harmed competition, but only that there is a *reasonable possibility* that they "may" have such an effect. [Emphasis supplied.]

Even though it has been said by two Supreme Court Justices that the distinction between reasonable probability and reasonable possibility "is not unimportant and in many cases would be decisive," as a practical matter most courts have used the terms interchangeably. Seldom, if ever, has the legality of a particular price discrimination turned upon distinction between the terms. If significance is to be attached to the distinction, however, the more appropriate term would be *reasonable probability*. If literally construed, the word *possibility* allows far too great a latitude to the courts and the commission by permitting them to make a finding of illegality even though the potentiality of the anticompetitive impact of the price discrimination is remote. The Supreme Court employed the more permissive "reasonable possibility" language in its recent *Utah Pie Co.* v. *Continental Baking Co.* decision.

Necessity of Causal Relationship

It must be remembered that the basic premise that must be established in order to permit a finding of unlawful price discrimination is that there must be a causal relationship between the differential pricing and the alleged competitive injury. In other words, it must be demonstrated that the price discrimination is legally responsible for the impairment of competition. As the Supreme Court said in its *Perkins* decision:

Before an injured party can recover damages under the Act, he must, of course, be able to show a causal connection between the price discrimination in violation of the Act and the injury suffered. This is true regardless of the "level" in the chain of distribution on which the injury occurs.

A supplier may be able to rebut, therefore, a prima facie case of the requisite adverse effect on competition by demonstrating that whatever misfortune may have befallen its rivals was caused not by the price difference, but rather by other factors or external influences such as differences in advertising success, marketing techniques, service, salesmanship, efficiency of operation, or the willingness to enter into price competition. All are relevant factors in determining the factual context in which the alleged competitive injury occurred. Moreover, the level of the injury—whether it is primary, secondary, or tertiary line or beyond— is of significance also. The impact of this factor was best summarized in *Shore Gas & Oil Co.* v. *Humble Oil & Refining Co.,* where a federal district court noted that:

> In the common "secondary" or buyer's-line injury case, the causal relationship between discrimination and injury to competition is obvious: defendant's difference in price to buyers places the one discriminated against at a competitive disadvantage, consequently prejudicing fair, vigorous competition in the affected market. . . .
> The situation in primary-line injury cases is quite different. Causation, which is equally essential to a cause of action, is more subtle and difficult to discern. Injury is not an "effect" of discrimination directly. Rather it is the result of a low price which a discrimination in price allowed the defendant to charge. High prices provide for the predatory defendant the profit margins with which to lower other prices and undercut competitors. The existence of a difference is essential to the injury. The injury is an effect of the discrimination.
> Contrariwise, if there is no relationship between high and low prices, the low prices and consequent competitive injury are not the "effect" of price discrimination.

In spelling out what has been termed the *aid from other markets* requirement in primary-level injury cases, the court reasoned that injury to competition cannot be considered the "effect" of the price discrimination, rather than merely of the lower price, unless it can be demonstrated that the price cut was made possible or "subsidized" by the higher prices received on other sales. According to the court, sales below cost would permit an inference of the "subsidy" element. If the seller's price is "self-sufficient" in the sense of being independent from other prices, however, then he "should be able to charge it without fear of primary-line injury and resulting treble-damage suits."

It may well be that this strict causality standard in seller-line injury cases is applicable only in private treble-damage suits where the plaintiff must establish that defendants caused actual harm to it. Such a dichotomy was suggested by the United States Court of Appeals in the *Lloyd Fry Roofing Co.* opinion, where in the context of a government action it rejected the contention that the commission must find that the higher price elsewhere supports the lower prices in the market under examination, stating: "Congress and the cases assume that the higher price to purchasers supports the lower price to others." But this dichotomy is by no means universally accepted even within the Seventh Circuit. In its recent *Dean Milk* decision, that court criticized the FTC for failing to introduce evidence indicating that "higher prices received by Dean from those accounts where discounts were small supported the lower prices received from those accounts where discounts were high."

Finally, brief reference should be made of the 1945 *Samuel H. Moss* decision, a case that is frequently described as the "aberrational Second Circuit doctrine" on competitive injury. According to the United States Court of Appeals, a prima facie case of primary-line price discrimination was established by the mere fact that the seller sold the same product at different prices to different customers. In other words, the party challenging a price difference need not demonstrate that the discrimination may have the proscribed inimical effects on competition. In the words of the court: "Congress adopted the common device in such cases of shifting the burden of proof to anyone who sets two prices, and who probably knows why he has done so, and what has been the result." Although the decision in *Moss* is clearly contrary to the massive body of law on competitive injury, it has never been overruled by the Second Circuit, and, therefore, must not be completely ignored.

6

Competitive Injury Under Section 2 (a)

Having identified the levels of competition susceptible to a Robinson-Patman price discrimination charge and certain facets of the competitive effects proviso common to all such levels, it remains to be determined when competitive injury occurs at each level. The problems in determining injury at each of the four levels described in the preceding chapter will now be examined in turn.

SELLER-LEVEL OR PRIMARY-LINE COMPETITIVE EFFECTS

It will be remembered that although the main thrust of the Robinson-Patman amendments of 1936 was directed against the abuses of the mass buying that resulted in competitive injury at the secondary line, the proscriptions in the original Clayton Act against price discrimination that precipitated primary-line injury were carried over also. That "an independent and important goal of Section 2(a) is to extend protection to competitors of the discriminating seller" was confirmed by the Supreme Court in the 1960 *Anheuser-Busch* decision. It is in the enforcement of Section 2(a) against competitive injury at the seller level that the potential conflict between the Robinson-Patman Act and over-all antitrust policies is most apparent. The core question is whether a seller's price differences constitute the competition fostered by the antitrust laws generally, or competition that is predatory and destructive to competition. A review of the significant primary-line injury cases will reveal that the courts' treatment of this problem has been by no means consistent.

At the outset it should be noted that an essential prerequisite to the demonstration of any primary-line injury is the existence of some competitive relationship between the discriminating seller and those said to be adversely affected by the discriminatory pricing. First, it must be established that those who are concerned with the price differentiation are selling the same product as the offending supplier. *Same* should not be equated with the like grade and quality requirement in Section 2(a). The latter relates solely to the products being sold by the offending supplier. Thus, a competitor need not sell products of a grade and quality identical to those of a discriminating seller as a prerequisite to bringing a private treble-damage action for a primary-line injury. Functional equivalence is all that is required in such a case. For example, in *McWhirter v. Monroe Calculating Machine Company,* which involved alleged price discrimination by one seller of business machines to the detriment of a rival, a federal district court concluded that, despite differences in appearance and design, the competing devices were "generally designed to perform the same functions in their respective classifications and hence were competitive." More recently, the United States Court of Appeals for the Sixth Circuit, in *Callaway Mills Co. v. FTC,* expressed this requirement in terms of the "saleability" of the products. In other words, the question was whether or not the defendant's products generate public demand at various price levels equivalent to that of its competitors' products. This is not to suggest, however, that the test of whether competion exists is one of product interchangeability or cross-elasticity of demand. To do so would expand the act into a device to regulate the entire business of a supplier. As a federal district court, in *Bolick-Gillman Co. v. Continental Baking Co.,* expressed it:

> . . . [I]f we were to view the term "competition" as does the academician in a university department of economics, we would have to say, at minimum, that every seller of a given commodity is in competition with every other seller of reasonably close substitutes. Thus, the seller of bread is, in theory, in competition with all sellers of bread substitutes, such as potatoes, spaghetti, and macaroni. We need say nothing more than that we are confident that the draftsmen of the Robinson-

Patman Act did not intend to give to Chef Boyardee a right to recover treble damages from the makers of "Wonder Bread" for having engaged in territorial price discrimination.

The same product test is designed for the purpose of including within the ambit of competitors those sellers who market goods of the same generic designation that differ only slightly in their physical·make-up.

Of course, not only do the sellers have to be marketing the same product in order to be competitiors in the Section 2(a) sense, they also must be competing against each other for the business of the same buyer. The significance of this requirement can best be illustrated by the *Bolick-Gillman Co.* case. The plaintiff, who was a wholesale distributor of bread in the Las Vegas, Nevada, area for an Arizona manufacturer, alleged that the defendant, a bread producer from Utah, had charged prices to its exclusive Las Vegas distributor that were lower than the prices charged its distributors elsewhere, resulting in primary-line competitive injury to the plaintiff. Noting that the goal of Section 2(a) with respect to primary-line competition was to extend protection to competitors of the discriminating seller, the court dismissed the action on the ground that plaintiff was not a competitor of the defendant. Moreover, Bolick-Gillman could not succeed on a secondary-line injury theory because it was not one of Continental's customers. Although there is no doubt that the concept of competition is sufficiently broad to include the rivalry between a manufacturer and a noncustomer wholesaler of competing products who sell to the same retailer, the two parties in this case did not sell to the same customers. The mere fact that Continental was materially interested in the outcome of the rivalry between its own independent distributor and the plaintiff wholesaler did not transform it into a competitor of Bolick-Gillman in the 2(a) sense.

Turning now to the problems of proof of primary-line injury, the cases can be divided into two basic groups, depending on whether or not the seller has acted with predatory intent. As we previously noted, it has been said that the courts have generally made a more conscientious attempt to assay the substantiality and probability of the competitive impact in primary-line cases, in contrast to the more lenient standards employed in determining the probability of secondary-line competitive injury. This generalization is true, however, only to the extent that it applies to nonpredatory pricing in primary-line cases. The presence of predatory intent has a substantial qualitative difference in the courts' analyses. Thus, our discussion of the cases shall be dichotomized accordingly.

Predatory Pricing

Predatory pricing can best be described as selling at a lower price than customarily profit-maximizing considerations would dictate, for the purpose of driving a competitor out of business or crippling his competitive power. In the *Porto Rican–American Tobacco* case of 1929, the United States Court of Appeals for the Second Circuit condemned predatory price slashing in selected areas as "foreign to any legitimate commercial competition." Little has changed in the judicial attitude since that time. Thus, even though a predatory intent on the part of a seller to injure a competitor's business is not a necessary element in a price discrimination case, the existence of such intent goes far to establish the competitive effects proscribed under Section 2(a). As the Supreme Court said in *Chicago Board of Trade* v. *United States*: "[K]nowledge of intent may help the court to interpret facts and predict consequences." The courts seem to have found competitive injury wherever predatory behavior has been found, thus implying a per se approach to the problem. In other words, it may be that the judge or a jury can find that a reasonable possibility of substantial competitive injury, which is all the act requires, automatically follows from predatory pricing. It may seem to some, that the element of predatory intent is but one of many factors that should be considered in determining whether the competitive injury requirement has been satisfied.

But because, in the words of the Attorney General's Committee to Study the Antitrust Laws, "Predatory price cutting designed to eliminate a smaller business rival . . . is a practice which *inevitably frustrates competition* by excluding competitors from the market or deliberately impairing their competitive strength" (emphasis added), reliance on a per se approach in those situations where evidence clearly reveals an intent to injure a competitor would be desirable. Such would accord with the act's purpose of eliminating anticompetitive conduct at its incipiency, particularly because there is greater likelihood that injury to competition will materialize where one intends to accomplish that result. As the United States Court of Appeals for the Seventh Circuit said in its *Anheuser-Busch* decision:

> If . . . the projection [as to the future effects of the price discrimination] is based upon predatoriness or buccaneering, it can reasonably be forecast that an adverse effect on competition *may* occur. In that event, the discriminations in their incipiency are such that they *may* have the prescribed effect to establish a violation of § 2(a). If one engages in the latter type of pricing activity, a reasonable probability may be inferred that its willful misconduct may substantially lessen, injure, destroy or prevent competition.

Moreover, the original aim of Section 2 of the Clayton Act—to prevent a strong national firm from engaging in selective territorial price reductions with a view to eventually eliminating all rivals one by one—is best effectuated by this approach, for clearly such a company would have the power to carry out its plan and divert trade from its local rivals.

It must be noted, however, that even though illicit intent, by itself, might result in a finding of competitive adversity, this issue has never arisen in the context of a litigated case; proof of predatory intent has generally appeared only in conjunction with some evidence of the actual injury to a competitor. Thus, under existing case law, predatory intent plus injury to a competitor constitutes, without more, the requisite possibility of injury to competition. On the other hand, injury to a competitor, without predatory intent, is not always enough; when predatory intent appears, the court is absolved of the necessity of examining market conditions and relevant economic factors in order to determine whether or not competition "may be" injured by the discrimination in price.

No case better illustrates the significance of predatory intent vis-à-vis the competitive injury requirement than the Supreme Court's 1967 decision in *Utah Pie Co.* v. *Continental Baking Co.*, where Continental and two other defendants, Carnation Company and Pet Milk Company —all national manufacturers—were charged with selling frozen pies in the Salt Lake City area at prices lower than those charged by them in other markets.

In 1957, Utah Pie was baking pies in its Salt Lake City plant and unprofitably selling them in Utah and surrounding states. In that year, however, the company entered the frozen pie business. By undercutting prevailing market prices by 15 to 20 per cent, Utah Pie achieved a 67 per cent share of the rapidly expanding Salt Lake City market within a year. During the 1959, 1960, and 1961 period covered by the suit, Utah's share of that market was 34.3, 45.5 and 45.3 per cent, respectively, its sales volume and financial position steadily improving during these years. Rather than accept elimination from the frozen pie market in the Salt Lake City area, the three defendant national suppliers responded with what the Supreme Court called "drastic" price cuts (10 to 15 per cent) and began selling at prices lower in Salt Lake City than those charged in other parts of the country.

The district court held that the responses were of a kind to permit a jury to find a violation of Section 2(a) and allowed the jury verdicts against the three defendants to stand. The United States Court of Appeals for the Tenth Circuit reversed on the ground that notwithstanding the existence of systematic price cutting, there was no actual or potential injury to competition because Utah Pie had consistently increased its sales volume and continued to make a profit. The United States Court of Appeals felt that because the defendants' actions had not actually injured competition during the four years in question, it was "quite unlikely that such a result would probably flow from such actions in the future." The court noted that Section 2(a)'s requirement that there be "reasonable probability" of injury to competition means something more than a "mere possibility."

The Supreme Court reversed and remanded the case to the lower court for further proceedings, holding that the improvement in Utah Pie's sales volume and financial position did not preclude a finding by the jury that the defendants' price discrimination resulted in a reasonable possibility of competitive injury. It said:

> In this case there was some evidence of predatory intent with respect to each of these respondents. There was also other evidence upon which the jury could rationally find the requisite injury to competition. The frozen pie market in Salt Lake City was highly competitive. At times Utah Pie was a leader in moving the general level of prices down, and at other times each of the respondents also bore responsibility for the downward pressure on the price structure. We believe that the Act reaches price discrimination that erodes competition as much as it does price discrimination that is intended to have immediate destructive impact. In this case, the evidence shows a drastically declining price structure which the jury could rationally attribute to continued or sporadic price discrimination. The jury was entitled to conclude that the "effect of such discrimination," by each of the respondents "may be [to bring about the proscribed injury to competition]."

Moreover, the Court was clearly unimpressed with the contention that the effect of the discrimination had been to create a competitive market. It said: "[T]he fact that a local competitor has a major share of the market [does not] make him fair game for discriminatory price-cutting free of Robinson-Patman Act proscriptions."

Although the Court's reasoning is sound, it would appear that Utah Pie's rising sales and profits rebutted the finding of an erosion of competition. Clearly, the controlling factor in this case was not the alleged erosion of competition, but rather the evidence of predatory intent in the form of drastic price cuts that contributed to a sharp decline in the price structure, sales below cost, and industrial espionage. Without this predatory intent, the mere decline in the price structure would not have constituted an erosion of competition sufficient to satisfy the competitive injury requirement of Section 2(a) when viewed in the context of a steady improvement in the plaintiff's business.

Although each company was found to have contributed to the "deteriorating price structure," one must differentiate the facts as to each of the three defendants in order to evaluate accurately the Court's decision. Pet was found to have engaged in nongeographic primary-line price discrimination when it sold pies to one of the largest purchasers, Safeway Stores, under Safeway's private brand, at a price lower than that charged by Pet for its regular brand. This incident probably colored the Court's determination with respect to Pet on the territorial price discrimination issue. As evidence of actual predatory intent, the Court noted that Pet's management, as early as 1959, had identified Utah Pie as an "unfavorable factor" in the market, one that "dug holes in our operation" and posed a constant "check" on Pet's performance in the Salt Lake City market. Moreover, Pet admitted that it sent an industrial spy into Utah Pie's plant in order to obtain information useful to Pet in convincing Safeway that Utah Pie was not worthy of its business. In addition to this evidence demonstrating actual predatory intent, the Court suggested that such intent could be inferred by the jury from the "surrounding economic circumstances, which would include persistent unprofitable sales below cost and drastic price cuts themselves discriminatory."

With respect to its below-cost selling, it should be noted that Pet's prices for its regular brand pies apparently were consistently higher than Utah Pie's regular brand prices. Moreover, there was evidence that the losses were the result of high expenses, rather than low prices. Pet asserted that it recovered its entire direct costs of production and distribution and failed to recover only the portion of its advertising and promotion expenses allocated to frozen pies. It was hoped that the large advertising expenditures would help build a market for the pies. The Court held, however, that the jury could conclude there was a relationship between the losses and prices charged, or, in effect, that the loss was incurred because the prices being charged were too low. Thus, despite the fact that Pet's prices were higher than Utah Pie's, and despite the impact of abnormally large advertising expenses on Pet's cost picture, Pet's below-cost selling contributed to the inference of predatory intent.

The importance of the finding of predatory intent in this instance cannot be overemphasized. Even though Pet's prices in the Salt Lake City market were at times lower than the prices it charged in California markets, the Salt Lake City prices were generally higher than Utah Pie's prices for comparable pies. Thus, although there was price discrimination, in a primary-line sense, it is doubtful that the requisite injury to competition could have been demonstrated but for the existence of predatory intent. For if predatory intent had not been present, thereby obviating the necessity of thoroughly examining and determining the probability of injury, it is doubtful whether the Court would have found sufficient evidence to support a jury finding of potential adverse competitive effect. The Court gave explicit recognition to the significant impact of predatory intent on the competitive injury issue when it cited with approval the United States Court of Appeals for the Seventh Circuit's opinion in *Anheuser-Busch*, where it was suggested that:

> If . . . the projection [to ascertain the future effect of price discrimination] is based upon predatoriness or buccaneering, it can reasonably be forecast that an adverse effect on competition *may* occur. In that event, the discriminations in their incipiency are such that they may have the prescribed effect to establish a violation of § 2(a). If one

engages in the latter type of pricing activity, a reasonable probability may be inferred that its willful conduct may substantially lessen, injure, destroy or prevent competition.

Although there was no direct evidence of predatory intent on the part of Continental, the Court found evidence of behavior sufficient to support an inference of predatory intent. In 1958, Continental had only 1.3 per cent of the market. In order to improve its position, Continental gradually reduced its prices by about 15 per cent during 1959. Meeting with no success, Continental then offered a series of short-term price concessions that brought its price per ounce to a level competitive with Utah Pie's regular brand, but still above Utah Pie's special low-priced brand for big buyers. Despite the existence of price discrimination, the Court had no objection to this behavior, probably because it met with little success. But in 1961, Continental made a substantial price reduction for a two-week period that assisted it in obtaining 8.3 per cent of the market in 1961. Its pies became the lowest priced in the market although they were equal to Utah Pie's special low-priced brand on a per-ounce basis. This action was the basis of the Court's finding against Continental because its price was now "less than its direct cost plus an allocation for overhead." Moreover, although Utah Pie increased its sales, it did so by undercutting Continental's price, thereby reducing its profit margin. The Court rejected the Tenth Circuit's opinion that Utah Pie was not damaged as a competitive force, a conclusion that apparently was based on the increase in the plaintiff's sales volume. According to the Court: "It [the jury] could also have reasonably concluded that a competitor who is forced to reduce his price to a new all-time low in a market of declining prices will in time feel the financial pinch and will be a less effective competitive force." Significantly, the Court noted that even if the impact on Utah Pie as a competitor was negligible, there had been an anticompetitive impact on the other sellers in the market. In addition to the litigants, there were nine other producers who had 12.7 per cent of the market in 1960. A year later, there were only eight other suppliers left with a mere 8.2 per cent of an expanded market. The Court held that there was sufficient evidence from which the jury could find a violation of Section 2(a) by Continental. Thus, in effect, the Court held that where there is evidence of predatory intent in the form of a discriminatory below-cost price cut to a new market low, the mere reduction in sales or profitability of any competitor, even one who is larger, or a decline of the market shares in an expanding market held by smaller competitors, will suffice to establish the requisite probability of injury to competition. A causal relationship between the price discrimination and the deterioration of a competitor's posture need not be demonstrated where a predatory intent can be inferred.

In examining the alternatives that were available to Continental, it could, of course, have based its competition on competitive factors other than price, such as quality and service. Or it might have engaged in aggressive price competition, taking care to keep its prices above cost. Such behavior might have improved Continental's position in the market and at the same time kept the case from the jury. If the price cut would have been "drastic," however, the result would probably have been the same as in the case of below-cost prices, because drastic discriminatory price cutting may create an inference of predatory intent also.

The Carnation situation can be described briefly because it closely resembles the case against Pet and Continental. The Court focused on a three-week "slash in price" of about 20 per cent that resulted in sales "well below" Carnation's costs and that made Carnation's prices lower than those then charged by any other leading seller. This action was followed by price reductions by the other major competitors. During the two years subsequent to the price cut, Carnation's below-cost prices, although lower than those charged in other markets, were generally above Utah Pie's special, big-buyer, brand price and seldom below the price charged for the plaintiff's regular brand. Without elaborating, the Court held that this evidence did not preclude the jury from finding it reasonably possible that Carnation's conduct would harm competition. Apparently, below-cost selling was the sine qua non of a probability of competitive injury, either in the form of a short-term below-cost "slash" under the other prices prevailing at the time or in the form of a long-term, below-cost price that was higher than the competitors' prices.

Justices Stewart and Harlan dissented, contending as did the Tenth Circuit that where an alleged victim's sales and profits are expanding, no probability of injury to competition can be found. In their opinion, Utah Pie's loss of some of its dominant market share from 66 to 45 per cent in 1961 and the drastic decline in the local price structure indicated that the market had been made more competitive, not less. "[T]he 1961 situation has to be considered more competitive than that of 1958." In their view, it was a fallacy to contend that Utah Pie was entitled to hold a "quasi-monopolistic" market share of over 66 per cent in the face of healthy competition. In the dissenters' opinion, the Court fell into the error of reading the Robinson-Patman Act as protecting competitors, instead of competition.

To summarize the holding in *Utah Pie,* it can be seen that a mere inference of predatory intent is enough to establish a prima facie probability of injury to competition, but does not make price discrimination per se unlawful. Significantly, the decision expanded the kind of behavior from which an inference of predatory intent can be drawn by the judge or a jury. As a result, a large national manufacturer will be much more reluctant to enter a new, local market if in order to do so he must make drastic (10–15 per cent or more) price cuts to a level below other prevailing prices, because such behavior may create the dangerous infer-ence of predatory intent. Moreover, that the market is expanding, that the defendant has obtained only a minor share of the market, that the plaintiff has thrived despite the discriminator's practices, and that the plaintiff contributed to the deteriorating price structure will not keep the case from the jury, apparently even in cases not involving predatory intent. Rather, these factors are to be considered in the determination of the cause-and-effect relationship between the proscribed behavior and the alleged damage to the plaintiff and in ascertaining the extent to which the plaintiff has in fact been injured. It must be remembered, also, that the *Utah Pie* decision left intact the act's good faith "meeting" (not "beating") competition defense, which was not raised by the defendant on appeal. Thus, although it is easier to establish a prima facie case of price discrimination where business buccaneering can be demonstrated, proof of predatory intent will not automatically result in victory by the commission or private litigant.

Inference of Predatory Intent

We have seen so far that "a price reduction below cost tends to estab-lish [predatory] intent." Sales below cost do not establish predatory intent in every instance, however. For example, distress sales or clear-ance sales of excess or obsolete merchandise would present a context in which sales below cost could serve a legitimate business objective.

Moreover, *Utah Pie* demonstrated the impact of drastic discriminatory price cuts on this issue, particularly when such reductions precipitate or contribute to a sharp decline in the price structure. In addition, several cases to be discussed subsequently have helped to provide some indication as to what evidence may create an inference of predatory intent.

In the *E. B. Muller & Co.* case, the first primary-line injury case to reach the courts under Section 2(a), the respondent was charged with cutting the price of chicory, frequently below cost, in the single area where its sole domestic competitor marketed, while maintaining higher prices elsewhere. In addition to cutting prices, the respondent was found to have disparaged the competitor's product. Correspondence between Muller's offices was introduced that revealed a plan to "ultimately curb this competition if we should not succeed in eliminating it entirely." Taken together, these factors evidenced a predatory intent on the part of the respondent and eliminated the necessity of demonstrating that the sole competitor had or probably would have suffered any loss.

In *Moore* v. *Mead's Fine Bread Co.*, plaintiff, who was engaged in the bakery business in Santa Rosa, New Mexico, threatened to move his bakery to another town unless the local merchants bought his products exclusively. Reacting to this boycott, the defendant cut the wholesale price of bread in the Santa Rosa area by approximately 50 per cent but did not reduce its prices in any other town. As a result of the price war, the petitioner was forced to close his business. Although the destruction of a competitor is proof of competitive injury for 2(a) purposes, the Court noted that there was evidence here to support a finding of a purpose to eliminate a competitor, as required by Section 3 of the Robinson-Patman Act. Although any attempt to explain the basis for the Court's inference of predatory intent would be conjectural, it is likely that the Court was significantly influenced by the fact that the defendant carried its reduction so far as to drive its competitor out of business rather than only to the extent that would have been necessary to regain its own market or reestablish competition. In this connection, it is significant to note that a different result obtained in the *Balian Ice Cream Co.* case, where the defendant, a large ice cream manufacturer distributing its products widely over the Western states, lowered its prices only in the Los Angeles area—the sole area in which the plaintiff competed with the defendant. The court refused to infer predatory intent on the part of Arden, whose new lower prices were found to have borne a realistic and reasonable relation to the prices charged by competitors. The court agreed with Arden that the price cuts were necessary to eliminate a great many of the chiseling cuts, special advantages, and rebates given by its competitors. Thus, unlike the *Moore* case, the court accepted the argument of reduction for defensive purposes. But unlike *Moore,* no competitor had been driven out of business by Arden. Having found an absence of predatory intent, the court then proceeded to examine the other data bearing on the question of possible injury to competition and found for the defendant. Even though the plantiff suffered a decline in sales during the period in question, it was found to be a result of the intensely competitive market situation to which Arden had responded, and not the product of the discriminator's prices in different areas.

The United States Court of Appeals for the Tenth Circuit suggested another source of inferential proof of predatory intent in *Atlas Building Products Co.* v. *Diamond Block & Gravel Co.* The crux of the plaintiff's charge was that the defendant, the largest manufacturer of cinder concrete blocks in the Texas-New Mexico area, sold its products to the building trade in Las Cruces, New Mexico, where Diamond Block competed, at prices substantially lower than those at which it sold its products in El Paso, Texas, where Atlas enjoyed a virtual monopoly. In this setting, the court said:

> . . . [I]t is fairly inferable that the appellant utilized its higher El Paso prices to stifle competition with its lower prices in the Las Cruces area. In other words, that the appellant utilized its . . . power for predatory ends.

Although the court did not mean to suggest that discriminatory pricing by a company with a dominant market position gives rise to an inference of predatory intent, it is clear that where a supplier has a virtual monopoly power in one market, is a dominant factor in another market, and charges substantially different prices in those markets, an inference of predatory intent may be drawn by the trier of fact.

In *Fry Roofing*, the United States Court of Appeals for the Seventh Circuit affirmed a commission ruling that the respondent roofing company, the price leader and dominant competitive factor in the sale of roofing products in the area served by the two small competitors, had occasioned competitive injury at the primary level by selling asphalt felt in that area at prices below the price at which the two smaller firms could profitably operate and by maintaining its prices at or below this level for over two years, while selling at substantially higher prices elsewhere. The commission inferred predatory intent from persistent selling below the smaller competitors' costs. In reaching the same conclusion, the Court of Appeals ruled that the persistent undercutting of a competitor's prices by one occupying a position of price leadership permitted the inference of predatory purpose.

Finally, the Seventh Circuit ruled in its recent *National Dairy* decision that the record evidence supported a commission finding of predatory intent in connection with a twenty-six-day sales promotion which provided for the unlimited giving of one case of fruit spread free with every case purchased at the regular list price by any customer in the Washington, D.C. market. The following facts were recited by the court as providing a legally acceptable basis for the inference of predatory purpose: the below-cost nature of the offer (National's price was below the cost of materials alone); National's knowledge of the comparable financial strength of it (National is the largest producer of food products in the U.S.) to its competitors as the result of experience and research; its knowledge that the competitors could not financially or otherwise compete with a below-cost and unlimited-quantity offer; its knowledge from a prior offer of its marshmallow product in a similar program in the Boston area which glutted that market; its failure, if not refusal, to control adequately the quantity of sales during the twenty-six-day period; its knowledge that to gain shelf space in the chains meant no reduction in the shelf space of the private brands of the chains but rather a reduction in the space allocated to the independent competitors; and the gearing of its production plant long in advance for a massive sale. The court concluded: "The Commission was warranted in finding that petitioner undertook an all out program, not caring what the effect would be on local competition and, in fact, fully intended to damage its competition."

Competitive Injury in the Absence of Proof of Predatory Intent

During the early years of FTC enforcement of the Robinson-Patman Act, a theory arose under which the diversion of a competitor's business from one supplier to another was sufficient, without more, to establish the requisite competitive effects on the seller level. The *diversion* theory reached its zenith in the commission's *Minneapolis-Honeywell* decision of 1948. In ruling that the respondent's cumulative quantity discount schedule on the sale of heat control merchanisms hindered competition, it said:

> The very nature of quantity price differentials is to divert business to the seller granting such differentials, and, insofar as they cannot be justified by cost differences or otherwise defended, any substantial injury to competition due to them falls within the ban of the Act.

The reversal by the United States Court of Appeals for the Seventh Circuit of the *Minneapolis-Honeywell* decision precipitated a decline in the diversion theory's popularity. Focusing on the continuing competitive vitality of M-H's rivals, the court said of the discount schedule:

> . . . [E]ven if it did succeed in retaining or diverting some business which might otherwise have gone to some of its competitors, where those competitors were able to enter its field and build thriving businesses in spite of M-H's commanding position and alleged wrongful practices, we think it cannot be said that the effect of those practices was substantially to injure competition. And we construe the Act to require substantial, not trivial or sporadic, interference with competition to establish violation of its mandate.

The Seventh Circuit again rejected FTC reliance on the diversion theory in its 1961 *Anheuser-Busch* decision. Stating that Section 2(a) is "not concerned with mere shifts of business between competitors," the court required proof of "substantial impairment of the vigor or health of the contest for business," as distinguished from mere injury to a competitor.

Despite these adverse decisions of the federal courts, the FTC has not altogether abandoned the diversion theory of competitive injury. In its 1965 *Dean Milk* decision, the commission stated that in the absence of predation:

> . . . [A] finding of possible substantial competitive injury on the seller level is warranted . . . where the evidence shows significant diversion of business from the discriminator's competitors to the discriminator or diminishing profits to competitors resulting either from the diversion of business or from the necessity of meeting the discriminator's lower prices, provided that these immediate actual effects portend either a financial crippling of those competitors, a possibility of an anticompetitive concentration of business in larger sellers, or a signifi-

cant reduction in the number of sellers in the market. In such a situation, the finding of possible competitive injury is not bottomed solely upon the fact that there has been or may continue to be diversion of business or loss of profits. Instead, the emphasis is placed upon the reasonably foreseeable results of the diversion or loss of profits.

More recently, in *National Dairy Products Corp.* v. *FTC,* the United States Court of Appeals for the Seventh Circuit agreed with a commission conclusion that an attempt by the country's largest distributor of food products to improve its disappointing fruit spread sales in the Washington, D.C. market by employing a "buy one case, get one free" offer resulted in a violation of Section 2(a). The offer was to have lasted twenty-six days and there was no limit on volume. The free goods were to be delivered after the end of the twenty-six-day offering period. The response was massive. Many retailers immediately began to sell the fruit spreads at half price. According to the commission, the program resulted in substantial losses to National's major and independent regional competitors despite the fact the competitors were "aggressive and informed merchandisers." No one could compete with such a selling program because of its below-cost nature. Setting aside the issue of predatory intent (the court's treatment of predatory intent as a separate, independent basis for supporting the commission's finding is discussed above), the court held that a finding of probable injury to competition was supportable in view of National's failure to limit the amount of goods that could be purchased (coupled with unlimited, free, postprogram delivery of the goods purchased during the promotion) and its lack of control over any reduction in the sales price to the ultimate consumer. The court agreed with the FTC that it was reasonably foreseeable by National Dairy that its product would glut the market and substantially affect competition both as to prices and sales for a considerable period of time. In effect, said the court, National Dairy, if not acting with predatory intent, clearly was attempting to buy shelf space, and "[a]ny shelf space it acquired had to be taken away from competitors. . . . It is further obvious that the shelf space of the chains' private brands would not be diminished under the program. In substance, the chains were being paid 'push money' to advance the sale of petitioner's fruit spreads over the sales of those of its competitors." Moreover, the court found it unrealistic to believe that any of the regional competitors, small or large, had the financial resources to counter with a competing price promotion because of the below-cost nature of the Kraft promotion. "Without such power to compete . . . there can be no other conclusion but that there was a reasonable probability that injury to competition would result for at least six months. . . ." The court rejected the contention that the program was of such short duration that there would have been only a temporary diversion of sales to achieve a lawful objective of competing in the chainstores and agreed with the commission's statement that to permit such promotions "would enable marketers to take short-range bites at the competitive apple which could have just as injurious an effect on competition as overt price cuts."

Even though the commission has modified its earlier views on business diversion to the extent that it now looks to the future results that the diversion or loss of profits may precipitate, this position still has the potential defect of possibly obscuring the very real requirement that there be a causal relationship between the discriminator's lower price and the injury to competition. While providing a relatively simple litmus test of legality, such an approach ignores, at times, the fact that the reduction in profits of a competitor who reduces prices in response to a rival's territorial price cut may have been greatly enhanced by the competitor's own inefficiency or because the previous prices reflected a monopolistic or totally noncompetitive pricing structure. Similarly, those who refuse to meet a price cut and consequently suffer a loss of business to the discriminator may have only to blame either their lack of imagination as to how to compete effectively or their unwillingness to compete. To predicate injury to competition solely on the diversion of sales from one business rival to another ignores the fact that the touchstone of antitrust legislation is to protect the health of the competitive process, not individual competitors. Moreover, it ignores the fact that changes in market position are a symptom of a dynamic competitive system and deters the operation of competitive processes by inhibiting a national seller from experimenting, entering new markets, or reacting to differing states of demand.

The United States Court of Appeals for the Seventh Circuit voiced objections similar to those above in reversing the commission's *Dean Milk* decision. The court ruled that the record did not show that the diversions of business to Dean and the losses of profits suffered by its competitors in the relevant market area were the "immediate actual effect" of Dean's discrimination, adding:

> The Commission focuses on Dean's discount system as "the prime factor in . . . [its] unusual growth." Underlying this position is the mistaken belief that all competitors in a market have a vested right to share in its growth in the same proportion as their existing shares of the market. The practicalities of competition, however, necessarily result in some competitors growing at the expense of their smaller or less efficient rivals. A more tenable explanation for Dean's growth can be found by analyzing a number of other factors. . . .

Among the factors considered by the court was the impact that *consumer preference* played in the relative growth of the competing dairies. Although it refrained from resting its conclusion on these points, the court suggested that technological changes, small size, and inefficiency may have impaired the ability of many dairies to engage in meaningful competition. It noted that Dean Milk's operation showed a substantial profit after the first two years, despite its volume discounts, suggesting that its profits must in some measure have resulted from efficient operations. Although not suggesting that these considerations concerning Dean's performance were determinative, the court was of the opinion that the commission did not give them the weight they deserved.

The market-analysis approach utilized by the Seventh Circuit evidences the present trend toward a more detailed analysis of competitive impact than required by the diversion theory. Rather than focus solely on a competitor's loss, the courts have looked to whether or not the price differential caused a substantial market dislocation. Such a determination, of course, is by no means easy. A fine line must be drawn to differentiate between attempts by companies to expand into new markets or increase their shares of existing ones on the one hand, and sustained geographic price discrimination by a dominant or monopolistic seller that has the effect of eliminating or impairing the competitive vitality of smaller, weaker competitors, on the other. In this context of substantial and permanent market dislocations, diversion of business away from a rival is clearly a relevant consideration, but no longer is regarded as the legal equivalent of injury to competition. Consideration may also be given to any one or all of the following factors: the number of competitors in the market; their relative size; the point at which a price difference becomes important with respect to the product in question; the volume of business done by each competitor both in the market affected and elsewhere; the market shares held by each competitor in the affected market; the difference between the prices charged by the seller in the different markets; the difference in the seller's costs in serving the various markets; the discriminator's profit margins both in the lower-price market and elsewhere; the profit margins of the competitors in the market affected; the relation of the prices challenged to the prices charged by competitors in the relevant locality; ease of entry by a new firm into the relevant line of commerce; the income of both the seller and its rivals in the affected market from other sources; the extent of consumer preference for one brand over another; the impact of advertising on consumer demands; and evidence as to the level of prices prior to the discrimination.

Although some market analysis is needed in most instances to determine whether the price difference may injure competition, one commentator has suggested the following relevant criteria as dispelling the existence of adverse competitive effects:

1. Decline in the seller's percentage share of the market, in the face of his price differentials.
2. Minor over-all market position of the seller.

3. Growth of the seller's competitors, in terms of market shares, absolute sales volume, or full capacity of their sales.

4. Prevalence of comparable price variations on the part of competitors.

5. Customer switches among sellers.

6. Ease of entry by competing sellers into the relevant market.

7. Keenness of competition among the sellers, or over-all dynamism in the market.

8. Competition by sellers against strongly entrenched regional competitors.

9. Intention of the seller to improve his deteriorating market position, or temporary price experimentation for this purpose.

The Causality Requirement

As we noted in the preceding chapter, there are really two aspects of the causality requirement in cases involving primary-line injury. First, there is an indispensable requirement, at least in cases not involving predatory intent, that there be a causal link between the seller's lower price and the alleged injury to competition. This requirement takes cognizance of the fact that the competitive impact could be the result of the supplier's superior marketing techniques, his rivals' internal problems, or competitive inertia, rather than of the supplier's lower price. For example, in the *Anheuser-Busch* case, the United States Court of Appeals for the Seventh Circuit pointed to the troubles plaguing the respondent's regional rivals as evidence of the absence of a casual relationship between the price difference and competitive injury. The court noted that one competitor's beer was "badly named, poorly merchandised, bitter in taste and 'wild'—that is with unstablized air content" and that it "was disliked by the consumer. . . ." Another competitor's "management had been maintaining a highly liquid cash position at the expense of renewal or replacement of production facilities." Secondly, it must be remembered that some courts require evidence demonstrating the causal relationship between the seller's higher and lower prices, often described as the subsidization or aid from other markets element. This requirement was discussed in the preceding chapter. The courts have generally dispensed with both aspects of the causation requirement when presented with evidence of predatory intent.

Territorial Price Discrimination at the Primary Level

Because territorial price discrimination is the most prevalent type of primary-line case, our discussion of seller-level injury would not be complete without focusing briefly on this subject. Generally speaking, the commission has approached geographic price cutting with an air of suspicion, fearing that even a temporary territorial price difference might have "immediate actual effects [that would] portend either a financial crippling of those competitors, a possibility of an anticompetitive concentration of business in large sellers, or a significant reduction in the numbers of sellers in the market." But as our review of primary-line injury has demonstrated, territorial or area-price differences are not per se unlawful. Regardless of whether the alleged injury at the seller level was precipitated by a cumulative quantity discount system or territorial price differentials, the same kind of qualitative analysis of various market factors must be made. Only through such analysis can one determine whether the seller's competitors suffered a decline in profits or a diversion of business because of the seller's territorial price cuts or because of the competitor's inefficiency, lack of ambition, imagination and aggressiveness, or poor management. Moreover, only by market analysis can one hope to make the crucial distinction between normal, legitimate pricing activities designed to gain a larger market share on the one hand, and activities that represent a destructive attack on local competitors and that impair the vitality of a competitive process, on the other.

A federal court in the *Balian Ice Cream* case, made such a distinction and sanctioned aggressive territorial price discrimination that was part of a move by the defendant to restore a market position that had deteriorated from 23 to 17 per cent in a four-year period. In the context of a declining price structure and keen competition in the relevant market, the court found that the defendants' actions, supported by legitimate business reasons, did not impair the health of the competitive process. In its opinion, Arden's lower prices "bore a realistic relation to previous changes by others in the field, either in the locality or elsewhere [and] . . . corresponded to factors relating to cost of production and demand for the article and the continuous shrinkage of Arden's customers. . . ."

A truly thorough market analysis in a classic territorial price discrimination case was made by a federal district court in *Heinz* v. *Beech-Nut*. Although the fact that a discriminating seller's gross sales and net worth are greater than his competitor's will count against the seller in determining the likelihood of injury to competition, even where the competitor adversely affected has a larger share of the market, the court refused to accept the converse. The fact that the rival's net worth and gross sales were larger than the discriminating seller's did not immunize it from liability under the act.

The *Beech-Nut* case involved what the plaintiff labeled a "price war in the baby food products market in the state of California." In 1957, the defendant reduced its prices on baby food in California to a level lower than its prices east of the Mississippi River. This action was followed by price reductions by the other two large baby food competitors in California, Gerber Products Company and the plaintiff. Heinz filed suit alleging that Beech-Nut's price reductions in California constituted an illegal territorial price discrimination. The plaintiff alleged that by reason of the defendants' reductions in prices in that market, it was forced to reduce its own prices, thereby sustaining a loss in revenue. The defendant moved for a summary judgment on the following grounds: It asserted that the classical case of potential injury to competition is the one in which a well-financed national distributor cuts its prices in an area where it has a weaker local competitor. Noting that the Section 2(a) primary-line injury cases have generally involved a situation in which there has been a great disparity in the relative economic strength of the two competitors, it contended that a territorial price reduction could not injure competition unless made against weaker competitors.

Under the facts of this case, where the three principal companies involved were large national companies with substantial sales, assets, and surpluses, the defendant reasoned that the statute had no applicability. It maintained that a company of the size and strength of Heinz, with the business investment Heinz had in California, had no alternative but to meet the price reduction. In further support of its position, Beech-Nut listed the market shares of each of the three companies, particularly in California, where it had less than 7 per cent at the time of the price cut. It further argued that Heinz had larger gross sales. The conclusion of the defendant was that if a price cut is used in a market where the competitors are of equal or substantially equal strength, there is no reason to suppose that normal competitive responses will not protect the competitive process.

Undeterred by this quantitative approach, the plaintiff denied that the companies were of substantially equal strength. In demonstrating that qualitatively speaking it was a weaker company, Heinz noted that before the price reduction, it had a long-term debt and was using its money for an expansion program whereas Beech-Nut had $25 million in capital. It pointed to the fact that in the areas in which they compete, Beech-Nut outsold Heinz 2 to 1. Heinz disputed the relevance of total sales and asset figures, emphasizing that in 1957 Beech-Nut had a profit of over $8 million whereas Heinz had a profit of $3 million. In addition, Heinz was engaged solely in the food business, which had a low profit margin, whereas Beech-Nut sold other types of products where the profit margins were significantly higher. With respect to the defendant's contention that Heinz could not afford to leave the California market, the plaintiff responded that its wealth in other lines may not be continually allocated to the baby food products line to support a losing fight, and that it had no capital surplus of high-profit products to bear the losses. In short, Heinz maintained that Beech-Nut was in a stronger competitive position than Heinz with a substantial "war chest" with which to fight a price war.

In rejecting Beech-Nut's contentions, the court stated:

Undue emphasis appears to be placed by the defendant on the fact that the plaintiff is also a nationwide competitor of substantial size. A competitor might sell on a nationwide basis and still be weaker. Price cutting in a specified area on a chosen battlefield in an attempt to drive a weaker competitor from that market could still substantially lessen competition in that market even if the injured party sold on a nationwide basis.

CUSTOMER-LEVEL OR SECONDARY-LINE COMPETITIVE EFFECTS

Having identified customer-level competition in Chapter 5, the question remains of whether the seller's discriminatory price concession to one or some of these competing customers runs afoul of the competitive-effects test built into Section 2(a), in the context of customer-level competition.

It will be recalled that legislative impetus for the enactment of the Robinson-Patman Act arose from evidence that large buyers used their economic power to coerce discriminatory price concessions from sellers. The act was designed to reduce this advantage based on economic power, not enjoyed by smaller competitors of such large buyers. It is, therefore, not surprising that the great percentage of price discrimination cases over the years since 1936 have involved this issue of competitive effects of price differentials at the customer level. It is also not surprising that the great bulk of controversy over the Robinson-Patman Act has arisen over the economic evidence necessary to establish that the price discrimination in issue "may be substantially to lessen competition . . . in any line of commerce. . . ."

Burden of Proof: The Balancing of Interests and Morton Salt

The statutory language itself offers a commodity seller precious little direct guidance in determining when a favored price concession "may be" anticompetitive at the customer level. There is, however, the implicit indication that the standard is easier to establish, than if the words *will be* were substituted for *may be*. As was indicated in the preceding chapter, the words *may be* suggest that a prediction is acceptable even if the adverse competitive effects have not already shown themselves. On the other hand, the words *substantially lessen competition* are also used. The word *substantially* suggests that the competitive injury that may arise, must be something more than a transient, inconsequential, or superficial effect on competition. The statutory language thus suggests that some price discrimination presenting insubstantial adverse competitive effects is acceptable. But the hard question is: "How much is 'substantial' in measuring competitive effects at the customer level?"

It will be remembered that the statutory standard speaks of injury to competition, not of injury to competitors. What is the difference in the context of injury at the customer level? When is competition *not* injured, although individual competitors suffer? We all know that the stuff of competition involves (although not exclusively) the conduct of competitors. As we noted in our previous discussion of the competition–competitor dichotomy, we have yet to see an economically satisfactory working distinction made between injury to competition and injury to competitors. Indeed, a criticism leveled against the customer-level injury cases under Section 2(a) is that the act has been enforced in a shotgun way to protect inefficient competitors of the favored purchaser, without adequate economic analysis of competition.

These and other questions of balancing competitive interests have confronted the FTC and the federal courts in interpreting the customer-level competitive effects requirement of Section 2(a) in particular fact situations. These adjudicators carry the responsibility for developing economically meaningful standards consistent with the over-all legislative purpose intended by Congress in enacting the Robinson-Patman Act— standards that should provide reasonable guidelines for the commodity sellers of American industry. With respect to secondary-line injury, the Federal Trade Commission and the courts have, in most cases, assumed that any price discrimination may substantially lessen competition.

We must also bear in mind that Congress has built into the Robinson-Patman Act *other* safety valves to prevent the fostering of "soft competition," apart from the adverse competitive-effects test in Section 2(a). These are the seller's affirmative defenses of meeting competition and cost justification, which will be discussed in later chapters.

In analyzing the case law that forms the guideposts for evaluating customer-level competitive effects, it will be useful to review the major Supreme Court decisions in this area, beginning with *FTC* v. *Morton Salt Co.,* decided in 1948. This landmark case constituted the first Supreme Court analysis of Section 2(a) in the context of customer-level competitive effects.

Morton brand table salt was and is a well-known household commodity, sold in grocery stores throughout the United States. Salt, like sugar, bread, milk, and gasoline, is a fungible product in the sense that no substantial quality differences generally exist between competitive brands. Table salt is but one of thousands of products sold in the retail grocery store. Salt sales account for but a nominal portion of any grocery store's sales volume.

Morton sold its best brand of table salt on a per-case price schedule that ranged from a high of $1.60 for LCL purchase to $1.50 for carload purchases, to $1.40 for 5,000–case purchases in any consecutive 12 months, and $1.35 for 50,000–case purchases in any consecutive 12 months. Only five national customers (large retail grocery chains like A & P, Krogers, Safeway, and National Tea) purchased in volume sufficient to receive the $1.35 price. Small chain competitors of these "Big Five" and independent retailers were unable to secure the same concessions, and these large retail chains were able to sell salt to consumers cheaper than wholesale customers could resell to competing retailers.

The FTC found these incremental "differences" gave rise to adverse competitive effects, and the Supreme Court agreed. Indeed, the $1.60 per-case price for LCL purchases compared to the $1.50 maximum charge for carload purchases (a 10-cent difference) was found to be anticompetitive. This 10-cent per case difference meant a ½-cent difference in the purchase price of a 26-ounce package of Morton Salt. The fact that the salt was a relatively minor item in the retailer's inventory was regarded as immaterial, because of the danger presented by the cumulative effect of several similar discriminations.

The Supreme Court held that it is unnecessary to show that competition had in fact been injured—this conclusion being consistent with the "may be" language of the statute. So far as the standard of evidence required, the Supreme Court gave its tacit blessing to a per se customer-level injury standard in concluding that a prima facie case of customer-level competitive injury is shown whenever the price differences in issue are sufficient to influence the resale price. In establishing what appeared to be an automatic inference of injury from the existence of a price difference, the Court said it was "obvious that the competitive opportunities of certain merchants were injured when they had to pay [Morton Salt Co.] substantially more for their goods than their competitors had to pay." Evidence of injury to individual competitors of the favored customers was sanctioned as a valid area of inquiry, the theory being that when secondary-line injury is at issue, discriminations always enable favored purchasers to resell at prices unrelated to operational efficiencies. It was felt that by permitting customers with superior bargaining power to obtain goods at prices lower than any cost savings their efficiency could provide the seller, these customers are gaining an unfair advantage over smaller individual rivals that will ultimately impair the vitality of the competitive process. Thus, the *Morton Salt* case established that in cases involving secondary-line injury, in sharp contrast to seller-line injury proceedings where a demonstration of a substantial adverse impact is required absent proof of predatory intent, the courts may rely on broad inferences of adverse competitive affects based on the mere existence of substantial price differentials among competing customers.

Although the 1948 *Morton Salt* decision set the framework for a low level of proof required to show customer-level anticompetitive effects, post-*Morton Salt* decisions by the commission and the courts have tended to predicate their findings of injury to competition on specific factors in addition to the price differences thereunder. For instance, the commission has taken the position that the requisite secondary-line injury proof exists where the seller's price differences are substantial and continuing in an industry where keen competition exists, especially where the percentage difference is a substantial portion of the customers' net profit. What if these factors are absent? Or some of them? Research has revealed no decision squarely ruling that no adverse competitive effects arose because no keen competition existed at the customer level, although a 1936 commission decision against Kraft-Phenix Cheese Co. alluded to this conclusion in evaluating the weak price competition for cheese products between retail grocers. It will, nevertheless, be useful to review specific topical standards to determine under what limited circumstances a price difference between customers may *not* be anticompetitive.

The Causality Requirement

To violate Section 2(a), the price discrimination must, of course, be the cause of the injury. As was noted in the preceding chapter, however, the causality requirement is made easier to establish in secondary- than in primary-line cases. As a federal district court said, in *Shore Gas & Oil Co.* v. *Humble Oil & Refining Co.:*

> In the common "secondary" or buyer's line injury case, the causal relationship between discrimination and injury to competition is obvious: defendants' difference in price to buyers places the one discriminated against at a competitive disadvantage, consequently prejudicing fair, vigorous competition in the affected market.

Inference of Competitive Injury from Low Profit Margins

As noted here, anticompetitive effects have, in some cases, been predicated on low profit margins in the industry in which the price cuts are employed. For example, the United States Court of Appeals for the Seventh Circuit affirmed the commission's 2(a) order where a defendant gave a 25 per cent discount to "stocking" jobbers, while giving only a 15 per cent discount to regular jobbers who did not warehouse its products. After noting that a wholesaler's profit margin in the business was "very, very low," the court held that it was "apparent from the difference [10 per cent] in discounts [that] . . . a 'reasonable possibility' [existed] that the regular Jobbers would be adversely affected by petitioners' discounting practice."

In the *United Biscuit Co.* case, the United States Court of Appeals for the Seventh Circuit held that the defendants' volume discount of 6 per cent, resulting in a price difference up to 6 per cent between independent grocers and grocery chain stores, had substantial anticompetitive effects in view of the "highly competitive nature of the retail food business and [the fact] that net profits are low. . . ." The fact that most of the independent store owners who testified stated that they would not be adversely affected by the discount differentials, did not overcome the commission's conclusion on the question of substantiality. The incipient harm to competition that may be present if the challenged discriminations should continue is not to be determined solely by the opinions of the store owners. That determination must be made by the commission through an exercise of its special competence and on the basis of all of the attendant facts and circumstances with particular reference to the type of business under investigation.

In another case, the United States Court of Appeals for the Fifth Circuit affirmed the commission's position that "if it can show a substantial price differential which is sustained over a significant period of time in a business where profit margins are low and competition keen [here, fluid milk], it is proper to infer that an injury to competition with the favored purchaser is probable." The court denied that it was, in effect, holding that price discriminations are per se illegal, but felt it "must defer to the Commission the task of drawing the inference of probable injury to competitors so long as that inference is supported by a reasonable quantum of evidence in the record." It concluded, "where the record indicates a price differential substantial enough to cut into a purchaser's profit margin and discloses a reduction which would afford the favored buyer a significant aggregate saving that, if reflected in a resale price cut, would have a noticeable effect on the decisions of customers in the retail market, an inference of injury may be properly indulged."

Substantial and Insubstantial Competitive Effects

It is standard competitive-effects dogma that a price discrimination must give rise to reasonable possibility of substantial anticompetitive effects for a violation of Section 2(a) to arise; although, as we previously noted, the term *substantially* means different things at different levels of competitive injury. The question of where nominal or *de minimus* leaves off and substantial begins, is an issue that has been given insufficient attention by the commission and the courts over the years. Generally, in secondary-line injury cases, there is an effort by the prosecutor, backed by the *Morton Salt* decision, to relate the percentage of the price concession to the percentage of profit margins among the competing customers, and sometimes to the influence of the price concession on resale prices. This latter point, however, has not been regarded as controlling, for courts have disregarded the customer resale prices as a necessary area of proof. Even though decisions as to what is substantial have been reached on this basis, there is little case precedent allowing price discriminations with insubstantial competitive effects.

Perhaps, because of the vagueness of this standard, the cases incline to lip-service toward determining whether the effects may be substantial, particularly where it is the large-volume buyer receiving the price concession, and there is no reason advanced for *any* difference in price.

Thus, in the Supreme Court's 1952 *Ruberoid* decision, a roofing product manufacturer's 5 per cent price differentials were found by the commission to violate Section 2(a), and respondent quarreled with a flat prohibition against *any* price differences in the commission's cease and desist order. Mr. Justice Clark responded for the Supreme Court:

> First, it is argued that the [FTC] order went too far in prohibiting *all* price differentials between competing purchasers, although only differentials of 5% or more were found. But the Commission found that very small differences in price were material factors in competition among Ruberoid's customers, and Ruberoid offered no evidence to the contrary. . . . In the absence of any indication that a lesser discrimination might not affect competition there was no need to afford an escape clause through which the seller might frustrate the whole purpose of the proceedings and the order by limiting future discriminations to something less than 5%.

Although the language in *Ruberoid* reflects a willingness to sanction a cease and desist order broader than the statutory measure of substantial, the language is tacit encouragement to the commission not to take the "substantial" language too seriously in formulating a case involving customer-level injury. Indeed, *Ruberoid* suggests that the burden shifts to the respondent in showing that the adverse effects are insubstantial if the price difference is shown, together with some other evidence relating the price differences to customer-level profit margins.

In *American Oil Co.* v. *FTC,* decided by the United States Seventh Circuit Court of Appeals in 1963, the court ruled that American Oil's discriminatory price concessions to gasoline retailers did not give rise to substantial adverse competitive effects at the disfavored gasoline retailer level of competition. Located in the area of two small towns in Georgia—Marietta and Smyrna—(adjacent to one another, about 15 miles outside of Atlanta) were ten Amoco gasoline-station customers of American Oil. During a seventeen-day period, there was a gasoline price war in the Marietta-Smyrna trading area.

The first day of the price war, a Shell gasoline station in Smyrna posted a pump price meeting the competition of another "private brand" station one block away, which just opened for business. The private brand station was located behind an Amoco station, and other major gasoline stations (Texaco, Sinclair, and Gulf) lowered their prices to match those of the Shell station. American Oil responded by granting its Smyrna Amoco dealers—but not its Marietta area Amoco dealers—*substantial* price concessions ranging, per day, from 3.5 cents per gallon (three days) to 5 cents per gallon (six days), and larger concessions up to 11½ cents per gallon (eight days). Following this price war of seventeen days, the situation returned to normal and all Marietta-Smyrna dealers paid the same price.

The court, seeking to determine whether the requisite substantial competitive injury was established, looked to the losses of the six disfavored Amoco dealers in the Marietta area: one had "a loss of gross profit . . . as much as $150"; one had losses that "would be slight"; one, who opened his station the day the price war started, lost about $50 gross profit; one lost "$500 over all in all business" with some unknown lesser amount in over-all profits.

The court then went on to observe that not only were these losses minimal, but

> . . . there is no substantial evidence to show that it was the result of American's price reductions to its Smyrna dealers rather than for the most part attributable to the fact that the major brands of gasoline were being sold in the Smyrna area for substantially less than in the Marietta area.

Finding no substantial, permanent competitive injury, the court refused to equate substantial price concessions to Smyrna dealers with substantial injury to competition. *American Oil,* thus, is a rare customer-level competitive-effects case where a United States Court of Appeals was persuaded that the facts showed no substantial customer-level competitive effects that had a causal connection traced to the seller's price differentials, rather than to general price declines of other retailers. *American Oil* shows, particularly, that where a price discrimination is not systematic and recurring, the courts will not follow a per se type of approach, but will make a realistic factual inquiry as to whether the statutory standard of substantial has been satisfied.

The 1967 *Borden Company* case presented a second situation in which price differentials were found to be not anticompetitive at the customer level. Since 1938, Borden had been producing and packaging evaporated milk under both its Borden label and under private brand labels owned by the customer. A significantly lower price was charged for private brand milk. Thus, private brand milk was identical to the Borden brand milk in all respects but the label on the can. The Federal Trade Commission ignored the labeling distinction and relied on *Morton Salt* in finding anticompetitive effects at the customer level. The commission held it sufficient for a violation that customers paid substantially more for the Borden brand than for the private brand. The United States Court of Appeals for the Fifth Circuit reversed on two grounds: First, the court felt that reliance on *Morton Salt* was erroneous, because in *Morton Salt* volume discounts were used to create price differentials, a practice that produced competitive effects far different from the Borden practice, which did not alter prices based on volume. Secondly, on the principal issue of whether label differences were a viable basis for price discrimination, the court stated:

> We are of the firm view that where a price differential between a premium and nonpremium brand reflects no more than a consumer preference for the premium brand, the price difference creates no competitive advantage to the recipient of the cheaper private brand product on which injury could be predicated.
>
> . . .
>
> And it is to be remembered that no customer who requested private-brand milk from Borden was denied the right to purchase it at the same price being charged to other customers.

The court, however, also noted the caveats that price differentials must neither exceed the consumer appeal of the premium brand nor be unreasonably low for the private brand; that is, Borden could not have used its profits from the premium brand product to subsidize its private brand.

Competing Customers

For secondary-line injury to occur, the discrimination in price must be given to a competing customer of the one against whom the injury is said to accrue. Thus, in the Federal Trade Commission case against William H. Rorer, Inc., Rorer was a drug manufacturer whose principal product during the years 1955–1963 was Maalox, an ulcer remedy. In 1962, Rorer's sales of Maalox amounted to about $15 million. During this period of time, Rorer sold Maalox direct to "independent" drugstores in minimum purchases of $100, at a 40 per cent discount (which was available by buying indirectly, through wholesalers) plus 15 per cent, plus a 2 per cent cash discount, ten days. This price was generally known to the drug trade. But Rorer had another price schedule, not generally known, that granted to "qualified" chain stores an extra 5 per cent discount—with no minimum purchase required. "Chain" drugstores were defined by Rorer as five or more registered pharmacies under single ownership, having a buying office and a warehouse. Others were independent.

The gist of the commission's complaint was that Rorer, in granting qualifying chain stores the extra 5 per cent discount, violated Section 2(a) of the Robinson-Patman Act, because of adverse competitive effects on competing independents who purchased Maalox from Rorer. In this connection, there was no requirement that the amount of Maalox ordered by the qualified chain stores exceed the amount normally ordered by the independents. There was also no provision or condition favoring a high-amount independent. It was also shown that there were instances of an independent paying the higher price even though the purchases of Maalox exceeded those of competing chain stores. With the price "difference" between competing purchasers (independents and chain stores) established, the bulk of the commission's case involved the proof that this price difference adversely affected competition of disfavored independent drugstores.

Retail drugstore operations were shown to be characterized by close profit margins, generally less than 5 per cent of gross sales. Retail drug prices were also shown to be significant in those cases where the drugstore —independent or chain—sells on the basis of comparative price advertising. Lost sales are not easy to trace in any particular discriminatory arrangement, and this fact was recognized by the FTC hearing examiner. Retail druggists commonly took advantage of the 2 per cent cash discount.

The typical retail price for Maalox was $1.49 a bottle, with independents paying about 89 cents and the chains paying about 84 cents per bottle under Rorer's pricing schedule. But commencing in 1962, Maalox came to be used as a discount item—with retail "specials" at approximately 90 cents or less and an everyday retail price of around 98 cents. This emerging discount practice (which had nothing to do with the 5 per cent discount in issue) destroyed in large measure the $1.49 retail price for Maalox. But there were some drugstores that did not get into the discount race for one reason or another.

The hearing examiner grounded the adverse competitive impact of this 5 per cent discount to qualified chain stores in five trading areas where *discount* chains and *discount* independents were in vigorous competition. The favored chain store, in selling Maalox just above its own cost (or own cost plus overhead), would compel the disfavored independent to sell below its own cost (or its own cost plus overhead) to meet competition. To the bargain hunter, a 5-cent difference in price was found to be significant, where the retail price is typically less than $1. The 5 per cent discount was, therefore, found to be, "substantial enough to have the requisite effect on competition and competitive vitality of unfavored customers." The retailer's image *as a discounter* was "an important matter in connection with requisite ability and vigor to compete at a low mark-up level."

The importance of the 5 per cent discount was further manifested by the fact that most customers took advantage of the 2 per cent discount for cash. But if "lost profits" by disfavored retailers were to be the test for finding adverse competitive effects, consistent with *Morton Salt* and its progeny, the hearing examiner declared that no violation could be established. Sales to the disfavored retail druggists in issue amounted to no more than $40–$50 per year in lost profits.

The hearing examiner thus ruled that although *discount* independents, and *discount chain stores,* as well as *nondiscounting* drugstores, all sold Maalox to the consuming public in the same trading areas, the area of adverse competitive effects excluded nondiscounting retail drugstores.

The FTC, on review, reversed this ruling of the hearing examiner and disregarded the discount-price-competition issue at the retail level as bearing on the measure of adverse competitive effects among *all* retail purchasers in the trading area.

> Where a retailer holds the prices on Maalox and consequently does not benefit from being able to sell at a price lower than his nonfavored competitors, his savings on the purchase of Maalox afford him additional profits which can readily be used for advertising or promotions which enable him to offer lower prices on other products. Such sums afford the favored recipients a definite competitive edge over their nonfavored competitors and this advantage exists regardless of whether the recipient sells Maalox at discount or at list prices. Where competition is keen, as it is in the retail drug industry, this edge may be decisive. Furthermore, the fact that certain favored chains did not discount Maalox at the time they were receiving the lower price did not mean that they would not do so in the future had the differential persisted.

The *Rorer* litigation raised a number of interesting issues, namely the extent to which *keen* competition among favored and disfavored competing customers is really regarded as a valid touchstone to finding customer-level injury where the price difference is substantial and continuing in a market where net profits are small. The commission found intense competition at the retail drugstore level. If we look to the economic indicators of competition: price, quality, and service, and acknowledge "quality" competition (all retailers in issue were selling the same Maalox product), Rorer's evidence of the absence of Maalox *price* competition by nondiscounting independents would be some evidence bearing on the keen competition issue. On the other hand, nondiscounting independents may have been providing *service* competition not offered by the discounters such as free delivery, credit, long hours, and so on. The point is that the question of keen competition was never fully resolved in an economic sense.

The *Rorer* case involves a situation where the commission adhered to the general approach of requiring independents and chains to start off on an equal price footing, which attitude is consistent with the over-all legislative mandate of the act. It would appear more forthright, in such a case as *Rorer,* to have disavowed frankly the controlling significance of intense competition among *all* competing customers of Rorer (in light of *Morton Salt*), and not to hold this carrot out as a relevant issue on which sellers can rely in good faith formulation of a discriminatory price structure that is not anticompetitive. Alternatively, the commission should have dealt with the keen competition issue in the light of the applicable economic indicators of competition, so that Rorer's evidence would have been more fully considered in its broader context.

Effect of Functional Discounts on Secondary-Line Injury

In assessing the existence of secondary-line injury, it is first necessary to determine if the injured customers are on the same level of competition. Because the Robinson-Patman Act prohibits only those discriminations that "lessen competition," the existence of a competitive situation must first be established. This involves classification of a seller's customers according to the functions they perform in the distributive process. A function can be described for purposes of this discussion as that operation unique to a particular stage in the marketing of a product. For example, the various operations involved in wholesaling—large-volume buying, storage, and so on—are not ordinarily repeated at the retail level and are traditionally considered functions of the wholesale level. Consequently, a customer of a manufacturer who performs those operations is considered to be on the wholesale functional level.

This division of customers according to work done has provided the basis for one of the most fundamental forms of legitimate price discounting—functional discounts. In reaffirming the essential legality of these price reductions, the commission, in its 1955 decision in *Doubleday & Co.*, clearly delineated the philosophy behind allowing these discounts:

> Functional discounts long have been a traditional pricing technique by which sellers compensated buyers for expenses incurred by the latter in assuming certain distributive functions. The typical functional discount system provided for graduated discounts to customers classified in accordance with their place in the distribution chain, namely, wholesaler, retailer and consumer in diminishing amounts. They were intended to reflect, at least from an economic viewpoint, the seller's estimates of the value of the marketing functions performed by the various classes of customers.

The idea of a discount system in this context can best be understood by treating a totally integrated vertical arrangement as the starting point. If we assume that a manufacturer performing all the distributive functions from production to consumer is the ordinary method of business operation, then the price charged to the ultimate consumer would be the cost of performing all the operations plus a reasonable profit margin. A functional discount would be the amount off that final price that the manufacturer considers the value of having one or more of the distributive functions absorbed by someone else. In effect, the manufacturer is willing to let someone else enjoy part of the selling price for doing part of the work.

Obviously, this description is imperfect. Not all manufacturers are capable of predetermining the consumer price of their products, and, therefore, their price to wholesalers is not a "discount" but simply their cost plus profit margin. The final price to the consumer is determined by subsequent cost plus profit increases added to the price at each stage of the distribution chain. It is, nonetheless, essential to keep the discount notion in mind in examining this area because that has been the traditional approach of the commission and the courts.

A functional discount is not simply the cost of performing the particular function. If this were the case, there would be little advantage to being anything but a manufacturer. Such discounts also contemplate a reasonable profit margin for the party performing the function. Operating from the premise that a functional discount, when given to the entire class, is legal because it is not anticompetitive, there is no necessity to justify the size of a particular functional reduction to any other class of customers operating on a different functional level. Thus, functional discounts to wholesalers can contemplate a wider profit margin than those to retailers without violating the act. What is essential is that everyone at the *same* functional level receives the *same* discount for absorption of the *same* function.

Difficulties in interpretation develop when a customer takes on several functions and, thereby, occupies more than one functional position in the distribution chain. For purposes of discovering the existence of competition, it is then necessary to place such a multifunction customer in some category. To accomplish this, the commission has established the practice of examining the last function performed by the customer before resale and assigning the customer to that functional level. It was described by the United States Second Circuit Court of Appeals in *Mennen Co.* v. *FTC,* as being "not the character of his buying, but the character of his selling, which marks him." Thus, a wholesaler-retailer would be in the retail functional class. If such a customer is given a lower price than a straight wholesaler, the requisite injury at the wholesale level might then prevail because both occupy that function. But if he is given lower prices than a straight retailer, this may be justified by reference to cost savings through assumption of the wholesale function. What is essential, however, is that such a multifunction customer can only receive a profit-margin discount (functional discount) for one level—in this case, the retail level. This is the true distinction in a functional discount and lends great importance to the determination of functional level.

It must be remembered that we are here discussing customers who ordinarily perform more than one function, such as the chain stores, and not a single-function customer who subsequently absorbs other operations. The multifunction customer, although competing with many functional levels, is generally entitled to only one discount, which contemplates a return over the cost of performing the operation that we have been calling a profit margin. This is not the only discount he may receive, but it is the only one that can reward him beyond cost.

The essential legality of functional discounts does not mean that the requisite competitive injury can never be found when the customers are on different competitive levels. Rather, the discount for functional levels will only be allowed when it fairly reflects the relative position of the two customers in the distribution chain. Under functional discount concepts, the wholesaler level will always receive a larger discount than the retail level because the wholesaler must subsequently give a retail functional discount. Therefore, a retailer who absorbs the wholesale function still may not receive a discount larger than the seller's wholesale customers because this would necessarily create injury at the retail level. This would be true despite the fact that the single-function wholesaler and the wholesaler-retailer are not technically on the same functional level. This will be the result whenever a seller reverses the normal progression of discounts in the distribution chain. As a federal district court declared in *Krug* v. *International Telephone & Telegraph Corp.,* "there can be no doubt that a violation of Section 2(a) may occur when a manufacturer sells his products to a retailer at a lower price than that charged to a wholesaler whose customers compete with the retailer." Thus, the functional discount is legal only so long as it respects the traditional structure of the distribution chain with regard to the relative size of the discounts given.

Another problem arises when a customer resells to two different competitive levels. May the supplier give a discount for the absorption of part of a function? This is permitted where the seller grants the discount in proportion to the actual cost such absorption has saved. This requires a dual pricing system by the manufacturer. Consider a distributor who sells to jobbers and also directly to consumers. A straight distributor discount would give an inordinate advantage over competing retailers, whereas a retail discount would seriously hinder his competition with other distributors. The solution is that the manufacturer must sell at two prices, in proportion to the amount the distributor-retailer sells in each capacity. In effect, these will both be functional discounts because his dual character prevents his being assigned to any one competitive level. Such a conclusion follows logically from the commission's policy of looking to the selling operation to determine function.

Until now we have been examining the customer who performs a number of distributive functions as a normal part of his marketing process. Our prototype has been a customer similar to a chain buyer who performs both wholesale and retail functions. Such a customer has been classified as operating on the retail level and as such is entitled to a discount for performing a function that includes reasonable profit. In addition, such a customer is entitled to an additional discount for absorption of the wholesale function, which would otherwise be an expense to the seller. This is equally true of the single function retailer who decides to integrate upward and assumes certain wholesale functions. These discounts are not technically functional discounts because the customer is defined as being on a different functional level. Instead, they are discounts for assuming additional functions and are subject to somewhat stricter requirements.

With respect to these additional functions, the commission stated in the *Doubleday* case:

> Only to the extent that a buyer actually performs certain functions, assuming all the risks and costs involved, should he qualify for a compensating discount. The amount of the discount should be reasonably related to the expenses assumed by the buyer. It should not exceed the cost of that part of the function he actually performs on that part of the goods for which he performs it.

The requirement is that the *seller* justify the discount to the buyer by reference to the savings to the *seller* in having the operation assumed by the buyer. The buyer might still obtain some profit from the wholesale operation, but it will have to be by performing it more cheaply than the seller was capable of doing. This cost justification will relate to all discounts given with respect to additional functions assumed beyond the functional level at which the customer ultimately sells. It is intended to prevent a customer from obtaining additional profit margin discounts that he can convert into price reductions to be used against competing customers who enjoy no such functional discounts. For example, if a chain grocery store were to receive functional discounts calculated to give it a profit on both its wholesale and retail functions, it could convert its wholesale profit margin into a price reduction, undercut competing retail grocers who must use independent wholesalers, and still enjoy its ordinary retail profit margin. The determination of whether such a discount given with respect to a function is legal will be determined under the criteria of the cost justification defense of Section 2(b), discussed in a subsequent chapter.

The approach of the commission to assumption of additional functions has created special problems for group buying arrangements. Often, small retailers will band together when making purchases in an attempt to avoid the wholesale stage of distribution and gain special discounts directly from the manufacturer. Their motive may be either to avoid the expense of dealing with wholesalers or to better compete with chain-store retailers. These collective groups are much more similar to wholesalers than the chain store is because they must still handle the redistribution of the product to numerous independent retailers. The question arises whether these groups can qualify as independent wholesalers entitled to separate functional discounts. If not, they may be hard pressed effectively to compete with other wholesalers while their member retailers would be disadvantaged by the chain-store techniques.

In the *Automotive Parts* cases, involving a classic series of group buying arrangements, the commission struck down the granting of any functional discounts to the "group" in its wholesale capacity because it was composed of nothing but members operating at a lower functional level. Under FTC interpretation, the functional discount for such a group would be the level on which its members, not the group, resell the product. It was precisely this type of interpretation that caused the farm cooperatives to voice such strident opposition to the functional discount section contained in the original Patman Bill. Although the section was not in the final bill, the commission has incorporated its philosophy into application of the act and has uniformly invalidated functional discounts to groups that are nothing more than cooperative buyers for lower-level customers.

The commission's cost justification approach to situations such as group buying has been the subject of much criticism. Dissatisfaction focuses largely on the FTC's method of determining the cost of a particular function. This is done by looking to the saving to the manufacturer in not having to perform the function. This could be described as a strict accounting-cost approach in that it examines only the operational figures for someone compelled to perform the function. It has been urged that the economic "cost" of a function is greater because it reflects what a seller will pay to have someone else perform the function, namely, cost plus some profit incentive. Because this is what the seller will pay an independent to perform the function it must be what he considers the value, or economic cost, of the function. Such a cost, it is argued, is a more accurate reflection of savings to the seller in having this function assumed by a customer. It is also asserted that a wholesaler who is willing to cut the profit margin incorporated in his functional discount can offer a lower retailer price than a retailer who has assumed the wholesale function can gain for himself. This is because the latter has no profit margin to cut at the wholesale level.

Despite this criticism, the commission has been invariable in prohibiting functional discounts to cooperative buying groups. This does not mean that an *independent* wholesale-level operation that simply services independent retailers could not obtain a functional discount. This has been permitted where the wholesale operation can be shown to be independently operated. Nor will mere stock ownership of a wholesaler by a retailer preclude wholesale discounts to the subsidiary. To be denied the discounts, the commission has usually required a degree of cooperation that would make the wholesale operation little more than a dummy buyer for the member retailers.

Although it will be discussed in far more detail in Chapter 10, absorption of the brokerage function by the buyer deserves some mention. Although traditionally falling within the description of a function, the unique language of Section 2(c) prevents any functional discount for brokerage services. If a buyer, in the process of integrating upward, should absorb the brokerage function, an elimination of that function would occur with a corresponding windfall to the seller. Both the commission and the courts have held that the fiduciary nature of the broker prevents his working for a buyer while being compensated through discounting by the seller. Similarly, the buyer is prevented from performing the function and accepting a discount from the seller. Even though this position has been somewhat eroded by the *Hruby Distributing Co.* case, it is still apparent that brokerage does not qualify for any of the ordinary functional discount treatment, nor will it justify a cost discount when absorbed by a customer. The only alternative to an independent functional level of brokerage would seem to be the complete elimination of that level.

Territorial Price Discrimination at the Secondary Level

The question of when customers compete with one another also arises in the territorial price discrimination context. Generally speaking, when a supplier charges different prices in different territories, an illegal competitive effect on the secondary level is rare because all the purchasers within each territory are given the same price. Thus, where the geographic areas are separate and the purchasers in one are not in competition with buyers in another, the only possible injury can be at the primary or seller's level. Where the territories are contiguous, however, secondary-level injury problems could arise because buyers on either side of the line dividing the two areas may in fact be competitors. A failure to offer equivalent price concession to a customer who in fact competes with a purchaser located inside the favored geographic market area will result in a violation of Section 2(a). For the supplier who desires to establish certain trade areas where customers will be offered reduced prices or promotional allowances, two questions arise: (1) What are the permissible methods by which a trade area may be drawn so as to not run afoul of Section 2(a)? (2) Assuming a trade area has been defined by a seller, what guidelines exist to determine whether purchasers located outside the perimeter of a trading area will be found to be in competition with preferred purchasers within that area?

Unfortunately, there has been a dearth of FTC or judicial comment as to factors or methods to be used in creating a legitimate geographic trade area. It has been stated by Sawyer that: "Geographic location of competitors is immaterial if competition actually exists." In other words, that the competing purchasers are located on opposite sides of trade-area boundary lines is of no consequence in determining whether or not a 2(a) violation has occurred. If literally applied, this approach would effectively preclude the creation of territorial markets with provisions for "feathering" out to make the price concession available to competing purchasers not located within the boundaries of the trade area. The feathering would, in turn, create additional purchasers who would qualify for the same price advantage by reason of their being in competition with those purchasers located just outside the favored trade area to whom the better offer was extended or feathered. The market area would, of necessity, have to grow until there were no competing purchasers beyond the perimeter of that area. Surprisingly, there has been some indication of acceptance of this extreme view. For example, in the *Forster Manufacturing Co.* decision, Chairman Dixon's majority opinion suggested that only natural geographic boundaries could be used to ascertain a legitimate trade area. Among other issues in the case was the legality of counter offers made by the respondents to retailer purchasers in the Pittsburgh area in order to match offers by its competitors. Instead of restricting its counter offers only to those particular buyers who had received a lower price from the competitor, Forster extended its lower prices to all buyers in the Pittsburgh area on the implied premise that such area-wide meeting of competition minimized the probability of secondary-line competitive injury. Chairman Dixon disagreed:

> Respondents' area-wide "meeting" of competition, on the other hand, widened the impact area and increased the likelihood of competitive injury not only at the primary level, but at the secondary level as well. As to the latter, even if respondents communicated the offer to sell at the 10% lower price to every buyer located within an arbitrary *perimeter* surrounding the Pittsburgh marketing area, there would always remain the likelihood that a few buyers located on one side of the "zone" line would compete with buyers located on the other side. To bring all these in, and thus avoid discrimination and competitive injury, respondents would have to continue widening the circle of favored customers, perhaps until they encountered some natural physical barrier (such as a mountain range) to protect the non-favored from the favored buyers. [Emphasis supplied.]

There is a strong probability that Chairman Dixon's description of Forster's trade area as "arbitrary" makes his statement inapplicable to justifiably drawn market areas. Recent advisory opinions by the commission suggest that this is the case. It would appear from these opinions that the commission will permit a price concession or promotional plan to be offered to all competing retailers within a given marketing area that is not arbitrarily created so long as "competing retailers located on the periphery of said market areas are considered . . . to be included within the . . . area if in fact they do compete with those . . . who are offered participation in the plan." Thus, once a legitimate market area is created, the seller must feather out beyond the periphery, but the clear implication from the advisory opinions is that this feathering out will not, in turn, necessitate additional expansion of the market area and so on until a natural barrier is reached. In other words, the seller need only feather once. But these advisory opinions provide no insight into how to draw or create a market area for differential pricing or promotional allowance purposes in such a way as to avoid making it arbitrary.

A somewhat ambiguous approach in determining what constitutes a legitimate trade area was taken by a federal district court judge in the recent case of *Ingram* v. *Phillips Petroleum Company,* where reliance was placed on both the natural physical barrier and the economic entity concepts. The plaintiff operated as a wholesaler for Phillips in the area surrounding Clovis, New Mexico, a town located nine miles from the Texas border. Ingram sought to enjoin the defendant from selling its product at a lower price to a wholesaler in Farwell, Texas, a town nine miles east of Clovis. There was evidence of a 1.8-cent differential on regular gasoline between the two dealers, primarily as the result of a sustained price war in Farwell. Phillips' position was that the state line was a logical trade-area boundary. It pointed out that if the injunction were granted, the Farwell price reduction would be extended into New Mexico. "This," Phillips claimed, "is contrary to the concept of the entire oil industry. . . . [A] state line is a proper boundary."

In response to the defendant's territorial boundary argument, the court stated:

> [D]espite the fact that defendant maintains that they operate in different market areas, we are of the opinion that *the Texas-New Mexico state line does not in this instance constitute a trade boundary which separates different trade areas.* . . . As previously noted, the towns of Clovis, New Mexico, and Farwell, Texas, are geographically close, and *the area is a single homogeneous economic unit* held together by its character as agricultural land. The *natural barriers are the sand hills and pasture lands that lie beyond the boundary of this agricultural area* served by underground water. The evidence shows that both the plaintiffs and Helton sell gasoline outside the territories prescribed to them. The farmers shop in both towns and patronize businesses in both places. In view of these facts, we are constrained to conclude that the plaintiffs and Helton are in practical competition. [Emphasis supplied.]

Which factor was most heavily relied on by the court cannot be determined. The "natural barrier" language indicates that this factor is important in determining the legitimacy of a trade area boundary. But most significant may be the "homogeneous economic unit" language. It suggests that the court refused to recognize the trade boundary based on the state line because it attempted artificially to divide a single economic unit in two. That this area was surrounded by natural physical barriers may have been incidental to the court's determination.

Assuming an acceptable trade area has been created, the question for a supplier then becomes how to determine which purchasers located outside of the favored trade area are in competition with the customers inside the area. There is no simple rule of thumb by which one can determine whether competition in fact exists, making the supplier's burden a heavy one. A number of cases involving gasoline pricing systems have arisen, and reference to three of them at this point may serve to demonstrate the problems encountered in this area.

In *Enterprise Industrial, Inc.* v. *Texas Co.,* price-war discounts were given to the defendant's dealers located within a trade zone defined as the greater Hartford area. The plaintiff was located a few miles south of the boundary line on the main road to New York City. In the court's view, the big factor in determining whether or not the plaintiff was in competition with the Hartford stations was whether or not the consumers had knowledge of the price differential. Because a substantial number of road users were commuters, and because they could look at the posted gasoline price signs as they drove back and forth, it was suggested by the court that stations up to twenty miles away were in competition with the favored Hartford dealers.

In another suit against Texaco, the plaintiff, Alexander, one of nineteen Texaco dealers in the Shreveport-Bossier City area, alleged that twelve of these stations received lower prices. In the court's view, the plaintiff failed to define what he contended was the so-called Shreveport-Bossier City trade area or to show that he was in competition with the favored dealers, many of whom were several miles away. The mere possibility of competition was not enough to satisfy the court. Because the station was located in a residential district in Shreveport, the court felt that it might have served only a relatively small area in its immediate vicinity. Competition with stations five or ten miles away could not be inferred. It must be clearly shown.

Sun Oil was charged by the commission with discriminating as to price between dealers located in the same market area, defined by it as the Duval County or Jacksonville, Florida, area. Sun Oil had divided this county into three separate trade areas, and, therefore, justified the gas-war price differential on the ground that the allegedly disfavored station was not in the same market area as the favored dealers. Strangely, neither the hearing examiner nor the commission commented on Sun Oil's trade-territory system. They merely looked to see if competition, in fact, existed between these various stations. Finding that motorists are particularly price conscious when they buy gasoline, and relying on the aggregate weight of a number of factors—the traffic flow in the sales territory, the 1.7-cent differential, and 2½ to 3½-mile distance between the favored and disfavored stations—the examiner found a 2(a) violation, and the commission agreed.

Because of the difficulties that could arise in determining whether two purchasers are competitors, possibly the best solution to a supplier's pricing-system problem from the secondary-line injury viewpoint would be to follow the advice given by Commissioner Elman in his dissenting opinion in the commission's *American Oil* decision. In discussing the various alternative courses of action which the respondent could have taken, he stated:

> American could have done what the Commission apparently thinks it was required to do by Section 2(a)—either reduce its prices equally to all of its dealers, or "feather" them out in some way, perhaps diminishing in concentric circles from the starting point of the [price] war, on the theory that the differentials between stations would then not have been sufficiently large to cause any diversion of business between competing stations.

In other words, Commissioner Elman suggests that the creation of what amounts to a buffer zone of diminishing price reductions between the favored trade area and the surrounding territory may eliminate the possibility of anticompetitive impact—the price differentials between the competitors being so small that it will precipitate no substantial market dislocation.

Lastly, with respect to notification of competing customers located outside a favored trade area, the seller has the clear, unequivocal obligation to make sure that each of those customers receives actual knowledge that the promotional allowance, service, or price concession is available to him. In other words, the seller bears full responsibility under the law for seeing that the method of communication selected by him gives each customer the notice to which he is entitled. It is not permissible to require that those customers located just outside one of the favored areas demonstrate that they compete with one or more of the favored purchasers before they qualify to have the same offer made available to them.

Sale of Components

There is, perhaps, a different standard of customer-level competitive effects when the customers are manufacturers and the product is a subassembly or component. In the 1964 *Quaker Oats* case, the commission held that Quaker's discriminatory low price of oat flour to a manufacturer gave rise to no reasonable probability of adverse competitive effects:

> There is no showing that the cost of oat flour is a sufficiently significant element in the price of the finished product [so as] to be a cause of adverse competitive effects; fluctuations in the price of oat flour seem

to have little or no competitive significance in the sale of the finished product. . . .

There is no showing that the ability of allegedly disfavored purchasers to compete with Gerber was, or will probably be, handicapped by respondent's sales . . . to Gerber. Gerber received so little practical benefit from purchasing run 14 at low prices from respondent that, after little more than a year, it discontinued using it and resumed the purchase of higher-priced blends.

In support of the *Quaker Oats* decision, finding no anticompetitive cause and effect from the Quaker price concession, the commission relied on a 1951 United States Court of Appeals decision involving the question of whether Minneapolis-Honeywell Regulator Co., in its discriminatory prices for automatic temperature controls, created adverse competitive effects between favored and disfavored oil burner manufacturers. The Court of Appeals grounded its *Minneapolis-Honeywell* decision of no requisite customer-level competitive effects on an extensive analysis of the relationship between M-H's component price differences and the oil burner prices of favored and disfavored manufacturer-customers. The Court of Appeals was particularly impressed with the following evidence of Minneapolis-Honeywell:

Prices Charged Oil Burner Manufacturers by M-H for Controls	Range of Prices Charged Wholesalers by Oil Burner Manufacturers for Burners with M-H Controls	
	Low	High
$17.35	$50.00	111.00
16.45	45.00	96.20
15.90	47.50	102.00
15.35	52.50	89.00
14.90	61.70	100.00
14.25	55.00	101.25
13.75	45.00	114.50

In refusing to accept the commission's contention that the record showed customer-level anti-competitive effects, the court pointed out that although some manufacturers did testify that the question of prices for controls was important in that they had lost business to certain competitors who enjoyed lower control prices, it was equally significant that other manufacturers who paid the higher prices testified that they did not lose business as a result of paying such higher control prices. These other manufacturers considered other factors of far greater importance in determining the price of the completed oil burner.

The court, therefore, found an absence of a causal connection between the price of oil burner controls and the price of the finished oil burners.

In Quaker Oats and Minneapolis-Honeywell adjudicators reflect a tacit willingness to consider more closely than otherwise the impact of price concessions for manufacturing components in the sale of the finished product, which, as we have seen in *Morton Salt,* is generally not regarded as a significant factor in weighing competitive effects among customers engaged solely in the redistribution of a product.

With this apparent exception of the subassembly or component parts cases involving sales to manufacturers, the commission and the courts have generally had little difficulty in finding the requisite measure of customer-level competitive effects where the price differences are substantial and continuing. Almost any continuing policy of substantial price differentials by sellers meeting the jurisdictional requirements attracts the commission's scrutiny, particularly where a seller's larger customers or chain stores receive the favored prices.

THIRD-LINE COMPETITIVE INJURY—
CUSTOMERS OF CUSTOMERS

As mentioned in the preceding chapter, this type of injury is suffered by a disfavored customer in his competition with customers of the supplier's favored buyer, three steps down the distribution chain. There are several factual contexts in which third-line competitive injury may occur:

First, suppose a supplier sells to an integrated jobber-retailer and a regular jobber at different prices. The retailers supplied by the jobber compete with the integrated jobber's retail outlets. If the integrated jobber (who performs the same wholesale functions as the other jobber) pays a higher price, and if the lower price to the favored jobber results in a lower price to its retailers, enabling them to underprice the integrated jobber's retail outlets, then the disfavored purchaser may be injured in his competition with the favored retailers who in this instance operate at the third level in the favored distribution system.

A second third-line situation exists when a supplier sells the identical product at different prices to two jobbers who, in turn, resell to competing retailers. Because of the difference in prices charged to the jobbers, suppose one retailer is able to purchase the identical goods at a lower price than his competing retailer. The disfavored retailer, who under the rationale of the Supreme Court's recent *Perkins* decision is clearly a "customer" of the supplier, may have a cause of action against the supplier if he was injured in his competition with the retailers who purchased from the favored buyer.

The third example of third-line injury is more controversial than the previous two: Suppose a supplier sells both to a direct buying retailer and to an independent jobber who, in turn, sells to retail stations which compete with the direct buying retailer. The supplier sells at a lower price to the independent jobber than to the retailer. If the lower price to the jobber results in a lower price to its retailers, enabling them to under-price the direct buying retailer, the requisite competitive injury may have occurred at the retail level. Counting the levels in the favored distribution system, it can be seen that this is third-line injury.

It is important to note that in the third situation, third-line injury can result only when the wholesaler-customer receives the lower price. If the retailer-customer receives a lower price than the wholesaler-customer, the discrimination is of a secondary-line nature, because only a customer of one receiving the benefit of a price discrimination comes within the statute's third-line wording. When the wholesaler-customer receives a higher price than a direct-buying retailer, he certainly cannot be the beneficiary of a price discrimination, and thus his retailer-customers are not purchasers from one who "either grants or knowingly receives the benefit of such discrimination." In this situation, a retailer purchasing from a disfavored wholesaler clearly has been discriminated against vis-à-vis a competitor in the same functional level—that is, the direct-buying retailer. Thus, he should be able to maintain a cause of action against the supplier for second-line injury, injury suffered in his competition with the favored direct-buying retailer.

For several reasons, few attacks have been made on price discrimination causing injury on the third distributional level. One reason is that, although the statutory language seems clear, congressional records and reports discuss only primary- and secondary-line problems and are silent as to whether third-line competitive injury is within the ambit of Section 2(a). Thus, there has always been some uncertainty as to the actual intent of Congress. Also, in order for a supplier to prevent his wholesaler-customers from selling to their retailer-customers at either a price below the supplier's price to his retailer-customer or at different prices (depending on which of the factual settings exist), the supplier may have to engage in resale-price maintenance, a practice prohibited by Section 1 of the Sherman Act. Because of these problems and because of the hostility of most commentators to third-line-injury enforcement, only one case, *Standard Oil Co.* v. *FTC,* has sustained a third-line price discrimination attack. This case involved a factual context similar to that discussed above in the third example of third-line injury.

Standard Oil, a refiner-supplier, sold its gasoline in the Detroit area to both retailers and wholesalers. Specifically, it had been selling gasoline to four jobbers at "tank car" prices, which were from .5 to 1.5 cents per gallon below the "tank-wagon" price offered to smaller purchasers who sold at retail only. Three of the four jobbers sold at both the retail and wholesale levels, although most of their sales were as wholesalers to independent retailers. The fourth jobber sold at retail only and did not at any time operate as a wholesaler. The FTC brought an action alleging a violation of the act not only as to the gasoline sold to the jobbers for retail sales (a secondary-line situation, because in their retail capacity the jobbers were clear competitors of those retailers who purchased directly from Standard at tank-wagon prices), but, also as to the gasoline sold to jobbers in their capacity as wholesalers (the third-line situation).

The commission found that Standard had violated the act, and in that portion of the cease and desist order dealing with third-line discrimination prohibited Standard from granting lower prices to the jobbers where the jobbers resold to retailers at a price below the tank-wagon price. On appeal to the United States Court of Appeals for the Seventh Circuit, this paragraph of the commission's order was altered to make Standard guilty under Section 2(a) only if it sold to the jobbers *knowing* that they planned to resell to retailers at below tank-wagon prices. The theory behind the alteration was that Standard did not have nor could it legally have any control over the prices at which jobbers sold to their retailer-customers. Thus, to impose liability on Standard for a jobber's resale price that is below tank-wagon prices would be unfair unless Standard had actual or constructive knowledge that such a price would be offered. Only if Standard had knowledge, could it take corrective action against the jobber—for example, refuse to sell at all or to sell only at tank-wagon prices. When the case came before the Supreme Court, the third-line injury issue was not considered; instead, the case was reversed on the legal significance of the meeting-competition defense. In dissent, Mr. Justice Reed stated he would have affirmed the FTC's order, albeit with some amendment in the wording of the order. Eventually, Standard Oil prevailed on its meeting-competition defense; the order was voided; and, in consequence, lawyers and businessmen have never been able to observe how a supplier would attempt to comply with such an order.

Standard Oil left several problems unresolved, but because third-line-injury enforcement has remained dormant for the twenty years since that case was decided, any analysis of these problems is necessarily somewhat speculative. First, it is uncertain whether the finding of a Section 2(a) prima facie violation is dependent on an actual "passing on" of lower prices by a wholesaler-customer to his retailer-customer, or whether the lower price to the wholesaler, which gives the wholesaler the capability of passing on the savings, is by itself sufficient. In *Standard,* only one of the three jobbers who resold to retailers had passed on the lower price. The FTC, however, held Standard liable for all three. Although no express reason was given why Standard's price granted to the other two jobbers were violative of Section 2(a), the probable theory was that the statute proscribes any price discrimination that "may be substantially to lessen competition," and thus demands only a showing of capability to pass on. One argument for the requirement of actual "passing on" is that no injury has taken place until one of the competing retailers has received an unfair competitive advantage—that is, a lower price. This view certainly must prevail in private treble-damage actions because it can hardly be claimed by one retailer that he has lost business to a second retailer as a result of the supplier's lower price to its wholesaler when the second retailer has not received the benefit of that lower price. When the government is the plaintiff, it can be argued that the statute's use of the word *may* indicates an intent that even potential discrimination can be proscribed; thus, *capability* is sufficient. However, even here it would appear that the sounder view is that there must be an actual passing on, because the word *may* should be construed to mean that a violation exists only when the retailers are receiving the product at different prices, even though it has not yet been shown that the direct-buying retailer has actually lost business as a result.

Secondly, the United States Circuit Court's alteration of the FTC order, which required proof that the supplier has either actual or constructive knowledge of the wholesaler's lower price to his retailer-customer, never has been examined further. However, this requirement seems quite reasonable because it would be almost impossible for a supplier to control sudden, discretionary price changes by his wholesaler-customer. In fact, any attempt to do so would probably give rise to a per se violation of Section 1 of the Sherman Act, which proscribes any resale price maintenance once title to the product has been transferred to the purchaser.

Criticism of this kind of third-line competitive injury has centered around the difficulty a supplier faces in trying to comply with a cease and desist order similar to the one in *Standard Oil*. Foremost among these criticisms is that, in complying with the Robinson-Patman Act, a supplier runs the risk of violating the Sherman Act. However, there are still several ways in which a businessman, faced with a third-line-injury problem, can comply with the Robinson-Patman Act without violating the Sherman Act. The most obvious, but perhaps least practical, way to comply with the act is to sell at identical prices to both wholesaler and retailer-customers. Secondly, a lower price may be granted a wholesaler-customer if it can be demonstrated that the amount of the differential is solely the result of lower distributional costs. If this is proved, then the supplier would be exonerated from liability even if the wholesaler-customer resold to his retailers at a price lower than the price offered by the supplier to his retailer-customers. There would be no illegal connection between the lower price offered by the supplier to the wholesaler and the price paid by the wholesaler's customer. The cost justification defense was argued by the defendant-supplier at the FTC level in *Standard Oil,* but was rejected because of inadequate evidence. Along the same lines, also available to the supplier, is the meeting-competition defense, and this defense was successfully maintained by *Standard Oil.* Thirdly, a supplier can alter his prices to retailer-customers to conform to the prices offered by his wholesaler-customer to its retailer-customers. However, this may be not only difficult but impossible where a supplier is selling to more than one wholesaler, because the wholesalers may be selling to their respective retailers at different prices.

Even more fundamental criticisms have been made of the third-line-injury concept in the *Standard Oil* situation. Generally, courts have found that to have a Section 2(a) violation, the disfavored purchaser must be both a competitor and on the same functional level as the favored purchaser. In the first situation, even assuming *arguendo* that the direct-buying retailer and the wholesaler-customer are competitors, it is impossible to say that they are on the same functional level of the distributional system. Therefore, a supplier should not be liable for discriminating in price between them.

However, it is far more reasonable that a third-line action should be maintainable in the first two examples of third-line injury discussed above. In the second example, it will be recalled, the two jobbers are receiving different prices, and the favored jobber is passing his lower price on to his retailer-customer, to the injury of a competing retailer who purchased from the disfavored jobber. It is arguable here also that the supplier should incur no Section 2(a) liability for his discrimination where the two jobbers are not direct competitors, because although they are on the same functional level, a discrimination between them would not ordinarily be actionable. However, this argument is offset by the fact that customers of the two jobbers are competitors. Conceivably, if the supplier knows or should know that competition exists on the third level, he should not be permitted to discriminate on the second level. Certainly, the retailer purchasing from the disfavored wholesaler is damaged by his competitor on the same functional level receiving a lower price.

The FTC's inaction with respect to third-line injury for the past two decades seemingly demonstrates a lack of interest in enforcement in this area, possibly because of the difficulty in reconciling in some instances, at least, antitrust law with an effective cease and desist order. However, in the recent *Perkins* decision, a fourth-line-injury case discussed previously, the Ninth Circuit clearly implied that third-line injury still has vitality. Because the possibility of private treble-damage actions still remains, the prudent businessman must guard against third-line competitive-injury violations.

FOURTH-LINE INJURY—CUSTOMERS OF CUSTOMERS OF CUSTOMERS

As we have noted previously, the applicability of the Robinson-Patman Act to competitive injury occurring below the third or tertiary level of competition was accepted by the Supreme Court in *Standard Oil Co.* v. *Perkins.* The problems and criticisms attendant to fourth-line injury and beyond are essentially the same as those arising in connection with third-line injury. Thus, the observations made in the section on third-line injury are apposite here also.

Because the *Perkins* decision is the sole basis for the extension of Section 2(a) to fourth-line injury and beyond, a careful examination of that case might be helpful. Perkins—formerely one of the largest independent gasoline wholesalers and retailers in the Pacific Northwest—brought this action against Standard Oil Company of California charging that Standard violated Section 2 of the amended Clayton Act by selling gasoline at substantially lower prices to a competing wholesaler. He alleged that as a result of Standard's discriminations he was driven out of business. The jury returned a verdict in favor of petitioner, and it assessed actual damages of over $330,000. The court of appeals set aside the entire verdict because some of petitioner's proof on the Section 2(a) aspects of his claim demonstrated (1) that the wholesaler obtaining the discriminatorily lower price, Signal Oil & Gas Company, resold the gasoline to one of its subsidiaries, Western Hyway Oil Company; (2) that that subsidiary, in turn, resold to one of its subsidiaries, a retail marketing chain, Regal Stations Co.; and (3) that Regal—to which the benefits of the discriminatorily lower price had been passed—precipitated a price war which adversely affected petitioner's overall wholesale and retail business. The Ninth Circuit ruled, as a matter of law, that "Section 2(a) of the Act, in terms, limits the distributing levels on which a supplier's price discrimination will be recognized as potentially injurious to competition. . . . Section 2(a) . . . does not recognize a casual connection, essential to liability, between a supplier's price discrimination and the trade practices of a customer as far removed on the distributive ladder as Regal was from Standard." The question presented to the Supreme Court was: Whether Standard's discrimination in price between competing wholesalers—which substantially lessened competition in the Pacific Northwest wholesale and retail gasoline markets—is immune from attack under Section 2(a) of the Clayton Act solely because the most direct and immediate competitive injury was felt at the retail level and, in reaching that level, Standard's gasoline was resold by the favored wholesaler to a majority-owned subsidiary which, in turn, resold again to its majority-owned retail outlets.

According to Section 2(a)'s concluding proviso, any price discrimination covered by Section 2(a) is unlawful where its effect may be

[1] substantially to lessen competition or [2] to tend to create a monopoly in any line of commerce or [3] to injure, destroy, or prevent competition with any person who either [a] grants [b] or knowingly receives the benefit of such discrimination, [c] or with customers of either of them.

Thus, Perkins contended, the statute contains three distinct and independent tests of illegality. The first two, the original Section 2 standard, focus on the overall "line of commerce" in which the competitive injury is felt. The third, the Robinson-Patman amendments, focuses on the specific competitors injured by the price discrimination. Perkins then argued that—accepting *arguendo* the Ninth Circuit's conclusion that this case involves so-called fourth-line injury not cognizable under the Robinson-Patman amendments to Section 2 of the Clayton Act—it is clear that under the original Section 2 standard, which was not altered by these amendments, the jury could properly have found that the effect of Standard's price discrimination was "substantially to lessen competition . . . in any line of commerce," *i.e.,* the wholesale and retail marketing of gasoline in the Pacific Northwest. Thus, the court erred since in effect it imposed the three-level limitation on cognizable competitive injury contained in the *amendments* upon the *original* Section 2 standard. Finally, said Perkins, effectuation of the act's broad remedial purpose requires that the "in any line of commerce" language be defined to prohibit a lessening of competition in any commercially significant product and geographic market—regardless of whether the favored purchaser is able to structure its distribution system so that the most direct and immediate competitive injury occurs two or more persons below it.

Perkins also contended that the court of appeals erred in failing to rule that the actions of Western Hyway (Signal's subsidiary) and Regal (Western Hyway's subsidiary) were not attributable to Signal because Signal did not exercise its power to control these firms. Perkins contended that the question of whether a parent corporation controls the operations of its subsidiaries is a factual one and that the jury could properly have inferred that Signal did, in fact, control Western Hyway and Regal to the extent necessary to accomplish Perkins' destruction. Under this theory, if the actions of one or both of the subsidiaries were attributable to Signal, at least one step in the distribution system would be eliminated, thereby transforming the case into one involving second or third-line injury.

In reversing the Ninth Circuit and reinstating the total verdict of $1,298,213, Justice Black, speaking for the majority, said that to view Perkins' "fourth level" injuries as not protected by Section 2(a) is to impose a "wholly . . . artifical" limitation which "is completely unwarranted by the language or purpose of the Act." The Court explained:

In *FTC* v. *Fred Meyer, Inc.,* 390 U.S. 341 (1968), we held that a retailer who buys through a wholesaler could be considered a "customer" of the original supplier within the meaning of §2(d) of the Robinson-Patman Act. . . . In *Meyer,* the Court stated that to read "customer" narrowly would be wholly untenable when viewed in light of the purposes of the Robinson-Patman Act. Similarly, to read "customer" more narrowly in this section than we did in the section involved in *Meyer* would allow price discriminators to avoid the sanctions of the Act by the simple expedient of adding an additional link to the distribution chain. . . . Had Signal . . . sold its gas directly to the Regal stations, giving Regal stations a competitive advantage, there would be no question . . . that a clear violation of the Robinson-Patman Act had been committed. Instead of selling directly to the retailer Regal, however, Signal transferred the gasoline first to its subsidiary, Western Hyway, who in turn supplied the Regal stations. Signal owned 60% of the stock of Western Hyway; Western in turn owned 55% of the stock of the Regal stations. We find no basis in the language or purpose of the Act for immunizing Standard's price discriminations simply because the product in question passed through an additional formal exchange before reaching the level of Perkins' actual competitor. From Perkins' point of view, the competitive harm done him by Standard is certainly no less because of the presence of an additional link in this particular distribution chain from the producer to the retailer.

Justice Marshall, joined by Justice Stewart, concurred in part and dissented in part. They agreed that a violation of Section 2(a) had occurred but on the limited ground that the favored Signal distribution chain consisted of majority-owned subsidiaries. "[I]t seems quite likely that the discriminatory price given Signal would have a vital effect on the pricing decisions of the stations which eventually marketed Signal's gasoline. . . . I see no reason to intimate . . . what the result would be if wholly independent firms had intervened in the distribution chain. I would therefore explicitly limit the holding to the facts of the case before us." Justices Marshall and Stewart dissented to the Court's decision to reinstate the jury verdict. Rather, they would have remanded the case for further consideration by the court of appeals.

In apparently eliminating the third-line limitation upon cognizable competitive injury contained in the Robinson-Patman *amendment* portion of Section 2(a), the Court went beyond the theory advanced by

Perkins—namely, that no such functional level limitation exists in the *original* Section 2 standard of illegality which was carried forward into the present Section 2(a). For the limited purpose of measuring competitive injury under 2(a), anyone who sells the supplier's product is a "customer" within the meaning of that section. Finally, it should be cautioned that the Court's decision in no way affects the existing law governing functional discounts or the problems raised by discrimination between purchasers operating at different functional levels since both purchasers in this case were wholesalers. The fact that Perkins was also a retailer does not diminish the fact that he was also a wholesaler performing functions similar to those performed by the favored purchaser, Signal.

7

Cost Justification
Defense

Even though the ten jurisdictional elements discussed in the preceding three chapters may have been established in a particular case, it does not automatically follow that a violation of the law has occurred. In the next three chapters, we shall consider certain defenses and exemptions that provide immunity to the charge of a violation of Section 2(a).

In the complex world of Robinson-Patman, no area has been more difficult to understand or less susceptible of practical application than the act's cost justification proviso that provides:

> Nothing herein contained shall prevent differentials which make only due allowances for differences in the cost of manufacture, sale, or delivery resulting from the differing methods or quantities in which such commodities are to such purchasers sold or delivered.

The legislative history of the Robinson-Patman Act makes clear that Congress, in enacting this statute, did not intend to "penalize, shackle or discourage efficiency or to reward inefficiency" by requiring sellers to charge all customers the same price. The cost justification proviso specifically was included in the act to effectuate this intent; it reflects the economic premise that a seller should not be required to charge an artificially higher price to a particular buyer if it actually costs less to sell to this particular buyer than to other buyers.

Although the basic economic premise on which the cost justification proviso is based can be stated relatively simply, application of the proviso to specific situations has been very difficult both because the FTC has generally taken a strict approach in implementing and applying the proviso, and because distributive cost accounting is far from an exact science. More than fifteen years ago, a commentator characterized the cost justification defense as "largely illusory," and many lawyers and businessmen might still agree. The more recent pronouncements of the courts, however, reflect a more practical and realistic approach and afford some encouragement to sellers desiring to utilize the cost justification proviso. Nevertheless, even today, some thirty years after the Robinson-Patman amendments were enacted, only very general guidelines exist regarding a number of difficult questions that are encountered in developing a cost study. For this reason, reliance by business executives on a cost study to justify a price differential can be dangerous unless experienced counsel, and if possible, the FTC accounting staff also, has approved the basic procedures employed in the cost study.

GENERAL EXPLANATION AND APPLICATION OF THE COST JUSTIFICATION PROVISO

Cost justification, unlike meeting competition, can only be employed to justify price differentials prohibited by Section 2(a); it is not available as a defense to alleged violations of Sections (c), (d), (e). Cost justification may, however, be utilized by a buyer charged under Section 2(f) with knowingly inducing or receiving a price discrimination, because 2(f) only makes unlawful the inducement or reception of a price discrimination that violates Sections 2(a).

Under the cost justification proviso, sellers are permitted, but are not required, to grant price differentials to buyers when the differentials can be cost justified. However, if a seller decides to grant a particular customer a lower price because of savings resulting from lower costs in selling to the particular buyer, the seller must then develop an over-all acceptable cost study and grant similar discounts to all competing buyers whose method of purchasing results in similar savings to the seller. Thus, although sellers need not pass on cost savings to buyers, if cost savings are passed on to one buyer, the seller is required to pass on similar cost savings to other competing buyers. In short, an acceptable cost study must include all competing buyers and generally result in equitable treatment of all acceptable groups of customers.

The seller bears the burden of affirmatively proving that the price discrimination shown to exist reflects only due allowance for difference in the costs of manufacturing, selling or delivering to the favored customers. In reaching this conclusion, the Supreme Court has relied on the rule of statutory construction which states that the burden of proving justification under a special exception to the prohibition of a statute generally rests on the one who claims the benefits of the exception. Requiring a seller to bear the burden of proving that his price differentials are cost justified appears fair and reasonable because the seller ordinarily has in his possession, or can obtain, the relevant information concerning his costs of manufacture, sale, or delivery and is, therefore, in a better position than complaint counsel or a disfavored purchaser to allocate his costs. In addition to the consideration of fairness and convenience and the principles of statutory construction, the Supreme Court has stated that its decision placing the burden of proving cost justification on the seller was compelled by the language of Section 2(b), a portion of which provides that:

> . . . the burden of rebutting the prima facie case thus made by showing justification shall be upon the person charged with a violation of this section.

Allocation of the burden of proof regarding cost justification in a proceeding against a buyer for violation of Section 2(f), however, presents an entirely different question. The considerations of convenience and fairness that justify placing the burden of proof on the seller in a Section 2(a) proceeding are totally absent. Complaint counsel for the FTC is in a better position than a buyer to obtain a seller's relevant cost data. Furthermore, as was noted by the Supreme Court in *Automatic Canteen Co.* v. *FTC,* requiring a buyer to prove his seller's costs "would almost inevitably require a degree of cooperation between buyer and seller, as against other buyers, that may offend other antitrust policies, and it might also expose the seller's cost secrets to the prejudice of arm's length bargaining in the future. . . ." It was because of such consideration that the Supreme Court held in *Automatic Canteen* that complaint counsel, in order to establish a prima facie violation of Section 2(f), must show that the lower prices received by the buyer could not be cost justified and that the buyer knew or should have known that the seller's cost savings could not give rise to savings sufficient to justify the lower prices.

Recently, the FTC set forth the rule of *Automatic Canteen* in allocating the burden of proof of cost justification in a Section 2(f) proceeding in the following language:

(a) Where a buyer knows that he buys in the same quantities as his competitor and is served by the seller in the same manner or with the same amount of exertion as the other buyer, the Commission need only show to establish its prima facie case, that the buyer knew that the methods by which he was served and the quantities in which he purchased were the same as in the case of his competitor; and (b) if the methods or quantities differ, the Commission must only show that such differences could not give rise to sufficient savings in the cost of manufacture, sale or delivery to justify the price differential and that the buyer, knowing these were the only differences, should have known that they could not give rise to sufficient cost savings.

Although the preceding statement of the rule regarding the burden of proof of cost justification in 2(f) proceedings appears clear enough, the *Surburban Propane* case divided the commission regarding the application of part (b) of the rule of *Automatic Canteen*. The majority held that complaint counsel satisfies his burden under 2(f) "by the introduction of such evidence that will create a prima facie showing that respondent, as a reasonable and prudent businessman, should have known that the differential it received could not be cost justified."

Commissioner Elman, in a strongly worded dissent, argued that the majority had rewritten *Automatic Canteen* and scrambled the equitable allocation of proof established by the Supreme Court. The majority, he believed, ignored the two-pronged nature of complaint counsel's burden of proof in cases involving differing methods or quantities of purchases. In such cases, Commissioner Elman said that the rule of *Automatic Canteen* requires that the complaint counsel show both (1) that the lower prices paid by respondent could not be cost justified, and (2) that respondent knew or reasonably should have known this. Apparently, the majority authorizes a finding of a violation of 2(f) (assuming, of course, there has been price discrimination) based solely on evidence of the buyer's guilty knowledge and without independent proof that the price differences could not be cost justified. To the extent that this is true, Commissioner Elman's dissent appears more acurately to interpret *Automatic Canteen*. In his dissent, Commissioner Elman made clear that he was not addressing the question of the quantum of evidence required to meet complaint counsel's burden of proof regarding absence of cost justification; rather, he agreed with the majority that complaint counsel is not to be required to present a detailed cost study to satisfy the burden of showing that the price differentials were not cost justified.

The result of the commission's decision in *Suburban Propane* is to lessen significantly, for the present, complaint counsel's burden of proof regarding the absence of cost justification in establishing a prima facie violation of Section 2(f). It is clear, however, that only additional court interpretations of *Automatic Canteen* will resolve the troublesome questions articulately raised by Commissioner Elman in his dissent, and it is probable that a heavier burden of proof regarding the absence of cost justification will ultimately be required of the FTC in 2(f) proceedings.

THE RELEVANT PRICE IS THE NET PRICE

The first essential task in the preparation of a cost study is determination of the relevant "price." Basically, the price of a commodity is measured by the value of the consideration that the buyer agrees to pay the seller. In determining price in a particular context "it is reality that counts, not form. . . ." The relevant price for cost justification purposes is the "net" price paid by the buyer to the seller after all applicable allowances, discounts, and rebates that the buyer receives or is entitled to receive. For example, cash discounts that are available to all buyers who pay their bills on time are deducted in determining the net price whether or not the buyer has taken advantage of such a discount. Indirect price concessions, such as payments for fictitious "services" allegedly rendered by a buyer should also be deducted in determining the net price. In situations where a seller's price schedule is replete with irregular discounts and ad hoc departures, however, no ascertainable price may emerge that is capable of cost justification.

CUSTOMER GROUPING FOR PURPOSES OF
COST JUSTIFICATION

Fortunately, it is now settled that some customer grouping and averaging is permissible in allocating costs for purposes of cost justification, although a number of years ago there were suggestions that customer by customer cost justification was required. Acceptance of the concept of appropriate customer grouping takes cognizance of the fact that even with sophisticated distributive cost accounting, it would be extremely difficult, if not impossible, for most sellers individually to cost justify each price differential as to each customer. Thus, in order to make cost justification more than an illusory defense, sellers now are permitted to allocate customers into homogeneous groups and average the relevant expenses of dealing with each group. Customer grouping in a cost study, however, necessarily raises a threshold question as to the acceptability of the customer grouping for cost justification purposes because if the customer grouping is improper, the cost study will be rejected. Consequently, the proper grouping of customers is probably the single most important job in preparation of a cost study. Given the critical importance of proper customer grouping to any cost justification defense, we shall now examine some of the earlier FTC and court decisions concerning customer grouping, as well as the more recent decisions.

In *Standard Oil,* one of the first FTC decisions dealing with customer groupings, Standard attempted to cost justify lower prices it had allowed one customer by comparing its cost per gallon of dealing with the one favored customer with the average cost of dealing with all of its other customers as a group. The commission specifically rejected this type of customer grouping with the observation that Standard had failed to take into consideration the fact that Standard's other customers fell into several different groups and that the cost of doing business would vary between these groups.

Three years later, in 1948, the FTC considered a cost justification defense in *Minneapolis-Honeywell Regulator Co.,* in which Minneapolis-Honeywell had granted many of its customers graduated volume discounts based on annual purchases. Commissioner Ayres, in approving the general principles of the cost study and the customer groupings, observed that:

> Where [cost studies] are made in good faith and in accordance with sound accounting principles they should be given a very great weight. . . . *Respondent's burden under the Act is very great and it should have a liberal measure of consideration when it becomes apparent that it has made sincere and extensive efforts to discharge that burden.* [Emphasis added.]

In 1951, two private treble-damage actions involving the same basic facts produced conflicting United States Circuit Court of Appeals' decisions on the question of proper customer groupings. The defendant in both cases, American Can Co., had a quantity discount program whereby two of its customers received lesser discounts and the great majority of customers received no discounts at all. The United States Court of Appeals for the Fifth Circuit found that the quantity discounts were not based on actual differences in the cost of selling to the customers, or classes of customers, and, in addition, that the system did not represent a good faith effort to make the price discounts functionally available to all customers. Noting that only two customers received the 5 per cent discount and only about 1 per cent of American's customers received any discount at all, the court affirmed the district court's finding that "the discount schedule was tainted with the inherent vice of 'too broad averaging'. . . ." The court also observed that "any discount system . . . which arbitrarily exclude[d] 98 per cent of the customers involved from qualifying for any discount whatever impose[d] a heavy burden on its proponent to justify its continued existence."

The United States Court of Appeals for the Eighth Circuit, on the other hand, dealing with the same quantity discounts, reversed a district court determination that the customers had been improperly grouped. Although the Eighth Circuit did not find that American's cost study should be accepted, it held, in effect, that the propriety or validity of American's customer groupings was irrelevant if the cost study had been adopted in good faith, had been honestly maintained, and reflected with substantial accuracy the differences in selling costs between the customer groups.

Still another attempt to cost justify was considered and rejected by the FTC in *Champion Spark Plug Co.,* because the customer groupings were not acceptable. Champion had granted two of its customers lower prices, and, in its cost study, treated the two as one group and its additional 485 customers as another group. The average cost of selling an individual spark plug to each group was computed and then compared to justify the price differentials. The commission noted that this type of customer grouping (two compared with 485) failed to take into consideration the fact that within the large unfavored group there were some customers on whom Champion expended a comparatively small amount of sales effort. The commission ruled that:

> A cost justification based on the difference between an estimated average cost of selling to one or two large customers and an average cost of selling to all other customers cannot be accepted as a defense to a charge of price discrimination.

A more authoritative pronouncement on the degree of homogeneity required for proper customer groupings for cost justification purposes was handed down in 1962, when this question was presented to the Supreme Court in *United States* v. *Borden Co.* In *Borden,* two Chicago dairies, Borden and Bowman, were charged with violating the Robinson-Patman Act because they had granted grocery-store chains lower prices than they had charged the independents. Sales by both dairies during the period in question were handled on plans that gave most of their customers—the independently owned stores—percentage discounts that increased with volume to a special maximum discount. The grocery-store chains, however, were granted a flat discount without reference to volume in an amount substantially greater than the maximum discount available to the independents under the volume plans. Both dairies introduced cost studies that purportedly justified the lower prices to the chains.

Borden's cost study divided its customers into two classes: the two chains with a combined total of 54 stores constituted one class and the 1,322 independents, grouped into four brackets based on volume, made up the other. Borden's cost justification was based on comparisons of its average cost per $100 of sales to the chains in relation to the average cost per $100 of sales to each of the groups of independent groceries.

Bowman, which serviced three chains and 2,500 independents, based its cost justification on differences in volume and methods of delivery. It relied heavily on a study of the cost per minute of the routeman's time. Bowman determined that a substantial portion of the routeman's time was devoted to services that were never performed for the chains. Bowman compared the cost of these services with the price differentials in an attempt to justify the·differentials. Bowman estimated that two thirds of the independents received some of the services and that most independents received others.

Justice Clark, writing for a majority of the Supreme Court, recognized that the only question before the Court was how accurate the cost justification must be in relation to each individual purchaser. A literal construction of the cost justification proviso, which would have required that any price discrepancy between any two purchasers be individually justified, was specifically rejected by the Court. The Court realized that complete rejection of class pricing as justified by class accounting would have the practical effect of eliminating the cost justification proviso as to sellers having a large number of purchasers and would thereby prevent them from passing their savings on to their customers. Such a result was considered to be at war with the congressional language and intent in enacting the proviso. The Court then explained:

> But this is not to say that price differentials can be justified on the basis of arbitrary classifications or even classifications which are representative of a numerical majority of the individual members. At some point practical considerations shade into a circumvention of the proviso. *A balance is struck by the use of classes for cost justification which are composed of members of such self-sameness as to make the averaging of the cost of dealing with the group a valid and reasonable indicium of the cost of dealing with any specific member. High on the list of "musts" in the use of the average cost of customer groupings under the proviso of § 2(a) is a close resemblance of the individual members of each group on the essential point or points which determine the costs considered.* [Emphasis added.]

The Supreme Court, applying the standards set forth in the preceding statement, rejected Borden's cost study because: (1) Borden had failed to show that the economies relied on were isolated within the favored class; (2) members of the classes were substantially unlike in some of the cost-saving factors relied on; and (3) some of the independents had volumes comparable to, and in some cases larger than, those of the chain stores, and the broad averaging created artificial disparities.

Bowman's customer-classification system had defects similar to Borden's. Bowman had failed to show that all the independents received the services daily or even on some lesser basis; actually, its study revealed that only a large majority of the independents took the services on a daily basis. The Court explained that the use of the cost factors across the board in calculating the independent store costs was not permissible because it possibly allocated costs to some independents whose mode of purchasing did not give rise to them. The Court then noted that the burden is on the one offering the customer classification to negate such a possibility and that this burden had not been met. Thus, the cost justification defenses of Borden and Bowman were rejected because both failed to satisfy the threshold burden of showing that the customers in each class were so homogeneous as to permit their being joined together for cost-allocation purposes.

In two recent post *Borden* cases, *FTC* v. *Standard Motor Products,* and *American Motor Corp.* v. *FTC,* the United States Circuit Courts of Appeal have reversed FTC decisions rejecting cost studies because of improper customer groupings and have upheld the customer groupings. In *Standard Motor Products,* Standard, a seller of automotive and electrical fuel-system replacement parts, employed a rebate plan under which it bracketed its customers according to their annual purchase volume and increased the rebate percentage as volume increased. On its "standard" line of products, the rebate was 4 per cent in the lowest volume bracket and went up to 17 per cent in the highest volume bracket. On its "hygrade" line the rebate moved from 0 to 12 per cent, depending on volume. Standard contended that the price differentials were cost justified and presented statistical data that purportedly represented the cost of four chosen activities for each volume bracket. The aggregate cost figures for each of the activities were divided by the year's volume of rebatable sales to customers within each bracket to show costs in terms of a percentage of volume.

In rejecting the cost study, the commission disapproved of the fact that Standard was relying on the purchasing ability of its buyers as the sole criteria of the rebates. The commission also noted that Standard had *first* established the volume brackets and then determined the cost attributable to customers whose purchases placed them within a particular bracket:

> While the successful establishment of a cost justification defense does not require the profferer to have put his horse first, one who has casually delimited available rebates must at least demonstrate that a significant majority of those customers relegated to a particular volume group most likely had costs supporting their inclusion in that group.

From Standard's own evidence the commission concluded that a majority of its customers had computed costs that should have resulted in their being placed in another bracket. A large number of customers whose purchases cast them into a particular bracket had costs equal to or lower than the average cost computed for the next higher bracket. The commission stated that the discriminating rebate schedule resulted in burdening a great number of low-cost customers with the expense of higher-cost customers, and, on this basis, the customer groupings and resultant averaging were rejected as discriminatory and arbitrary.

On appeal, in the United States Second Circuit Court of Appeals, Standard argued that the practical effect of the commission's decision and order prohibiting it from utilizing its volume rebate system was to make cost justification unavailable to it because it would be compelled to cost justify its rebates with respect to each individual purchaser. The court agreed with Standard and it criticized the commission for its failure to suggest any practical, alternative means of classifying customers that might be available to Standard. The court reasoned that it was not enough merely to find that the volume rebate schedule discriminated against some low-cost customers vis-à-vis higher-cost customers because:

> This "economic discrimination"—charging low-cost and high-cost purchasers the same price . . .—*must be weighed against that which would result from enforced uniform prices, which seem likely to load more of the expense of serving high-cost purchasers upon low-cost purchasers, and which might lead Standard to decide not to sell to small-volume purchasers.* [Emphasis added.]

The court also rebuked the commission for: (1) not analyzing more carefully the economic discrimination resulting from Standard's volume rebates; and (2) not attempting to determine whether the standards of customer classification it was requiring of Standard could realistically be met by other sellers in the automotive replacement parts industry and in other industries. The court stated that:

> . . . [B]efore rejecting Standard's cost justification studies the Commission should have brought its experience and expertise to bear on the problem of defining practicable standards of customer classification for cost justification purposes which reconcile the objectives of the cost justification proviso and of the Robinson-Patman Act as a whole.

The FTC's contention that Borden supported its approach to Standard's customer classification was specifically rejected. The court found Borden to be inapposite because the issue raised in this case was not before the Supreme Court in *Borden*—namely, what degree of homogeneity is required within each class of a volume discount program when a reasonable number of classes has been established. In *Borden*, a reasonable number of classes had not been established.

In *American Motors,* American was charged with discriminating in its sales of electrical appliances to some of its retailers. American had classified its retailers into two groups for pricing purposes: merchandising distributors and regular dealers. The merchandising distributors were charged uniformly lower prices than the regular dealers. Four retailer customers were classified as merchandising distributors. All were multiple outlet retailers and each usually carried American's line exclusively, or along with the line of one other competitor. American classified all of its additional 6,000 retailer customers as regular dealers. These regular dealers fell roughly into two categories: department stores with appliance divisions, and appliance stores or stores with appliance outlets. Some of the regular dealers had multiple outlets; some were as large as the merchandising distributors; and some limited their line exclusively to American, or carried, at most, only one other competitive line of appliances.

In its cost study, American did not differentiate between the customer groups as to their relative size, number of outlets, competitive lines handled, or manner of delivery. Rather, American asserted that there were basic differences in the functions its salesmen performed for its merchandising distributors and its regular dealers that justified their classification into separate groups and accounted for the differences in time, and, therefore, in cost of servicing the two groups. More specifically, American claimed that there were six sales functions that it had to perform for its regular dealers but did not have to perform for the merchandising dealers. Time studies conducted by American in seven of its nineteen sales areas supported the contention that it took more time to perform such functions for regular dealers, which resulted in proportionately higher costs in selling to the regular dealers. The costs analyzed included (1) direct selling expenses (salaries, bonuses, travel expenses); (2) compensation and expense of servicemen; (3) credit and collection and bad debt expenses; and (4) office expenses in connection with the preceding.

The FTC hearing examiner accepted American's cost study and found that the discounts were cost justified. The commission, however, rejected the hearing examiner's conclusion on the ground that American had failed to satisfy its threshold burden of establishing a reasonable basis for the classification of its customers on which it had rested its cost justification defense. The commission found that the functions relied on did not, in fact, constitute differentiating factors between the two classes of customers. The commission repeatedly stated that American had made no meaningful showing that the 6,000 regular dealers should be treated as a single group and pointed out that among the regular dealers there were many large multiple-outlet dealers who probably could and did perform many of the functions for themselves.

The commission explained that members of a group whose costs are being averaged must "have a sufficient homogeneity so that averaging the cost of dealing with them as a whole will fairly represent the cost of dealing with each member in the group." Applying the standards set forth in

Borden, the commission found that American had not shown that the 6,000 retailers grouped together had the requisite self-sameness on the cost-determining points to constitute them a single group for purposes of comparison with the merchandising distributors. In its order, the commission explained:

> . . . our decision here is limited to our holding that respondent failed to establish that some of its "nonfavored" customers were not discriminated against insofar as they, too, may have saved respondent the identical selling expenses that respondent claims is saved in servicing its merchandising distributors.

The commission specifically disclaimed that sellers with many purchasers had to individually cost justify each one out in each area he had selected for his cost justification defense, although it did feel that a detailed representative study should be made by the seller.

The United States Sixth Circuit Court of Appeals, in a 2-to-1 decision, reversed the Federal Trade Commission and specifically approved American's customer groupings. The majority stated that the requisite homogeneity of customers for cost justification purposes is not dependent on the customers' size or style of doing business "but in the uniformity and 'self-sameness' of American Motors' cost of doing business with them." The court affirmed the findings of the hearing examiner that the regular dealers were unable to perform certain functions and that this required American Motors to spend more time and perform more sales functions for the regular dealers. The majority concluded that the departures from the otherwise uniform differences between American's method of dealing with its two classes of customers by regular dealers who, at times, did not require certain of the sale functions, were minimal, and, therefore, did not impair the substantiality of the cost study.

The majority in American also concluded that the cost study and customer groupings presented in *Borden* were clearly distinguishable. The majority specifically noted that American had not lumped its favored retailers together and merely averaged the relevant selling costs as was done in *Borden,* but had separately analyzed the cost savings experienced in doing business with each of the merchandising distributors as compared with the cost of doing business with the regular dealers. Moreover, the majority was impressed with the fact that American's cost study did not rely on "majorities, estimates or approximations" but was based on a study of all customers in a particular zone. The majority chastised the commission for reverting to its former, harder policy regarding customer grouping, which was rejected by the Supreme Court in *Borden* by requiring American to demonstrate that the higher cost of doing business with the regular dealers equals or exceeds the price differential to each and every regular dealer.

Judge Battisti, in a brief, cogent dissent, noted that it is not sufficient under *Borden* merely to show that all or most regular dealers received the services not received by the favored merchandising distributors; it also must be shown that the cost of providing the services was reasonably uniform to all members of the group.

This latter element, he stated, had not been proved and it would be improper for the commission or the court to speculate that such was the case. Thus, because American had not shown that the cost of providing the six additional services to regular dealers was reasonably uniform to the individual regular dealers, he would have affirmed the judgment of the commission. The Solicitor General filed a petition for a writ of *certiorari,* which was denied by the Supreme Court.

As can be seen from the review of the two most recent cases involving customer groupings, there is widespread disagreement as to how to achieve proper customer grouping. The general test set forth in *Borden*—whether there is substantial homogeneity within the customer groups on the critical cost-determining factors—can be and is cited as authority both by those accepting and rejecting a particular customer grouping. To date there has been no indication that the commission accepts the *Standard Motor Products* and *American Motors* decisions as the proper approach, and it is unlikely that the commission will accept the rationale of the Court of Appeals' decisions. Consequently, sellers contemplating cost studies are under great pressure to follow the stricter commission standards to avoid expensive litigation. The only aspect of customer grouping that is presently settled is that some grouping is permissible. Hopefully, the Supreme Court will take another case involving customer grouping for cost justification purposes soon and provide lawyers and businessmen with some much-needed workable guidelines in this area.

PRODUCT AVERAGING FOR COST JUSTIFICATION PURPOSES

The FTC's position on averaging of prices and costs for a broad line of products was set forth in the *Sylvania* case. The issue in *Sylvania* involved the legality of price differentials in the sale of hundreds of types of radio tubes by Sylvania to its own distributors for resale and to Philco, the favored purchaser, for resale through its marketing organization. Sylvania, in its cost study, employed a *weighted-average* method, whereby the average price per tube to its distributors and to Philco was determined and then compared, although the price differences were great on certain tubes and there was no price difference on others. Both the distributors and Philco had to carry the full line of tubes, and there was no showing that the tubes that were in greatest demand were the ones on which the price spread was the greatest; in fact, the evidence showed the opposite to be true. Sylvania then demonstrated that it incurred greater costs in selling to its distributors than in selling to Philco and that such costs justified the average price difference. The commission approved of Sylvania's cost justification and its weighted-average system because the challenged price discriminations were commercially significant only in terms of Sylvania's entire line of tubes and not in terms of individual tubes. On this basis the differentials were cost justifiable.

In its *Sylvania* opinion, the commission also indicated that one challenging a cost study should be required to rebut the reasonableness of an averaging method like Sylvania's by showing that the price differentials on particular types of tubes had competitive significance. Thus, in situations where the seller is distributing a number of products, reasonable short-cut methods designed to determine the price to be justified may be employed by sellers. Such is consistent with a flexible, realistic approach and is designed to make this proviso meaningful to those interested in employing the proviso for legitimate purposes.

CATEGORIES OF COSTS THAT MAY BE USED IN JUSTIFICATION

The proviso permits costs to be established on a relatively broad basis with the fundamental requirements being that the differentials must arise from "the differing methods or quantities" in which commodities are sold or delivered and must result from lower costs of "manufacture, sale or delivery." Of course, the cost item also must be larger per unit sold for the customers paying the higher price in order to represent any actual "justification" and the differences in methods or quantities must, in turn, be differences as between customers paying lower prices and those paying the higher price.

At least one seller has contended that, in preparing a cost study, it had the right to include and exclude such cost categories as it chose. The FTC's staff, however, opposed the attempted exclusion of the cost item because its inclusion might have significantly undermined the cost justification study in issue; and the respondent acceded to the staff's objection. On the other hand, neither the FTC nor the staff has objected to the omission of many items of cost in cases where it appears that their inclusion would not be harmful to the study. For example, the successful cost justification defense in *Minneapolis-Honeywell* consisted of evidence covering only about 7 per cent of the company's selling and administrative costs. A requirement that all costs be ascertained and included would create almost insurmountable problems to businessmen interested in employing the cost justification defense. Although definitive guidelines cannot be set forth in this area, it appears that a cost study based on reasonable and consistent accounting procedures that are not designed to exclude unfavorable cost factors will probably be acceptable by the FTC and the courts.

Distribution Costs

Differences in distribution or direct selling costs have been and undoubtedly will continue to be the most fertile source of cost savings. Most cost justification defenses presented to the FTC have been based primarily on distribution costs. Distribution costs encompass a wide variety of expenses including the following specific unit costs of sale and delivery that experience has shown frequently vary with the size of orders: (1) transportation, (2) warehousing and storage, (3) sales promotion and advertising, (4) sales accounting, (5) sales management, (6) sales administration, such as clerical work, (7) salesmen's salaries and expenses, and (8) special services for the customer.

In its recent decision in *Eleanor G. Morton* v. *National Dairy Products Corp.*, the United States Court of Appeals for the Third Circuit upheld a district court decision that price differentials granted by a Pennsylvania dairy to Philadelphia stores at low, state-regulated New Jersey platform rates, rather than higher, into-the-store Pennsylvania rates, were cost justified. The dairy's savings in platform sales "expressed as a percentage of the sales dollar" was 21.8 per cent broken down as follows: "delivery expense 14.4%, selling expense 5%, and general and administrative expense 2.4%. . . ."

Manufacturing Costs

Although the proviso speaks in broad terms, few sellers have relied on differences in manufacturing costs because of the difficult problems of proof presented by the requirement that the costs being used must be related to "differing quantities or methods" of distribution. For example, it is especially difficult for a manufacturer who produces a uniform line of products for inventory to develop cost justification proof from differences in manufacturing costs. There are situations, however, where manufacturing costs are cognizable for cost justification purposes. The increased cost of dealing with a customer who orders from hand to mouth during the rush of the season—compelling the employment of expensive overtime labor—while other customers order far in advance—thereby permitting the manufacturer to use cheaper off-season prices—may be charged to such a customer requiring such additional expenses.

In situations where the products are made on a customer order, manufacturers are more likely to be able to justify price differences on the basis of differences in the cost of manufacture. In such instances, the cost per unit of product may decrease as the size of the order goes up. As a practical matter, however, cost elements such as product development, design, and materials rarely are major factors in cost justification defenses. Once such differences become substantial, they tend to establish that the products sold at different prices are not of like grade and quality within the meaning of Section 2(a). Sellers would rather rely on the like grade and quality requirement whenever possible because: (1) it is less expensive to litigate on this basis, and (2) such differences when established immunize any price differential, no matter how unrelated to quality or cost.

Incremental Costs

The legislative history of the Robinson-Patman amendments clearly establishes that incremental costs—that is, the mere out-of-pocket cost of the additional activity incurred in making the commodities involved in the particular transaction—are not the only manufacturing costs to be allocated to a particular customer. The statutory requirement that cost differences result from differing methods or quantities was included to ensure that all customers be taxed with their aliquot share of relevant manufacturing costs. The House Judiciary Committee report succinctly states that the cost justification proviso "precludes differentials based on the imputation of overhead to particular customers, or the exemption of others from it, where such overhead represents facilities or activities inseparable from the seller's business as a whole and not attributable to the business of particular customers or of the particular customers concerned in the discrimination."

Brokerage

The Justices of the Supreme Court disagreed as to whether brokerage savings are cognizable cost savings in *FTC* v. *Henry Broch & Co.* The majority, in dictum, indicated that the legitimacy of brokerage is governed entirely by Section 2(c), and that the language of 2(c) is sufficiently broad to prohibit allowances to buyers in the form of price concessions that reflect a differential in brokerage costs. The four dissenting Justices, on the other hand, found that Congress intended in Section 2(a) to permit sellers to pass through to buyers in the form of reduced prices any actual savings in the cost of distribution of their goods, including savings on brokerage costs. The minority's position is supported by Wright Patman, co-author of the act, who has listed the "elimination of . . . brokers" as a factor to be taken into consideration in determining whether a special price cut has merely made due allowances for differences in costs. The commission, nevertheless, has reversed a hearing examiner who allowed inclusion of savings on brokers' commissions and ruled that "savings in costs resulting from the elimination of brokers' commissions are not allowable cost savings under Section 2(a)." Thus, although no final determination of the appropriateness of including savings on brokerage commissions has been made, as a logical matter, it would seem that if savings on sales commissions and salaries can be employed in justifying a lower price, brokerage savings should similarly be cognizable. Nevertheless, if one desires to avoid challenge by the FTC, brokerage savings should not be included in a cost study.

Costs That Vary with Price

Certain costs such as patent royalties and excise taxes vary directly with the price charged, and it has not yet been finally determined whether such cost savings can be deemed to result from differing methods or quantities of sale or whether they should be treated as a by-product of the lower price unrelated to any differences in the arrangements between the customers. In *Sylvania,* the seller had included as a cost saving the lower royalties it had to pay as a result of charging his favored purchaser a lower price. The FTC's staff objected to the inclusion of such savings on the ground that they did not arise out of the differing methods or quantities by which the commodities were sold. The case, however, ultimately was decided on other grounds and this question was never finally resolved. One commentator has suggested a reasonable and logical approach that would involve prorating the royalty or excise tax expense between the justified and unjustified portions of the price differential, and this approach may ultimately be adopted.

Miscellaneous Costs

In *Standard Oil of Indiana,* Standard unsuccessfully attempted to include certain "landlord" costs and advertising costs that were incurred only by its favored buyers in its cost justification defense. As to the landlord costs, Standard wanted to show that the expenses of owning and keeping up a station exceeded their rent revenue. This was rejected on the ground that such costs are not costs of sale and delivery, and, therefore, are not properly able to be included in a cost study. Standard's rationale for inclusion of its favored buyers' advertising costs was that it received a reciprocal benefit from their advertising that justified a discount. This argument was rejected because such costs were not the seller's, and the favored buyers' costs must be excluded. Thus, it appears that the commission will require a seller to justify his price differences on the basis of his actual cost savings and that it will not permit a seller to utilize the favored buyers' costs in performing a function that the seller would have to perform for the buyer if the buyer did not perform it.

The differing methods or quantities requirement has been interpreted to prevent sellers from using many types of expenses as elements of a cost study, such as return on investment and dealer training. In the *Thomp-*

son Products case, the seller attempted to include as a cost of selling to his disfavored wholesalers a projected profit on his $9 million investment in facilities employed only in doing business with such wholesalers. The commission held that inclusion of projected profit on an investment was not a cost resulting from differing methods or quantities of selling even though the money, if otherwise invested, would yield a profit. The commission has reaffirmed its rejection of inclusion of a reasonable return on an investment in facilities used only in selling to disfavored buyers, despite criticism by some commentators.

In *Shell Oil Co.*, the seller wanted to show that its lower prices to dealers owning their stations were justified on the basis that because of the constant turnover among its lessee dealers, it was required to spend substantially more money in training such dealers. The commission rejected this offer of proof on the grounds that "insofar as the cost of making the original sales contract is concerned, there is nothing to show that the method of making such contracts differed or that the costs of making sales contracts differed between different classes of customers." The vital fact was that the same training methods were used for both types of dealers and both types of dealers received such training.

Despite the rather strict approach of the FTC to the differing methods or quantities requirement regarding dealer training, return on investment, and other costs, the legislative history of the cost proviso suggests that this requirement need not be so strictly applied, and it may be that the courts will take a more practical and flexible approach to this requirement than the FTC has. It appears that only further litigation will finally resolve whether the preceding and numerous other expenses related to selling may properly be included in a cost study.

QUANTITY DISCOUNTS

Suppose manufacturer M sells to three buyers—B_1, B_2, and B_3—and discriminates in favor of B_1. In seeking to cost justify his price to B_1, M contends that the total purchases by B_1 make M's total volume great enough that certain cost economies are possible in M's over-all production process. This is not permissible. M cannot say that the goods sold to B_1 reflect the entire savings in the unit cost of manufacturing. Because the extra volume necessary to the cost economies would vanish if B_2 and B_3 withdrew their business, B_2 and B_3 have just as much right to a price reduction as B_1 on this basis. On the other hand, if M, as a service to his buyers, maintains warehouse facilities for goods after they are sold, and B_1 agrees to take over the warehousing of the goods he buys, or if B_1

accepts less expensive crating, M can pass these cost savings on to B_1 in the form of a price concession.

It is difficult, if not impossible, to cost justify special treatment to new customers or discounts based on the cumulative volume of business per year that have no relationship to the size of individual shipments. A new customer normally is as expensive to serve as an old customer. Annual volume bears no necessary relationship to shipping costs. Quantity discount schedules must be developed with care if they are to be protected by the cost justification defense. Only if these schedules accurately reflect cost differences will the defense be available.

DUE ALLOWANCE

The cost justification proviso allows price differences that make "only due allowance" for differences in costs of manufacturing, selling or delivering to customers and does not, by its terms, require precise and complete justification for a price difference. Despite a rather conservative early decision, the commission has observed that "cost studies . . . do not afford precise accuracy" and that "there is inherent in them a reasonable margin of allowable error." In *United States Rubber Co.*, the commission enunciated a *de minimis* doctrine, whereby competitively insignificant price differentials not justifiable by cost differences will be disregarded where the substantial portion of the price differential is justified. This *de minimis* doctrine has been applied in a number of cases and has even been extended to justify the ignoring of an entire discount bracket where the sales in that bracket were so small as to make it extremely unlikely that they would have any significant competitive consequences.

Application of the *de minimis* doctrine, however, depends on the particular facts and industry involved and cannot be carried too far. In one case, the commission found unlawful price discrimination where all but 3 to 7 per cent of a rather sizeable discount was cost justified. The commission held that *de minimis* doctrine was not applicable because the competition in this particular industry was exceedingly keen and the margins of profit were low. Thus, although the *de minimis* doctrine is available to sellers, it should be used only in reserve, because certain cost items that the seller is relying on may ultimately be excluded for one reason or another, and because its scope remains unclear.

8

The Meeting Competition Defense

A seller who has discriminated in price in the terms of Section 2(a), or who has granted disproportionate promotional benefits within the meaning of Sections 2(d) or 2(e), may, nevertheless, avoid liability by affirmatively establishing the defense of meeting competition in good faith. The meeting competition defense is not available to sellers who have violated Section 2(c). This defense has the effect of sanctioning certain instances of discriminatory concessions and constitutes a congressional resolution of encouraging "hard competition"—lower prices—in certain competitive situations even though, by definition, adverse competitive effects continue. The meeting competition and cost justification defenses constitute safety valves against excessive pressure for "soft competition" capable of being read into Section 2(a).

Meeting competition is not an easy defense to establish. As with all defenses, the burden of proof is on the defendant, and the FTC has built a record over the years of taking a narrow view of its application. It was not until the 1951 decision of the Supreme Court in the famous *Standard*

Oil litigation, that the commission was required to accept the defense as an absolute one to a finding of price discrimination. It was not until 1961, in the United States Court of Appeals for the District of Columbia's decision in *Exquisite Form Brassiere,* that the commission was required to accept the defense in a 2(d) proceeding. And, it was not until the 1963 decision in *Continental Baking*—almost thirty years after the Robinson-Patman Act was passed—that the FTC first accepted a respondent's factual proof of meeting competition in a litigated Section 2(a) case.

Let us now explore the highlights of the seller's absolute defense to a violation of Sections 2(a), 2(d), or 2(e). Section 2(b) of the Robinson-Patman Act provides:

That nothing herein . . . shall prevent a seller rebutting a prima facie case . . . by showing that his lower price or the furnishing of services or facilities to any purchaser or purchasers was made in good faith to meet an equally low price of a competitor, or the services or facilities furnished by a competitor.

WHOSE COMPETITION CAN THE SELLER MEET WITH A LOWER PRICE?

Although a seller is free to meet the competition of his direct competitor, the existence of multifunction or vertically integrated sellers competing with single-function sellers has raised questions as to the expanse of Section 2(b)'s "price of a competitor" statutory language. In the 1963 case of *FTC* v. *Sun Oil Co.,* the Supreme Court was confronted with interpreting the meeting competition defense in the context of a gasoline price war in Jacksonville, Florida. This case involved the question, "Can a seller lawfully meet the lower price of a party who is not the seller's own competitor, but a competitor of his customer?"

Sun Oil, a major oil refiner, was integrated forward as a gasoline jobber or wholesaler. Sun sold Sunoco gasoline to one Gilbert McLean, a Sunoco service station lessee in Jacksonville. There were a large number of other Sunoco dealers in the Jacksonville area; seven others were in McLean's sales territory, the closest being about eleven blocks away. Sun sold to McLean and all other Jacksonville Sunoco dealers at 24.1 cents per gallon, the retail price for "regular" Sunoco gasoline being 28.9 cents per gallon in this trading area. Shortly after McLean opened his station, Super Test Oil Company opened its first Jacksonville service station across the street from McLean. The record was unclear as to the distribution role of the Super Test. The Supreme Court assumed Super Test was a retailer only, not a vertically integrated jobber or refiner-jobber.

Super Test started a gasoline price war, with sporadic retail price reductions to as low as 20.9 cents per gallon. McLean's sales suffered whenever more than a 2-cent per gallon retail price spread existed. A few months later, Super Test dropped its regular gasoline retail price to 24.9 cents per gallon. Following McLean's pleas to Sun for help, Sun gave McLean a price reduction of 1.7 cents per gallon, and McLean then reduced his price to 25.9 cents per gallon. Sun gave no other Jacksonville retailers the 1.7 cents per gallon discount. Finding a Section 2(a) violation in this Sun-McLean transaction, the commission rejected Sun's meeting competition defense.

The Supreme Court agreed with the commission and ruled that Sun, being a refiner-jobber, in not meeting *its competitor's* price, but the price of a competitor of Sun's customer, was not within the meeting competition shelter of Section 2(b). This conduct was regarded as not embraced by the meeting competition defense, which the Supreme Court ruled to be available only to the price competition of the seller, and not the seller's customer.

The Sun Oil decision thus imposes a duty on a seller to establish that the lower price in issue is its competitor's lower price, and not the lower price of its customer's competitor. The Supreme Court avoided saying specifically that Sun Oil, a refiner-jobber, would have won on the meeting competition defense if Super Test competed against Sun at least at the jobber level, by virtue of being an integrated jobber-retailer. Also, the Supreme Court did not speculate on the outcome if Sun would have made a good faith effort to determine the distribution role of Super Test and was wrong—and whether under these circumstances Sun still might have won under the good faith standard to be discussed shortly.

A controversial sequel to the *Sun Oil* decision arose with the 1967 FTC report governing gasoline marketing. Here the commission answered the question left by the Supreme Court: whether a refiner-distributor can meet competition under Section 2(b) by assisting its retail customer in meeting a lower retail price a competing retailer receives from its distributor, or in meeting the lower retail price of a competing distributor-retailer? The commission majority said the meeting competition defense is available in these circumstances.

This "whose-price-can-I-meet" problem was raised in a different context in a case involving a New Mexico tobacco wholesaler who bought cigarettes from the manufacturers and resold them to retail accounts, including large chain stores. The cigarette manufacturers also sold to the chain stores on a direct basis, generally at the same price as sold to the tobacco wholesaler. New Mexico passed a cigarette stamp law requiring tax stamps for cigarette sales in New Mexico to be affixed within the boundaries of that state. The chain stores, thus, had to decide whether to buy direct and set up New Mexico stamping facilities or buy tax-stamped cigarettes from the New Mexico tobacco wholesaler. A wholesaler, because of this situation, sold stamped cigarettes to chain stores "at a price slightly higher than the manufacturer's price applicable to competing customers in the relevant trade areas." Charged with price discrimination, the wholesaler defended on the ground of meeting the competition of its supplier-competitors, the dual-distributing cigarette manufacturers. The commission agreed, and ruled that, based on "economic reality," the meeting competition defense was available to the tobacco wholesaler.

IS THE DEFENSE AVAILABLE TO SECURE "NEW" CUSTOMERS OR JUST TO KEEP "OLD" CUSTOMERS?

Sunshine Biscuits sold its Krun-Chee potato chips to grocery and drug chains in Cleveland, Ohio. Potato chip competition in Cleveland was "extremely sharp." Competitors of Sunshine Biscuits were granting discounts of 5 and 2 per cent to certain favored customers in the trading area and 5 per cent to others. Sunshine Biscuits responded by granting discounts of 5 and 2 per cent to four customers and 5 per cent to fifteen customers, all other competing customers receiving no special discounts. In a number of these instances, Sunshine Biscuits granted the matching discounts to those granted by its competitors to their own customers (rather than to Sunshine Biscuits' own customers), and was able to obtain new Krun-Chee retail customers in Cleveland.

The Federal Trade Commission charged Sunshine Biscuits with violating Section 2(a), and Sunshine Biscuits defended on the ground of meeting competition. The commission majority relied on a line of earlier cases and ruled that the meeting competition defense was available, defensively—to retain old customers, not offensively—to secure new customers. Commissioner Elman dissented, pointing out how the prior decisions do not lead to this conclusion, and then turned to an appeal to economic logic:

> First, it is practically unworkable. The line between "old" and "new" customers is far easier to state than to apply to the myriad situations that develop in actual business relations between sellers and buyers. It has been aptly said that a "concept of 'retainable' customers leads into statutory bogs. A customer may be one who negotiates with a view to buying, one who has bought at some time in the past, or one who currently buys."
>
> Indeed, this is a conservative description of the probable difficulties

Does an "old" customer retain that status forever, regardless of the infrequency or irregularity of his purchases? Suppose an "old" customer transfers his business to another seller offering a lower price; how long a period of grace does the first seller have in which to meet the lower competitive price? If he waits too long, will the "old" customer be regarded as a "new" one, and hence unapproachable because Section 2(b) no longer applies? If so, how long is too long? And if not, does it suffice that the buyer has at *any* time in the past, no matter how remote, been a customer of the respondent?

Even if these problems are satisfactorily solved (and, it seems to me, the Commission will have to solve them in such a way as to give reasonable guidance to businessmen who are entitled to know what they may or may not lawfully do), the evidentiary burden placed upon the seller, especially one whose business consists of a multitude of small individual transactions, seems virtually insurmountable. The point need not be labored. Whatever its verbal simplicity, the "defensive" versus "aggressive" test will inevitably produce uncertainty and confusion in application.

Even more important, the test adopted by the Commission appears to be economically unsound. Let us suppose the presence in an area of two or three big buyers of a particular product and a number of small ones. Suppose further that producers of this product tend to make discriminatory price reductions to the big buyers alone. If one of those producers can manage legitimately to underbid its rivals (let us assume as a result of lower costs) for the business of the big buyers, under the Commission's ruling competing producers may also lower their price to the big buyers if they have previously dealt with them; otherwise they may not. Does this make economic sense, and does it accord with the basic policy of the statute? I venture to suggest that it does not. [Citations omitted.]

The case was appealed by Sunshine Biscuits, and the United States Court of Appeals reversed the commission majority and adopted Commissioner Elman's dissenting position. Although there remains some lack of clarity in this area of meeting competition, arising principally from the fact that a line of earlier cases reached a contrary position, judicial opinion now supports the *Sunshine Biscuit* decision. It is reasonable to disregard any distinction between old and new customers in the context of a price discrimination charge that alleges competitive injury among disfavored customers. However, if a violation of Section 2(a) is shown to exist in reference to a finding of primary-line competitive injury, there remains sufficient latitude in the meeting competition statute to explore the good faith of the seller, as might dictate distinguishing the *Sunshine Biscuit* doctrine, such as a situation where predatory intent to destroy competition (bad faith) is found in what is ostensibly a meeting competition pricing program.

ONCE A DISCRIMINATORY LOWER PRICE IS GRANTED TO MEET COMPETITION, FOR HOW LONG MAY IT BE CONTINUED?

It is simple enough to say generally that if the competitor's lower price offer is no longer available to the favored customer, the discriminatory lower price must also be withdrawn at that time. But, in its application to particular marketing facts, qualifications may arise with respect to such matters as the seller's duty to inquire as to the continuance of the lower price offer.

In a Federal Trade Commission proceeding against Beatrice Foods Co., Beatrice granted a grocery chain in Denver, Colorado, a discriminatory lower price on fluid milk, to meet a competitive offer by Fairmont Dairy. Prior to May 1, 1958, Beatrice was selling to the grocery chain on an exclusive basis at discounts of 7 per cent off list price. Fairmont offered to sell to the chain on an exclusive basis, at a 14½ per cent discount on Fairmont label products and 14½ per cent plus 2 cents per unit on private brand milk. The Denver grocery chain informed Beatrice it would accept the Fairmont offer, and Beatrice countered with a discount of 10 per cent on its Meadow Gold milk and 12 per cent on its private brand milk. The Beatrice offer was accepted, and Beatrice received the business "for an indefinite period." The discriminatory discounts were still in effect 1½ years later when the commission hearings were commenced. Nothing occurred after the Fairmont offer to warrant Beatrice to reconsider whether its preferred discount to the Denver grocery chain was necessary in order to maintain the business. The commission ruled that the meeting competition defense was not lost under these circumstances, and that there was no duty to inquire as to the subsequent availability of the Fairmont Dairy offer. However, the commission indicated that if "changing conditions" took place as a consequence of a subsequent milk price war, a duty to inquire would have arisen:

If, after this price war, milk prices had readjusted themselves downward, or if some other change in the competitive situation in Denver had occurred, either as a result of the price war or of some other event, respondent [Beatrice] clearly would have been under a duty to inquire or otherwise test out whether the Fairmont offer was still a competitive reality. . . . In an ordinary situation, respondent's inaction in not at least testing out by some means whether its lower price was still necessary, might by the sheer passage of time, vitiate or cancel out the original justification for its good faith meeting of competition defense.

However, on the facts of this case, respondent was meeting a lower price offered by Fairmont on condition that it may be made the exclusive supplier of [the Denver grocery chain] and we find nothing in the record to suggest that the offer was not a continuing one or had become impracticable or was withdrawn.

Chairman Dixon was the lone dissenter in the 3 to 1 *Beatrice Foods* decision, taking issue with the majority's approval of the continuation of the Beatrice discounts 1½ years after they were initiated on the ground that there was nothing in the record to show that they were needed at that time. The chairman regarded such a practice to constitute a writing of the good faith requirement out of the meeting competition statute, and he would have found a duty, under the facts of the case, for Beatrice Foods to test out whether the Fairmont offer to the Denver grocery chain was still a competitive reality.

MUST THE COMPETITOR'S LOWER-PRICED GOODS BE OF LIKE GRADE AND QUALITY?

Section 2(a) of the Robinson-Patman Act prohibits price discrimination in the sale of commodities of like grade and quality. As we have seen in the analysis of Section 2(a), minor physical differences in size or composition (rather than trademarks or brand names) may allow a seller to escape Section 2(a) liability. In the meeting competition context, however, does the same requirement follow—or may the seller avail himself of the meeting competition defense where the competitors' commodities are not of like grade and quality under Section 2(a) standards, but are, nevertheless, directly competitive? One court has answered this question in the affirmative. In *Callaway Mills,* a "tufted"-carpet manufacturer reduced his carpet prices to meet the competition of certain old-line woven-carpet manufacturers. These two kinds of carpet constructions were not of like grade and quality because of different materials and construction. But they were, in fact, competitive. The commission ruled that the meeting competition defense was not available. On appeal, however, this narrow reading of the meeting competition defense was rejected. The court dealt with the issue as follows:

The Commission committed error on this point by equating "grade and quality" with "saleability." The two are not synonymous. It is obvious that the consuming public, being far less aware of such factors as "craftsmanship and materials" than professional carpetmakers, cannot easily discern differences in quality between comparable carpeting. Furthermore, the public is greatly influenced by such intangibles as color, design, display, advertising, and similar factors. So long as petitioners conclusively show that their products at various price levels generate public demand (or "saleability") substantially equivalent to that of competitors' carpeting at the same price levels, considerations of "grade and quality" become unnecessary and indeed superfluous, for the most "grade and quality" can do is tend to show "saleability." . . . Moreover, the Commission completely ignored abundant unrebutted testimony in both cases which clearly demonstrated or would support the inference that petitioners' products at the various price levels possessed qualities of "saleability" comparable to that of its competitors' products. It also surprisingly ignored *substantial* evidence actually showing "like grade and quality." For instance, Mr. Brenner in the CC hearing said its carpets were "interchangeable" with those of the competition.

It is interesting to note that the Federal Trade Commission held, in another recent case, that a wholesaler selling cigarettes with New Mexico tax stamps was free to meet the lower price of the same kind of cigarettes without the New Mexico tax stamps. The grade and quality of the cigarettes was the same but there was a definite cost differential involved because of the state tax stamps.

WHEN IS A SELLER BEATING RATHER THAN MEETING A LOWER PRICE?

The statutory provision for meeting competition expressly declares that a seller's discriminatory price concession may be reduced to that price necessary to *meet* his competitor's lower price offer. Therefore, if the seller's discriminatory price is lower than necessary to *meet* competition, the seller has lost his meeting competition defense. What starts out as a simple rule can end up as a very complicated one depending on the particular industry, commodities and products involved. The rule is easy to apply where competing sellers of fungible commodities such as sugar, bread, milk, and salt are in fact competing solely on the basis of price. But what about the situation where the commodities in issue command price differentials among consumers because of trademarks or good will? This brings us into the thicket of premium versus nonpremium products, and situations where the premium seller reduces his price to that of a nonpremium seller. This issue is closely related to the like grade and quality issue previously discussed.

A leading case in this area involved Anheuser-Busch, which markets Budweiser premium beer in different trading areas across the nation. In the St. Louis, Missouri, trading area, three regional brewers sold beer at $2.35 per case, while Budweiser was sold in this trading area at $2.93 per case, a differential of 58 cents per case. Anheuser-Busch then reduced its price in June, 1954, to $2.35 per case, the same as its nonpremium St. Louis competitors, following an earlier reduction in January, 1954, to $2.68 per case. This lower price continued for some months, until March, 1955, when the Budweiser price was raised to $2.80 per case and its competitors raised their price to $2.50 per case, a 30-cent per case differential. One of the defenses advanced to this primary-line competitive injury case involving geographic price discrimination was the defense of meeting competition. The commission rejected this defense, noting that the public was willing to buy Budweiser at a higher price.

> Clearly, therefore, respondent's reduction from the premium price to match the prices of the regional beers on the market was not a meeting of competition. The effect was to undercut competition. The huge gains which respondent made at the lower prices testifies to that fact.

Other situations where meeting competition turned out to beat competition because of preexisting price differentials involved Lucky Strike cigarettes being reduced to a price equal to a "poorer grade of cigarettes," and a reduction in the price of "premium" automatic controls to a price that is above the price of less acceptable controls.

The 1955 Attorney General's report recommended that the flexible point of focus be on the question of whether "actual competition not merely a nominal price quotation is equalized."

In today's consumer goods marketing era of product differentiation, there remains a need for further guidance as to when a premium seller's price reduction passes from the safe area of meeting competition into the forbidden jungle of beating competition. The cases, most of which involve solely primary-line competitive-injury charges, offer precious little guidance to members of an industry that is not selling fungible goods. This is the result, in large measure, of the fact that meeting competition in such a context is closely related to the finding of competitive injury. The following factors illustrate, however, lines of inquiry to be made that may help to sharpen the determination:

> What is the established range of price differences between the competing products in the particular trading area at the retail level as well as at the seller's level? Is it relatively stable or has it fluctuated in recent years? Does the premium seller's proposed price reduction remain within the fluctuating area of premium—non-premium differences which have existed in recent years? If not, do other "good faith" reasons exist? Is there any evidence of the probable effect of the proposed price reduction gained from market testing of selected price reductions?
> What is the anticipated purpose and effect of the proposed premium price concession? Is it defensive, aimed at maintaining a market position rather than increasing a market share?

HOW DOES THE GOOD FAITH–BAD FAITH STANDARD WORK?

The meeting competition defense incorporates a good faith test. If the seller acts in bad faith, he cannot avail himself of the defense. It follows that the state of the seller's "corporate mind," as it were, becomes a matter of relevant inquiry. In *Continental Baking,* a leading Federal Trade Commission decision in this area, Commissioner Elman characterized the good faith requirement as a "flexible and pragmatic not a doctrinaire" concept. The standard of good faith was regarded by Commissioner Elman as simply a standard of the prudent businessman responding fairly to what he reasonably believes is a situation of competitive necessity.

The courts, similarly, have recognized the pragmatic nature of buyer-seller relationships in the market place as a touchstone of good faith standards. In one case, a United States Court of Appeals took issue with the commission requirement that, in order to establish the defense, a seller must have proof positive of the lower prices offered together with the names of the competing dealers who made the lower price offers, before he initiates the discriminatory price concession. This was a case where the only meeting competition evidence was the word of respondent that a buyer would abandon his regular supplier and take on a new one rather than to divulge the name and price quotation of the latter. The court said:

> We may not be in as intimate touch with the ways of commerce as the Commission, but we would be naive indeed if we believed that buyers would have any great solicitude for the welfare of their commercial antagonists, sellers. The seller wants the highest price he can get and the buyer wants to buy as cheaply as he can, and to achieve their antagonistic ends neither expects the other, or can be expected, to lay all his cards face up on the table. Battle of wits is the rule. Haggling has ever been the way of the market place. The Commission's requirement is unrealistic.

Good Faith in Primary-Line Competitive-Injury Cases
Compared to Secondary-Line Competitive-Injury Cases

Where a seller is charged with price discrimination that injures his competitors, the issue is one usually involving geographic price discrimination practices. Consider the situation where a national seller is charged with destroying competition in a specific trading area by a blanket-price reduction in that trading area, driving out competition in that trading area. In this situation, if it is established that the seller exercised a predatory intent to destroy competition, there would be no good faith meeting of competition. Competition was destroyed, not met. Predatory intent means bad faith; conversely, good faith motives for the discriminatory concession would negate predatory intent. Thus, in primary-line competition cases, good faith evidence will bear on the issue of whether a 2(a) violation is established, and would not necessarily resolve itself into a separate issue in terms of meeting competition. Good faith becomes more significant as an identifiable issue in secondary-line competitive-injury cases, where the competitive injury is alleged to arise among buyer-level competition on the disfavored class of customers.

Good Faith—But Wrong

Suppose that the seller in good faith believes he is meeting his competitor's lower price offer but was deceived by the customer so that he actually beat his competitor's offer? Is the meeting competition defense lost when the seller acted in good faith? Did the seller act at his peril? The courts have indicated that the defense is not lost under such circumstances. The seller must, of course, make a good faith effort to determine the competing sellers' low price offer. In *Knoll Associates,* the commission described this good faith effort as "simply the standard of the prudent businessman responding fairly to what he reasonably believes is a situation of competitive reality."

The question of whether the competing seller's lower price offer was or was not lawful involves the question of whether good faith was exercised. It can be argued that the seller should be free to presume that his competitor's lower price was lawful absent an adjudication to the contrary. But recent case law indicates that such a presumption, without substantiation by the seller, fails to satisfy the defense. Thus, in *National Dairy Products Corp.* v. *FTC,* the United States Court of Appeals for the Seventh Circuit held that it was proper for the commission to reject the defense where the seller failed to verify a low competitive offer communicated by a customer. Even though the seller must verify the competition he meets, he is not obliged to document every competitive price to which he responds. The same court held this to be an unreasonable burden and beyond the requirements of 2(b). Several other appellate courts have reversed lower court requirements that the seller prove that his competitor made "a definite offer" of which the seller was specifically aware. It is sufficient that the seller verify the general competitive situation.

That verification is essential to a finding of the good faith requirement necessary to a successful meeting of competition defense, was emphasized in the recent decision of the United States Court of Appeals for the Third Circuit in *Viviano Macaroni Co.* v. *FTC,* in which petitioner appealed a commission order based upon a determination that Sections 2(a), 2(d), and 2(e) had been violated by Viviano in connection with the sale of macaroni products to wholesalers and retailers. The main point on appeal was whether the discriminations in issue were made in good faith to meet competitive offers from rival macaroni companies. In conducting its limited review to determine whether the commission's findings as to the petitioner's alleged Section 2(b) defense were supported by substantial evidence in the record, the court relied upon the 2(b) standard set forth in *FTC* v. *Staley Mfg. Co.*, and agreed with the commission decision that Viviano had failed to demonstrate the existence of facts which would lead a reasonable and prudent person to believe that the granting of the lower prices and more favorable advertising allowances would in fact meet the equally low price of a competitor. With respect to the price concessions given the Loblow supermarkets, Samuel Viviano testified that he had no understanding as to how much money the discriminatory free goods arrangement would amount to. The Third Circuit responded: "It is difficult to imagine that petitioner's offer was made in good faith to meet competition when Samuel Viviano had no idea of how much a significant part of his offer was worth. He would have no way of comparing his offer with those of [his rivals] in order to insure that his company was only making an equally low offer and not a lower one. It is clear . . . that [the] offer was made in an effort to obtain additional business." As to the Fox Grocery Co. radio-TV program, Viviano relied upon testimony by a Fox official that "other companies" before petitioner had offered to buy radio and television spots for Fox. The commission rejected the 2(b) defense because petitioner failed to establish that it knew who its competitors were or that it knew the amount of the competitors' offers and because the petitioner continued its participation in the Fox program for three years. The court of appeals agreed that such testimony was not sufficient to justify the petitioner's participation without further investigation, stating: "We think that it is clear from the Supreme Court opinion in *Staley* that petitioner was under a duty to investigate or verify the oral communication of [Fox] as well as the reliability of [Fox] himself in view of the 'tendency of buyers to secure the most advantageous terms of sales possible.' *Staley, supra* at 759. Moreover, that duty continued throughout the period of the discriminatory payments. Therefore the fact that petitioner continued to participate for three years on an annually renewable contract, without making any further inquiries as to outstanding offers of other macaroni companies, is further evidence that petitioner did not participate to stave off competition, but rather to accommodate a large customer." Finally, Viviano's 2(d) discrimination in favor of State Food Stores was found by the commission not to be based upon a good faith meeting of competition because of the petitioner's failure to show diligence in verifying the reports of competitive offers received from its salesman. Petitioner attempted to justify its reliance upon this unverified information by pointing to the salesman's 18 years of service and the insignificance of the dollar amount involved. The court agreed with the commission that "Viviano's failure to corroborate the information given by [the salesman] showed a lack of good faith."

Good Faith in the Context of Adopting Industrywide Pricing Practices

It is basic dogma of the meeting competition defense that the discriminatory price reduction should be one which is responsive to an individual competitive situation rather than, on the other hand, mere adoption of an unlawful industrywide discriminatory pricing program without regard to individual competitive situations.

The Supreme Court first took this position in the *A. E. Staley* case. Decided by the Supreme Court in 1945, the case involved the meeting competition defense of a corn syrup manufacturer. Staley, operating a corn syrup plant in Decatur, Illinois, adopted the existing pricing system of competitors who delivered corn syrup in Chicago at a lower price than elsewhere, charging other buyers outside Chicago a price equal to the Chicago price plus the published freight rate from Chicago to the destination of delivery. This pricing practice was followed regardless of the place (outside Chicago) from which the corn syrup was actually shipped. There were overtones of collusion and price fixing, the pricing practices ensuring industrywide price uniformity.

The Supreme Court refused to apply the meeting competition defense to Staley's adoption of the "Chicago-plus" pricing system on the rationale that the Robinson-Patman Act "places emphasis on individual competitive situations rather than upon a general system of competition;" it was the purpose of Congress "not to sanction . . . the excuse that the person charged with violation of the law was merely adopting a similar unlawful price of another;" and, the meeting competition defense presupposes establishing nondiscriminatory pricing methods, with concessions to meet competition rather than following a pricing policy resulting in systematic discrimination. In *Staley,* the Supreme Court held that the seller must show the existence of facts that would lead a reasonable and prudent person to believe that the granting of a lower price would in fact meet the equally low price of a competitor.

In the *Callaway Mills Co.* case, decided some twenty years later, however, a seller was successful in advancing this defense in a competitive situation that involved no attempt to meet specific lower prices of specific competitors.

Callaway Mills was a Georgia-based carpet manufacturer that, in 1950, pioneered the manufacture of tufted carpets, and commenced competing against the large, old-line woven-carpet manufacturers. For many years the old-line carpet manufacturers had granted annual graduated volume discounts to purchasers—mostly retail department stores and home furnishing stores. Interestingly, this volume discounting practice was perpetuated in the carpet industry because of a 1939 Justice Department consent decree that forbade any agreement or conspiracy to refrain from giving volume discounts to purchasers of rugs and carpets.

Thus, Callaway, a small, new entrant with a new carpet design commenced competing with large, established competitors in an industry where an almost infinite variety of prices, colors, and designs was sold on volume discounts. For five years, until 1955, Callaway refused to grant volume discounts, but it, then, yielded to customer pressures with the following schedule:

Aggregate Annual Purchases	Discount
$ 5,000 – $ 7,999	1%
$ 8,000 – $14,999	2%
$15,000 – $29,999	3%
$30,000 – $49,999	4%
$50,000 and over	5%

Callaway carpeting sold in the $4.95 to $13.95 per yard price range, whereas its competitors (tufted and woven) sold carpeting up to $49.95 and more. The effect of the discount schedule was to allow retailers to sell at a net per-unit price for comparable quality the same as their competition. These dollar volume levels of stated discounts were "appreciably lower" than those of its competitors, which latter group embraced both woven and tufted carpets.

The FTC charged Callaway with violating Section 2(a), and the case was decided on the question of whether Callaway satisfied the meeting competition standard of Section 2(b).

The commission refused to accept the meeting competition defense on a number of grounds: (1) Callaway failed to show that its carpets at various price levels were "comparable in materials and construction to the products of competitors at similar price levels;" (2) Callaway's volume discount plan involved a simple adoption of a formal pricing system, and thus was not a good faith effort to meet a competitor's price; (3) because of the lower minimum volume purchase per discount class, Callaway was beating not meeting competition; and (4) Callaway failed to produce price lists comparing its net prices after discounts with those of the competition.

The United States Fifth Circuit Court of Appeals rejected the commission's position on each of these points, and reversed.

With respect to number 2 above, the commission had sought simple application of the *Staley* case, implicitly requiring Callaway to lower its prices on carpeting "in a wholly piecemeal fashion," meeting the exact price at which any given competitor sold a certain type or style of carpeting to any particular customer. The Court of Appeals found three reasons for distinguishing *Staley*. First, the court said there is nothing wrong, per se, with adopting a pricing system used by competitors. Second, the commission was considered to have disregarded the competitive conditions in the carpeting industry that were different from *Staley*. Third, the commission ignored certain key facts.

The Fifth Circuit, thus, limited *Staley* by focusing on "industry conditions," and the commercially impractical feasibility of meeting individual competitive situations. The *Calloway* approach, which involved a generous but realistic construction of the good faith standard, may find application in comparable industries where an entrenched discriminatory policy exists incident to marketing a multitudinous product line and it is commercially impractical to deal with individual competitive situations. However, as subsequent cases demonstrate, it is unlikely to constitute even a ripple in the settled waters of meeting individual competitive situations where it can be shown that it is commercially feasible, especially in "staple goods" industries. Thus, in *Ingram* v. *Phillips Petroleum Co.*, a federal district court, although acknowledging that, if applicable, Section 2(b) "is an absolute bar to the granting of relief even though price discrimination injurious to competition has been shown," accepted the plaintiff's contention that the "defendant's price reductions were made pursuant to an established pricing system rather than competitive demand." The court concluded: "If it was pursuant to a pricing system it was not made in genuine response to an individual competitive demand. . . . Therefore, the 2(b) 'good faith' defense must be ruled out."

The price *versus* price rather than plan *versus* plan approach has also been affirmed with respect to the defense's applicability under Section 2(d). In *Exquisite Form Brassiere,* an FTC respondent appealed a commission ruling that a 2(b) defense had not been established with the argument that "if the accused company establishes that its competitors have plans or systems whereby they make advertising allowances to their customers, any company in the industry can combat such systems by inventing and operating a system or plan of its own." The court, however, although recognizing factual differences between price discriminations and advertising allowances, found no "compelling reason for different treatment." As in a 2(a) case, for the meeting of competition defense to prevail, the combative acts must, therefore, not consist of general plans but should rather be specific acts aimed at advertising practices on the part of a competitor in "individual competitive situations."

In *Surprise Brassiere Co.* v. *FTC*, the petitioner appealed a commission decision that Surprise Brassiere had not met its burden under Section 2(b) of establishing that its higher promotional allowances to some of its customers were granted in response to allowances offered by other sellers in individual competitive situations. Surprise Brassiere contended that it was sufficient under Section 2(b) to demonstrate that the variances in its cooperative advertising program in favor of certain large customers were made to meet competition in general. The petitioner relied primarily upon *Callaway Mills,* where the allowance of volume discounts according to a plan or system, as distinguished from individual competitive responses, was not condemned per se. Callaway Mills was found by the court to be acting in "good faith" in attempting to meet competition since no workable alternative was apparent. The court of appeals contrasted Surprise Brassiere's situation from that presented in *Callaway Mills,* however, on the ground that the former was not confronted with the problem of trying to match its prices with the prices of competitors that varied according to the cumulative annual purchases of each customer. "It was faced with specific competitive situations but its proof did not show that it limited its variance to specific competitive situations." The decision noted, also, the existence of recent decisions in other circuits which upheld the view that a "seller cannot deviate from promotional advertising programs in order to meet competition generally as opposed to meeting competition as individual competitive situations."

FEATHERING—MEETING COMPETITION UNDER SECTION 2(A) RATHER THAN SECTION 2(B)

In the *Sun Oil* decision, the Supreme Court stated:

Since Sun made no attempt here to utilize a so-called "feathered" discount to its dealers, under which the amount of the price allowance diminishes as it reaches stations further away from the center of the price war, we need not expressly pass upon such practice. However, it may be noted that a properly designed and limited price reduction system fashioned in such a manner might, under appropriate circumstances, be found to have obviated substantial competitive harm to the other Sun dealers and thereby negated a violation of § 2(a) such as is here charged. Of course, improperly designed or too sharply drawn "feathering" gradations may produce precisely the same effect as no gradation at all, and consequently fall within the same ban as an outright illegal discrimination.

In effect, the Supreme Court was pointing to an alternative means for meeting competition, under Section 2(a) rather than Section 2(b). In a situation where price feathering might be considered, the seller would, in effect, be revising his price structure to meet competition and basing his defense not on Section 2(b), but on the rationale that the feathered price structure does not give rise to the requisite adverse competitive effects under Section 2(a). In this connection, reference should be made to Chapter 6 where this theory is discussed in detail.

Difficulties are presented by this approach principally arising from the argument that the partial beneficiaries of feathered prices (which are not so great as the most favored concession) did not receive enough, so that pressures will be generated for the seller to grant greater concessions to the other purchasers. But the issue of adverse competitive effects at the customer level tends to be an easy matter of proof where the price differences are substantial, continuing, and the competing customers operate on close margins of profit. The Supreme Court seems to be suggesting that the adverse competitive effects might not be established where disfavored buyers pay a higher price in a trading area, although that same differential might in other cases give rise to adverse competitive effects. The olive branch of feathering is thus one not without its own difficulties. The Supreme Court's feathering suggestion appears to open the door for a double standard on secondary-line competitive effects, with a higher standard somehow involved where feathering takes place in response to competitively localized lower prices. Even though this may or may not ultimately prove to be a desirable rationale, there is little judicial guidance for sellers at this stage of the development in the law, apart from general trading area principles discussed in Chapters 5 and 6.

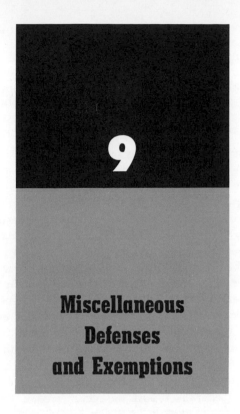

9

Miscellaneous Defenses and Exemptions

In addition to the affirmative defenses available under the provisions of 2(a) and 2(b), special amendments and later judicial interpretations have established certain exemptions from the Robinson-Patman Act that can be pleaded as defenses. Three of these exemptions are the result of direct statutory exception enacted in response to the legitimate needs of special industries and market circumstances. The fourth has evolved from the judicially observed distinction between a price differential and a competitive injury. All these miscellaneous defenses are narrow in scope and limited in application, thereby providing little in the way of judicial analysis.

CHANGING CONDITIONS DEFENSE

Secton 2(a) of the Robinson-Patman Act concludes with the observation:

> That nothing herein contained shall prevent price changes from time to time in response to changing conditions affecting the market for or the marketability of the goods concerned, such as but not limited to actual or imminent deterioration of perishable goods, obsolescence of seasonal goods, distress sales under court process, or sales in good faith in discontinuance of business in the goods concerned.

This provision was inserted to mollify the perishable foods interests and seasonal goods producers who feared that the price fluctuations characteristic of their industries would fall under the strict language of Section 2(a). Despite the prevailing congressional intention that such price variations were not within the scope of the act, the proviso was, nonetheless, added by incorporating both the broad language concerning changing conditions and the specific mention of certain factors of particular concern to the affected industries. The exemption was intended to deal with all the possible contingencies fostered by a fluid market situation, but its actual application has been far less comprehensive.

The provision contemplates two possible eventualities that might justify a price differential: (1) an alteration in the conditions of the market and (2) an alteration in the marketability of the product. Both alternatives reflect congressional intent that the fluctuation stem from market conditions fundamentally beyond the control of the seller. The Attorney General's report has characterized the situation as a "spontaneous shift in market conditions" that forces the seller to make "commercial adjustments."

Where the condition is a factor of the market, such as the dual purchasing system encountered in the *Fruitvale Canning* case, it lacks the necessary spontaneity to constitute the type of changing condition envisioned by Congress. Fruitvale attempted to justify different prices to direct-buying chains and broker-represented independents by asserting the highly fluid conditions of the West Coast fruit market. Because the two methods of purchase were a regular factor in the market they hardly constituted a change. Rather, the commission viewed them as the defendant's "customary and normal method of business."

Similarly, situations in which competitors' practices foster retaliatory price cuts are not market conditions within the meaning of the statute. Thus, in *Moore* v. *Mead,* the defendant could not justify retaliatory price cutting by asserting a local retail boycott. In the view of the United States Court of Appeals for the Tenth Circuit, "the plain language of the statute limits the exceptions to those which are 'such as' or similar to those named."

In like manner, the United States Ninth Circuit Court of Appeals denied the defense to a seller who varied his price to meet a local competitive situation. In the *Balian Ice Cream* case, the defendant attempted to offset a Los Angeles area practice of list-price rebates by reducing his prices. The court ruled the defense unavailable to that type of competitive situation.

Even though all three cases appear correct in their rejection of changing conditions affecting the market, they all employed an unfortunately restrictive interpretation of the proviso. By making the proviso's specific examples serve as the measure of its broad language, these cases have tended to require that the conditions of change must closely parallel, if not duplicate, those enumerated in the statute. Such a narrow reading was completely unnecessary to the decision in these cases because all focused on the fact that the condition was not one engendered by the "market" but rather by a specific competitor. It was unnecessary to explore the nature of the condition once this was determined. The result of this strict judicial view of changing conditions has been substantially to limit the availability of the defense in the framework of the market conditions exception.

The exemption for "changing conditions in . . . the marketability" of the product has enjoyed more success. Here the focus is not on some uncontrollable market variable—such as a local substitute product—but rather on the alteration in the product's own desirability. Perhaps the classic application of this concept is in the automobile industry's practice of reducing the price on the remaining new car stock from a previous year once the following year's models have come out.

In *Valley Plymouth* v. *Studebaker-Packard Corp.,* the defendant, Studebaker, sold over 400 1960-model automobiles to dealers competing with the plaintiff. These sales were made late in December, 1960, some three months after the 1961 models had been introduced. Because of Studebaker's good faith miscalculation early in 1960, it found itself with an unusually large inventory of close to 1,400 cars at the time of the model changeover. The December sales to the plaintiff's competitors were at discounts of 25 to 30 per cent below the price generally quoted to dealers for such automobiles. The court held that these December sales were in response to a changed condition "affecting the marketability of the goods concerned," that is, the model changeover and the consequent obsolescence of the 1960-model automobiles. The specific statutory example of "obsolescence of seasonal goods" was held to be directly on point. The situation was also deemed to be of a sufficiently spontaneous character to constitute a true fluctuation outside the control of the seller.

An examination of the existing case law, although sparse, nonetheless, indicates certain minimal prerequisites to a successful assertion of either market change or a change in marketability. The situation alleged, and specifically the activity in question, must constitute a variation from prior, usual market circumstances. It is not enough that the situation differs from other markets, it must be an alteration from prior conditions in the same market. The condition of change must stem from a source outside the control of either the seller or his competitors. Competing sellers cannot "manufacture" the requisite changing conditions. Finally, the market, itself, must resemble in character one of those enumerated in the proviso. This is usually an easier task where the change occurs in marketability rather than the market itself, because products affected by seasonal buying tastes appear to be those most clearly covered.

THE DEFENSE OF AVAILABILITY

Sellers charged with a violation of Section 2(a) have sometimes contended that their price differentials were made available to all customers and were, thereby, incapable of creating competitive injury. Although denominated a seller's "defense," the contention is actually an affirmative rebuttal of one of the jurisdictional prerequisites—competitive injury.

The theoretical foundation of the defense has been somewhat confused by recent judicial pronouncements on the definition of price discrimination. It was at first thought that the distinction between a price difference and a price discrimination turned on the relative availability of the differential to all customers. Some commentators have suggested that this view was seriously curtailed by the Supreme Court in *Anheuser-Busch,* where the majority equated a differential with a discrimination. As a result, the defense is more popularly rationalized as a negation of the jurisdictional requirement of competitive injury.

The problem is largely semantic. In *Anheuser-Busch,* the Supreme Court was concerned with the limited question of whether the existence of a price differential always constituted a price discrimination. In responding affirmatively, the Court did not in any way conclude that this was tantamount to a violation of the act. Courts have consistently recognized that not all discriminations violate the act, but only those that work a competitive injury. It is at this latter stage—demonstrating competitive injury—that the defense of availability applies. Essentially it is an assertion that no one need have been injured by the price difference because it was equally available to all. Thus, *Anheuser-Busch* never reached, and, therefore, did not limit the defense of availability.

Whatever the theoretical basis for the defense, it is clear that in order to succeed, the seller must show that the lower price was actually and practically available to the nonfavored buyers. Virtually all the cases considering the defense of availability have turned on the issue of practical, as opposed to mere formal, availability. In *FTC* v. *Morton Salt Co.,* the Supreme Court rejected the defense where it appeared that the seller's lowest price, although offered to all, was available only on purchases of carload quantities. Because this volume of purchase was beyond the needs of all but a few large buyers, the price was realistically unavailable to all. Similarly, in the *Dayco* case, the commission found the respondent in violation of Section 2(a) when he sold to an association of jobbers at a lower price than that available to nonmember competitors. The argument that the nonfavored jobbers could have joined or formed group buying associations of their own and, thereby, have obtained the more favorable prices was rejected on the ground that "Lower prices are not 'available' where a purchaser must alter his purchasing status before he can receive them."

Recent case law indicates that a seller may well have a duty to inform all customers of lower prices if he hopes to assert the defense of availability. In *Tri-Valley Packing Association,* the price discrimination was between large buyers of canned fruits and vegetables who maintained purchasing agents in California, and other smaller buyers, who did not maintain California agents. The commission found that the California prices were not in any way communicated to the nonfavored buyers and that many of them did not even know about them. Hence, it was held that the lower prices were not, in fact, available to them.

The commission's *Tri-Valley* decision appears to impose a duty on the seller specifically to offer a price concession to all his competing purchasers before he can raise an availability defense. Tri-Valley had argued that, even though several of the nonfavored buyers did not know of the lower California prices, they could have learned of these prices through the exercise of reasonable diligence. The commission's rejection of this argument raises questions about what affirmative actions a seller must take to apprise his customers of the availability of lower prices. Even though *Tri-Valley* is presently unique, future assertions of the defense may necessitate promulgation of FTC guidelines similar to those already applied to Section 2(d) "availability" cases.

At present, the defense has been confined to situations involving a discount to a buyer based on the buyer's status. The seller ordinarily asserts that the favored status, and, consequently, the discount, was readily attainable by all competing buyers. Scant attention has been given to the defense's application to situations in which alternate products, physically identical but differently priced, are readily available to all buyers. This possibility is highlighted by the recent Supreme Court decision in *FTC* v. *Borden Co.* In that case the Court held that a product sold under a nationally known brand is of like grade and quality with a physically identical product sold under a private label. This would suggest that the availability of the private label may constitute an adequate availability to offset price reductions on the brand name product. In the *Borden* case, itself, the Court recognized the possibility of an availability question, and the court of appeals, on remand from the Supreme Court, noted that the injury "may not be the result of price discrimination but of the buyer's failure to take advantage of the opportunity . . . to buy at the same prices as other customers."

Future cases may see the defense raised in the context of other pricing systems. One system that could possibly be justified by reason of the availability of its lowest price to all comers is the incentive-type discount, the size of which is based on the percentage increase in the buyer's present purchases over those of a previous period. In an advisory opinion, the commission has held such a discount plan to be, on its face, a violation of Section 2(a). Such a plan has not arisen in the context of any litigated case, either before the commission or before the courts, however. It is possible that, where all purchasers enjoy equal sales potential in the seller's product, the plan might be upheld. Although the plan has the obvious merit of giving smaller customers a better opportunity to get larger discounts by attaining percentage increases, such may prove to be the plan's greatest defect. The larger purchasers can certainly argue that the higher discounts are not practically available to them if offered for percentage increases that are beyond their capacity but that are within the capacity of the smaller concerns. Problems of availability could also arise where the plan is offered to competing retailers, some of whom specialize in the product while others conduct a general retail business. The general retailer may claim that it is easier for his competition to concentrate his efforts and, thereby, increase his sales of the product involved. Unfortunately, all of these unsettled possibilities are necessarily inhibited by the commission's sole pronouncement in the advisory opinion on incentive discount plans.

One further aspect of the availability defense remains to be considered. It is possible that an equally low price may be available to the nonfavored buyers through some source besides the seller. May the seller defend his price differential by asserting that a competitor would have given a similarly low price to the nonfavored buyers? Such a situation normally arises as a seller's attempt to meet competition and is, therefore, handled under Section 2(b). But circumstances might occur in which the meeting competition defense is technically frustrated, thereby, forcing the seller to resort to the availability defense.

There appears to be nothing to prevent the successful assertion of such a defense, and several commentators have supported its application. The rationale seems fully compatible with the fundamental basis of the availability defense—the negation of competitive injury. Certainly no new anticompetitive effect can be created if the lower price is already available in the market. The seller would have to demonstrate that the goods available from alternate sources are equal in all respects to his product, but having done this the defense should be viable. As the total absence of litigation would seem to indicate, the most difficult aspect of the theory is constructing a factual situation having an identical availability of price and product while failing to satisfy the meeting competition defense.

COOPERATIVE ASSOCIATION EXEMPTION

The cooperative association is a purchasing method employed by smaller businessmen to combat the purchasing leverage of the chain buyers. Essentially, it has functioned as a group buying association for its members and frequently enjoys a profit based on its performance of certain distribution functions. This profit would then be distributed to the association's members. During the consideration of the Robinson-Patman Bill, considerable concern was voiced that this practice of profit distribution might violate the act. Consequently, Section 4 of the Robinson-Patman Act provides that:

> Nothing in this Act shall prevent a cooperative association from returning to its members, producers, or consumers, the whole or any part of the net earnings or surplus resulting from its trading operations in proportion to their purchases or sales from, to or through the association.

This section in no way exempts the methods by which the cooperatives operate to acquire their profit—such is governed like any other commercial arrangement under the act. Rather, this exemption merely provides that profits legally obtained by the cooperative may be distributed to members without violation of the act. Conversely, where the initial transaction engaged in by the cooperative violates the act, as where the cooperative accepts illegal brokerage, a distribution of that money will not exempt the transaction. Similarly, where a cooperative is formed so that its members can take advantage of illegal volume discounts, Section 4 gives it no protection against a charge based on Section 2(f) for "knowingly . . . receiving a discrimination in price which is prohibited by this section."

PURCHASES BY NONPROFIT INSTITUTIONS AND GOVERNMENTAL AGENCIES

Nonprofit Institutions

In 1938, two years after its enactment, the Robinson-Patman Act was amended to preclude from its application:

. . . purchases of their supplies for their own use by schools, colleges, universities, public libraries, churches, hospitals, and charitable institutions not operated for profit.

Litigation involving this section has primarily focused on interpretation of the phrase "for their own use." Plaintiffs, in treble-damage actions, have sought to exclude from the exemption practices that are only tangentially related to the purpose of the eleemosynary institution and have succeeded where the activity has an independent profit motive. For example, in the *Student Book* case, the United States Court of Appeals for the District of Columbia refused to exempt the sale of law books by a "self-sustaining campus bookstore" that competed with retail bookstores. In contrast, a university bowling facility constructed primarily "to fulfill the needs of the . . . students, faculty, and staff" was considered to be within the exemption in *Logan Lanes, Inc.* v. *Brunswick Corp.*, where the United States Court of Appeals for the Ninth Circuit ruled that purchases of bowling equipment by Utah State University were exempt from the Robinson-Patman Act, despite the facility's availability to the general public. But instead of turning on the question of whether or not there existed a broad exemption for purchases by state agencies, the case turned on the issue of whether or not a specific statutory exemption of "supplies" purchased by nonprofit schools applied to a situation in which the bowling alleys at the University were open to the public. The plaintiff, who sought treble-damage relief on the ground that Brunswick's lower price for the state caused him to lose customers to the University's bowling alleys, claimed that the public's use of the alleys for a fee meant that the purchases were made neither for the University's "use" nor by a "nonprofit" institution, as the exemption requires. The court rejected these contentions, because it was shown that the income derived from the bowling operation was used exclusively to finance the expansion and improvement of the school and was not distributed to any private person as a profit. It noted that the exemption applied to:

. . . anything required to meet the institution's needs, whether it is consumed or otherwise disposed of, or whether it constitutes, or becomes part of, a material object utilized to enable the institution to carry on its activities.

Governmental Agencies

Shortly after the passage of the Robinson-Patman Act, the question arose with respect to its application in cases where the favored purchaser is a governmental body. The Attorney General of the United States, in a letter to the Secretary of War, concluded that the act "is not applicable to Government contracts for supplies." His opinion was based principally on the lack of any discernible indication that Congress intended to prohibit the practice, then prevalent, of quoting special discount prices to agencies of the federal government.

Although this opinion appears to have settled the matter where the federal government is concerned, some controversy has arisen over the applicability of the act to purchases by state and local governments. One state attorney general has ruled the act to be generally applicable to government purchases; while two others have rendered opinions holding it inapplicable. Still another has considered separately those cases where the state acts in a business or proprietary, rather than a governmental, capacity. Purchases by a state in its governmental capacity are held exempt, but all other purchases are held covered by the act. In spite of these contrary indications, it is generally believed that the exemption applies to governmental purchases at any level and at least one federal district court has affirmed that belief by exempting a purchase by a municipal housing authority.

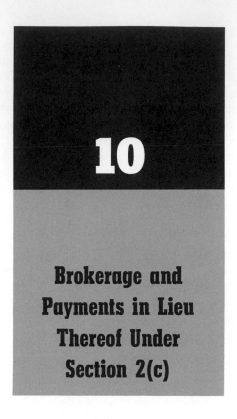

10

Brokerage and Payments in Lieu Thereof Under Section 2(c)

The regulation of brokerage fees under Section 2(c) represents the clearest statutory proscription in the Robinson-Patman Act. The section was intended to prevent large chain buyers from extorting "dummy" brokerage fees that constituted little more than price rebates because no brokerage services were performed. These practices were considered sufficiently obnoxious to competition that the section afforded none of the traditional defenses relating to cost justification, meeting of competition, or lack of anticompetitive effect. As a result, early application of the section centered on definition of the statutory terms and interpretation of the section's internal exceptions. Within these interpretive confines, application of the section was uniform and rigorous. This approach persisted until the Supreme Court, in the *Broch* decision, indicated the possibility of a more expansive interpretation of the exceptions to the section. This decision has precipitated a good deal of reexamination of 2(c) and has introduced a certain measure of uncertainty as to the present scope of the section's application. A discussion of 2(c) will, therefore, largely concern the developing interpretation of the various elements of 2(c) and the resultant impact of the *Broch* decision.

According to the terms of 2(c) it is unlawful to (1) pay or grant, (2) or receive or accept, (3) anything of value as a commission, brokerage, or other compensation, or any allowance or discount in lieu thereof, except for services rendered (4) in connection with the sale or purchase of goods, wares, or merchandise (5) either to the other party to such transaction or to an agent, representative, or other intermediary therein (6) where such intermediary is acting in fact for or in behalf, or is subject to the direct or indirect control, of any party to such transaction other than the person by whom such compensation is so granted or paid.

INDEPENDENCE OF SECTION 2(C)

The structure of 2(c) would seem to indicate a congressional intent to make it a totally self-contained prohibition. The section reiterates the commerce requirement and contains no cross references to other subsections. Similarly, the other sections, particularly 2(b), conspicuously avoid cross reference to 2(c) or inclusion of any mention of brokerage. The commission and the courts have, for the most part, adhered to the position that 2(c) would be interpreted without reference to any defenses available under other sections and with attention only to the elements specifically contained in 2(c).

The most unique result of this judicial approach is that a violation of 2(c) can be found in circumstances involving only a single transaction, making Section 2(c) distinct among the prohibitions of the Robinson-Patman Act. The case of *Jarrett* v. *Pittsburgh Plate Glass Company* illustrates the significance of this distinction. In that case, Jarrett agreed to be the exclusive distributor of Pittsburgh Plate Glass Company's products in certain geographical areas. Under the contract, Jarrett would buy the products on his own account and then resell them to retail enterprises. At the end of the year, Pittsburgh was obligated to give Jarrett percentage rebates based on the volume of sales. Because these rebates were deemed payments in lieu of brokerage, a United States district court ruled that the contract constituted a violation of 2(c). It was not even alleged that such payments to an *exclusive* distributor could be discriminatory or injurious to competition. These considerations were inconsequential; the 2(c) violation was proven with reference only to the contract.

The potential severity of this interpretation of congressional intent is clear. Once it is determined that brokerage or anything resembling it has been transferred, the sanctions of the act will automatically be imposed unless such brokerage falls within the purview of the strictly limited "for services rendered" exception. Thus, a transaction may, in fact, tend to encourage competition, yet be violative of the Robinson-Patman Act.

Similarly, the frequent efforts of defendants accused under Section 2(c) to seek the shelter of the defenses applicable to 2(a) or 2(b) actions has been met with constant rebuff. On the surface, at least, the failure of these defenses is somewhat surprising. Because the primary purpose of the Robinson-Patman Act is to prohibit discriminatory treatment causing injury to competition, the arguments, made in the *Biddle* and *Oliver* cases, that an action based on 2(c) was ill-advised because the suspect discounts were neither discriminatory nor injurious to competition, seem appealing. Similarly, the defendant in the *A & P* case maintained that the policy of encouraging economic efficiencies delineated in the cost justification provision of 2(a) merited application to other sections of the act. Specifically, A & P contended that the discounts and payments at issue were made possible only because its efficient purchasing system enabled its suppliers to save the usual costs of brokerage services. The commission and the courts, however, remained unpersuaded. Although significant in 2(a) actions, proof of discrimination, cost justification, and lack of competitive injury were deemed wholly immaterial to proceedings under the brokerage provision.

Not until the decision in *Washington Fish and Oyster Company*, however, was there a direct holding that the brokerage provision was similarly independent of the meeting competition defense contained in 2(b). In that action, the company charged sought to introduce evidence to show that the price advantage given direct-dealing customers in preference to those purchasing through brokers was compelled by economic pressures to meet competition. In dismissing the motion to adduce further evidence, the United States Court of Appeals for the Ninth Circuit simply rechanted what had been said frequently as dictum in prior decisions and held that "the defense based on meeting competition, set out in subsection (b), is inapplicable to Section 2(c) violations."

RELATIONSHIPS WITHIN COVERAGE OF SECTION 2(C)

Section 2(c) prohibits any person from transmitting brokerage or concessions in lieu of brokerage either directly to the other party to the transaction or indirectly through "an agent, representative, or other intermediary [when the latter] is acting in fact for or in behalf, or is subject to the direct or indirect control," of the other party. The phrasing of this portion of 2(c) made mandatory a close scrutiny into the exact nature of the parties involved in a particular transaction.

The decision in the *Independent Grocers' Alliance Distrib. Co.* case exemplifies this scrutiny. Independent Grocers' Alliance (IGA), a brokerage firm that had accepted discounts in lieu of brokerage from sellers, was found to be affiliated with the buyers by means of a complex tracing of corporate ownership and management. Indeed, the court found that IGA was controlled by two holding corporations whose stock was controlled by individuals, partnerships, and corporations who in turn owned the buying companies. As further proof of this affiliation, it was shown that, with one exception, the officers and directors of IGA were also officers and directors of the companies buying through IGA. Once this connection between the broker and the buyer was established, no alternative remained under the traditional view but to find a violation of 2(c). Acceptance of brokerage by the buyer's "agent, representative, or other intermediary" was per se illegal.

Even though little doubt remains that 2(c) should not be subverted by devious disguises, it is of questionable wisdom to apply the sanctions of the act to practical business devices that, although within the literal meaning of the section, do not controvert its policies. By way of example, in the *Oliver* case, the phrase "agent, representative, or other intermediary" was interpreted to include an independent brokerage concern that, after accepting commissions from suppliers, indirectly bestowed some of the benefits upon its customers—a group of small companies. Yet, this practice, if anything, tended to increase the competitive status of small enterprises in a market generally dominated by larger corporations.

RECENT DEVELOPMENTS IN APPLICATION OF 2(C): THE BROCH DECISION

Because of the prolonged and vociferous dissatisfaction with the traditional view, the slightest questioning of its validity could ignite a complete reappraisal of the section. On its first confrontation with Section 2(c) issues, the Supreme Court kindled a spark of dissent. Indeed, on June 6, 1960, the *FTC* v. *Henry Broch & Company* decision upset, but did not overturn, many of the theretofore unyielding principles. Exactly what the Court intended by this disruption is unclear even today.

Among the clients of the brokerage firm, Henry Broch & Company, was Canada Foods, Ltd., a processor of apple concentrate. Because Broch performed certain special services, the commission rate was set at 5 per cent instead of Canada Foods' usual rate of 4 per cent. The selling price of the concentrate was set at $1.30 per gallon. Seeking a lower price, J. M. Smucker, a buyer, negotiated with one of Canada Foods' other brokers, Jensen & Phipps Co., eventually offering to purchase 500 drums at $1.25 per gallon. The broker immediately relayed this offer to Canada Foods, which indicated that the price could be lowered only through a reduction of the brokerage assessment. Jensen & Phipps Co. was unwilling to make the reduction.

Upon learning of these negotiations, Broch contacted Smucker in an attempt to secure the order. Smucker remained steadfast to its offer of $1.25 per gallon. Canada Foods again insisted that the lower price could be achieved only by reducing brokerage from 5 to 3 per cent. Broch consented to these terms and the sale was consummated.

The FTC initiated an action against Broch, charging it with a violation of 2(c). After a hearing, the commission ruled that 2(c) prohibits a seller's broker from passing any portion of his fee to the buyer "in any manner, directly or indirectly." Because the reduced brokerage was contemporaneous with the price reduction, the commission applied the usual presumption and concluded that the price reduction was an illegal allowance in lieu of brokerage. The commission found that the economic effect of Broch's action was exactly the same as when a broker pays a portion of his brokerage fee directly to the buyer. Because the latter practice clearly is violative of Section 2(c), the commission concluded that to be consistent with the purposes of the provision, Broch's action must similarly be condemned.

In reversing the commission, the United States Court of Appeals for the Seventh Circuit ruled that the brokerage provision was never intended to cover a seller's independent broker. From a purely policy standpoint, the court considered the commission's resolution undesirable, because it encouraged price uniformity and rigidity by foreclosing negotiations on brokerage rates as a variable in setting sales prices. Finally, the court asserted that because the case was essentially "a private grievance between rival brokers," there was no public interest to justify the commission's attention.

The Supreme Court reversed the Court of Appeals in a 5 to 4 decision. The opinion of the majority initially addressed itself to the contention, relied on by the Court of Appeals, that 2(c) was inapplicable to a seller's independent broker. Placing the seller's broker outside the scope of Section 2(c) was considered to be in derogation of the text of the section that specifically delineates its prohibition against "any person." Moreover, the Court asserted that the lower court's interpretation, in effect, condoned activities that significantly transgressed the policies of the act. Indeed, one purpose of the Robinson-Patman Act was to relieve sellers and their brokers from the economic pressures placed on them by large buyers to grant unfair price advantages. In this case, the Court took the view that the buyer, relying on the leverage of an unusually large order, prompted the seller's broker to concede part of his brokerage fee, which ultimately led to a discriminatory price reduction.

Although agreeing that Section 2(c) could be applied to the seller's independent broker, the dissent argued that the provision was never intended to affect "legitimately negotiated rates of commission for broker's services." According to the dissenters, the amount that a principal compensates his own agent is a matter not embraced by Section 2(c), and, therefore, that section has no applicability to "any" case of this type. The dissent, therefore, concluded that the price reduction received by the buyer could be tested only under Section 2(a). Finally, the dissent charged that the majority's decision would, in fact, have the anticompetitive effect of freezing brokerage rates.

Even though the applicability of Section 2(c) was the focal point of disagreement between the majority and the dissent, it was not the cause of the precipitating controversies. Rather, the significance of the case lies in the Supreme Court's willingness to question old rules and to experiment with new approaches. For example, the Court went out of its way to cast doubt on the validity of the traditional interpretation of the services rendered exception. Under established law, a buyer could never perform services for the seller that would justify discounts in lieu of brokerage. Although it found no evidence in this case that the buyer had rendered any services to the seller, the Court asserted that such evidence would present "quite a different case." Unfortunately, the Court did not explain in what circumstances the exception might be applicable.

Even more significant was the language of the Court in limiting its holding to a situation where a seller's broker accepts a reduced commission in order to obtain a "particular" order. The Court remarked that not every reduction in price coupled with a reduction in brokerage "automatically compels the conclusion" that an allowance in lieu of brokerage has been granted. Even though a reduction in brokerage rates on all sales to all customers would be legal, a reduction made only to obtain a particular order is "discriminatory" and, therefore, would be violative of 2(c). Indeed, the Court's standard for determining the legality of price reductions under Section 2(c) was "whether such a reduction is tantamount to a discriminatory payment of brokerage." The Court implied that if the buyer's practices enabled the seller to realize cost savings other than brokerage, price discounts based on such savings could be legal under 2(c) as long as they were allowed to all parties similarly situated. At first glance, this reference to discrimination and this implied statement as to services rendered would suggest an intent to incorporate the standards of 2(a) into 2(c). Yet, the Court specifically disclaimed such fusion and expressly rejected a defense based on cost justification.

The Court obviously was not at peace with the workings of the traditional view. The established interpretation of the services rendered exception was questioned and the per se illegality of price discounts subsequent to reductions in brokerage costs was rejected. Moreover, instead of basing its decision on seemingly applicable traditional rules, the Court invoked a new standard of discriminatory impact. Possibly inhibited by the unyielding text of 2(c), however, the Court did not enlarge on or even define this new test. In fact, its meaning was obscured in the many internal inconsistencies of the opinion.

With all its enigmas, the *Broch* decision, nevertheless, did inject a concept of reasonableness into a domain previously ruled by absolutism. For example, the Court asserted that imposition of the sanctions of 2(c) to transactions involving no discriminatory effect would be wholly "absurd." Moreover, as precedent for the principle of discriminatory ends, the Court cited approvingly the few decisions of the traditional era, such as *Main Fish Co.* and *Robinson* v. *Stanley Home Products, Inc.,* where flexible rules were applied in order to accommodate reasonable business transactions. Whatever else may be said of the *Broch* decision, it weakened the shackles of the traditional rules and, thereby, opened the gate for change.

IN LIEU OF BROKERAGE PROVISION

Not satisfied merely with a prohibition against outright dummy brokerage, the text of Section 2(c) was drafted so as to make illegal "any allowance or discount in lieu of" brokerage. That Congress' fear of ingenious manipulation was not unfounded is evidenced by the *A & P* case. Even though condemnation of A & P's dummy brokerage scheme followed naturally from the language of 2(c), application of the in lieu of brokerage provision to less transparent transactions has caused considerable difficulty.

In many of the pioneering decisions, the courts would recite as the test of determining the applicability of the provision whether the discounts or payments in issue furthered the same purpose and effect as the illicit brokerage. The transfer between parties of a separate outright payment of a sum of money was apparently viewed by the courts as a brokerage fee violative of 2(c), unless there existed clear and convincing evidence of some other purpose. With this convenient standard, the courts have applied the sanctions of the act to payments that bear little resemblance to traditional notions of brokerage.

For example, in *Freedman* v. *Philadelphia Terminals Auction Co.,* it was alleged that defendant, an auctioneer, took unfair advantage of his economic leverage by levying and accepting tributes from plaintiffs, fruit retailers, in the form of terminal charge payments. Notwithstanding the dissimilarity between these payments and usual conceptions of brokerage, the court apparently relied on the general remedial impact of the brokerage provision and held that, because the auctioneer had already received commissions for his services from the fruit suppliers, the payments from the retail buyers would violate 2(c).

Perhaps the most startling application of this rationale is *Fitch* v. *Kentucky-Tennessee Light and Power Co.* Tempted by kickbacks, a corporate officer used his influence to see that his corporation bought certain supplies from the contributing concern. When the corporation discovered that it had been victimized, it sought retribution. An action was instituted against the employee seeking treble damages under 2(c). A sympathetic, if not logical, court sustained the action holding that the kickbacks were payments in lieu of brokerage and thus violated 2(c).

Although the application of 2(c) to separate payments has failed to arouse significant controversy, the effect of the in lieu of provision to *discounts* has presented more challenging problems. Here, the central issue is whether the discount should be tested against the strict prohibition of 2(c) or the more lenient standards of 2(a). The cases finding 2(c) applicable generally involve the granting of discounts by the seller in a context of reduced or eliminated brokerage. Doing some business with a broker is seemingly the pivotal element connecting the discount at issue with the brokerage provision. More frequent are the cases where the acts of a broker are scrutinized for possible evasion of 2(c)'s prohibition. The section has been applied when a seller's broker secured commodities on his own account and, nevertheless, accepted his normal brokerage commission for the transaction. The sanctions of the section were similarly applied to a distributor's broker who passed on part of his commission to a company that had bypassed the usual practice of purchasing goods through a subbroker and bought the goods directly from the broker. Indeed, all types of brokerage fee-splitting have been held to be within the purview of Section 2(c).

Once it was determined that 2(c) was applicable, the test for identifying the discount as brokerage was generally the same as that for determining the legality of outright payments. If a seller who customarily retains a broker gives a direct-dealing buyer a discount, any similarity between the discount and usual brokerage commissions usually has led to a presumption that the discount was in lieu of brokerage. Some similarity rather than mathematical equivalence has been the test. Mathematical equivalence, as in *A & P*, would make the presumption almost irrebuttable; yet, the burden for exercising the presumption based on mere similarity was substantial. Successful defenses were rare. In fact, prior to *Broch* there are only two decisions in which one accused of violating 2(c) in presumptive circumstances has been able to avoid its sanctions because of failure of proof.

In *Main Fish Co.*, a wholesaler of fresh fish required most of its other customers to buy through sales brokers. A few concerns, however, were allowed to buy directly. When brokers were used, Main Fish would pay a 5 per cent commission. In about one third of fifty-two transactions with one of the direct purchasers, the price charged was lower by 4 to 6 per cent. In dismissing the complaint, the commission emphasized that the marketing of fish, a highly perishable product, was characterized by frequent and substantial price fluctuations. The commission simply did not apply the presumption ruling; instead, it ruled that in the absence of specific proof connecting the lower prices with the brokerage savings, an action based on 2(c) must fail. As might be expected, however, the impact of this case has been limited to similarly volatile markets.

The only other pre-*Broch* decision sustaining the validity of a discount because of failure of proof was *In re Whitney & Company*. A seafood distributing company, which used a broker in some transactions and not in others, allowed a 5 per cent discount to a direct purchaser. Because the distributing company was already subject to an outstanding cease and desist order, the commission initiated a criminal contempt proceeding based in part on the preceding transaction. Again, all the elements for a presumptive conclusion were present. The evidence against the distributing company was particularly persuasive because many of the invoices covering these transactions were marked "Less 5 Per Cent Brokerage." The severity of a criminal charge is the probable explanation for the court's dispensation of the usual presumption. After pointing out the difficult burden of proof in such actions, the court concluded that "it has not been proved beyond a reasonable doubt" that the discounts were in lieu of brokerage.

Distinct from the two decisions that dismissed 2(c) actions because of failure of proof, the decision of the Court of Appeals for the First Circuit in the case of *Robinson* v. *Stanley Home Products Co.* represents a unique legal exception to the presumptive quicksands. A manufacturer of plastic cups completely terminated his connections with his broker and reduced prices to his now direct-dealing customers. The broker then brought an action for treble damages against his former principal claiming a violation of 2(c). Elements that usually had sufficed to find a violation were present—reduction in price following elimination of broker's services and absence of a convincing explanation that the reduction was caused by anything other than brokerage. Nevertheless, the Court of Appeals was able to avoid the result seemingly compelled by the then current interpretation of 2(c).

Later decisions viewed *Robinson* v. *Stanley Home Products Co.* as clearly establishing a rule of law: When a seller completely discontinues doing business through brokers, the in lieu of brokerage provision is not applicable to subsequent price reductions and any challenges against the reduction must, therefore, be tested under 2(a).

The potentially unsatisfactory effect of the *Broch* decision was first realized in *Thomasville Chair Co.* v. *FTC.* Thomasville Chair, a manufacturer of household furniture, marketed its products exclusively through a staff of about forty salesmen who worked strictly on a commission basis. Each was assigned a particular territory and each had to pay all his expenses, including travel expenses. On sales to the approximately 4,500 "carload customers," the salesmen would receive 6 per cent; but on sales to the large volume customers, referred to as the "J" account, the rate was set at only 3 per cent. On all sales to these J customers, Thomasville Chair would allow a 5 per cent discount off the price regularly charged to the other customers.

In 1959, the FTC initiated a complaint against Thomasville Chair Company, charging it with a violation of 2(c). It was alleged that the 5 per cent discount granted to the large J customers was derived in part from the reduced commissions, and, therefore, was an illegal discount in lieu of brokerage. At the hearing, the company sought to admit cost data to establish a cost justification defense and to negate the inference that the reduced brokerage commission was passed on to the buyer. On an interlocutory appeal of the examiner's exclusion of this data, the commission, although reasserting the rule that cost justification is no defense in a 2(c) action, remarked that all evidence tending to rebut the inference of a violation is relevant, "including evidence to show that the lower prices charged certain buyers actually did not result from a passing on of a part of salesmen's commissions but was in fact due to some other cost difference."

The commission apparently adopted the reasonable view that the "in lieu of" provisions should not be indiscriminately applied to strike down all discounts that should occur contemporaneously with a reduction of brokerage costs. If the discounts could be related to cost savings other than brokerage, they should stand and be accorded the dignity of cost efficiency subject only to the limitations of 2(a).

In reviewing the case on its merits, however, the commission jumped two steps backward to make up for the one step forward. The hearing examiner, abiding by the directive from the commission in the interlocutory decision, admitted the cost data and, thereupon, concluded that there was insufficient evidence to support an inference that the lower prices were partially derived from the reduced brokerage commissions. Furthermore, he indicated that even if such an inference were warranted, it would have been rebutted by the cost data introduced by the company. In reversing the determination of the hearing examiner, the commission applied the traditional presumption with utmost severity. It concluded that 2(c) had been violated because Thomasville Chair had not completely accounted for the discount with savings other than brokerage, and, therefore, it is "conclusively established" that the discounts were actually related to the reduction in brokerage. Even though the commission did imply that the presumption could be overcome, the burden imposed on defendants appears almost impossible.

Drawing from its interpretation of the Supreme Court's *Broch* decision, the United States Fifth Circuit Court of Appeals set aside the commission order and remanded the case to the commission for further proceedings.

Judge Tuttle, speaking for the court, pounced on *Broch's* emphasis on the "discriminatory" effects of the price reduction and construed it as indicative of a new element necessary to actions under Section 2(c). The commission, therefore, had erred in assuming that a price reduction, not completely derived from cost savings independent of a contemporaneous reduction in brokerage, is a per se violation of 2(c).

Looking to Section 2(a) for guidance, Judge Tuttle defined a discriminatory price reduction as one without cost savings "resulting from the differing methods or quantities in which such commodities are sold or delivered." In remanding the case, the court directed the commission to determine whether the smaller commissions to the salesmen on sales to the large volume customers "could be legally justified." If it could be so justified, the court remarked, "then there is no violation of Section 2(c)."

The court seemingly injected Section 2(a)'s cost justification defense with all its ramifications into 2(c). Indeed, the court appears to say that a seller now can pass reduced brokerage costs on to the buyer by a reduction in price. Such a reduction would be cost justified. This interpretation, however, arguably cannot happily coexist with much of the language and the result of the *Broch* decision. The cost justification implied in the *Broch* decision seemingly referred only to cost savings other than brokerage. The court, therefore, apparently went beyond the *Broch* dicta. Indeed, if the cost justification theory of Thomasville had been applied in the *Broch* case, the reduced brokerage fee would have provided invaluable evidence in demonstrating the legality of the price reduction. Indeed, the defense would have probably prevailed. In digesting the *Broch* decision, the Fifth Circuit arrived at an interpretation that, if applied to the facts of the *Broch* case, probably would lead to a result in direct contradiction to the resolution of the Supreme Court.

It is highly improbable that this doctrine will be widely adopted. The *Broch* decision implicitly rejects this interpretation of discrimination and the commission has already voiced its emphatic disapproval of the *Thomasville* dicta. In finally dismissing the complaint, the commission sought to limit the precedential impact of the decision by construing its holding simply as a disapproval of the commission's presumptive techniques. To this purpose, the commission issued a memorandum accompanying the dismissal order that stated:

We read the Court of Appeals' decision as holding that the Commission, in a case in which it is alleged that a seller has violated Section 2(c) of the Clayton Act by passing on a reduction in brokerage to favored buyers in the form of a discriminatory price reduction, may not rely solely on the fact that the seller has paid less brokerage on the sales at the lower price, but must establish a causal relationship between the reduced brokerage and the reduced sales price.

As to any other statement of the Court of Appeals, the memorandum remarked that the commission did not necessarily agree "with such 'dicta.'"

FOR SERVICES RENDERED EXCEPTION

One provision of Section 2(c) specifically exempts commissions, brokerage, or payments in lieu of brokerage from the sanctions of the act if for services rendered. The meaning of this exception stands preeminent among the many mysteries of the Robinson-Patman Act.

Through all the confusion surrounding the section one fact is clear: Cooperative buying groups were primarily responsible for incorporation of this exception in the belief that it would allow them to continue receiving brokerage payments for their services. Without this exception it was felt that Section 2(c) would be tantamount to "class legislation" favoring independent brokers.

Representative Utterbach, Chairman of the House Conferees, apparently agreed with the position of the cooperatives by noting that the for services rendered exception would allow economic efficiencies to be "expressed in price differentials in favor of the particular customers whose distinctive methods of purchase and delivery make them possible."

The position of the cooperatives was not clearly reflected in the reports issued on the section. In fact, the committee interpretation, eventually followed by the FTC, was far narrower than that urged by the cooperatives. The report of the House Judiciary Committee implied that even with the inclusion of the exception, 2(c) would never permit brokerage payments to flow between the buyer and seller, for "it is a contradiction in terms incompatible with his natural function for an intermediary to claim to be rendering services for the seller when he is acting in fact for or under the control of the buyer." This was further defined by the conference report, which suggested that the exception simply meant that a buyer or seller could only pay his own agent for services rendered.

Taken literally, the principles announced in these reports would affix a purpose to the for services rendered exception quite unlike that intended by the cooperatives and inconsistent with the view of many legislators. One conclusion may be drawn from this cryptic legislative history—because evidence of congressional intent is inconclusive, the FTC possessed considerable flexibility in fashioning a meaning to the exception.

When the issue first confronted this tribunal—which occasioned the initial cease and desist order under 2(c)—the interpretation proposed in the conference report came to the forefront. The case arose in the following context. Biddle Purchasing Company, operating primarily in the food industry, provided market information services for about 2,500 relatively small enterprises. Biddle was affiliated with the buyers. Its entire income was derived from fixed monthly assessments charged each client for use of the services. Acting on the request of its clients, Biddle frequently would place orders for merchandise described in the market catalogs. In these transactions, Biddle would collect brokerage commissions from the sellers and, then, pass them on to the client-buyer in the form of credits toward the monthly charge.

In sustaining the commission's cease and desist order against Biddle, the United States Court of Appeals for the Second Circuit held that the arrangement was proscribed by 2(c) because the brokerage payments were ultimately received by the buyers. Thus, even before the *A & P* case, 2(c) was regarded as an absolute prohibition; if any brokerage is transmitted between the buyer and seller, the section is automatically violated. The services rendered exception could offer no relief, because the same insignificant role assigned to the exception in the conference report was adopted in toto by the court.

Neither tribunal, however, specifically found that Biddle did, in fact, provide services for the sellers. Hence, even after the *Biddle* decision, it was not certain that a buyer could not receive compensation for brokerage if for actual services rendered.

This uncertainty was prolonged in subsequent cases. In the *A & P* case, both the commission and the United States Court of Appeals for the Second Circuit found that A & P never performed any services for the sellers. Any benefits derived by the seller from the chain's operations were characterized as "purely incidental." Similarly, in *Oliver Bros., Inc. v. FTC,* a company, whose operations were similar to those of the Biddle Company, was held not to be performing "genuine services" for the buyer.

Because of judicial failure to rule directly on the point, a slight possibility remained that a buyer could pay brokerage to the seller, or *vice versa,* if *actual* services were rendered. However, in *Webb-Crawford Co. v. FTC,* even this possibility vanished. In that case, grocery food suppliers transacted business with Webb-Crawford Company through Daniel Brokerage Company. The brokerage company was a partnership whose members owned 95 per cent of the corporate stores of Webb-Crawford. Relying on this identity of interests, the United States Court of Appeals for the Fifth Circuit concluded that brokerage commissions paid to the

Daniel Company were tantamount to payment to the buyer, Webb-Crawford, and, therefore, were barred by 2(c). What is of particular interest is that, for the first time, the court admitted the obvious: The brokerage partnership did in fact provide real services for the sellers.

After conceding the existence of services rendered, the court performed another novel feat. It met head-on the difficult problem of comparing its conclusion with the plain meaning of the words used in 2(c). A literal reading suggests that the for services rendered exception qualifies the whole subsection. Hence, a brokerage payment or discount in lieu of brokerage, if for services rendered, would be lawful irrespective of the relationship between the parties. Confronted with such statutory language and believing that the purpose of the statue would be defeated by a literal construction, the court could justify its conclusion only by offering a repunctuation of the subsection. Specifically, the court asserted:

> The words can, by transferring a comma, be attached to those immediately preceding: "or any allowance or discount in lieu thereof except for services rendered." The statute would then prohibit "a commission, brokerage, or other compensation, or any allowance or discount in lieu thereof except for services rendered, in connection with the sale or purchase, etc." The punctuation as published is confusing. We think the true meaning is better indicated by taking the comma out after "thereof", and inserting it after "rendered." Commas are not to be suffered to defeat the legislative meaning.

COOPERATIVES

The aftermath of the *A & P* case had one immediate prophylactic effect: Chain organizations discontinued the practice of exacting dummy brokerage. Enforcement proceedings under 2(c), therefore, have rarely involved members of the powerful economic groups to which the provision had been addressed. Instead, the principal focus of Section 2(c) shifted to small enterprises, which, in their zest for economic survival, realized that in unity there was strength.

In 1940, however, the courts struck their first direct blow against cooperatives. Before enactment of the Robinson-Patman Act, Quality Bakers of America, an association of seventy relatively small wholesale baking concerns, had formed a corporation that functioned as a buying agent and a management consultant. The corporation would finalize orders for its members, collect brokerage from the suppliers, and credit one half of the brokerage income to the member who had placed the order, the other half being contributed to the expenses of the cooperative or to a general fund. When the brokerage provision became law, the corporation did not alter its practices other than to designate as "services fees" those sums that previously had been referred to as brokerage commissions. By the time that the United States Court of Appeals for the First Circuit confronted the issue of the validity of these service fees, the decision called for by the traditional view appeared obvious. Clearly, the text of 2(c) forbidding payment of brokerage to one who is "acting in fact for or in behalf, or subject to the direct or indirect control of the other party," seemed to apply directly to cooperatives. In *Webb-Crawford Co.* v. *FTC,* for example, the United States Court of Appeals for the Fifth Circuit had struck down brokerage payments under less blatant facts. In that case, the payments at issue were made to a brokerage concern that was affiliated with the buyer only through stock ownership. The payments were not actually passed on to the buyer. Nevertheless, the court held that the mere receipt of brokerage by an affiliate of the buyer constituted a violation of 2(c). In *Quality Bakers,* the United States Court of Appeals for the First Circuit found that the cooperative buying corporation formed by Quality Bakers had been "accepting brokerage fees from sellers on purchases of commodities made by its stockholders through it, while acting as the agent for them and in their behalf and while owned and controlled by such stockholders," and, thus, had contributed to a violation of Section 2(c).

In the shadow of the *Broch* opinion's upheaving dictum, the commission's tenacity to the traditional view was prolonged. In the *Central Retailer-Owned Grocers* case, the commission resorted to an unprecedented hard-line approach on a subject that had been the primary recipient of the critics' wrath—application of 2(c) to cooperatives. In reversing the order, the United States Court of Appeals for the Seventh Circuit chastised the commission for its "shoddy analysis" and injected renewed hope for the relief that cooperatives had long sought.

Central Retailer-Owned Grocers, Inc. (hereinafter referred to as Central), was owned and operated for the benefit of thirty-five relatively small retailer-owned warehousing and distributing companies. After integrating the seasonal estimates of members, Central would negotiate directly with suppliers for discounted prices. A member would then simply issue an order to Central, which immediately forwarded it to the supplier. The merchandise was shipped directly to the member company, but the invoices were billed to Central. After paying these obligations, Central would restore its capital by charging the member company a somewhat higher price. At the end of the fiscal year, any excess funds remaining in Central's account would be distributed to the member companies as special dividends.

That the practices of the cooperative were found illegal is entirely consistent with prior commission rulings. Because Central's stock was wholly owned by the member buying companies, Central was clearly an intermediary or representative of the buyer within the purview of 2(c). The discounts, which the cooperative admittedly sought and accepted, were viewed by the commission as mathematically correlated to the supplier's usual brokerage expenses. The absence of any reference to brokerage in negotiations had never precluded a finding that discounts were in lieu of brokerage. Indeed, the traditional presumption of invalidity clearly would be applicable to these circumstances.

After observing Central's corporate charter and its business practices, Chairman Dixon speaking for the commission, concluded that,

> . . . the attempt to segregate such cost savings and ascribe them to CROG's [Central's] business methods in order to rebut an inference that these sums constituted savings in brokerage is irrelevant.
>
> In light of the above record facts, it is unnecessary to document a pattern whereunder the lower prices, allowances and discounts granted CROG may be correlated mathematically with the brokerage rates of CROG's suppliers in order to infer the payment of brokerage or amounts in lieu thereof to that respondent. *The inferences to be drawn from the interrelationship of CROG and its members and the manner of their transactions with CROG's suppliers are conclusive on this point.* [Emphasis added.]

In dissent, Commissioner Elman viewed as wholly unjustified the majority's conclusion that the discounts were illegal simply because Central performed certain brokerage functions. This holding, in effect, would condemn all price concessions to cooperative buying organizations. Citing the *Broch* decision, Commissioner Elman argued that the price concessions were legal if they reflect cost savings *other than brokerage* that the seller has realized because of the buyer's special mode of operation. According to the dissent, Central had submitted, and the majority ignored, persuasive evidence that the price concessions in issue were, indeed, derived from such independent cost savings.

On appeal, the United States Seventh Circuit Court of Appeals reversed the commission's order on substantially the same grounds posed in Commissioner Elman's dissent. Like the *Thomasville* decision, the court relied on a cost justification principle to sustain the validity of price discounts. The similarity, however, ceases there, for the substance of the principles were quite different. Unlike *Thomasville,* the cost savings justifying the price allowances to Central were limited to savings *other than brokerage* realized by the seller because of the cooperatives' business practices. Rather than actually asserting that cost justification is a defense to actions under 2(c), the court relied on the cost-savings data as persuasive evidence in proving that discounts were not in lieu of brokerage.

Any remaining question as to the reality of a revolution in the interpretation of 2(c) was finally settled in *Empire Rayon Yarn Co.* v. *American Viscose Corp.* American, a major producer of quality yarn, had established a distribution system whereby two companies were authorized to function as jobbers for the resale of the yarn at prices set by American. The jobbers performed such services as maintaining substantial inventories, providing a widespread selling organization, assuming risk of loss and credit, and assuming the risk of price fluctuations. In consideration of these services, American allowed the selected jobbers a "functional discount" equal to 5 per cent of the list price of the yarn.

Empire Rayon Yarn Co., both a processor and jobber of yarn, was repeatedly denied its request to become another of American's selected jobbers. Consequently, Empire brought an action against American and its jobbers claiming that the discounts allowed the selected jobbers were illegal commissions in lieu of brokerage. The federal district court, relying on *Broch,* ruled that the jobbers performed brokerage services justifying the discounts and "the fact that they take title in the interim does not detract from the value of the services."

On appeal, the United States Court of Appeals, with one dissent, reversed on the ground that Section 2(c) prohibits the transfer of brokerage or discounts in lieu of brokerage between the parties of a transaction. Apparently ignoring the significant cases of the post-*Broch* era, the court relied on the stringent traditional rule on buying brokers reminiscent of the *Southgate* decision. Moreover, the court asserted that 2(c) is applicable whenever a "price discrimination is effected by a discount which is related to a sale by the person receiving the discount." Although not entirely clear, the statement apparently meant that 2(c) could be applied to discounts irrespective of their causal relationship with the partial or total elimination of brokerage.

Upon rehearing *in banc,* the Second Circuit reversed its previous decision and affirmed the district court. The court found that the jobbers performed a vital function by facilitating the movement of commodities to small businessmen who found it economically difficult to buy direct. In these circumstances, the discounts should be viewed as functional discounts, "the validity of which should be judged under Section 2(a)." To find that the in lieu of provision encompasses such discounts would exceed the limited purpose of 2(c) to prevent powerful buyers from taking unfair advantage of their bargaining leverage. Moreover, the court thought this interpretation probably would "render all functional discounts illegal per se," and, thereby, prohibit the use of price differentials at different noncompeting business levels.

Perhaps the most significant aspect of the decision, however, was the court's adoption of Judge Moore's dissenting opinion in the prior case, which asserted that the jobbers' business practices and the "resultant advantage to the supplier" rebut any inference that the discounts were causally related to a reduction in brokerage expenses. Moreover, Judge Moore had indicated that the discounts involved in the *Central* and

Hruby decisions were justified because of distribution services performed by the buyers. By placing primary emphasis on the value of the services instead of cost justification or competitive injury, Judge Moore may have given lift to the for services rendered exception.

BUYING BROKERS

Business expedience at times dictates an unusual method of distribution. One such deviation is represented by the buying broker, a term generally referring to a broker who, while performing his distributive functions, for some reason takes actual title to the transferred goods. Hoping to receive additional orders while the goods are in transit, the broker buys some of the commodities *on his own account* in order to receive the transportation cost differentials. Even when sufficient quantites were on order, sellers often persuaded their brokers to assume legal ownership of transported commodities for various credit and processing reasons.

As early as 1940, the commission condemned the buyer-broker practice in *Albert W. Sisk & Sons,* where field brokers for sellers of canned fruits and vegetables accepted brokerage commissions on purchases made on their own account. The brokers would then resell the goods to jobbers, wholesalers, retail chain stores, and other purchasers. The undesirable economic results of these transactions are apparent. With respect to the commodities actually purchased, the broker was on the same competitive level as wholesalers who had received no commission discount. The resulting difference in price was clearly a reflection of brokerage. The commission, however, did not attempt to explain the economic evil inherent in Sisk's practices. Instead, it merely asserted, without explanation, that brokers violate 2(c) "in receiving and accepting brokerage fees . . . upon their purchase of commodities." In later cases, the commission similarly dispensed with economic analysis and relied wholly on a per se prohibition.

The legality of brokerage fees accepted by the buying broker was first tested by the courts in *Southgate Brokerage Co.* v. *FTC*. During the course of transacting business with a fish packing concern, Southgate Brokerage Co., in addition to placing orders for purchases, purchased substantial quantities of goods on its own account.

In sustaining the commission's order, the United States Court of Appeals for the Fourth Circuit looked no further than the principles of the traditional view. In brief, the court relied on the iron-clad rule that 2(c) "forbids the payment of brokerage on a sale or purchase of goods to the other party to the transaction." A broker buying on his own account becomes the "other party," and, therefore, any commissions fall within the purview of 2(c)'s prohibition. The defendant's contention that the brokerage fees were justified because of services rendered was unhesitatingly rejected.

At first glance, the facts do not present what is called a hard case. Southgate was more a brokering buyer than a buying broker, and many of the persuasive arguments in favor of striking an exception for the buying broker were inapplicable to this case. However, one highly controversial element adds considerable complexity to the facts. Because Southgate sold only to wholesalers who paid the same price that they would pay if purchasing through usual brokerage channels, Southgate functioned at all times on the same level as brokers who had similarly received commissions. By competing with brokers as another source of supply, Southgate probably encouraged competition on all functional levels. Nevertheless, the court refused to depart from the traditional view. Simply citing such cases as *A & P, Biddle* and *Oliver,* it asserted that "price discrimination which is covered by Section 2(a) of the Act . . . is not necessary to a violation of Section 2(c)."

The undercurrent of discontent so apparent in *Broch, Thomasville,* and *Central* had little or no effect on the commission until its decision in *Hruby Distributing Company,* in which the commission, for the first time, demonstrated a willingness to depart from the old and undertake the task of redefining the brokerage provision. Paralleling the *Central* decision, the commission protected another victim of the traditional view by adding what seems to be a new dimension to the in lieu of brokerage provision.

In conducting its business of purchasing foodstuffs and reselling them to wholesalers, Hruby took title to the goods, assumed all risks incident to ownership, and set its own resale price. Although Hruby received all the bills and invoices, half of the orders were drop-shipped from the suppliers directly to Hruby's customers. The remaining orders were stored and sold from Hruby's own warehouses. Because Hruby sold exclusively to wholesalers, its operation was on a functional and competitive level with brokers. Consequently, Hruby's survival as an economic entity was dependent on its ability to offer prices competitive with brokers' quotations. Cognizant of this economic straitjacket, suppliers allowed Hruby a reduction in their regular wholesale price—a reduction that usually was equivalent to the standard brokerage rates.

These price reductions soon became the basis of an FTC complaint charging a violation of Section 2(c). Unquestionably, evidence identifying the price reductions as in lieu of brokerage was more than sufficient to meet tests previously applied by the commission. Not only were the reductions generally equivalent to the suppliers' brokerage expenses, but in a number of transactions, the suppliers specifically labeled the discounts as brokerage or in lieu of brokerage. Moreover, in response to a commission questionnaire, one supplier expressly characterized the reduction as in lieu of brokerage.

Confronted with such damning circumstances, the hearing examiner had little choice but to abide by the analogous *Southgate* decision and find a violation of Section 2(c). The commission, however, did not consider itself so restricted, for in a 2 to 1 decision, it held that Hruby's practices did not violate the brokerage provision.

Citing the *Broch* decision, the majority, through Commissioner Elman, initially insisted that the practices of Hruby did not resemble the evils that Congress sought to eliminate by enactment of Section 2(c). Without a showing of injurious circumstances, therefore, application of Section 2(c) was inappropriate. Hruby's practices provided a useful and economic alternative for the intermediate distribution of goods between producers and wholesalers. If anything, Hruby sharpened competition at its functional level and offered a competitive source of supply for small businessmen.

The broad implication of the opinion was that discounts serving a useful business purpose and causing no competitive injury are not within the purview of the in lieu of brokerage provision. The opinion, therefore, contains a new flexible test under 2(c) involving a genuine inquiry into the competitive injuries caused by a suspected practice. Even as *Central* had injected a type of cost justification into the in lieu of brokerage provision, *Hruby* added the lack of competitive injury as another possible line of defense.

In an apparent effort to construct an opinion more palatable to those members of the commission more reluctant to abandon the old, Commissioner Elman detracted from the import of his basic rationale by phrasing much of his discussion in purely evidential terms. Notwithstanding the dissent's seemingly faultless observation that the majority had embarked on a course directly contrary to the *Southgate* decision, Commissioner Elman chose neither to expressly degrade nor deny its precedential authority—in fact, he merely ignored it. Mr. Elman asserted that the price reductions were not proved to be brokerage but in fact represented "the difference in the functional competitive level at which Hruby and his wholesaler customers operate." The only commissioner to concur in Elman's opinion subsequently asserted that the decision represents only that the facts failed to justify a finding that brokerage had been transferred.

In *Western Fruit Growers Sales Co.* v. *FTC,* another case involving the validity of discounts to buying brokers, the commission argued before the United States Ninth Circuit Court of Appeals that the *Hruby* rule was inapplicable where the parties concede that the discounts were in lieu of brokerage, an argument seemingly based on an interpretation of *Hruby* that is relegated to evidentiary issues. Finally, even though the discounts granted by Western seemingly were discriminatory and anticompetitive, the court did not distinguish nor even mention the *Hruby* decision. In fact, the court found that the discounts were illegal by applying the simple traditional standard of determining "whether a seller-buyer relationship existed."

The commission's decision in *Garrett-Holmes & Co., Inc.,* represents still another manifestation of the lasting impact of the *Hruby* and *Broch* decisions. Functioning as a buying broker, Garrett-Holmes often received discounts approximating brokerage commissions in its purchases of food commodities on its own account. Unlike Hruby, however, this company resold these products to purchasers on all functional levels including wholesalers, retailers, chain stores, and jobbers. Because of the wide range of customers, Garrett-Holmes was in active competition not only with brokers in its sales to wholesalers, but also with wholesalers in its sales to retailers. The hearing examiner's decision, adopted by the commission, recognized this distinction from the *Hruby* case. Accordingly, the examiner ruled that "whether considered in the light of old precedents such as the *Southgate* and *A & P* cases or in the light of more recent Commission decisions such as the *Hruby* and *Flotill* cases, the receipt of . . . brokerage . . . was a violation of Section 2(c)." Implicit in this remark is the recognition that *Hruby* does not merely represent an instance where brokerage was not proven, but, in fact, provides a distinct standard for assessing the validity of discounts.

The commission's final order against Garrett-Holmes, instead of reciting traditional verbiage that a buyer cannot accept discounts from a seller, focused on the discriminatory aspects of the case by quoting the most controversial language of the *Broch* decision, which reads, "there is no evidence that the buyer rendered any services to the sellers . . . nor that anything in its method of dealing justified its getting a dsicriminatory price."

Considering the language adopted in *Hruby* and *Garrett-Holmes,* one would surmise that the commission was about to discard much of the traditional view and admit the advent of a new era. Nevertheless, in a recent publication of the *Trade Practice Rules for the Fresh Fruit and Vegetable Industry,* the commission did not choose to venture from the past. Without recognizing the flexible standards applied in recent cases, the rules appear to to be mere restatement of traditional dogma. For example, Section 74.2, entitled "Prohibited Brokerage," provides as follows:

(a)(1) The foregoing provision [Section 2(c)] prohibits, in connection with the sale of goods, the payment of a brokerage fee or the granting of an allowance or discount in lieu of a brokerage fee—
    (i) By the seller to the buyer; and
    (ii) By the buyer to the seller; and

(iii) By the seller or the buyer to an agent,
representative or other intermediary who is working for or in behalf of the other party to sales transaction, or is subject to such
other party's direct or indirect control. . . .

(b) The paying or granting or receiving or accepting of any commission, brokerage fee, or allowance or discount in lieu thereof, such
as is proscribed by paragraph (a) of this section is unlawful without
regard to whether or not the practice—

(1) Causes or is likely to cause competitive injury. . . .

(2) Was employed to meet any payment, allowance or discount
furnished by a competitor.

The fate of *Hruby* and the principles it represents, therefore, are as
yet uncertain. Even though the possibility of escaping seemingly unjust
applications of 2(c) has increased, a businessman would be ill-advised to
formulate his practices in reliance on a total or even partial rejection of
the traditional view. A wiser course would be to await clarification before
treading new waters. The many pitfalls engendered by the conflict between the traditional and modern view necessitate cautious evaluation.

CONCLUSION

To describe what has replaced the traditional view as a modern view
would be a misnomer. Indeed, if a modern view means a system of newly
developed principles, a modern view does not exist. Although a meta-
morphosis, no doubt, has taken place, it has not assumed any discernible
form. Although diverging from the traditional view, the recent decisions
have done little to construct a basis for developing a logical approach to
2(c). Instead, they seem to represent uncoordinated rebellions against particular injustices of the traditional view. By rectifying some of the past
ends in this manner, the courts and the commission have left the business world without clear rules on which to formulate plans and direct
activities.

The confusion that exists today stems from the cryptic opinion of the
Supreme Court in the *Broch* decision. Obvious displeasure with the traditional view could have presented an occasion for the Supreme Court
to direct a wholly new approach. Instead, the Court chose to cast asper-
sions on the past rules by mere implication and left an undefined,
although distinct, desire to enrich the law with more flexible standards.
For example, the Court suggested, but did not explain, that a new and
more meaningful significance should be given to the for services rendered
exception. Perhaps even more important was the injection of discriminatory impact as an element to be considered in actions under 2(c). In

short, even though the Court showed restraint in retreating from the past, the unalterability of the traditional view at last had been questioned and the avenues for change were opened.

In granting relief from the sanctions of 2(c), subsequent decisions employ these many avenues. In *Empire Rayon,* the United States Court of Appeals for the Second Circuit seemingly injected new life into the for services rendered exception. Notwithstanding the Supreme Court's specific rejection of a fusion of 2(a) defenses into 2(c), lower courts and the commission have looked to Section 2(a) as a source of guidance in determining the meaning of the *Broch* decision's reference to discrimination. *Thomasville* and *Central,* therefore, allowed different types of cost justification defenses, and *Hruby* followed suit with the defense of no competitive injury. It would not be wise, however, for the business world to assume that such a fusion has been consummated. The decisions in *Central* and *Hruby* were affected by a desire to render relief to particular groups who had been severely restricted by the traditional view. Rather than having broadened the application of *Hruby,* subsequent cases and the commission's Trade Rules have probably restricted its impact. The broad cost justification defense announced in *Thomasville* has been openly denounced by the commission and has never been followed by the courts. In summary, the status of the decisions embodying the so-called modern view is uncertain. Each decision adopted a somewhat different approach in avoiding the injustices of the traditional view. Hence, although the traditional view has been discredited, not even one principle contained therein has expressly been overruled. Until the law is clarified, the business world must function in limbo.

There seems to be, however, one thread that does connect the diversified nature of the modern cases. For the present, this single theme may provide the only basis for evaluating business practices. As discussed in detail above, the traditional view required little evidence for permitting application of an almost irrefutable inference that discounts are in lieu of brokerage. Recent cases uniformly have rejected such an automatic application of the in lieu of provision to discounts wholly unrelated to the purposes of the act. Hence, discounts that are part of an arrangement with reasonable business motives and effects are now less likely to be subjected to per se condemnation under the brokerage provision.

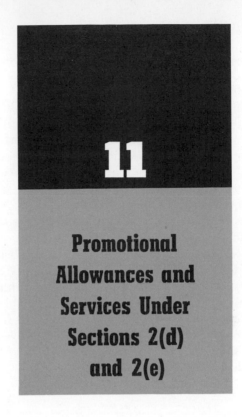

11

Promotional Allowances and Services Under Sections 2(d) and 2(e)

In addition to the regulation of indirect price discrimination *via* brokerage fees, the Robinson-Patman Act seeks to prevent discriminatory advantages through the inequitable granting of promotional allowances or services. By means of Sections 2(d) and 2(e), Congress sought to eliminate three prevalent forms of discrimination: (1) payments to a customer for promotional services when none had been performed, (2) payments to a customer greatly in excess of the services actually performed, and (3) payments for promotional services to some purchasers while denying proportional assistance to competing purchasers. Although originally enacted in response to the evils created by big buyers, such as the chain grocery stores, Sections 2(d) and 2(e) are directed at sellers who grant services or allowances to such buyers, rather than directly at the buyers. When this initial indirection is coupled with the "hopelessly vague" language of the act, several threshold problems of interpretation develop. Neither section completely describes an intended violation, and it has been necessary for the courts to read the two sections together in order to resolve ambiguities. As the United States Court of Appeals for the District of Columbia explained in the *Exquisite Form Brassiere* case, "the economic evil sought to be outlawed by [the Robinson-Patman Act] is the same whether the services and facilities are furnished to the customer or by the customer with reimbursement, so long as discrimination is practiced." Approached under such a philosophy, courts have read the two sections to have completely parallel application with regard to elements and defenses.

To trigger the application of either Section 2(d) or 2(e), there must be (1) two or more consummated sales, (2) reasonably close in point of time, (3) of commodities, (4) of like grade and quality, (5) by the same seller, (6) to two or more different customers, (7) in interstate commerce, (8) where the seller pays for, (9) or furnishes, (10) promotional services or facilities, (11) in connection with the sale of his product, (12) without making proportionately equal treatment available to all competing customers. Both sections are considered per se, and it is no defense to allege either cost justification or lack of anticompetitive effect. The only available defense under either section is to assert that the payment or service was provided to meet competition.

PREREQUISITES UNCHANGED FROM SECTION 2(A) CAUSE OF ACTION

Several of the elements of a cause of action under Section 2(a), which have already been discussed, remain unchanged in Sections 2(d) and 2(e). The requirements of two or more reasonably contemporaneous, consummated sales remain necessary preconditions where promotional allowances or services are involved. Similarly, the seller preserves the right to refuse to deal with a given customer under the *Colgate* doctrine. Refusals to deal may not be interpreted as any sort of a promotional preference to those who are customers of the seller. The seller is also free to refuse to sell select items in a given line to certain customers without fearing that this will be interpreted as granting a promotional benefit to those receiving the full line.

The requirements that the sales be of commodities of like grade and quality, to two or more different customers, and by the same seller remain essentially undisturbed. The definition of *customer* is different for promotional discrimination, but this will be explored later under an examination of competing customers. The balance of the elements for a 2(d) or 2(e) cause of action are unique to those sections and will be discussed in detail.

COMMERCE REQUIREMENT

Unlike the strict requirement of Section 2(a) that one of the sales must cross a state line, the commerce requirement for Sections 2(d) and 2(e) more nearly approaches traditional concepts of interstate commerce. The phrase "engaged in commerce" does not appear in Section 2(e), but the Supreme Court has, nonetheless, read the commerce requirement into that section from 2(d) where the phrase does appear. In interpreting this requirement, courts have ignored the absence of any evidence that a particular sale crossed a state line and have looked instead to the general interstate character of the business entities involved. This certainly would seem to be the logical construction, because these sections are not directly concerned with the sale of a specific commodity that can be traced readily through its physical transit across state borders. Rather, the sections are directed at promotional arrangements the effect of which cannot be easily ascribed to a particular geographic locale.

The standard to be applied in ascertaining the necessary effect on commerce was amply demonstrated in the *Corn Products* case. There, the Supreme Court examined the dollar volume of business that was of an interstate character and noted the existence of interstate competitors. Furthermore, the Court pointed out that some of the sales that did not contain promotional benefits were in interstate commerce. It would seem, therefore, that it is never necessary to place the particular sale involving the promotional scheme directly in interstate commerce so long as it can be demonstrated that the seller's general business activities have an effect on interstate commerce.

PROMOTIONAL SERVICES OR FACILITIES

Perhaps the broadest limitation on the application of Sections 2(d) and 2(e) is implicit in the definition of promotional services and facilities. These sections have been described by the United States Court of Appeals for the Second Circuit as applying to all "promotional allowances which have the effect of price adjustments." At least three separate prerequisites have been recognized as necessary to establishing the existence of a promotional service: (1) a cooperative promotional arrangement, (2) in connection with a sale, (3) for customer resale. The outer perimeter of the sections' coverage can best be described by an examination of these three criteria.

Cooperative Promotional Arrangement Allowances

The program must be one that has a beneficial effect on one or both of the participants through encouragement of the resale of the product. The activity must be reasonably calculated to promote the resale of the seller's product, but, otherwise, may be anything that encourages the purchase of the commodity by means of facilitating a lower resale price or by providing advertising encouragement to the ultimate consumer. In 1969, the Federal Trade Commission adopted guidelines that list several categories of services or facilities that would qualify under the two sections. Where the seller provides allowances, the commission ruled that 2(d) would apply to: (1) any kind of advertising, (2) handbills, (3) window and floor displays, (4) special sales or promotional efforts for which "push money" is paid to clerks, salesmen, and other employees of the customer, (5) demonstrators and demonstrations. This list is essentially a compilation of the most characteristic subject matter for the granting of a promotional allowance; Section 2(d) has by no means been limited to the situations described in the commission's Guides. Far more subtle methods of promotional reimbursement have fallen within the proscription of 2(d). In one case, a manufacturer of golf balls paid "royalties" to the Professional Golf Association (PGA) in order to obtain the association's mark on those balls sold by customers who were also members of the association. The mark was considered to be a stamp of approval that greatly enhanced the marketability of the golf balls. The payment of the royalties was interpreted by the FTC as a promotional allowance to those favored customers of the manufacturer who were members of the golfer's association and who were, thereby, better able to market the favorably marked balls.

Particular problems arise in the area of a seller's purchase of "any kind of advertising" when the seller purchases very general ads for his product in a publication owned by one of his customers. The leading case on this point is *State Wholesale Grocers* v. *Great Atlantic & Pacific Tea Co.* There, the seller bought advertising space for its product line in *Woman's Day* magazine, a wholly owned subsidiary of its customer, A & P, without naming any specific retailers. However, the magazine was distributed solely in A & P's retail outlets. The United States Court of Appeals for the Seventh Circuit combined the advertisement with the restricted distribution and found a promotional activity that peculiarly benefited A & P. The payments for such an activity were classified as being the type of promotional allowance contemplated by Section 2(d). The decision hinged on the finding of a special *promotional* benefit flowing to the customer owning the publication. In the *A & P* case, the general nature of the ads was irrelevant because only A & P's customers would see them and be encouraged to purchase. This essential ingredient was further clarified in a later Seventh Circuit decision that appears, on the surface, to contradict the result in *A & P*. The cases are, however, fully compatible. In the second decision, a manufacturer advertised in a trade publication owned by the president and controlling shareholder of a customer. Unlike *A & P*, however, the publication was independently operated and received industrywide circulation. In finding that such broad circulation could afford no special *promotional* advantage to the customer-owner, the court reiterated the requirement that "there must be a showing that some benefit accrued to, or was intended to accrue to the customer." A failure to demonstrate such intended benefit negates the possibility of a cooperative promotional arrangement.

Services and Facilities

Services and facilities under 2(e), although nominally the counterpart of promotional allowances, nonetheless encompasses a far wider range of activities than 2(d). Because the seller frequently controls the packaging, loading, and distribution of the product, he is in a unique position to render a great number of promotional services that a customer could not possibly otherwise purchase with a promotional allowance. The 1969 Federal Trade Commission's Guides lists the following as services or facilities when provided directly by the seller: (1) any kind of advertising, (2) catalogs, (3) demonstrators, (4) display and storage cabinets, (5) display materials, (6) special packaging or package sizes, (7) accepting returns for credit, and (8) prizes or merchandise for conducting promotional contests.

The most prevalent promotional service provided by sellers has been in the form of demonstrators. The question of whether trained specialists provided by the supplier to work in selected customers' stores was a promotional service was settled in the *Elizabeth Arden* case. Special sales personnel dispatched by the seller to work in selected large department stores that stocked Arden products were found by the FTC to be the subject of a promotional service provided to those customers. This area has been expanded to include programs of on-the-job training of customers' sales personnel by a supplier's fieldmen, and the stationing, by the seller, of trained repairmen in selected customer outlets.

As a general rule, credit arrangements will not be construed as promotional services unless they are particularly tailored to encourage the resale of the product. Several recent decisions have predicated their refusal to consider preferential credit treatment as a form of promotional service on the tenuous connection between credit arrangements and resale promotion.

In addition to direct promotional aids and credit services, a seller might attempt to engage in a unilateral advertising program in which he makes mention of available outlets for his products. Or he might be tempted to use an advertising campaign of one of his customers to promote those parts of his customer's products that he supplied. This latter alternative was precisely what occurred in the landmark *Corn Products* case. A manufacturer of dextrose, a sweetener used in the production of candy, secretly arranged with one of its customers, the Curtiss Candy Company, to conduct an advertising campaign for Curtiss' candy that would include mention of the fact that the candies were "rich in dextrose." Overcoming other interpretive difficulties, the FTC found such an arrangement, when subsidized by the seller, to be a promotional service or facility within the meaning of 2(e). The commission has similarly attacked billboard advertising by a seller that featured the names of selected retail customers.

Tripartite Arrangements and the Intended Benefit Theory

The requirement of a cooperative promotional arrangement has enabled the commission to reach advertising schemes that employ a third person to conduct the service or facility for the benefit of the customer. The *Chain Lightning* cases established this theory of finding a cooperative promotional agreement where it can be shown that the customer is a sort of third-party beneficiary of the sellers' promotional activities. In those cases, certain broadcast networks negotiated with retail grocery chains to provide local "spot" air time in return for the stores' consent to conduct in-store promotions of products designated by the broadcast networks. The networks then negotiated with the suppliers of those grocery chains for national broadcast time using the arrangement with the grocers for in-store promotion as an incentive to undertake the national broadcast advertising. The Federal Trade Commission regarded the two agreements as one and asserted that the suppliers had negotiated a promotional contract that rewarded selected retail customers with local spot broadcast time in exchange for promotion of the suppliers' products.

The ingredient of intended promotional benefit has been described by at least one United States Circuit Court of Appeals as a prerequisite to finding a cooperative promotional arrangement. In the *NuArc* case, the United States Court of Appeals for the Seventh Circuit declared that, "there must be a showing that some benefit accrued to, or was intended to accrue to the customer." This would seem fully to comport with the commission's own view with regard to payments under 2(d). In the *Yakima* case, the commission held that payments made without reference to any particular promotional scheme were not within the ambit of 2(d) because "payments made for other types of consideration or for which no tangible consideration was expected would not violate Section 2(d)." The doctrine would seem to have only limited application to Section 2(e) because the direct provision of a promotional service or facility is not nearly as ambiguous as the payment of money for such services or facilities. Nevertheless, in those situations, such as the indirect service arrangement of the *Chain Lightning* cases, where intent can become a prime factor, *Yakima* and *NuArc* will operate to require a showing that the activity was intended to have a beneficial promotional effect.

"In Connection with"

Once it is found that the activity under investigation is a promotional arrangement, it must then be shown that it was given in connection with a sale of the commodity intended for resale. In addition to the exceptions of refusals to deal and sales on consignment already discussed, there are other situations involving promotional allowances or services that will prevent the arrangement from being considered in connection with a sale. Chief among these are (1) refusals to furnish one item in a product line and (2) unilateral sales promotions by the seller.

Refusals to Furnish One Product in a Sales Line. Retailers recognize that it is more attractive to the consumer to carry a complete line of a manufacturer's products, especially where a popular brand name is involved. For this reason, there have been a number of complaints that manufacturers who provide their entire line to only a limited number of competing customers are rendering a promotional service to those customers. Relying essentially on the philosophy of the *Colgate* doctrine, the courts have fully protected a seller's right to customer selection, even down to individual items in his product line, in spite of the commission's attempts to rule to the contrary. In the *Chicago Seating* case, the United States Court of Appeals for the Seventh Circuit went so far as to allow a manufacturer to deny sale of a specially designed product, which was a highly attractive commodity, to one of its competing customers.

Unilateral Sales Promotions. A seller is completely free to conduct promotions of his product on either a local or national scale through whichever media he desires. Such advertising campaigns are an everyday fact for nationwide industries and were never intended to be proscribed by 2(e). As the House Judiciary Committee observed: "There is nothing in this section or elsewhere in the bill to limit or restrict the widespread custom of manufacturers and others selling sources of supply to engage and pay for exhibit space at trade association exhibitions, or for advertising space in trade-association publications, nor to limit the freedom of newspaper or periodical advertising generally, so long as not employed in ways calculated to defeat the purposes of this bill." The purposes of the bill will be defeated, however, when the supplier includes references to selected customers in his advertising campaign. As was demonstrated in the *Corn Products* case, association of the customer's product in the seller's otherwise unilateral advertising campaign falls within 2(e) even though the reference is as remote as the phrase "rich in dextrose."

Demonstration of "Connection." In addition to not being a refusal to deal or a unilateral sales promotion, the arrangement must evidence an association or a course of business with the customer in order for liability to attach. If the promotional arrangement does not have any connection with the sales transactions conducted with the customer it will not be regulated by 2(d) or 2(e). The most obvious example is an allowance or service provided with the original sale to the customer as an inducement for that sale, as when a manufacturer provides an initial free delivery to induce a store to begin carrying his product. Such arrangements are more properly measured against the standards of 2(a).

Not all connections are so readily dismissed as the original sale situation. Ordinarily, the courts will examine the time sequence of the sales and the promotional schemes to determine whether the promotions relate in time to any particular sales to the customer. This was the approach of the United States Seventh Circuit Court of Appeals in the *A & P* case, where it rejected a finding of connection with regard to the 2(e) count by observing that the ads were "not concurrent with the beginning, or with the ending, of A & P stores' handling of each supplier's products on its shelves." Not all courts, however, have required such chronological perfection. The *Corn Products* case condemned a promotional scheme that was not contemporaneous with any particular sales between the parties but rather was arranged quite independently. This issue is far from settled, although the later cases appear to consider separately negotiated and bargained for promotions as not being in connection with a particular sale where the defendant can demonstrate a lack of concurrence with any sales.

Another dimension of the in connection with requirement relates to the functional connection between the alleged promotional arrangement and the sale for customer resale. If the alleged arrangement is one not likely to promote such resale, it will not be considered as having a connection with a sale for that purpose. This approach stems largely from the *Skinner* case and appears to represent a situation that could be more properly dismissed as not being sufficiently *promotional*. The preferential credit arrangement in that case was held not to have been rendered with respect to any specific commodity, although it quite obviously related to every commodity on which credit was granted. The gist of the opinion of the United States Court of Appeals for the Fifth Circuit seemed to focus on connection with sales rather than connection with promotion for resale. Later cases have clarified the situation by recognizing that the condemned arrangement must be connected with the promotional resale of the product as well as connected with the sale of the product to the customer.

Customer Resale

The product that is the subject of the promotional favoritism must have been bought with the intention of resale. Thus, if an ultimate consumer purchases directly from the supplier and is given a promotional service not given to any customer of the supplier who purchases for resale, there is no violation of 2(d) or 2(e). The requirement of resale does not, however, mean that the retailer can be nothing more than a commercial conduit for the goods. The two sections contemplate that the commodities may be subject to processing or handling while held by the customer, and provide that alteration by the reselling customer will not avoid application of the act. This would be the case where the seller only supplies one ingredient in the customer's product. In the *Corn Products* case, the seller was a manufacturer of dextrose, a cornstarch condiment, which the customer used as a sweetener in the production of candy. The Supreme Court noted that, "the evils of the discrimination would seem to be the same whether the processing results in little or much alteration of the commodity purchased and resold."

A second category within the scope of the "customer resale" requirement is a resale under private brand. The entire area of private brands in relation to promotional allowances and services has been unnecessarily confused by its association with the commission's refusal to consider a brand name as a distinction in the grade and quality of the goods. The sole issue to be determined here is whether the application of a private brand by the customer is a sufficiently complete alteration of the product originally supplied by the seller that the original product cannot be considered to have been sold for resale. Because a brand name in no way alters the physical characteristics of the commodity, but only its commercial attractiveness, it more closely resembles a promotional additive than a substantive alteration. The logic of arguing no alteration in the context of resale is far more palatable than the commission's stand that a brand name by the customer is considered to be a form of processing that will not exempt the transaction from the requirements of 2(d) and 2(e).

AVAILABILITY

To avoid the proscriptions of the act, all promotional allowances and services must be made available to all competing customers on proportionately equal terms. The concept of availability, when used in connection with promotional services, includes both the buyer's knowledge of the services and his ability to employ them to promote the seller's product, or to take advantage of them at all. A failure of either condition will make the promotional service unavailable to that customer.

Notification

The first essential of availability is that the customer knows of the existence of the promotional service allowance. The leading case in the area of notification is *Vanity Fair Paper Mills,* where the United States Court of Appeals for the Second Circuit held that a promotional allowance is not "available" where steps have been taken to conceal it from discovery by some competing customer. In that case, Vanity Fair used a standard contract in selling its household paper products that contained a "Cooperative Advertising Agreement" clause. Vanity Fair then advanced promotional allowances to one customer at rates in excess of the clause in the standard contract. Vanity Fair alleged that such rates were available to any other of its customers who so requested them. In rejecting Vanity's argument, the court noted that the requirement is that the allowance *actually be available* rather than *potentially be available* depending on the initiative of individual customers. The existence of the standard clause served to mislead customers to the extent that any alternate service or allowance not similarly contained in the standard contract was effectively concealed from the customers.

The *Vanity Fair* case further indicates that the burden of producing evidence of notification shifts to the seller once the government demonstrates that an allowance was paid to some customers and was not paid to other competing customers. This shift in the burden of proceeding is sufficient to sustain an inference of unavailability from the weakness of the seller's case in demonstrating notification. The effect of these rather stringent evidentiary burdens on the seller is to place a premium on documentary proof that notice was given to all competing customers. Even though it is questionable whether an individualized and formal offer must be made to each and every competing customer, the 1969 FTC Guides, after announcing a "good faith" standard, indicate that a seller is obligated to take some form of affirmative action to ensure that all of his competing customers are notified. After suggesting a number of possible means of notification, the Guides continue: "however, if a seller wants to be able to show later that he gave notice to a certain customer, he is in a better position to do so if it was given in writing." Exactly where this leaves a seller is unclear, but it appears that the only way to prevent a shifting of the burden of proceeding is to produce a written notification directed to the individual customer concerned. This appears perilously close to the individualized, formal offer that *Vanity Fair* rejected as a prerequisite.

The duty to notify customers is a continuing one and a seller is required to employ methods calculated to apprise later-acquired customers of all available promotional allowances and services at the earliest possible time. Where possible, the general offer should be renewed periodically to guarantee continued notice. Thus, the FTC has approved a notification to newsstand operators, a particularly fluid occupation, that would periodically be made in the form of a "slug" accompanying the packaged magazines as they arrived at the stands.

The obligation to notify is not subject to the individual interest of a particular customer, and a seller cannot neglect to notify certain customers simply because it is unlikely that they will be interested in the promotional scheme. The only exception to this rule would be in those cases where the seller is completely convinced that an offer of promotional assistance would be futile.

A recent Supreme Court decision has had an as yet uncharted effect on the commission's notification requirements. Thus, in the *Fred Meyer* case, the Court held that a seller who deals directly with both retailer and wholesaler and with wholesalers who in turn sell to competing retailers must afford *all* the retailers proportionately equal treatment. This would appear to require that the seller must now ensure that his promotional offer is transmitted through the wholesaler to the retailers handling his product. Because he can never be certain which retailers will buy from the wholesaler during a given period, direct offers to the retailers would seem highly impractical. The seller may well be required to segregate those commodities going to wholesalers and attach a promotional offer to each item or at least to the smallest bulk package ordinarily sold by the wholesaler. The 1969 FTC Guides adopted in response to *Fred Meyer* attempt to clarify the new obligations of sellers in this regard, by establishing a general rule that the substance of the notice must either cover all features or give essentials with some sources for details. As to the mechanics of notice, the new Guides accept publication of essentials plus sources in a trade journal as adequate notice where more direct methods fail.

Ability to Take Advantage of the Allowance

The programs offered by the seller must be of a type that can be used by all competing customers. If a supplier offers one service or facility based on a quantitative measure and the program has all the earmarks of being available to all competing customers in relation to their purchases, it may, nonetheless, prove unavailable to certain customers because they cannot possibly employ it to their advantage. A promotional allowance or service can be functionally unavailable in two ways: (1) the activity is of a type or on a scale that the customer cannot afford or use or (2) the minimum requirements to qualify for the program are beyond the particular customer. The best example of the first category is illustrated by the *State Wholesale Grocers* v. *Great Atlantic & Pacific Tea Co.* case, where the seller took ads in a magazine owned by the customer and sold only in the customer's retail outlets. Competing customers of A & P had no comparable exclusive publications, and, therefore, could not possibly have obtained advertising allowances from the seller. The United States Court of Appeals for the Seventh Circuit ruled that the payments for the ads were promotional allowances and were not available to competing customers of A & P who did not have the financial resources to operate similar publications. In the words of the court: ". . . the Act requires a frank recognition of the business limitations of each buyer. An offer to make a service available to one, the economic status of whose business renders him unable to accept the offer, is tantamount to no offer to him."

The exclusive promotional advantage need not be as extreme as in the *A & P* case. Whenever a seller tailors a promotional plan to suit the needs of its largest customers and, thereby, goes beyond the economic reach of smaller competing customers, the act is violated. In the *Elizabeth Arden* case, the seller provided a specialized plan of demonstrators for in-store promotion. These demonstrators were practically available only to the larger department stores that had sufficient volume to justify their presence. The court there held that the inability of the smaller customers to make any use of demonstrators made the plan unavailable to them no matter what degree of notification was achieved. A similar plan for in-store "stylists" was invalidated as unavailable to smaller competing customers in the *Exquisite Form Brassiere* case.

The area of minimum requirements has proved to be the most susceptible to abuse by sellers. Minimum requirements can be of two types: The seller can limit any promotional allowance to a certain quantity of advertising or a certain minimum value on the promotional scheme, for example, by paying an allowance only if newspaper ads exceed 100 lines. The seller can also restrict promotional services or facilities to customers that do a certain minimum volume of business with him. If either method should act to exclude a competing customer from ever having the opportunity to participate in the plan, then it is functionally unavailable to that customer. This should not be confused with the area of proportionately equal treatment, to be discussed later, where the concern is with the degree of comparative availability to competing customers. Here the concern is whether the minimum requirements are so restrictive as to completely exclude any possible participation by certain competing customers.

In *Exquisite Form Brassiere,* the seller agreed to reimburse 60 per cent of the cost of any newspaper advertising that exceeded 400 lines in length in a given ad. No payments were made for any smaller advertisements or in any other media. The Federal Trade Commission observed that several of the seller's customers were much too small to employ feasibly any newspaper advertising and others could not possibly afford the 400-line minimum. Such a plan, in the commission's view, was completely unavailable to both these classes of customers. This conclusion was entirely consistent with the attitude reflected in the famous *Soap* case of 1953. There, the commission established that the unavailability of a plan could only be justified by the existence of equally acceptable alternative plans. Where only one plan exists and it is functionally unavailable to some because of a minimum limit placed on compensable promotion, then the plan is not available within the meaning of the act.

While some sellers seek to ensure maximum return on their advertising dollar by placing minimum limits on reimbursible promotion, still others seek to ensure that their advertising dollar is giving preference to the greatest concentration of business. This is usually accomplished by making promotional allowances or services depend on some minimum volume of business with the customer. However, for purposes of a discussion of the availability concept, we are only concerned with those volume requirements that effectively preclude certain low-volume customers from ever participating in the program. The effect of disparate minimum volumes or progressive rates dependent on volumes will be discussed under the treatment of proportionate equality.

When some customers of a seller traditionally never purchase more than 100-lot quantities and the seller institutes a promotional program with participation requiring a 500-lot volume of business, the seller has managed to give a competitive advantage to his larger customers even though he fully informs all customers of the plan. The smaller buyers simply cannot meet the minimum-volume requirements. Thus, the plan is effectively unavailable to them even though no other limits are placed on the nature or amount of advertising to be done. Problems arise when the seller establishes a minimum in order to make the plan economically possible for him to conduct, and it is *possible* for all buyers to meet the volume requirements, although some have not done so in the past. Just when such a plan becomes inconvenient rather than unavailable is still not completely clear.

It is clear, however, that prohibitive volumes are forbidden. The 1969 FTC Guides describe the need for a plan that is "suitable for and usable by all competing customers . . ." and absolutely condemns any plan that might "eliminate some competing customers." Although the Guides are not completely clear on the question of what is suitable and usable *under reasonable terms*, the FTC has given some indication of its attitude on such plans, albeit in fact patterns that have tended to be somewhat extreme. As the commission observed in the *Atlantic Products* case:

> While the inclusion of a minimum-purchases requirement in an advertising allowance plan is not *per se* a violation of 2(d), where, as here, 85–90% of the seller's customers do not purchase in sufficient amounts

to qualify for the allowance and it is not demonstrated that a lower minimum, under which a great many more such customers would qualify, would be impractical or burdensome for the seller, the conclusion seems inescapable that the seller has not made his allowance available to competing customers. . . .

The most disturbing feature of the commission's reasoning is the apparent insertion of a quantitative standard. Under both the Guides and the leading case law, it should be sufficient if *one* customer is effectively precluded from participation by the requirements, and any remedy that includes less than all of the customers would still be illegal. The commission also seems to weigh the cost factor to the seller of complete coverage even though such a consideration is irrelevant to either 2(d) or 2(e). The best analysis of how the commission might determine the case in which the seller asserts that all customers can afford it despite past purchasing practices can be obtained from a series of recent decisions concerning availability of alternate plans, a subject subsequently treated at greater length.

In *Advisory Opinion Digest No. 94,* a seller offered an alternate plan to all those customers functionally unable to employ the primary promotional scheme. One customer, capable of using the primary plan, nonetheless, desired to employ the alternate for purely private reasons. The commission ruled that the seller could refuse to make the alternate plan available to that customer because he *could have used* the primary plan.

In *United Banana Co.* v. *United Fruit Co.,* the complainant charged discrimination in the defendant's free loading of railroad cars while charging a wharfage fee for truck loading. The United States Second Circuit Court of Appeals denied recovery on the theory that the complainant's selection of trucking was based on its own choice of speed and economy rather than any lack of opportunity or ability to employ rail shipment.

Both of these decisions indicate that the essential ingredient is the functional utility of the plan to a customer and not its attractiveness. Thus, it would seem that if a seller can demonstrate that a customer is economically capable of profitably meeting the minimum requirement he is safe, even though the customer might prefer to purchase in a different quantity. The *opportunity* to participate would then be universal and participation would be the subjective decision of the individual purchaser. Admittedly, this does not solve the problem of determining when the plan is merely unattractive and when it is unavailable, but it does indicate that the commission has demonstrated a new willingness to give the factor of convenience to the customer limited weight in assessing the availability of a plan to all customers.

In spite of these recent indications, the fundamental principles of minimum purchase requirements remain unchanged. Any plan that would preclude participation to a customer based on that customer's business volume in the previous year is invalid. Similarly, any plan that would seasonally eliminate certain customers by requiring a minimum seasonal purchase is invalid, and the commission has refused to acknowledge any distinction between in-season and off-season buyers that would justify making a promotional plan available only to one group.

COMPETING CUSTOMERS

The act has been interpreted as providing that allowances and services must be made proportionately available to *all competing customers.* As originally passed, only Section 2(d) contained a specific requirement of competing customers. However, the Supreme Court, in the *Simplicity Patterns* case, inferred such a requirement in 2(e) from an integrated reading of the two sections. The requirement of competing customers presents two points of inquiry: (1) what is a customer for purposes of 2(d) and 2(e), and (2) when are customers in competition?

What Is a Customer?

The old-1960 Guides were extremely broad and, consequently, extremely vague in their definition of customer: "A 'customer' is someone who buys directly from the seller or his agent or broker." This appeared to be a most precise standard, but the Guides continued to state that "sometimes someone who buys from the customer may have such a relationship with the seller that the law also makes him a customer of the seller." This second pronouncement is a capsule statement of the commission's indirect purchaser doctrine, and its easy description belies the confusion that has surrounded this area. The problem of indirect purchasers developed over sellers who conducted sales both to wholesalers and directly to retailers and provided promotional allowances or services to only one of the two groups. Retail customers of the wholesalers objected to allowances or services given to the direct-purchase retailers, claiming that they should qualify as customers of the seller within the meaning of the act. The FTC's first resolution of this problem was to construe the wholesaler as a conduit purchaser for the retailer and make the necessary connection between retailer and seller through application of agency principles, which would compel the seller to pass the competitive benefits on to purchasing retailers. This entire concept was completely overhauled in the recent Supreme Court decision in *Fred Meyer,* which created an entirely new category of customer under 2(d) and 2(e). The Court held that retail customers of a wholesaler were also customers of the seller when they competed with direct customers of the seller.

The effect of the decision has been to eliminate the indirect-purchaser doctrine and replace it with a new category of competing customer directly entitled to receive proportionately equal promotional assistance. To reflect the impact of *Fred Meyer,* the FTC has adopted new guides to expand the definition of customer to include "any buyer of the seller's product for resale who purchases from or through a wholesaler or other intermediate reseller." However, this expanded definition still exempts sporadic purchasers of the seller's product where the seller has no notice that such sellers are selling his product.

What Is a Competing Customer?

The act limits the necessity of proportionately equal treatment to those customers of the seller who are actually in competition with one another. In order to compete, two customers must be both (1) geographically located within the same market area and (2) functionally operating at the same competitive level. These dual requirements permit a seller to narrow the intended scope of his promotional program to geographic regions or certain sales levels.

The 1969 Guides, while clearly recognizing that distance is capable of eliminating competition between customers, are unclear as to the exact spatial gap necessary to insulate a seller's offer to just one region. Admittedly, such a determination rests largely on the size of the customers and the nature of the product involved, but the examples cited in the Guides all carry the caveat of ensuring protection for competing customers on the periphery of the selected region. This, of course, is the essence of many problems developing in this area. Just when a customer is no longer considered to be on the periphery of a market area can be an extremely difficult determination in the context of the East Coast industrial region. Clearly, retail stores in New England do not compete with those in New Jersey or Maryland. Just as clearly stores in Manhattan probably do compete with stores in Brooklyn or the Bronx. But whether an urban retail store competes with a suburban shopping center still requires careful individual consideration with little help from the Guides or the prior case law. This area has provided an excellent application of the commission's advisory opinion practice by affording sellers the opportunity to have their contemplated market areas approved by the commission. In certain recent opinions, the commission has indicated a willingness to accept a "reasonable trading area, even though limited" provided there was a competitive basis for its boundaries. The commission also indicated that it would not accept a noncompetitive basis for such a trading area, such as a geographic or political subdivision.

The definition of competing customer also contains certain implicit functional limitations. The customers must compete on the same level. As a general rule, customers at different levels of the distribution system do not compete with one another. Thus, a seller could encourage wholesale purchasing by offering allowances or services to wholesale customers without having to make similar offers at the retail level. It soon became apparent, however, that when a seller had both wholesale and retail customers, promotional assistance to one of them might give competitive advantage at the retail level. If the assistance was given to the wholesaler it could be passed on to the retail customers and then direct-purchase retail customers would be disadvantaged. If the aid went to the direct-purchasers, then the damage occurred to the retail customers of the wholesalers. In response to this problem, the commission and the courts developed the indirect-purchaser doctrine mentioned here. Under an involved formula requiring tracing of the seller's product through the wholesaler to the shelves of the retailer and demonstrating prior direct dealings between the seller and the retailer, a wholesaler could be considered a conduit for indirect purchases by the retailer. This would then require the seller to afford proportionately the same promotional assistance both to the wholesaler and the direct-purchase retailers, relying on a passing-on of the benefits by the wholesaler to balance the competitive effect at the retail level. The doctrine was also employed to require direct assistance to retail customers of wholesalers where the seller could be shown to have effectively supplanted his distributor in dealing with the retail customer. This latter application generally required seller control over the distributor's resale arrangements with the retail customers.

This entire doctrine, with all its variations, may well have been eliminated by the recent Supreme Court decision in *Fred Meyer*. The Court ruled that whenever the customers of a wholesale distributor compete with the seller's direct-purchase retailers, such customers will be considered to be competing customers of the seller. There is no longer any need to show the seller's influence in the distributor's sales or to trace the product through the wholesaler to the retailers' shelves. In the words of Justice Fortas' concurrence, the decision "can best be squared with the language of Section 2(d) by the device of regarding the wholesaler and his retail customer as a unit for purposes of that section." Although purporting not to question the validity of the indirect-purchaser doctrine, the Court provided an alternative approach that drastically limits the viability of that doctrine, at least in instances involving allowances or services to direct-purchase retailers. It would appear, however, that the doctrine will still be operative where the allowances are given to the wholesalers but not to the retailers who purchase directly. In that situation it might still be necessary to demonstrate that the competitive benefit of the allowance is being passed on to the wholesaler's customers at the competitive retail level. This area is still very much uncertain, but the present attitude of the commission, as reflected in the Guides, is that *Fred Meyer* is the controlling law for all situations involving multidistributional sellers.

Attempts to avoid a finding of competing customers have also focused on classification of customers by the seller with promotional benefits only going to one class. In the *Liggett & Meyers* case, a tobacco company attempted to distinguish between vending machine customers and wholesalers in the granting of promotional allowances. The commission held that the two customers were not seeking sales at the same customer level, and, therefore, the classification was valid. The tobacco company had also distinguished between vending machine operators and over-the-counter retail sales. However, the commission observed that the two were competing for the same consumer dollar and the classification was insufficient to justify offering promotional allowances only to the retailers. This case is a prime example of the commission's approach to customer classification. The validity of the class is determined by an examination of the next customer level—if it is identical to another class' customer level, then the two classes must be given equal treatment. In *Liggett,* both the retailer and the vending machines sold to smokers and competed for that purchasing dollar, whereas the wholesaler sold to another selling level rather than to an ultimate consumer level and was, therefore, in a different functional category.

A similar attempt to argue different classes of customers was rejected by the Supreme Court in its *Simplicity Patterns* opinion. There, the manufacturer tried to argue that certain of its customers favored with promotional services and facilities carried its product for large-volume profit sales, whereas the other customers not so favored merely carried the product as a consumer convenience and did not seek competitively to market the product for profit. The Court refused to examine the competitive intent of the parties and looked only to the physical proximity of the retail outlets and the consumer level competition in finding the two classes to be competing customers. The Court reaffirmed the precept that the only test for valid classification of customers is whether they seek to sell directly to the same buying public.

In a most unusual application of classification, the defendant in the *Dantzler* v. *Dictograph Products* case, sought to distinguish between his new and old distributors during the period when both were handling his products and to give promotional services only to the new distributors. The United States Court of Appeals for the Fourth Circuit held that the mere fact that the seller was in the process of switching his distribution outlets did not negate the customer status of his old distributor and justify giving preference only to the new one. Although the decision employs impeccable logic, it does raise some practical difficulties for the supplier attempting to build up a market for his new distributor or seeking to avoid customer confusion during the switch-over period.

The most recent pronouncement on customer classification was that of the United States Court of Appeals for the Ninth Circuit in *Clairol, Inc.* v. *FTC.* Clairol sought to distinguish between retail customers and beauty salon customers by reasoning that the former purchased for resale while the latter were actually consumers. Rejecting this distinction, the count concluded that both types of customers resold the product to the ultimate consumer, the only distinction being the location at which consumption occurred. Thus, the customers competed for consumer patronage and an allowance to only one class was discriminatory.

PROPORTIONATELY EQUAL TREATMENT

Our discussion, thus far, has examined those situations in which a customer is denied *any* promotional allowance or services because of the seller's promotional plan. But the act does not simply provide that *some* promotional assistance be given; rather it requires that *proportionately equal treatment* be given to all competing customers. This constitutes an additional antidiscrimination factor in the operation of Section 2(d) and (e). Proportionate equality requires not only that the amount of promotional allowances or services have some fair relationship to the customers' volume of business, but also that alternate modes of participation be afforded where a promotional scheme would otherwise be unavailable to certain competing customers.

The commission has never required a strict formula to determine the allocation of promotional benefits among competing customers and has admitted that "no standard could be laid down which would insure exact proportionality with the mathematical accuracy of a slide rule." Instead it has sought to give a "relatively broad scope to the standard of proportional equality." Nonetheless, the 1969 Guides observe that it "can best be done by basing the payments made or the services furnished on the dollar volume or on the quantity of goods purchased during a specified period." This commission preference for a formula based on business volume constitutes one of the clearest and most specific pronouncements in the Guides, and interpretation of the standard has, therefore, been rather clear-cut.

Equally clear-cut are the formulas that are unacceptable to the commission. Participation based on rates graduated with the volume of business is unacceptable as favoring large-volume buyers. Disparate rates resulting from individual negotiation with competing customers are equally unacceptable to the commission.

The issue is not quite as well defined when the seller attempts to make a qualitative distinction between various types of promotional activity and reflects that distinction in the rates offered for each. A typical case would involve a fixed percentage of business volume as a promotional allowance for newspaper advertising and a smaller rate for in-store advertising. If both forms of advertising are functionally available to all competing customers, then the seller should be free to select the media of his preference. This was exactly the conclusion of the commission in the *Soap* cases in which the competitive advantage of newspaper advertising over in-store display was acknowledged as justifying a disparity in the rates assigned to the two media. The relative liberality of the FTC on this question of advertising preference has led one prominent commentator to observe that: "Any properly measurable basis is acceptable if it is not artificially tailored into proportionally equal terms by fitting it into some imaginary basis or standard that never, in fact, existed."

If the seller's plan contemplates a promotional allowance for *any* form of advertising, it will suffice to formulate an acceptable quantitative standard on which to base participation. If, instead, he wishes to provide services or facilities directly or wishes to reimburse only selected forms of promotional activity, he must take steps to determine that the selected forms of promotional activity are available to all the competing customers. If they are unavailable to some customers, the seller is obliged to provide alternate forms of participation for those customers unable to employ the original plan. The *Soap* cases recognized that alternate plans may be necessary for compliance with proportionate equality and indicated a wide range of potential alternatives. The *Lever Brothers* decision authorized alternatives that ranged from newspaper ads to handbills and from radio spots to in-store displays. Also, the seller may offer allowances or services to cater to the varying needs of his customers.

The Guides recite that the customer must be free to select from among the alternate plans the one best suited to his needs. This has not, however, been the consistent interpretation of either the commission or the courts. In *Simplicity Patterns,* the Supreme Court noted with favor a "tailoring of services and facilities to meet the different needs of two classes of customers" and indicated its belief that this might constitute proportionalely equal terms. More recently, the commission has acknowledged a seller's right to deny an alternate plan to a customer who was functionally capable of profitably employing the basic plan. Both of these decisions raise some doubt as to the customer's ability to choose among alternate plans when the seller clearly prefers one and is offering the alternate only to assure the requisite proportionality.

As was the case with the notification requirement, the burden of producing evidence to demonstrate proportionally equal treatment shifts to the seller after it is shown that one customer has suffered discrimination in promotional allowances or services. This was the rule set down in the *Vanity Fair Paper Mills* case.

Furthermore, a showing that one customer has not received a proportionate allowance or service will create an inference of discriminatory treatment sufficient to support a verdict if not rebutted by adequate evidence of the seller. The basis for this evidentiary rule is that the provision permitting proportionately equal treatment is an exception to the otherwise general prohibitions of Sections 2(d) and 2(e), and as an exception the burden of demonstrating it will rest on the party seeking its protection.

CHECKING CUSTOMERS' USE OF PAYMENTS

When the seller gives proportionately equal promotional allowances to competing customers, his obligations under the act are not at an end. The seller has the additional duty of checking to ensure that the payments advanced for promotional activities were actually used by the customer for that purpose, and that the rate charged the seller was not excessive for the promotional activity conducted. This duty is intended to eliminate two of the major evils sought to be regulated by Sections 2(d) and 2(e)—namely, promotional allowances where no services are rendered and overpriced promotional allowances. The commission acknowledged this seller's duty in the *General Foods* ruling, where it stated that "there must be a discernable relationship between the amounts paid and the cost or reasonable value of the services rendered." Because the act itself involves an absolute prohibition, those seeking to come within one of the exceptions would naturally have the obligation of seeing that their conduct strictly conforms with the statutory requirements. The 1969 Guides eliminate any lingering doubt that this was an affirmative duty on the seller by requiring that, "the seller should take reasonable precautions to see that services he is paying for are furnished and also that he is not overpaying for them."

The recent *Fred Meyer* decision has created additional problems for a seller seeking to fulfill this obligation. By requiring that the seller give promotional assistance on a proportionately equal basis to competing retailers who purchase from his wholesale customers, the decision has also necessarily extended the duty to check to the same retail level. Obviously, the seller will have to make some arrangements with its wholesale customers to obtain lists of the retail purchasers of its products. Although it is very easy to say, the functioning of such an arrangement might create serious problems of vertical integration that could overstep other antitrust laws. The rationale of *Automatic Canteen* and *Parke, Davis* concerning buyer-seller cooperation and information-sharing may well put the seller in an extremely sensitive position. There is also the additional problem of a wholesaler's unwillingness to surrender accurate, current customer information to a seller who could easily use the information to vertically integrate, and, thereby, eliminate that wholesaler. Furthermore, because the duty to check is a continuing one, the information-sharing would have to be constantly updated, an operation that "would almost inevitably require a degree of cooperation between buyer and seller, as against other buyers, that may offend other antitrust policies. . . ." The commission has thus far given no indication as to the exact degree of seller-wholesaler cooperation that will fulfill the obligation to check while avoiding any embroilment in other antitrust violations.

DEFENSES

Cost Justification

The interpretation of Sections 2(d) and 2(e) as per se statutes has ruled out any application of a cost justification defense to a charge of a discriminatory promotional allowance or service. Both the courts and the commission have consistently refused to read this 2(a) defense into either of the promotional sections. This does not mean, however, that cost justification is never a consideration in examining an allegedly discriminatory promotional allowance or service. Often the issue of cost will play an important role in the conclusions of law on some other element of a 2(d) or 2(e) offense. Insertion of the cost factor has produced some rather ingenious interpretations of what constitutes a promotional allowance or service. In *American Can Co.* v. *Russellville Canning,* a supplier delivered to a neighboring customer via a conveyor belt between their respective plants. The customer received a reduced delivery rate as a result of this rather unique method of delivery. Competing customers alleged that this constituted either a delivery service or the provision of a facility for promotional advantage. In rejecting these allegations, the United States Court of Appeals for the Eighth Circuit noted that the mode of delivery was not a service or facility within the meaning of the act, and the allowance given on a per-thousand basis would constitute a price discrimination if anything. Although it is not particularly unusual for a court to reject such a borderline case as not being a service or facility, its reference to 2(a) clearly indicates that a cost justification defense would be available there, and that it was an important consideration in the court's finding of no 2(d) cause of action. The impact of the cost justification factor is further increased by the definition of warehouse facilities as a promotional facility in the 1960 Guides and its subsequent deletion from the 1969 Guides in response to *Fred Meyer.* It is difficult to conceptualize a promotional advantage gained by warehouse facilities that would not be similarly provided by a rapid and comparably inexpensive delivery service over a conveyor belt. The case is, thus, far from a unique example of consideration of cost factors in construing other elements of a 2(d) or 2(e) offense. Naturally, none of these secondary considerations of cost justification has compromised the unavailability of it as a formal defense—the factor of cost may only be considered as a relative factor in assessing the other elements of a cause of action under one of the promotional sections.

Lack of Competitive Effect

The Supreme Court's decision in *Simplicity Pattern* reflected a legislative determination that the activities sought to be controlled by Sections 2(d) and 2(e) were such pernicious evils that there would be no inquiry into competitive impact regardless of the effect in a particular case. As a result, the sections are considered as an absolute ban on the activities proscribed. Lke the cost justification defense, however, elimination as an independent defense does not preclude its consideration in conjunction with other elements of a 2(d) or 2(e) violation. Thus, at least one court has weighed competitive injury in determining whether a promotional plan was available to a competing customer. In the recent *United Banana* case, the complainant charged discriminatory promotional services in the defendant's practice of loading rail cars for free while charging a wharfage fee for loading trucks. The court concluded that the complainant had voluntarily selected truck loading for reasons of economy and speed, and to illustrate the voluntariness of the complainant's selection, the court conducted an examination of the injury suffered by the complainant. In ultimately finding no violation, the court observed that "there was no showing of competitive effect." The case indicates that courts do not disregard the competitive factor in their over-all examination of a charge of discriminatory promotional allowances or services.

Good Faith Meeting Competition

This defense is recognized as available under 2(d) and 2(e). The defense was originally thought to be limited to 2(e) because that was the only promotional section referred to by 2(b). This interpretation was reversed in the *Exquisite Form Brassiere* case, when the United States Court of Appeals for the District of Columbia Circuit read the meeting competition defense into 2(d) by a parallel reading of the two sections.

The result in *Exquisite Form Brassiere* did not greatly increase the commission's willingness to accept such a defense. The stringent requirements surrounding the availability of the defense in a 2(a) action have been applied, when possible, to use of the defense in the framework of promotional allowances or services. Thus, the commission has required that the seller demonstrate the existence of a specific competitive practice rather than any general industry practice. A failure to prove a particular competitive situation, or the existence of other motives for the promotional scheme, will cause the defense to fail. The limitation on the availability of the defense can best be seen in an examination of the very case that extended its application: In *Exquisite Form Brassiere,* the defendant had provided stylists to certain customers to aid in the sale of Exquisite's products. These stylists were not made available on a proportionately equal basis, and Exquisite contended that this was the result of its efforts to meet competition and that the stylists were only assigned to areas where competitors had instituted similar plans. When the Court of Appeals ruled that the defense was available to Exquisite and remanded the case, the commission, on remand, heard and rejected Exquisite's arguments for meeting competition, observing that, "the meeting competition defense does not sanction the fortuitous meeting of competition which occurs when the manufacturer discriminates and then in hindsight points to the previously unknown fact that another was granting similar allowances at the same time." The commission then concluded that, "there is every indication that respondent's business by meeting competitive efforts was instead an aggressive, competitive measure designed to attract additional business and enhance respondent's position in the market."

The *Exquisite Form Brassiere* decision was followed by a flurry of commission decisions that quickly limited the scope of the meeting competition defense. The necessity of prior knowledge, and the reasonable belief that the payments were legal, quickly became prerequisites to a showing of good faith.

The present state of the defense would seem to closely parallel its application to 2(a). There must be (1) prior knowledge of a competitive promotional situation, (2) which the seller attempts to meet, rather than beat, in an effort to preserve his existing market position, (3) in good faith and without any reason to believe that the promotional activities he is competitively meeting are in themselves illegal.

As a result of the fact that promotional activities are naturally aggressive rather than responsive programs, the meeting competition defense is less likely to receive wide success and far more likely to stumble on the requirement that it be solely in response to existing competitive promotional schemes.

Finally, the commission's Guides are emphatic in requiring that any promotional scheme desiring to avoid attack must be conducted pursuant to a plan. Basically, the plan format provided by the Guides is little more than a recitation of the basic prerequisites to conforming with proportionate equality. The one particular benefit of a plan, especially a plan in writing, is its ability to establish the motives of the seller should it later be necessary to assert a meeting competition defense.

12

Buyer Inducement or Receipt of Discriminations

Until now, our discussion has involved those statutory prohibitions aimed at preventing sellers from engaging in discriminatory pricing. We will now direct our attention to those proscriptions aimed at regulating a buyer's involvement in such discriminatory practices. Because the original motivation for the Robinson-Patman Act was the excesses of the chain stores in their buying practices, it is not unnatural that the act should contain a specific provision relating to buyer activity. What is unusual is that the provision should have been little more than a legislative afterthought, whose vagueness has seriously limited its effective application to many types of buyer misconduct with regard to discriminatory pricing. This has led to the use of other statutory powers to implement the control of buyer inducement of price discriminations. In addition to Section 2(f), therefore, we will also consider the regulation of buyer activities under the provisions of Section 2(c) of the Robinson-Patman Act and Section 5 of the Federal Trade Commission Act. Each of these three methods of regulation parallels one or more of the controls on seller discrimination, and, therefore, will be considered in the same order as the discussion of sellers.

SECTION 2(F) AND PRICE DISCOUNTS

The original Patman proposal contemplated only seller regulation. The buyer regulation contained in Section 2(f) was only added at the late stages of congressional consideration of the measure. In its initial form it was merely an amendment to Section 2(a), which would make the restrictions of that section equally applicable to buyers. For this reason the amendment only referred to discriminations in price. It was anticipated that similar amendments would be made to the other sections of the bill to make each of them applicable to buyers as well. Instead, the original amendment was incorporated in a separate section with the intention of making a blanket application of all the act's provisions to buyers. By apparent oversight, the final form of the section retained the original language of the amendment to Section 2(a), and thereby, only specified discriminations in price. Even though it was the professed intention of Congress to have buyers liable for inducing any seller violation of the act, the "price" language of Section 2(f) raised considerable doubts about that section's applicability to discriminatory promotional allowances and services. Although the early cases under Section 2(f) succeeded in attacking such promotional arrangements, subsequent judicial restrictions placed on 2(f) caused the FTC to limit its use of 2(f) to those situations where a buyer knowingly induces a violation of Section 2(a). As a practical matter, therefore, Section 2(f) prohibits a buyer from knowingly inducing or receiving a price reduction that would cause a seller to violate the provisions of Section 2(a).

In order to prove a violation of Section 2(f), it is necessary to first establish all the elements of a 2(a) violation, which are (1) two or more consummated sales, (2) one of which crosses a state line, (3) reasonably close in point of time, (4) of commodities, (5) of like grade and quality, (6) with a difference in price, (7) by the same seller, (8) to two or more different purchasers, (9) for use, consumption, or resale within the United States or any territory thereof, (10) that may result in competitive injury. It is then necessary to show that (11) the buyer deals in interstate commerce, (12) the buyer's purchase was in interstate commerce, and (13) that the inducing buyer knew or should have known that the price would cause the seller to violate the provisions of Section 2(a). The law governing the first ten elements is identical to that already discussed in the chapters on Section 2(a).

Commerce Requirement of Section 2(f)

The commerce requirement of Section 2(f), on its face, appears measurably more difficult than that for Section 2(a). The unique wording of 2(f) creates two entirely independent criteria for a finding of interstate commerce, both of which must be met before the buyer's conduct is covered by the section. Much of the law governing this commerce standard is highly speculative because there has been scant litigation of the commerce requirements of Section 2(f). In all likelihood, however, it can be anticipated that courts will take the same broad approach to finding commerce under 2(f) that they have already taken with regard to the other sections of the Robinson-Patman Act.

The first requirement is that the buyer himself must be engaged in commerce at the time he induces or receives the differential. A harsh literal reading of this language would appear to exclude consideration of the seller's involvement in commerce in determining the status of the buyer. However, at least one case has indicated that such will not be the reading of this provision. In *Mid-South Distributors* v. *FTC,* the United States Court of Appeals for the Fifth Circuit dismissed a buyer's contention that it was the character of his resale business rather than his relationship with the seller that should determine the commerce status of the buyer. The court reasoned that the discrimination occurred on the sale to the buyer and that sale must be examined for its interstate characteristics. Because 2(a) requires that at least one of the sales must cross a state line, it was not difficult for the court to find the buyer within the flow of interstate commerce already engaged in by the seller.

The second requirement of 2(f) is that the discriminatory price be obtained "in the course of such commerce." Although this would seem to exempt the buyer whose purchase does not cross a state line, it seems highly unlikely that courts will be willing to apply the test of interstate commerce in such a limited and arbitrary fashion. Admittedly, the vast majority of cases will moot this issue by having both of the sales cross state lines. But in those cases where one of the sales is truly local in nature, it, nonetheless, seems probable that a court will still find the commerce requirement satisfied. This conclusion stems largely from the court's traditional concern with the discrimination rather than the individual sale in testing for commerce. A local sale will still engender an interstate discrimination where the out of state sale is at a higher price. Well-established doctrines of "effect on commerce" are certainly broad enough to encompass such a situation and prevent a buyer from insulating his receipt of discriminatory prices solely on the grounds that he is the local half of the discrimination.

Knowing Inducement or Receipt

The Federal Trade Commission's original approach to prosecutions under 2(f) followed the theory that the commission's burden of proof consisted of showing a violation of Section 2(a) by the seller and a receipt of a price differential by the buyer pursuant to the 2(a) violation. Under this very light burden, the FTC was quite successful in its early prosecutions of receipt of both price and promotional discriminations. All this quickly changed when the commission's approach was first tested before the Supreme Court in *Automatic Canteen Co.* v. *FTC.*

The Automatic Canteen Company was a vending machine concessionaire that dominated the market in vending machine sales of candy products. In its investigation of the candy industry, the FTC discovered that Automatic Canteen had solicited and received discounts from candy manufacturers that occasionally amounted to one third of the price. Having successfully prosecuted the sellers for their part, in the *Corn Products* case, the commission then instituted a suit under Section 2(f) against the buyer. Adhering to its traditional position, the commission alleged only the seller violation of 2(a) and Automatic Canteen's solicitation and receipt of the discriminatory price. The commission further sought to limit the buyer's defenses to a showing that the initial sale was not discriminatory.

In reversing the FTC's position, the Supreme Court conducted an exhaustive reappraisal of the administrative application of Section 2(f). Writing for the majority, Justice Frankfurter expounded two new rules to govern future suits under Section 2(f).

The Court's first concern was with the existing FTC interpretation of "knowing inducement and receipt" as an element of 2(f). By emphasizing receipt rather than culpability, the commission was placing an onerous burden on the buyer who had bargained for his price in good faith and without knowledge of the prices given to others. The Court described 2(f) as requiring a demonstration of guilty knowledge in the buyer of the discriminatory nature of the price he was soliciting and receiving. In the words of the Court, "the buyer whom Congress in the main sought to reach was the one who, knowing full well that there was little likelihood of a defense for the seller, nevertheless proceeded to exert pressure for lower prices." Justice Frankfurter did not consider it an "undue administrative burden" to require the commission to demonstrate that the buyer "is not an unsuspecting recipient of prohibited discriminations."

The assignment of this burden to the commission raised certain problems of proof that the Court was quick to recognize. An adequate demonstration of the buyer's guilty knowledge can rarely be made through direct evidence. Even assertions by the seller that he informed the buyer would have to be carefully scrutinized for indications of a "puffing" of bargaining position rather than a sincere communication of knowledge of discrimination. Consequently, the commission would ordinarily be in the position of having to establish the requisite *scienter* by inference—that is, by demonstration of a sufficiently suspicious set of circumstances that the buyer should have known that the price he was inducing violated the act. The Court did not elaborate on just what quantum of proof would satisfy this inference or what facts were pertinent to such a consideration, choosing instead to leave this to future judicial development.

The knowledge requirement, itself, involved two aspects. As formulated by the Court, the discrimination would have to be significant enough to cause competitive injury and also apparently big enough to create knowledge in the buyer that it was capable of creating competitive injury. In addition, the very character of the transaction must be such that the buyer knew or should have known of its illegality. Thus, the knowledge to be proved by the commission was not only that the buyer knew he was getting a discriminatory price, but also that the differential in his price was substantial enough to create competitive injury. Considered in this fashion, there could arguably be a dual showing of competitive injury necessitated by Section 2(f). The first would be the competitive injury needed to sustain the charge of violation of 2(a), and the second would be the demonstration of competitive injury through the discount to the individual buyer. This might conceivably be an issue where the seller grants a discount to a group of buyers large enough to create competitive injury, but the discount that filters to the individual members approaches *de minimis*. In such a case, the group might have to be collectively attacked in order to sustain an inference that they had knowledge that their discount was creating competitive injury.

The second element considered by the Court was the availability to the buyer of the seller's defenses under Section 2(b). Should the buyer be able to defend on the basis of cost justification or meeting competition, and if so, should the FTC have to establish that the buyer also knew that none of these defenses were available to the seller? In affirmatively answering both of these questions, the Court concluded "that a buyer is not liable under § 2(f) if the lower prices he induces are either within one of the seller's defenses such as cost justification or not known by him not to be within one of those defenses." This added another dimension to the commission's burden of proof by necessitating a showing of sufficient information on the part of the buyer to negate his believing that the discounts he received were cost justified or the result of an effort to meet the competition of another seller. This rather onerous burden was diminished somewhat by two qualifications added by the Court. In requiring the commission to negate the possibility of cost justification, the Court employed a "balance of convenience" test that assigned the burden to the party most likely to have the pertinent information regarding the particular defense. Because cost justification required elaborate technical data not likely to be in the buyer's possession, fairness dictated that the commission, a prodigious collector of such information, be obliged to show the impossibility of the buyer having relied on such a theory in accepting the discount. On the other hand, the buyer would be the party most likely to be aware of other outstanding prices on the same product, and, therefore, would be well qualified to handle the issue of meeting competition. Consequently, the Court did not consider it unfair for the buyer to be obliged to affirmatively establish another competitive offer at the lower price in defending his receipt of the discount. One FTC staff authority questions, in light of Footnote 23 of the *Canteen* case, whether the Court even required the government to show that the buyer "knew or should have known" that the discounts it received were justified by meeting competition.

The second qualification on the commission's burden of proof was the Court's willingness to acknowledge the buyer's practical familiarity with the traditional marketing devices employed for the reduction of cost. Aware of these factors, a buyer receiving a discount in their absence would be considered to be on notice that there was a strong likelihood the discount was unjustified. The Court gave sufficient weight to this *trade experience* to constitute it "a sufficient degree of knowledge to provide a basis for prosecution." Thus, a buyer who receives a solicited discount with no change in mode, quantity, or quality of delivery could be inferentially proven to have knowledge that no cost justification was available to the seller. His trade experience should tell him the seller has done nothing to warrant this price cut to him.

The initial commission reaction to *Automatic Canteen* was a complete abandonment of its existing enforcement policy under Section 2(f), including dismissal of four pending suits. Section 2(f) was relegated to a limbo of nonuse while the commission attempted to devise alternate methods of attacking buyer activity in price discrimination. Practically speaking, this was an overreaction to the new doctrines of *Automatic Canteen*. Admittedly, the FTC's burden of proof was enormously increased and the likelihood of success in promotional allowance cases was almost nonexistent. Nonetheless, insufficient weight had been given the qualifications placed on the new burden of proof by the Supreme Court. The factors of *balance of convenience* and trade experience would provide potent tools for softening the blow dealt by *Automatic Canteen*. However, the Court also appeared to recognize that in situations where the favored buyer bought in larger quantities or was served differently than its nonfavored competitors, the prosecution would be held to a much stricter standard of proof. Specifically, the Court noted that, under the preceding situation:

> . . . the Commission must only show that such differences could not give rise to sufficient savings in the cost of manufacture, sale or delivery to justify the price differential and that the buyer, knowing these were the only differences, should have known that they could not give rise to sufficient cost savings.

After a period of inactivity, the commission once again initiated a series of actions under Section 2(f), aimed primarily at group buying associations. In the first of these cases, *American Motors Specialties Company* v. *FTC*, a group of automobile parts distributors had grouped together for the purpose of soliciting lower prices for members of the association. In finding a violation of 2(f), the United States Court of Appeals for the Second Circuit observed that "by the very fact of having combined into a group and having obtained thereby a favorable price differential, they each, under *Automatic Canteen*, were charged with notice that this price differential they each enjoyed could not be justified." Thus, trade experience was adequate to create notice in the individual buyers and completely satisfy the commission's burden of proof with regard to both knowledge and the 2(b) defenses, because there were no differences in the quantities of purchase or methods of sales and delivery between favored and nonfavored purchases as contemplated by the Supreme Court in the *Automatic Canteen* case.

The United States Court of Appeals for the Fifth Circuit soon confirmed that *Automatic Canteen* could be a two-edged sword. In *Mid-South Distributors* v. *FTC*, knowledge that the price was substantially lower, coupled with the knowledge that their orders were otherwise similarly handled, sufficed to hold a group buying association liable under 2(f). The *Automatic Canteen* decision was once again employed to describe the limits—rather than the quantum—of the commission's burden of proof. This reflected an almost uniform willingness on the part of appellate courts to retreat from the strict application of *Automatic Canteen*. Under the influence of this favorable judicial climate, the FTC experienced a series of successful 2(f) suits in which it limited its burden of proof to a "reasonable man" standard. This was simply a demonstration of the seller's cost situation coupled with a showing that no reasonable buyer could have anticipated that his discounts were cost justified. It was the commission's position that this interpretation would satisfy *Automatic Canteen* even in those instances where there was a difference in quantity or methods of purchase.

The commission received a setback to its post-*Automatic Canteen* approach to 2(f) in the case of *Alhambra Motor Parts* v. *FTC*. A cooperative buying group was formed among automobile parts dealers and the association that actually performed additional services and employed different purchasing methods. Adopting what was by now its traditional view, the commission sought only to show the seller's cost factors and, thereby, demonstrate the unreasonableness of Alhambra's belief that the discounts were cost justified. No evidence was introduced specifically to negate cost justification. The United States Court of Appeals for the Ninth Circuit, in reversing the commission's finding of a 2(f) violation, stated that, "since it is established in the evidence that there were differences in the methods by which manufacturers sold to jobber members, as compared to independent jobbers, the burden was on the Commission to show that the cost saving could not be commensurate with the price differential." On remand, complaint counsel was required to make a detailed showing of actual manufacturing costs as well as the trade experience with variations of such costs—a far stricter standard than previously applied by the commission. The *Alhambra* case has been described as a reversion to the strict application of *Automatic Canteen,* but two factors mitigate against such a conclusion. First, the court in *Alhambra* employed some unusual language in placing the burden on the FTC. Rather than hold the commission to an initial burden of producing such evidence, the court indicated that detailed cost justification evidence was necessitated by the existence of evidence that tended to support a reasonable belief by the buyer that the discount might be cost justified. This would be completely consistent with prior 2(f) decisions because they largely concerned buying groups that did not perform any services of a degree that would support a reasonable belief in cost justification. Secondly, cases subsequent to *Alhambra* continue to support the commission's position where there is nothing in the evidence reasonably to support a belief in cost justification.

As further evidence that its *Alhambra* decision was not a retreat to a strict reading of *Automatic Canteen,* the United States Court of Appeals for the Ninth Circuit subsequently gave a very broad reading to the standards of 2(f) in *Fred Meyer* v. *FTC.* In attacking a chain store that had induced several suppliers to cooperate in a promotional scheme involving seller rebates, the court supported the commission's position that the performance of the promotional service by the buyer necessarily possessed that buyer of "information sufficient to put upon [him] the duty of making inquiry to ascertain whether the suppliers were making such payments available on proportionately equal terms to competitors." In effect, the court allowed examination of the buyer's cost situation to give rise to a buyer's duty to examine the seller's cost situation, with a failure to do so constituting a reasonable inference of knowledge. Furthermore, the court scrupulously avoided any mention of its *Alhambra* decision when discussing the commission's burden of proof in a 2(f) proceeding. Any attempt to read *Alhambra* as a restriction, therefore, must necessarily conflict with the expansive attitude demonstrated by the same court in subsequent 2(f) cases.

It is possible to read *Alhambra* as a purely procedural case. As such it is fully consistent with the liberalization of Section 2(f) burden of proof requirements. The court indicated that the burden it imposed on the commission was the result of evidence in the record supporting a reasonable belief of cost justification. It appears that the FTC was required to respond to this evidence or fail in its burden of negating cost justification. Under such an interpretation, there would be no *initial* burden on the commission to negate cost saving by detailed evidence. Rather, this burden would arise when evidence appeared in the record supporting a contrary conclusion. This closely parallels traditional evidentiary notions of shifting the burden of going forward with the evidence and would seem to imply that the commission need only negate cost justification when there is some evidence introduced by the buyer to support such a proposition. Thus, in a *Mid-South* or *American Motors Specialties* situation, the commission would never have to assume the burden of going forward with detailed evidence because no facts have entered the record reasonably to support a buyer's belief in cost justification.

Whatever the ultimate interpretation placed on *Alhambra,* the case is a singular setback in an otherwise highly successful series of prosecutions of 2(f) under the FTC's post-*Automatic Canteen* position on buyer inducement and receipt of price discriminations. With regard to the cost justification defense, that position can be summarized only in relation to the context in which the discount occurs. Where the buyer experiences no alteration of his method of purchase or delivery and does not vary his quantities, the *Mid-South* rationale that a substantial discount will put the buyer on notice of a discrimination in price is still the applicable law. Where the buyer alters his method or amount of purchase, as in *Alhambra,* evidence of such differences will put the burden on the commission of introducing detailed cost information to negate any possible reliance on cost justification by the buyer. In those instances where the buyer induces a discount, knowledge of which is peculiarly available to him (as with a promotional allowance), he incurs a corresponding duty to make inquiry of the seller to determine if the transaction circumvents the act. A failure to make such inquiry, as demonstrated by *Fred Meyer,* will impute the requisite culpability to the buyer. It also appears that certain promotional discounts violative of Sections 2(d) and 2(e) will once again be attacked under 2(f) despite the commission's previous preference for Section 5 of the Federal Trade Commission Act in such cases. Although this is a quite recent development, it has proved successful and may lead to combined suits under both sections, as occurred in the *Fred Meyer* case. Such a possibility is already reflected in the commission's new Guides on promotional allowances and services. Incorporating the changes wrought by the *Meyer* decision, the Guides now caution buyers against prosecution under both Section 5 and Section 2(f).

The remaining defenses available to a buyer are allocated in accordance with the "balance of convenience" test announced in *Automatic Canteen*. Since the Supreme Court expressed a willingness to impose the burden of asserting the meeting competition defense on the buyer, there has been no subsequent litigation challenging the allocation of that burden. When a buyer interposes this defense he must show that the seller granted the alleged price discrimination in order to meet the legitimate price of a competitor of the seller and that the buyer knew or should have known that the seller was meeting competition. If the competitor's price is itself illegal and the buyer is aware of this, then clearly he cannot avail himself of the defense any more than the seller could.

A more difficult question is involved when the buyer is unaware that the price of the seller's competitor is illegally low. May the buyer in such circumstances avail himself of a defense that would be unavailable to the seller? The clear language of *Automatic Canteen* would seem to limit the buyer's defenses to those available to the seller. Because this would clearly be unavailable to the seller, it seems likely that it will be similarly unavailable to the buyer. The one disturbing feature of such a result is its apparent contradiction of the essential holding of *Automatic Canteen*—namely, that the knowledge requirement of Section 2(f) seeks to penalize only *culpable* buyers. Clearly, a buyer knowing of the competitive price and ignorant of its illegality does not seem to fall into the general definition of culpable one would expect to have applied to the act. Yet, it would seem that knowledge of prices of competitors of the seller being uniquely in the buyer's hands, would make it clear to the buyer, most of all, whether the seller was meeting "legal" prices. Thus far, neither the commission nor the courts have given any indication of which position will be taken, but the consistent reference to the buyer's defenses being those otherwise available to the seller apparently would support a denial of that defense to the buyer.

The last defense available to a seller under the Robinson-Patman Act is based on the assertion that the price reduction is the result of changes in market conditions or marketability of the product. Under the *Automatic Canteen* formulation of balance of convenience, this defense has ordinarily been allocated to the buyer. In the United States Court of Appeals for the Ninth Circuit's decision in *Fred Meyer,* the court cited the buyer's failure to introduce certain evidence concerning a change in marketing conditions as a reinforcement of the commission's case and as an indication of the unavailability of that defense. Although the case treatment of this burden of proof is limited, it is clear that the type of information involved will almost invariably be more accessible to the buyer, and, therefore, under a balance of convenience, will warrant assigning the burden of proof on that defense to the buyer. Whatever the assignment in the individual case, the resolution of such questions as proximity in time of the two sales causing the differential and other similar points will be governed by the same rules of law applicable when the seller asserts this defense. Because this has already been treated in Chapter 9, there is no need to repeat the discussion here. However, it would seem logical that if a buyer intentionally misleads a seller as to competitive offers and the seller, relying on good faith, meets, but in reality beats, competition, the seller might still maintain a defense of good faith. The buyer, because of culpability, might not do so.

The preceding discussion of defenses available to a buyer under Section 2(f) in no way limits the buyer's ability to challenge the jurisdictional basis of the commission's action. Thus, a buyer may also allege as a defense that one or more of the elements necessary to a 2(a) violation is missing. For example, he is free to question the determination that the goods are of like grade and quality or to challenge his status as a competing buyer. A failure of any one of the ten necessary elements, outlined earlier, that go into a Section 2(a) cause of action will also serve as a complete defense to a Section 2(f) suit. Assertion that an element is missing is not, however, a "defense" in the technical sense, but rather a challenge to the existence of any violation in the first place. Consequently, such assertions were not within the contemplation of *Automatic Canteen* and would not be treated under any of the tests announced therein. Rather, the commission has the sole and complete burden of alleging and proving every one of the ten elements in a 2(a) violation as well as the commerce and knowledge requirements of 2(f). A failure to prove any one warrants dismissal, and it is only after all are demonstrated that the availability of defenses becomes an issue in the case.

This dichotomy between elements and defenses has created a certain amount of confusion with regard to proof of competitive injury. Such proof is a prerequisite of both 2(a) and 2(f) causes of action, and, except in rare cases, the same proof will establish this element for both. What has caused difficulty is the entanglement of competitive injury in judicial discussions of knowledgeable receipt. Because a buyer must know of a violation of 2(a) in order to violate 2(f), he must also have some knowledge of the elements of a 2(a) violation, including the potential competitive injury of the discount he receives. This can be circumstantially established, usually from the size of the differential, just as guilty knowledge of the absence of cost justification may be shown by inference from trade experience. This does not, however, mean that assertion of lack of anticompetitive effect is the type of defense contemplated by

Automatic Canteen in its formulation of the balance of convenience test. The competitive injury of the seller's activity and the buyer's knowledge of the competitive injury of the discount he received are basic elements of a 2(f) cause of action that must always be alleged and proved by the commission regardless of the buyer's convenience or trade experience.

BUYER INDUCEMENT AND RECEIPT OF BROKERAGE UNDER 2(C)

The provisions of Section 2(c) are completely independent of the remainder of the act in their application to both sellers and buyers. Consequently, there is no application of the statutory defenses and no concern with allocation of the burden of proof in this regard. The section has been described as having a per se effect, without any need to demonstrate competitive injury. Because the elements of Section 2(c) and its application to both sellers and buyers are fully discussed in the chapter on brokerage, our discussion here will focus on the propriety of employing 2(c) where the factual situation supports a suit under 2(f) as well.

The selection of the proper section often turns on the form of the arrangement employed by the seller and buyer. In order for the transaction to come under 2(c), it must be in a form that is characteristic of a brokerage arrangement. This is because the courts have been unwilling to impose the harsh standards of 2(c) on an activity that could be defended under another section of the act. For example, in *Atlas Supply Co.*, the buyer was involved in two different methods of purchase from the seller, one as an agent and one involving his independent ownership. The discount in both instances reflected the seller's savings from the elimination of the brokerage fee, but prosecution under 2(c) was only permitted in those cases where the buyer acted as agent. Whenever Atlas actually took title to the goods it was possible, and, consequently, required, that suit be brought under 2(f).

In general, suits against buyers under 2(c) will follow the classic format of *Great Atlantic & Pacific Tea Co.* v. *FTC*, in which A & P coerced sellers to rebate discounts in the exact equivalent of the brokerage fees that otherwise would have been paid by the sellers. Such discounts were clearly in lieu of brokerage and justified suit under 2(c). More difficult questions arise when the elimination of brokerage becomes one of the factors in a much larger price differential. In such circumstances, the commission has demonstrated a preference for treating such discriminations under 2(f).

RECEIPT OF DISCRIMINATORY PROMOTIONAL ALLOWANCES AND SERVICES

One of the collateral effects of the *Automatic Canteen* decision was the abandonment by the FTC of its attempts to prosecute violations of Sections 2(d) and 2(e) under the provisions of 2(f). The knowledge requirements announced in *Automatic Canteen* created the apparently impossible task of demonstrating that the buyer knew or should have known that the discounts he was receiving were not being proportionately given to his competitors who dealt with the same seller. Because this would require a familiarity by the buyer with the seller's relative sales volume to all his customers, the commission concluded the task was insurmountable.

Faced with this apparent loophole in buyer enforcement, the commission resorted to Section 5 of the Federal Trade Commission Act. Waiving application of 2(f), the commission attacked all discriminatory receipts of promotional allowances and services as "unfair methods of competition." It was the position of the FTC that Section 5 was capable of punishing activities on the periphery of the Robinson-Patman Act that would be outside the strict letter of that act. In the landmark case of *Grand Union Co.* v. *FTC,* the United States Court of Appeals for the Second Circuit sustained that viewpoint.

Grand Union had arranged with the owner of a large billboard in Times Square that the latter would provide Grand Union with advertising space at greatly reduced rates if Grand Union would induce its suppliers to purchase the remaining space on the billboard at substantially higher rates. Grand Union's suppliers were totally unaware of the arrangement with the billboard owner when they agreed to purchase the advertising space. The commission brought suit against Grand Union alleging that by "knowingly inducing or receiving . . . special payments and benefits from suppliers which were not available on proportionally equal terms to [its] competitors," Grand Union had committed "unfair methods of competition and unfair acts and practices" that violated Section 5. By directly quoting the language of Section 2(f), the commission sought to show that the provisions of Section 5 went beyond the strict language of the Robinson-Patman Act. The commission claimed that "the very purpose of §5 is to permit it to make such a determination and to bolster other antitrust statutes by outlawing acts which violate their 'spirit,' but not their letter."

In upholding the commission's finding of liability under Section 5, the

United States Court of Appeals for the Second Circuit observed that the underlying concept of unfair competition "was left flexible, so that the Commission could apply the broad Congressional standard to the myriad fact situations which would arise." Relying primarily on the fact that the buyer had originated and solicited the plan, and understood it to be a long-term arrangement, the court found Grand Union's activity susceptible to prosecution under Section 5. In reinforcing its conclusions, the court explored similar parallel applications of Section 5 to violations not precisely within the ambit of other antitrust laws, explaining this to be the very reason for the enactment of Section 5. The court then continued with an exploration of the legislative history of 2(f), demonstrating that the omission of promotional allowances and services from its coverage was purely a "legislative oversight" that Section 5 was particularly well equipped to correct.

Judicial acceptance of the commission's Section 5 approach to buyer receipt of discriminatory promotional allowances or services reestablished a balanced enforcement of the Robinson-Patman Act. Once again it was possible for the commission to attack the buyer's involvement in any activity that would hold the seller liable under the act. Cases that followed *Grand Union* clearly established the commission's power to handle every sort of promotional scheme that violates either Section 2(d) or 2(e). The best definition of the present application of Section 5 to these circumstances can be found in the United States Court of Appeals for the Second Circuit's 1964 reaffirmation of the Grand Union rationale in *R. H. Macy & Co.* v. *FTC:* "In Grand Union . . . this court held that a buyer who knowingly induced a seller to violate Section 2(d) of the Robinson-Patman Act through solicitation of special promotional and advertising payments had committed a per se violation of Section 5 of the Federal Trade Commission Act." This rationale has subsequently been adopted by a number of other federal circuit courts without addition or alteration, and can now be said to reflect accurately the state of the law with regard to Section 5.

The most recent case involving the application of Section 5 to the receipt of discriminatory promotional allowances is the United States Ninth Circuit Court of Appeals decision in *Fred Meyer, Inc.* v. *FTC.* This case indicates that judicial thinking on the scope of Section 2(f) may well have come full circle. Fred Meyer, Inc., a grocery chain, was prosecuted for accepting promotional rebates on an in-store promotional scheme that involved cash redemption of certain suppliers' product labels. Suit was brought under *both* 2(f) and Section 5, and succeeded in both instances. The court was unwilling to read the unusual language of 2(f) in such a way as to restrict its application to purely cash discount transactions. Rather than turn to Section 5, the court simply viewed the transaction as an indirect price discrimination within the coverage of 2(f). Although this conclusion was greatly facilitated by Meyer's cash receipt of rebates from the suppliers, the rebates were, nonetheless, technically a promotional allowance rather than a Section 2(a) price cut. The court's subsequent acceptance of a Section 5 cause of action as well was somewhat perfunctory once an actual violation of 2(f) was found. In accepting Section 5, however, the court did not cite the 2(f) holding, but rather simply relied on the rationale in *Grand Union* without further comment. This would seem to provide the commission with two potent weapons against buyer inducement of promotional allowances or services, each somewhat independent as to proof. Just how frequently the commission will resort to the more difficult Section 2(f) route in the light of its success with Section 5 still remains an open question.

In summary, it can be observed that the general state of the law regarding application of Section 5 to receipt of promotional allowances and services is reflected in the *Grand Union* and *R. H. Macy* cases. Where a buyer induces a seller to grant promotional allowances and services that have the effect of achieving indirect price discriminations, evidence that the buyer knowingly did so, without any demonstration of competitive injury, will satisfy the requirements of Section 5.

13

Criminal Sanctions Under Section 3

From their inception, the criminal provisions embodied in Section 3 of the Robinson-Patman Act have been attacked for vagueness and characterized as both inconsistent and redundant with the other provisions of the act. Although the Section 3 sanctions—fines up to $5,000, imprisonment not exceeding one year, or both—are relatively small in comparison to those under the Sherman Act, the percipient business-man would be unwise were he to overlook the application of these provisions.

LEGISLATIVE HISTORY

The principal purpose of Section 3 was to place criminal sanctions on unscrupulous sellers who persisted in illegitimate predatory pricing practices through the use of discriminatory price concessions and rebates,

266

territorial price discrimination, or below-cost selling of products to destroy competition or eliminate a competitor. Originally introduced as the Borah-Van Nuys Bill, the criminal provisions of Section 3 were intended as an alternative approach to the civil liabilities proposed through the Robinson-Patman Bill. In contrast to the Robinson-Patman Bill, the Borah-Van Nuys Bill imposed harsher and more categorical restrictions to a specific and limited class of evil pricing practices. The bill was designed to afford relief through local prosecution by the United States Attorney as opposed to the infrequent and less practical enforcement of the Federal Trade Commission. It was to operate as a more vigorous deterrent to those involved in predatory pricing practices.

Although introduced as an alternative approach, the bill was engrafted onto the Robinson-Patman Bill and became Section 3 of the act. As a consequence, confusion has been the hallmark of the development of Section 3. Representative Emanuel Celler's prediction that the courts would face a "herculean task to make it yield sense" has proven accurate.

ENFORCEMENT EVOLUTION

As a result of the patent incongruities and doubtful constitutionality of Section 3, it was rarely enforced by the federal government. Prior to 1955, only five cases were filed alleging Section 3 violations, and four of these were supplemental allegations in Sherman Act prosecutions. In addition, the FTC often chose to attack the practices prohibited by the first clause of Section 3 as "unfair methods of competition" under Section 5 of the Federal Trade Commission Act. Indeed, Section 3 found its greatest application in suits brought by private litigants seeking treble-damage relief under Section 4 of the Clayton Act.

In 1958, the Supreme Court was confronted with the "possibility of abuse inherent in a private cause of action based on this vague provision." In *Nashville Milk Co.* v. *Carnation Co.,* the Court closed the door to the availability of Section 3 as a predicate for private treble-damage recovery. The Court concluded that the section was not one of the antitrust laws within the purview of Section 4 of the Clayton Act, which establishes the right to private recovery. Section 3 provided "exclusive" sanctions and was not intended to amend the Clayton Act. Consequently, neither private parties nor the Federal Trade Commission could enforce its provisions. Enforcement powers rested solely with the Department of Justice.

In extracting Section 3 from the antitrust laws, the Supreme Court examined its relationship to Section 2 of the Clayton Act, partially resolving the claims that their provisions were redundant and inconsistent.

> The fair conclusions to be drawn from [the legislative] history are (a) that [Section] 3 of the Robinson-Patman Act was not intended to become part of the Clayton Act, and (b) that the section was intended to carry only criminal sanctions, except that price discriminations, to the extent that they were common to both that section and [Section] 2 of the Clayton Act, were also understood to carry, *under the independent force of the Clayton Act,* the private remedies provided in [Sections] 4 and 16 of the Clayton Act. In other words, although price discriminations are both criminally punishable . . . and subject to civil redress . . . , selling "at unreasonably low prices" is subject only to the criminal penalties provided in [Section] 3 of the Robinson-Patman Act.

The elimination of Section 3 as a tool for private litigants coupled with the Justice Department's reluctance to enforce it, resulted in its virtual disappearance in antitrust litigation. Doubts as to its constitutionality persisted.

It was not until 1963, in *United States* v. *National Dairy Products Corp.,* that the Supreme Court granted a carefully limited recognition to the constitutionality of Section 3 as applied to "below cost" sales made "without legitimate commercial objective and with specific intent to destroy competition." Asserting its power to construe a statute in a limited manner, the Court upheld the "unreasonably low price" provision, holding that the phrase was not unconstitutionally vague when applied to sales made below cost with an illegitimate purpose.

Despite the *National Dairy* case, Section 3 continues to remain vague, in principal part. Its redundancy and inconsistency with other antitrust provisions coupled with its arduous development make it imperative for the businessman to be aware of its proscriptions, especially when confronted with decisions to sell his product at a loss or negligible profit. It is within this context, and keeping in mind the criminal penalties that attach to Section 3 violations, that the decisions dealing with the prohibited practices are examined.

INTERSTATE COMMERCE REQUIREMENT

Unlike the strict requirement of Section 2(a) that one of the sales cross a state line, the commerce requirement for Section 3 more nearly approaches traditional concepts of interstate commerce. Section 3 provides: "It shall be unlawful for any person engaged in commerce, in the course of such commerce. . . ." Thus, practices that affect interstate by one engaged in interstate commerce come within the purview of Section 3.

PRACTICES PROHIBITED BY SECTION 3 AND THEIR APPLICATION

As summarized by the Supreme Court, Section 3 prohibits three kinds of trade practices, "(a) general price discrimination, (b) geographical price discriminations, and (c) selling 'at unreasonably low prices for the purpose of destroying competition or eliminating a competitor.'" Although no longer relevant within the context of private antitrust suits, the earlier Section 3 private treble damage actions are helpful in providing a predictable basis for determining the scope of Section 3's application.

General Price Discrimination

The first clause of Section 3 provides that it shall be unlawful for any person engaged in commerce, in the course of such commerce:

> To be a party to, or assist in, any transaction of sale, or contract to sell, which discriminates to his knowledge against competitors of the purchaser, in that, any discount, rebate, allowance or advertising service charge is granted to the purchaser over and above any discount, rebate, allowance or advertising service charge available at the time of such transaction to said competitors in respect of sale of goods of like grade, quality and quantity.

Predatory intent to achieve the unlawful act is a prerequisite and it is not enough that a product has been sold below cost. There must be a specific intent to sell the product below cost. Cutting prices is not unlawful per se and will not supply the intent that must be found in order to justify the issuance of an injunction under the Clayton Act. The government carries a heavier burden when it elects to challenge local price cutting under Section 3, because unlike Section 2(a) it expressly requires affirmative proof of a "purpose of destroying competition, or eliminating a competitor."

To date, only knowing sellers who afford indiscriminate concessions to one customer and not to their customer's competitor have been held liable under the act. In past cases, the government has named both buyer and seller in Sherman Act violations, but charged only the seller in Robinson-Patman Act counts. However, Representative Patman is of the view that this clause places liability on, "not only the parties to contract of sale and purchase, but any other party connected with negotiations resulting in a transaction that proves to be discriminatory, whether in fact performed or not." Furthermore, future cases may hold corporate executives individually liable under this section's definition of "any person." The Supreme Court has held that a corporate officer, a "person" under the Sherman Act definition, "is subject to prosecution under [Section] 1 of the Sherman Act whenever he knowingly participates in effecting the illegal contract, combination, or conspiracy—be he one who authorizes, orders or helps perpetrate the crime—regardless of whether he is acting in a representative capacity." Although the question of individual liability has not appeared in past Section 3 prosecutions, precedent exists for its application in future litigation.

In order for criminal liability to apply, the seller must refuse to make the bonus or concession given to one of his purchasers "available" to another purchaser. In a decision by a federal district court, Bowman Dairy was found liable for entering into a contract with the Great Atlantic and Pacific Tea Company, under which Bowman agreed to pay "a secret lump sum rebate, discount and allowance of $50,000 and a continuing, secret percentage rebate, discount, and allowance of 11% of Bowman's sales price" on all purchases made by A & P. Comparable concessions were not made available to the competitors of A & P and there was an apparent unwillingness by Bowman Dairy to give the same discount. Future litigation on this aspect of the intent requirement will predictably follow that discussed in our consideration of Sections 2(d) and 2(e). Suffice it to say that, where the seller secretly conceals concessions from competitors of his purchaser, a violation will have taken place.

The construction placed on the term *purchaser* in this section parallels that applied to Section 2(a). Thus, competitors refers to competing purchasers from the same seller. In the *Lionel* case, Lionel sold its products to jobbers, middlemen, and to some retailers at a reasonable discount based on the type of purchase—that is, jobber, middleman, or retailer. Klein, a retailer in Wilmington, Delaware, purchased Lionel's products for resale from jobbers or middlemen, but did not receive the same size discount as retailers who purchased directly from Lionel and with whom he competed. The court held that Klein failed to state a cause of action on which relief could be granted, because he was not a direct purchaser from Lionel; therefore, he was not a competing purchaser with those who did purchase from Lionel.

The Supreme Court's recent decision in the *Fred Meyer* case, which involved Section 2(d) of the act, may well have an impact in this area. In *Meyer*, the Court held that a supplier who grants promotional allowances to a direct-buying retailer must make them available on comparable terms to customers who buy through wholesalers and compete with the direct buyers in the product's resale. Section 2(e) of the act employs the term *purchasers*, as do Sections 2(a) and 3, which has been interpreted as synonymous with Section 2(d)'s term, *customer*. Within the context of an *in pare materia* treatment, it could be contended that the *Meyer* rationale is applicable to Section 3.

Unlike the civil liability of Section 2, which deals with price discriminations in the sale of goods of like grade and quality, Section 3 adds the additional criterion of quantity. It is believed that liability under this section "may be avoided by an insignificant variation in the quantities sold." Representative Patman noted at the time of the section's enactment that the law could be circumvented "by just taking one case out of a carload or putting one case more in the carload." The complaint must include the allegation that the seller discriminated against the competitors of the purchaser by not permitting or making available discounts or rebates and so forth, in sales of like quantities. On the other hand, it has been successfully contended that the total purchases of two area competitors at differing prices need not be equal to invoke liability under Section 3. It was sufficient that the quantities purchased by the complainant and the particular grocery chain, which was the complainant's day-to-day competitor, were like quantities. A prima facie case was established when the complaint alleged that the grocery chain purchased milk at one price whereas the complainant purchased it at another.

In summary, in order for liability to be found under the first clause of Section 3, the government must establish (1) a knowing discrimination; (2) by the seller to a preferred customer (purchaser); (3) of a discount, rebate, allowance or advertising service charge, over and above any bonus; (4) not made available at the time of such transaction; (5) to a competing purchaser; (6) selling goods of "like grade, quality and quantity"; (7) in interstate commerce.

Geographic Price Discrimination

The second prohibition of Section 3 relates to regional price cutting to destroy competition. It makes unlawful the selling of goods in any part of the United States at prices lower than those exacted elsewhere in the United States for the purpose of destroying competition. More specifically, it prohibits anyone "engaged in commerce, in the course of such commerce,"

> . . . to sell, or contract to sell, goods in any part of the United States at prices lower than those extracted by said person elsewhere in the United States for the purpose of destroying competition or eliminating a competitor.

The substance of this offense is the subsidization of a destructively low price from sales made in other markets where the seller is strong and can command higher prices for his product. Thus, a seller violates this provision where as a result of operating in a number of geographic markets, he lowers his price in one market while maintaining higher prices elsewhere, under circumstances that, as a matter of reasonable business probability, result in destroying competition or eliminating a competitor.

The best illustration of the prohibited conduct of this clause of Section 3, is the Supreme Court case of *Moore* v. *Mead's Fine Bread*. Moore operated a local bakery solely in intrastate commerce in Santa Rosa, New Mexico. Mead's was one of several interlocking corporations having plants in Texas and New Mexico, all of which sold their bread under the name Mead's Fine Bread. Mead's serviced a town in Texas from its Clovis, New Mexico, plant. Both Moore and Mead's were in competition in the Santa Rosa, New Mexico, area. As a result of Moore's threat to move his bakery to another vicinity, the local merchants placed a boycott on all other bread and agreed to purchase Moore's products exclusively. In an attempt to circumvent this boycott, Mead's cut the wholesale price of its bread in the Santa Rosa area in half, but did not cut the prices of bread in any other market. Moore was forced to close his business and subsequently brought a treble-damage action under Section 2(a) and 3 of the Robinson-Patman Act on the basis that Mead's had maintained its prices in interstate commerce while unlawfully lowering his prices in intrastate commerce. The Supreme Court rejected the lower court's decision, which determined that the injury was to a purely local competitor whose business was in no way related to interstate commerce and, therefore, beyond the reach of the statute. Although no interstate sales were utilized to eliminate Moore's competition, the Supreme Court held that the pricing methods employed by Mead's coupled with predatory intent to destroy competition and eliminate its competitor fell within the framework of practices prohibited by the Robinson-Patman Act:

> We think that the practices in the present case are also included within the scope of the antitrust laws. We have here an interstate industry increasing its domain through outlawed competitive practices. The victim, to be sure, is only a local merchant; and no interstate transactions are used to destroy him. But the beneficiary is an interstate business; the treasury used to finance the warfare is drawn from interstate, as well as local, sources which include not only respondent (Mead's) but also a group of interlocked companies engaged in the same line of business; and the prices on the interstate sales . . . are kept high while the local prices are lowered. If this method of competition were approved, the pattern for growth of monopoly would be simple. . . . The profits made in interstate activities would underwrite the losses of local price-cutting campaigns. No instrumentality of interstate commerce would be used to destroy the local merchant and expand the domain of the combine. But the opportunities afforded by interstate commerce would be employed to injure local trade.

Thus, it is not necessary that specific interstate transactions result in the destruction of a competitor; it is enough that an interstate business enterprise increases its domain through the use of anticompetitive practices to establish a violation of this clause of Section 3. Furthermore, sellers cannot intelligently assume that their intrastate pricing policies are immune from the Robinson-Patman Act on the ground that the transaction complained of did not take place in the course of interstate commerce where it is alleged that the lower intrastate prices are subsidized through higher prices obtained in interstate commerce. In the *National Dairy* case, the government successfully alleged that National utilized the advantages it possessed through operation in many different localities to finance and subsidize a price war against small local dairies by intentionally selling milk at prices below its cost.

It is relevant to note that Section 2(a) of the act prohibits geographic price discriminations and affords injured parties the right to bring treble-damage actions against those who employ such discriminiations. Section 2(a) requires only a showing of a price discrimination and the requisite effect on competition. Under Section 3 area price discriminations, the government is faced with a heavier burden than the private litigant under 2(a) and must make an affirmative showing that the seller lowered his prices for the purpose of destroying competition or eliminating a competitor; and neither provision is dependent on the other. In 1957, the Federal Trade Commission issued a cease and desist order against Anheuser-Busch, a national brewery, on grounds that Busch had lowered prices in the St. Louis, Missouri, market without making similar price reductions in other markets, in violation of Section 2(a). In response to Busch's argument that the government had established that "high prices in one area have subsidized low prices in another," and that such a showing constituted a violation of Section 3 of the Robinson-Patman Act as opposed to Section 2(a) of the Clayton Act under which the action was brought, the Supreme Court stated: "The fact that activity which falls within the civil proscription of (Section) 2(a) may also be criminal under (Section) 3 is entirely irrelevant. . . . [T]his Section [3] does not restrict the operation of the prohibitions, with civil sanctions, of the Robinson-Patman amendments to (Section) 2(a) of the Clayton Act." Thus, the major distinction between these prohibitions is the mandatory requirement under Section 3 that the discriminatory practices were committed for the purpose of destroying competition with specific, predatory intent to accomplish that purpose. In spite of the additional showing of intent under Section 3, it appears that the meeting competition and cost justification defenses available to Section 2(a) violations are equally applicable as valid defenses under Section 3. Thus, a showing by a seller that his reduction in price was made in good faith to meet a lawful and equally low price of a competitor, to restore his position in the market, or to follow the prices of his competitors, would negate the predatory intent required to establish a geographic price discrimination.

Furthermore, there are numbers of instances in which it can be demonstrated that area price differences are not destructive or unfair. Suppose a firm operating in a number of geographic markets desires to enter a new market where it has not sold before. In order to obtain a foothold in the new market and stimulate competition with the well-entrenched seller, it may be necessary for the firm initially to sell its product at a low price. Unless the firm is in a position to subsidize its initial low price from higher prices maintained elsewhere, entry into the new market would be virtually impracticable. In this instance, the purpose of the reduction in price is to breed new competition in a new market as opposed to the illegal purpose to eliminate a competitor or destroy him. It may, therefore, be permissible under the criminal provisions of Section 3. However, such conduct by an interstate supplier might result in competitive injury in violation of Section 2(a) of the act, which imposes civil liability and does not require any showing of illegal intent.

In summary, for liability under this clause to attach, the government must establish (1) a lowering of prices in one market; (2) by an interstate supplier; (3) while maintaining higher prices in another market; (4) with the specific purpose; (5) of destroying competition or eliminating a competitor.

Selling at Unreasonably Low Prices

The third clause of Section 3 makes it unlawful for persons engaged in interstate commerce, in the course of such commerce, to sell at "unreasonably low prices for the purpose of destroying competition or eliminating a competitor." There is no overlap in this prohibition with any of the other prohibitions of Section 2 of the act. This clause has been the center of controversy because of its vagueness and indefiniteness. The requisite elements for the composition of liability under the clause were succinctly outlined by Judge Matthes in the *National Dairy Products* case:

(1) sales at prices below some level of cost and intent to destroy competition or eliminate a competitor;
(2) the question whether sales are "unreasonably low" so as to impose liability . . . must be determined on the facts of each case—on an ad hoc basis; and
(3) the predatory or competitive nature of the seller's price, rather than the theoretical cost considerations, is the real index of its legality. The question resolves itself into one of intent and purpose, not a choice of accounting method.

It was the second element that had raised a serious constitutional question because of the absence of any definite standards applicable to "unreasonably low" pricing practices. As a result of its doubtful constitutionality, the Justice Department had largely abandoned any serious attempts at enforcement of this provision. Moreover, the Supreme Court's *Nashville Milk* decision ended the utilization of private treble-damage enforcement, which also contributed to the temporary demise of this provision. However, in 1963, the Supreme Court revitalized this clause of Section 3 in the *National Dairy Products* case.

National Dairy, a supplier of dairy products throughout the United States, competed with a number of local and national concerns in the Kansas City, Missouri, area. The small local dairies were able to sell gallon jugs of milk at lower prices than National could sell in its paper half-gallon containers. In an attempt to offset the marketing advantage, National substantially reduced its prices, which caused the loss of business by the local dairies—and in some instances their ultimate destruction. The government charged that National had violated Section 3 by selling milk "at unreasonably low prices for the purpose of destroying competition." It claimed that National, because of the advantages it possessed as a result of its operation in a great many geographic markets, had financed and subsidized the price war in the Kansas City area by intentionally selling milk at prices below cost.

The Supreme Court upheld the constitutionality of this provision against the vagueness attack because the indictment had charged National with selling below cost rather than utilizing the more general statutory language. The Supreme Court pointed to the congressional intent to prohibit sales below cost unless "mitigated by some acceptable business exigency." The Court held that a showing of the requisite intent coupled with the resultant destruction of competition was sufficient to come within the prohibition of the act. These combined elements provided the "specificity of warning" required of criminal statutes under the Constitution.

The Supreme Court's revitalization of this antitrust weapon will likely result in future government attempts at Section 3 enforcement. Consequently, businessmen should acquaint themselves with the pitfalls inherent in this provision of Section 3. A brief examination of the two basic elements required to establish a violation is essential to a proper understanding of its application.

Sales at Unreasonably Low Prices. Prior to 1955, the treble-damage cases initiated under Section 3 went a good distance in determining what the "unreasonably low price" clause represented. In *F & A Ice Cream Co.*, a federal district court stated:

> Whether a price is high or low, and if so, whether it is unreasonably so, can be determined by ordinary business and accountancy methods which take into consideration cost, market, usual profits and other elements. The unreasonably low price which the statute considers an

evil would rarely, if ever, be an *initial* price, except in the rare instance where it would relate to a product not previously marketed.
In most instances, it would involve a sudden and unexpected change
of price in a staple article of commerce by one engaged in a competitive field. So, in determining its character, and whether it was put into
effect as a means of destroying competition, additional elements other
than those already mentioned, such as cost, usual profits and the like,
would be available for consideration. Among them might be mentioned the suddenness of the price change, its relation to previous
prices charged by the merchant or by others in the field in the particular locality or elsewhere, the existence or non-existence of new economic factors relating to cost of production, demand for the article,
seasonal or other, the consequent need for expansion or contraction of
the field for the particular merchandise and other factors, financial or
economic, which might or might not warrant a precipitate reduction
in price.

The early application of Section 3 left some uncertain yet helpful
guideposts relating to the predatory intent required to establish liability.
Thus, reductions justified by reasonable business and economic considerations, in a legitimate attempt to keep customers or gain others, have
been permitted. Some early considerations were the length of time the
price cut was contemplated: its relation to competitors' prices in the
field; and, the cost of production and demand for the article. Thus,
where a coal processor uniformly reduced its prices of coal in a declining
market in the absence of design and purpose to destroy competition, no
violation of Section 3 existed. As was noted by the United States Court
of Appeals for the Tenth Circuit: "One who reduces his prices in defense of his economic life cannot be guilty of eliminating competition
or his competitors." Reasonableness is the test used under Section 3 to
determine how "low" prices actually are. The legitimate objective of
operating a business is to produce profits. It logically follows that sales
that do not produce profits are unreasonable unless there exists a "legitimate commercial objective." It is quite difficult for a businessman to
keep or maintain an exact knowledge of the cost attributable to particular products and often the relationship of cost and price can only be
determined over a protracted period. As the United States Court of
Appeals for the Eighth Circuit observed in the *National Dairy* case,
"whether sales are 'unreasonably low' so as to impose liability . . .
must be determined on the facts of each case—on an *ad hoc* basis."

The legitimate commercial objectives test has not yet been clearly defined. Future litigation will have to be relied on to mark the boundaries
of the test. Would liability result where sales are made below cost when
the supplier can prove legitimate business aims but where predatory
intent was admittedly used? The same question would arise where a
manufacturer deems it profitable and expedient to sell below cost to

absorb overhead, cognizant that a competitor may be eliminated; or where below cost sales are made to increase sales and decrease unit-production cost despite the realization that a competitor will be ruined.

To date, the courts have determined whether sales are unreasonably below cost by a cursory examination of whether they are below fully distributed costs or direct cost. In the *National Dairy* case, National contended that a below cost sale was one made at a price lower than direct cost—obtaining milk, processing, and container costs. The government, on the other hand, asserted that a below cost sale was one made below fully distributed cost—that is, cost of production plus allocated delivery and selling and administrative costs. Although the Supreme Court did not decide the question in the intermediate appeal, the United States Eighth Circuit Court of Appeals, stated, ". . . we have no great difficulty in concluding that even though appellant made no sales below direct cost . . . the question whether it violated (Section 3) *by selling below fully distributed cost* was, in view of all the facts and circumstances, one to be resolved by the jury under proper instructions."

Thus, selling at unreasonably low prices means selling at prices somewhere below fully distributed cost. Exactly where a jury will determine the extent to which the low price, below fully distributed cost, becomes unreasonable, is open to speculation. With the proper utilization of modern business accounting methods, the fastidious businessman should be able to keep a concise and accurate accounting of his costs, which would be a major factor in establishing reasonableness in price. Pertinent here is the definition of production cost, which includes raw materials, labor and overhead, distribution costs, income or replacement cost, plus the cost of doing business. In any event, the standards of reasonableness permit below cost sales that have a legitimate commercial objective "such as the liquidation of excess, obsolete or perishable merchandise, or the need to meet a lawful, equally low price of a competitor."

Future cases will undoubtedly face questions relating to loss operations during start-up periods for new units or sales below cost for promotional purposes—that is, loss leaders, two-for-one sales, and heavy promotional devices for new products. These cases will predictably turn on an analysis of the (1) duration and timing of promotional sales below cost; (2) whether or not a new product is being advanced into a new or old market; and (3) the extent of the business loss as determined by the expected future volume, profit and sales, and so on. An evaluation or determination of reasonableness should take into account the characteristics surrounding injurious competition and other unilateral forces on prices that competition generates from time to time. Yet to be answered are the questions pertaining to limited sales—that is, one isolated sale below or above costs, and the length of time a violator must sell at an unreasonably low price to incur liability.

Intent. As to intent, the United States Court of Appeals for the Eighth Circuit stated in the *National Dairy* case that, ". . . the predatory or competitive nature of the seller's price, rather than theoretical cost considerations, is the real index of its legality. The question resolves itself into one of intent and purpose, not a choice of accounting methods."

Thus, in addition to finding that the sales were unreasonably below cost, liability turns on a finding of *specific, predatory* intent to destroy competition or eliminate a competitor in the market. It is incumbent on the government to offer evidence and prove beyond a reasonable doubt that such below cost sales were concomitant with a predatory intent. This may be difficult to prove. However, as one court observed:

> . . . [I]t would ignore the economic facts of life to say that one in business for a profit would deliberately and consistently sell at a loss without some ulterior motive. It would be equally inadmissible to say that one who consistently sells at a loss without competitive compulsion is not selling at unreasonably low prices. And, one who consistently sells at unreasonably low prices is vulnerable to the inference that he is doing so for the proscribed purpose of destroying competition or eliminating a competitor.

In the past, the government has placed considerable emphasis on improper statements, both documentary and verbal, made by officers and employees; animosity between the destroyer and destroyed; demand for the product; lack of the reduction in price to stimulate sales; loss suffered by the alleged discriminator; and the methods of cost accounting. On the other hand, these considerations might prove decisive in providing a sound explanation of the background and motive for a legitimate price reduction. Presumptions are insufficient to establish unlawful intent; however, a sudden, severe reduction in price would be difficult to explain.

Thus, unlawful intent is a prerequisite to the imposition of liability. It is a question for the jury to be resolved on an ad hoc basis depending on the facts and circumstances of each case.

In summary, for liability under this clause to attach, the government must establish (1) sales below cost; (2) in interstate commerce; (3) without legitimate commercial objectives; (4) with the specific intent; (5) of destroying competition or eliminating a competitor.

DEFENSES

Essential to any Section 3 violation is the over-all requirement of specific, predatory intent to commit the prohibited practices. Whether the violation is premised on secret price concessions, rebates, area price discrimination, or selling at unreasonably low prices for the purpose of destroying competition or eliminating a competitor from the market, the government must establish a knowing participation in the unlawful price discrimination by the accused. There must be a showing of deliberate anticompetitive motive and intent, which is legally rebuttable with proof of a legitimate commercial objective.

Furthermore, even though Section 3 contains no express defenses to charges of price discriminations, for the most part, the express defenses inherent in Section 2 of the Robinson-Patman Act are implied and available to disprove a claim of predatory price discrimination under Section 3. If the allegations are based on the general price discrimination clause —that is, secret discounts, rebates, or advertising service charges, however, the government need not prove adverse effect on competition as required of the private litigant seeking redress under Section 2(a). Furthermore, the cost justification or good faith meeting of competition defenses available to the Section 2(a) violator, in the face of showing of predatory intent, may not be used to refute allegations premised on this clause of Section 3. On the other hand, where Section 2 defenses are adequate to avoid liability in a civil suit, it stands to reason that conviction under Section 3 could not be obtained. It would be fatally inconsistent for lawful conduct under Section 2 to be held unlawful and subject to criminal sanction under Section 3.

In summary, the absence of either (1) a specific predatory intent to destroy competition or eliminate a competitor, or (2) sales of products at unreasonably low prices for the purpose of destroying competition or eliminating a competitor will constitute a complete defense to alleged violations of Section 3.

CONCLUSION

To a great extent the criminal provisions of Section 3 duplicate the civil provisions under Section 2 of the Robinson-Patman Act. Section 3 has been criticized as vague, duplicative, and possibly unconstitutional. In 1955, the Attorney General's National Committee to Study the Antitrust Laws called for its repeal. Although some of the questions concerning Section 3 have been resolved, it remains an enigma in antitrust legislation. Consequently, there have been recent attempts to bolster its provisions through statutory amendment.

In February of 1967, Senate Bill 877 was introduced as an amendment to the Clayton Act, which would make Section 3, in modified form, one of the antitrust laws. This would reopen the door to private enforcement through treble-damage actions under Section 4 of the Clayton Act. A similar proposal had also been introduced in the Senate in 1965—Senate Bill 995. In January of 1967, House Bill 2348 was introduced, which would amend the Federal Trade Commission Act to prohibit certain discriminatory practices including sales at unreasonably low prices. These bills manifest the dissatisfaction over the efficacy of the present state of Section 3.

Therefore, it is readily apparent that Section 3 remains unclear in its application and uncertain as an antitrust tool. Moreover, it provides little guidance to the businessmen who must conform their conduct to its mandates. Some form of revision would seem inescapable if it is to become a viable and effective piece of antitrust legislation.

14

Enforcement by the Federal Trade Commission

The principal enforcing agency of the Robinson-Patman Act is the Federal Trade Commission, which was established by Congress, in 1914, as an independent regulatory agency. The commission is composed of five commissioners, appointed by the President and confirmed by the Senate for terms of seven years. No more than three commissioners may be members of the same political party. Since 1950, the President has by law designated one of the commissioners to serve as chairman. The chairman has broad authority over most commission personnel, including appointments and promotion. The chairman, subject to the policy guidance of his four colleagues, also has broad authority over the use and expenditure of funds and the distribution of business within the commission. Under the direction of the chairman, the executive director is the chief operating official, who exercises supervisory authority over the various bureaus within the commission and over the staff of the commission. The secretary of the commission has among his many responsibilities the coordination of liaison activities with Congress and government departments and agencies. The general counsel is the commission's chief legal expert. His office is responsible for representing the commission in the federal courts, preparing legal memoranda, and advising the commission. Within the commission are various bureaus and divisions designated to fulfill the commission's broad responsibility in guiding and policing the economy. The Bureau of Industry Guidance, for example, attempts to secure voluntary compliance with the statutes administered by the commission by the education of the business community. The commission's employees total over 1,150, of which 473 are attorneys and 130 are other professional personnel. The commission's headquarters is in Washington, D.C., but over 300 employees are located in eleven field offices throughout the country.

Apart from the Bureau of Industry Guidance, with its divisions of Advisory Opinions and Guides, Trade Practice Conferences, and Trade Regulation Rules, there are five other operating bureaus, with divisions as follows: (1) Bureau of Deceptive Practices—divisions of Compliance, Food and Drug Advertising, General Advertising, General Practices, and Scientific Opinions; (2) Bureau of Economics—divisions of Economic Evidence, Financial Reports, and Financial Statistics; (3) Bureau of Field Operations, supervising the eleven field offices; (4) Bureau of Restraint of Trade—divisions of Accounting, Compliance, Discriminatory Practices (Robinson-Patman), General Trade Restraints, and Mergers; and (5) Bureau of Textiles and Furs—divisions of Enforcement and Regulation, as well as various field stations for investigations.

Violations of the Robinson-Patman law are brought to the commission's attention in a variety of ways. Letters are received from consumers, business competitors, suppliers, and customers, sometimes directly, sometimes from other agencies of the government. The procedure for filing a complaint is very informal. All that is necessary is a letter to the commission detailing the facts that are believed to constitute a violation of the law. The commission possesses extremely broad investigative powers under the Federal Trade Commission Act. This act provides the commission with the power of access to documentary evidence, the authority to require annual and special reports from any firm, and the power of subpoena. The power to require special reports from corporations has been exercised in several ways during the history of the commission. Reports have been used to gather information for the *Quarterly Financial Report for Manufacturing Corporations,* prepared jointly by the Federal Trade Commission and the Securities and Exchange Commission. Extensive use of this special report power has been made in connection with general economic surveys conducted by the commission. In recent years, the commission has used its special report power to conduct general investigations of alleged widespread violations of the antitrust and trade regulation laws throughout an entire industry.

When a possible violation of the law comes to the commission's attention, either through its own investigation or through one of the media mentioned here, the procedures for enforcement are varied and flexible. The Federal Trade Commission Act provides that if it appears that a formal proceeding would be in the interest of the public, the commission may issue a complaint against the alleged offender and set a hearing date. Such hearings are conducted before hearing examiners, and the proceedings are similar to those employed in federal courts. The rules of evidence are somewhat relaxed in such hearings, yet they remain subject to due-process requirements of fairness. The respondent is given an opportunity to cross-examine witnesses and to present evidence in rebuttal. After the hearings are completed and evidence has been received from the commission's lawyers and the lawyers representing the respondent, the hearing examiner makes an initial decision. This decision becomes final if not appealed from or modified by the commission within thirty days. If the initial decision is appealed to the full commission for review, or if the commission reviews the matter of its own volition, the commission may modify the order in any way it sees fit. If the decision is against the respondent, the commission may issue an order to *cease and desist*. Such an order is like an injunction and remains in effect indefinitely, unless later modified or dismissed for reasons of changes in the circumstances of fact or law. If violated, the respondent may be prosecuted in a district court for civil penalties, which may run as high as $5,000 for each violation, with each day of a continuing violation counting as a separate offense. A cease and desist order does not become final until sixty days after it has been served on the respondent. During this period, the respondent may appeal to a federal court of appeals. Before such courts, the commission's findings regarding the facts are conclusive if supported by substantial evidence. Cease and desist orders include a provision that respondents file, within sixty days from the date of the service of the order, a report of compliance setting forth the manner of compliance. Other statutes under the commission's purview, such as the Clayton Act, of which Section 2 of the Robinson-Patman Act is a part, also provide for this procedure.

The commission seeks to encourage compliance with the requirements of the laws it administers by a number of means other than the formal proceedings just outlined, as informal techniques may be quicker, cheaper, and equally effective. These methods include administrative treatment, trade practice conferences, trade regulation rules, the issuance of guides, advisory opinions, and consent settlement procedures. It is important to note that there is a commission policy of effecting industry-wide compliance, whenever possible or practicable, if alleged violations of law are extensive. This policy is a most important one in the agency's current program.

Administrative treatment is the simplest and one of the newest of the informal methods. Letters of discontinuance or affidavits signed by responsible officials of the offending concern, accompanied by evidence of compliance with the law and assurance that the questioned practices will not be resumed, are accepted in settlement of many smaller infractions. In this connection, it is important to note that currently the commission's eleven field offices have authority in proper instances to accept administrative settlements of alleged violations. However, the field office must obtain enough facts to disclose a probable violation and may not accept a settlement tendered by a businessman seeking to avoid further government involvement, without regard to whether or not the facts indicate that a violation has occurred.

Until the change in its rules of practice effective August 1, 1963, the commission did not apply informal voluntary compliance procedures to Robinson-Patman and other antimonopoly violations. With the removal of this restriction, however, commission spokesmen made it clear that such procedures would be sparingly used in such areas of law enforcement and that first violators would be the most likely subjects. The rules state:

> In determining whether the public interest will be fully safeguarded through such informal administrative treatment, the Commission will consider (1) the nature and gravity of the alleged violation; (2) the prior record of good faith of the parties involved; and (3) other factors, including, where appropriate, adequate assurance that the practice has been discontinued and will not be resumed.

In 1962, provision was made for the issuance of trade regulation rules applicable to unlawful trade practices. These rules are designed to express the judgment of the commission, based on facts of which it has knowledge derived from its past experience, regarding practices clearly violative of the law. Such rules may be sharply limited to particular areas or industries or to particular product or geographic areas, as appropriate. Provision is made for reliance on these rules in litigated cases if the respondent is given a fair hearing on the legality and propriety of applying a particular rule to a particular case. Also, there is the usual provision for formal due-process procedures prior to the final issuance of the rules. Although not yet subjected to a court test, rules of this nature increasingly are being used by the commission to solve industrywide problems.

For many years, the commission has provided procedures for trade practice conferences on the application of businessmen and their trade associations in a particular industry or on the commission's own motion. If the commission concludes that such a conference would be useful and proper, notice is given to members of the industry concerned. They and other interested parties appear and freely express their views regarding practices that are prevalent in the industry, practices that perhaps should be eliminated. Such conferences may, where appropriate, voluntarily repudiate widespread illegal practices in a particular industry. Conferences always involve formal trade practice rules with which members of a given industry may signify their willingness to comply. Recently, such trade conference procedures have been merged into the industry guides program. Compliance with such rules is not permissive, since they express what the law already prohibits. Other rules, which the members of an industry may voluntarily agree to follow, condemn practices that the particular industry deems to be harmful or unethical even though such practices are not illegal. Trade practice rules on adoption, often become the basis for the settlement of investigative matters pending against members of the industry concerned.

In recent years, the commission has published a series of guides in an effort to make clear to businessmen those practices that the law prohibits and that should be avoided. Illustrative are the 2(d) and 2(e) guides, reprinted in the Appendices. Guides, unlike the trade practice rules, may deal with practices common to many industries. Although the preparation of guides that are both informative and accurate is not an overnight task, there is no necessity for hearings or conferences concerning them. The guides are not intended to cover gaps in the law by dealing with factual situations that have not yet come before the courts or before the commission in any form. Rather, they set forth in an easily understood language the principles already established by the courts and the commission in decided cases. Their purpose is to give the businessman some knowledge of what the law requires of him. Additionally, the guides, by delineating areas of potential trouble, should alert the businessman to consult his lawyer when a problem arises and before a violation of law occurs. The commission has sought the greatest publicity for its guides in an effort to reach as many businessmen as possible. Copies are available without charge on request to the commission. The trade practice rules and guides, together with special conferences called by the commission staff from time to time, are all designed to educate businessmen in the requirements of the law and to encourage them to avoid illegal practices.

In this age of increasing business complexity, it is often extremely difficult for businessmen and their legal counsel to determine accurately the legality of proposed business action. Some assistance may be obtained by seeking an advisory opinion from the commission. Informal advice may be obtained from members of the commission's staff or from its field offices in Atlanta, Boston, Chicago, Cleveland, Kansas City, Los Angeles, New Orleans, New York City, San Francisco, Seattle, and Washington, D.C. Although such advice is not binding on the commission in regard to future activity of the requesting party, such advice will normally allow the businessman to proceed with greater certainty.

In connection with the advisory opinion procedure it is important to note the circumstances in which the commission will not give advice:

. . . (1) where the course of action is already being followed by the requesting party; (2) where the same or substantially the same course of action is under investigation or is the subject of a current proceeding by the Commission against the requesting party; (3) where the same or substantially the same course of action is under investigation or is or has been the subject of a proceeding, order or decree initiated or obtained by another government agency against the requesting party; or (4) where the proposed course of action is such that an informed decision thereon could be made only after extensive investigation, clinical study, testing or collateral inquiry.

Texts or digests of advisory opinions of general interest may be published "subject to statutory restrictions against disclosure of trade secrets and names of customers and to considerations of the confidentiality of facts involved and of meritorious objections made by the requesting party to such publication." Digests of selected advisory opinions dealing with Robinson-Patman matters are reprinted in Appendix VI here.

Finally, the commission may employ the consent decree procedure to halt illegal practices. Following notification by the commission of its determination to issue a complaint, a party may indicate to the commission its willingness to have the proceedings disposed of by the entry of an order. The consent decree, by which the objectionable practices may be effectively prohibited, is negotiated currently with the trial and investigative staff, advised in this connection by the General Counsel. If an agreement is approved by the commission, the complaint and proposed order will be issued. If the proposed consent settlement is rejected, the complaint is issued and the matter set down for adjudication in regular course.

The commission shares with the Department of Justice the task of enforcing the Robinson-Patman Act. To avoid duplication of action, a working relationship has been arranged between the two. This relationship has been characterized by willing interchange of information, avoidance of the duplication of effort, and the careful assignment of cases to the agency whose action will be likely to do the most good. At the same time, in recognition of their mutual and separate responsibilities, each agency has preserved its individual freedom to take independent action whenever it believes it to be necessary. In practice, and by common consent, the Federal Trade Commission has become the primary enforcer of the Robinson-Patman Act. However, only the Justice Department can enforce the criminal provisions of Section 3. And, on occasion, the Justice Department couples Robinson-Patman charges with charges of other violations of the antitrust laws.

If either agency begins an investigation, the other agency is promptly notified. If the commission schedules a trade practice conference, the division is immediately informed. If the agency notified has any objections, a conference is held to effect a workable compromise. Even though each agency retains its right to initiate separate proceedings, in practice their working agreement has wholly prevented wasteful duplication. Similarly, only rarely will either the division or the commission institute action when a private suit has been brought against the same conduct.

Certain ground rules have been established to govern the normal way in which cases are handled. The commission normally enforces the provisions of the Robinson-Patman Act, unless the violation is part of a larger pattern of illegality characterized by Sherman Act violations. For practices violative of both the Sherman Act and Section 5 of the Federal Trade Commission Act, a number of factors are considered. For example, if criminal proceedings are in order, the division naturally will be the agency of enforcement. Similarly, the magnitude of the violation or its per se character may dictate division action. In an area where the commission's economic *expertise* can be profitably put to advantage, however, the division may stand aside. The nature of the relief required may be of importance. If immediate interlocutory relief is desirable, the division will probably handle the case. Finally, that agency with prior experience and, therefore, familiarity with a particular company or industry will in all likelihood deal with future violations by that company or in that industry.

This working relationship is obviously tailored to avoid duplication-of-enforcement effort. Prior expertize is utilized whenever possible, and other means of increasing the effectiveness of both agencies are readily embraced. The system has been remarkably effective in practice, and this alone is a tribute to the practical bent of those charged with the enforcement of the act.

15

Enforcement by the Department of Justice

Although, as indicated in the preceding chapter, the principal governmental enforcing agency of the act is the Federal Trade Commission, Robinson-Patman charges occasionally accompany Justice Department complaints alleging other antitrust violations. Also, the Justice Department alone is vested with responsibility for enforcing the criminal provisions of Section 3 of the act. It, therefore, appears appropriate at this point to consider enforcement procedures, both civil and criminal, of the Antitrust Division of the Department of Justice. In this connection, we shall discuss the means by which the division discovers possible violations of the laws, the methods by which it investigates such possible violations, the standards governing the division's decision to proceed formally in court, the nature of a proceeding, the nature of decrees entered in Robinson-Patman suits, and the informal methods of dealing with the division.

The businessman will first learn that he is suspected of a possible violation when he is approached, or hears that his customers or competitors have been approached, for information concerning his business or his competitors' businesses by representatives of the division or agents of the Federal Bureau of Investigation (FBI). Occasionally, the businessman will not learn of the division's interest until he receives orders to produce certain documents before a grand jury or to the division pursuant to a civil investigative demand (a method of pretrial discovery that will be discussed later in this chapter). In whatever manner he learns of the division's concern, however, he will first want to know what started the division's desire to investigate him and his industry.

Robinson-Patman proceedings are usually initiated by the complaint of a customer or a competitor. Often, of course, the complaints turn out to be groundless. Initially, therefore, the division makes a preliminary analysis to determine whether a more detailed investigation is warranted. If the complaint itself reveals that the questioned conduct does not violate the law, the whole matter can be dropped immediately. For example, if a customer complains that a manufacturer would not afford him the identical discount as offered to a large competitor, but the discount is, in fact, cost justified and the customer alleges nothing more, no Robinson-Patman violation has taken place, and further investigation would be fruitless. Another consideration is whether the challenged conduct is in or affects interstate commerce. Broad as the present definition of interstate commerce may be, some conduct will still be outside the reach of the Robinson-Patman Act.

The division must decide whether a proceeding would be in the public interest. Because stopping any violation would appear to benefit the public, this question may seem out of place. But more is involved than the simple truth that all violations should be prevented. Like all government agencies, the division receives only a limited amount of money each year. Necessarily, therefore, only a limited number of investigations and actions can be undertaken. Accordingly, the division must choose cases that will derive the greatest public benefit from the money expended. In short, the division aims to spend its enforcement dollar wisely. Cases will be chosen with a view to reaching situations of the greatest magnitude. The division also seeks to prosecute those cases that will lead to an orderly growth in the scope and content of the laws themselves. By pursuing these joint goals, the division attempts to ensure maximum compliance with the laws.

As a final preliminary step, the division checks with the FTC to see if that agency is interested in the same matter. Naturally, an investigation will not be undertaken or an action begun if the commission is already working on the same case. Double enforcement serves neither the public nor the industry involved.

The scope of the investigation necessary will determine the next step taken by the division attorney. If only limited investigation is required, the attorney may carry it out himself. Where more extensive research is indicated, the services of the FBI will probably be used. The bureau may conduct interviews of potential defendants, their customers, suppliers, and competitors. Additionally, any other people who could have knowledge of the violation or of the industry in which it is alleged to have occurred might be contacted. The bureau might also request the opportunity to examine the documents of anyone interviewed.

Quite possibly, the investigation carried out by the attorney or the bureau will provide enough information to determine either that an action should be instituted or that the matter should be dropped. Whenever either decision is taken, of course, further investigation is halted. If further information is necessary, it may have to be obtained through the use of procedures requiring a potential defendant to produce the data in question. There are several methods of compulsory discovery available to the division. The choice will depend mainly on the initial determination whether to try the case civilly under Section 2 or criminally under Section 3. We shall have more to say about the considerations underlying this decision later in this chapter. What is important to note here is that the initial determination is only provisional in nature. From the evidence the division possesses at the time compulsory discovery is initiated, a decision may be made to seek a criminal indictment. If the data and testimony obtained by a grand jury investigation reveal that the character of the offense is not sufficiently pernicious to warrant criminal prosecution, the division retains the right to institute civil proceedings instead. Similarly, information obtained through a civil investigative demand may reveal a far more flagrant violation than the division had at first suspected. A criminal action might then be sought.

First, let us consider what the businessman might expect if the division feels that criminal prosecution is warranted. Assuming the Attorney General's concurrence in the division's recommendation, grand jury proceedings will probably be instituted. A grand jury is a frightening thing to those who have never experienced such an investigation. Grand jury proceedings are carried on in absolute secrecy, and a potential defendant will know nothing of the probable outcome until an indictment is returned or the grand jury is dismissed.

The businessman will probably first become aware of the threat of criminal prosecution against some or all members of his industry when he receives a subpoena *duces tecum* requiring him to assemble certain documents and transmit them to the grand jury. Typically, subpoenas are extremely broad in their demands for documents. Thus, if territorial price fixing is suspected, the subpoena might direct submission of all documents relating to prices and pricing of certain products for a period of four or five years. Some subpoenas are even more broadly drawn. The process of assembling the required documents often imposes a tremendous burden on a company. Many personnel will be required to sort through the mountain of paper that is amassed over the years by the normal corporation. Additionally, some means of copying or otherwise noting the documents that are produced must be devised.

Before any document search is instituted, legal counsel should be obtained. The language of subpoenas is often very technical, and legal advice on just what documents must be produced will save a company wasted hours of searching. Furthermore, a company's attorney can often work out ambiguities by contacting the division attorney responsible for the subpoena. For example, the subpoena might call for "all" documents relating to a certain subject. In practical effect, this might require a company to produce a literal carload of paper that appears to have no conceivble relevance to any possible subject of investigation. By contacting the division attorney and describing to him the particular documents that appear valueless, a company's lawyer might be able to avoid their submission to the grand jury. This will not only save the time of the company's employees but also minimize the inevitable disruption of the company's business attendant to the delivery of company documents to a grand jury. Finally, a lawyer can examine those documents that the company believes are called for by the subpoena and determine if any unnecessary documents are being produced. Not only will this prevent the submission of irrelevant documents, but it will also serve to familiarize the attorney with the facts concerning any potential liability of the company.

Failure to produce documents requested under a grand jury subpoena is a contempt of court and subjects the violator to severe criminal penalties. Identical penalties await those who destroy documents in order to avoid producing them before the grand jury. In short—and this cannot be overemphasized—documents called for by a grand jury subpoena must be produced in good faith.

Often the documents requested by the grand jury will not, after examination, satisfy all the questions that must be answered. Alternatively, new areas of investigation might arise. In either event, a second subpoena may be issued. The whole procedure just described must be undertaken a second time.

After consideration of a company's documents, the division attorney might decide to call officers of the company as witnesses before the grand jury. One called as a witness in such circumstances has no right to take his attorney with him into the grand jury room.

Suppose now, that the Antitrust Division had decided that any potential action will be civil rather than criminal in character. In such a case, information will probably be sought by a civil investigative demand. As this method of discovery was inaugurated as recently as 1962, the scope of its use by the division has not yet been fully explored. Prior to 1962, the division had no really suitable way to obtain data if voluntary cooperation was not forthcoming from the persons possessing the data. Use of the grand jury process for a case obviously destined to be civil had been held by the Supreme Court to be an abuse of process. The other possibility was to file a skeleton complaint in the district court and then use discovery methods available under the *Federal Rules of Civil Procedure* to obtain the information necessary to prove the violation. But because it is improper to bring a proceeding to see if a proceeding should be brought, this alternative scarcely satisfied the division's need to obtain information. To answer this need, Congress created the civil investigative demand especially for the Antitrust Division.

This statute permits the Attorney General or the Assistant Attorney General in charge of the Antitrust Division, whenever either has reason to believe that a person under investigation has documents relevant to an investigation being made to determine if the antitrust laws (and thus the Robinson-Patman Act) have been violated, to issue and serve on such a person a civil investigative demand requiring production of the documents for examination. The demand must state the nature of the conduct being investigated and the statute that it is alleged to violate; describe the documents to be produced with sufficient "definiteness and certainty as to permit such material to be fairly identified;" prescribe a reasonable return date; and identify the custodian to whom the material should be made available. The demand may not contain requirements that would be held unreasonable in a grand jury subpoena and may not require production of documents that would be exempt from disclosure to a grand jury. Persons receiving demands that are unreasonable may petition the local federal court for an order modifying or setting aside the demand. Finally, failure to comply with the demand subjects a person to severe criminal penalties.

A number of procedural rules are embodied in the statute. For example, a demand may be issued only before a complaint is filed. Any time after this, of course, the regular discovery rules of the *Federal Rules of Civil Procedure* are available, thus obviating any need for a civil investigative demand. Also, the statute permits the division only to inspect or copy the documents. This salutary rule prevents the complete disruption of a business through deprivation of vast numbers of important documents for a substantial period of time, or, alternatively, avoids the tremendous cost to the company of having to copy all the required documents. Documents copied by the division are to be kept secret.

When the division has completed its investigation, a decision must be made on the type of enforcement action, if any, to be used. Of course, if the investigation reveals no violation, then no action will be instituted. If a violation exists, there is the question of whether enforcement should be pursued by civil or criminal means, or both. A number of factors are taken into consideration. Criminal actions can be brought under Section 3 after specific intent to drive out a competitor is shown or on evidence of extremely predatory practices. Finally, the chances of criminal prosecution are much greater if the defendant has been guilty of similar violations in the past or if the defendant is aware that his conduct has been declared illegal in an action against other persons. If none of these criminal indicators are present, the division is almost certain to institute civil proceedings and forego a grand jury indictment.

Even though a decision is made to prosecute criminally, a civil action might also be brought. A court might find that the conduct is not criminal—even though it may constitute a civil violation—because the exacting criminal standard of proof beyond a reasonable doubt of injury to competition might not be made, whereas injury to competition might be shown by the preponderance of the evidence and thus sustain a finding of a civil violation. A more important justification for filing a companion civil suit, though, is the need to secure injunctive relief against future violations. If the division feels that the imposition of criminal penalties against the defendant is not adequate to deter future misconduct, civil remedies will also be sought.

Let us assume that the division has instituted action against a company for alleged violations of the Robinson-Patman Act. What should the officers of that company expect during the preparation for trial and during the trial itself? They should expect to spend a great deal of time educating their attorneys on the facts of the case. And, they should expect months or even years of having to deal with the case. To discover what the company and its officers will face, let us follow the normal course of an investigation.

The first thing that must be done, of course, is to familiarize the company's counsel with the operations of which the division has complained. If the same attorney who aided the company in the production of documents under a grand jury subpoena or civil investigative demand is used, the task will be easier. The education of the attorney in the relevant facts will be a continuing process, extending over the life of the case. The facts are the raw material out of which the company's counsel will attempt to develop a defense to the action. Only by being completely open and candid with him can a company hope to prevail.

Not all the facts relevant to the action, however, will usually be in possession of the company attacked. The company's attorney will have to use the discovery devices available to him to obtain from the government and from other persons the data necessary for him to prepare his case and for him to discover the nature of the division's case. This can be a long and costly process, but it is absolutely essential to a proper presentation of a company's case.

The extent to which discovery will be available to a company depends primarily on whether a civil or a criminal case is involved. The *Federal Rules of Civil Procedure* provide for the liberal use of pretrial discovery. The first discovery device available to the company is the deposition. Officers of competitor companies may be required to appear and give testimony with respect to relevant facts. The deposition may be taken on oral examination or written interrogatories. In either case, the deponent will be required, except as he is protected by certain privileges, to answer all relevant questions. If he cannot answer a question, he may be required to give the name of a person in his company who can. He may also be required to reveal the nature and description of documents that could have a bearing on the case. The use of depositions is tremendously important in preparing a case, because it is both the easiest and most reliable method of developing the facts.

Other tools are available to the civil defendant for obtaining information from the government. For example, written interrogatories may be served on the government to learn relevant facts. After showing good cause, documents in the possession of the division may be obtained to aid in the company's preparation. Finally, the division may be required to admit facts that are not in dispute, thus relieving the company of the burden of producing evidence on these matters at trial.

In a Section 3 case, unfortunately, many of these useful devices are not available to the defendant company. Without going into details, it is sufficient to say that the use of discovery in such circumstances is severely limited. This difficulty would be obviated by the use of the civil devices in a companion civil case. If that alternative is not available, then a company will have to prepare without the aid of liberal discovery.

During the time that the facts of the case are being prepared, the company's counsel and the division's attorneys, with the aid of the court, will be attempting to frame and narrow the issues properly so that a speedy resolution of those issues at trial can be accomplished. Commonly, factual issues that are not in dispute will be admitted by the parties. Procedural matters, such as the date of trial, will be arranged. In short, everything possible will be done to facilitate the handling of the case.

If a violation is found, separate hearings are usually held on the relief to be granted to the government. In a criminal case this will relate simply to the amount of the fine and the extent and necessity for jail sentences. In a civil case, however, a hearing can involve such a knotty question as the proper scope of an injunction order. The scope of the relief is of tremendous importance to a company, and great care must be exercised to obtain a decree that will prevent Robinson-Patman violations but at the same time allow the company a maximum of competitive freedom.

Because of the tremendous cost of an antitrust trial, as well as the business uncertainty attendant to it, many companies prefer to attempt settlement of the case through the division's consent decree program. Obviously, the urge to take advantage of this program increases directly as the probability of proof of violation increases. In addition to the cost savings and the avoidance of business uncertainty, the acceptance of a consent decree has two other major advantages. First and most important, a consent decree cannot be used in a private damage suit to prove that the defendant company has violated the antitrust laws. As we will discover in the next chapter, Section 5 of the Clayton Act provides that a final judgment in favor of the United States in an antitrust suit shall be prima facie evidence of violation of the law in any other antitrust action based on the same facts, except if the judgment was entered by consent or before any testimony had been taken. This provision relieves the private claimant of a tremendous burden of proof. Naturally, companies are loath to invite treble-damage suits, and a consent judgment offers one means of avoidance. A second advantage of a consent judgment is that it keeps a company's dirty linen from being aired in court and in the newspapers. Consumers may well become incensed at what appears to be business duplicity. To avoid such public castigation, a company may wish to embrace a consent settlement.

A decree, whether entered by consent or after contest, provides a guide by which the defendant company must live. Not surprisingly, problems often arise concerning the need to modify the terms of the decree. Normally, the terms of a decree are relatively easy to understand. Occasionally, however, an ambiguous provision in a decree must be construed by a court to determine the meaning intended. The rule of construction followed is that specific provisions should be read in a way that furthers the general purposes of the decree. This rule of construction does not permit a court to modify a decree silently under the guise of construing its meaning. At times, though, courts have appeared to do just this.

Sometimes conditions will have changed so markedly since the decree was entered that a company bound by the decree may desire its modification. Modification is not easily obtained from a court. If the conditions existing at the time of the entry of the decree have not changed sufficiently, modification will not be granted. And, not every changed condition will warrant modification. As one court put it: "Change is inevitable, but it is only change that reaches the underlying reasons for the decree that is relevant. Conditions existing at the time of the original entry must be compared with conditions at the time of requested modification, and the significance of the difference measured in the light of those original reasons." In short, "nothing less than a clear showing of grievous wrong evoked by new and unforeseen conditions" will lead a court to relax and modify the provisions of a decree.

So far we have discussed the problems that the businessman may have with the Antitrust Division. But in other contexts the division can be most helpful to a businessman faced with antitrust problems.

For example, a company experiencing business difficulty because of the violations of its competitors, customers, or suppliers may wish to file a formal complaint with the division. All that is necessary to accomplish this is to write to the Attorney General the facts that the company believes to indicate antitrust violations by another. The division will handle the matter thereafter. One danger in taking advantage of this right of complaint should be mentioned. If the division becomes interested in the industry affected by the violation, it may institute a full-scale investigation of that industry. This investigation may reveal that the complaining company has also been guilty of violations. In such a situation the division will not hesitate to prosecute. Accordingly, a company should ensure that its own house is in order before complaining of the antitrust violations of others.

16

Private Enforcement

In addition to the enforcement of the Robinson-Patman Act by the Federal Trade Commission and, to a limited extent, by the Department of Justice, there is always the possibility of action by private parties. Indeed, private action has often been praised as the most effective means of enforcing the law, for two reasons. First, it has been thought that violations will be more readily detected by persons who are directly affected by them. Secondly, private parties often will be able to bring suit with greater ease than the governmental enforcement agencies, which are burdened by budgetary problems. To encourage such private enforcement, Congress has provided that a successful litigant can recover three times the actual damages sustained by his business as a result of the violation, plus a reasonable attorney's fee. Not surprisingly, this has been a tremendous incentive to private suits, and the importance of such suits has increased markedly with the passing years.

Private actions to enforce the Robinson-Patman Act may be brought only in federal district courts. This requirement precludes an injured

297

company from bringing suit in a state court and even prevents the company from counterclaiming in a state court when sued by the violator on some other cause of action.

Although suit is normally brought directly by the injured company or companies, actions may arise in other ways. In a recent interesting case, a group of miners, on their own behalf and for those similarly situated, sued two mining companies, alleging, among other things, that they had been damaged by the conspiracy between the companies to fix at an unreasonably low level the price at which the companies would purchase raw ore. By suing both for themselves and for others similarly situated, the miners had brought what is termed a *class action*. Eventually, the miners recovered. Because a class action was involved, miners who were not parties to the original action could intervene in the proceedings and recover simply by proving that they were members of the class and injured by the violation. The necessity of proving that the defendants had violated the law was no longer essential, as this had been accomplished by the original plaintiffs. Additionally, the original action suspended the statute of limitations for those miners later intervening in the proceedings.

Another unusual means of private enforcement is an action by shareholders of the injured company. If the directors of the company arbitrarily refuse to bring suit, the shareholders may then bring what is commonly termed a *derivative suit* in order to recover for the company the damages to which it is entitled. For example, in a recent case the shareholders were allowed to enforce the company's cause of action, even though the directors of the company had voted not to bring action, because it appeared that the directors of the company were under the control of the corporation that had been violating the law. In short, shareholders are allowed to enforce a company's rights when those in control of the company unreasonably fail to do so. To be distinguished from such a derivative suit is an action by the shareholders seeking to recover on their own account damages to the value of their stock interest caused by a violation. The basis for such an action is that the violation has so injured the company that the value of its stock has declined and the shareholders have thereby been directly injured. But such a cause of action has never been allowed, because courts have felt that the likelihood of such an injury was too tenuous to warrant the grant of relief. An additional ground for the denial of relief will be discussed subsequently.

Section 4 of the Clayton Act provides that "any person who shall be injured in his business or property by reason of anything forbidden in the antitrust laws may sue therefore . . . and shall recover threefold the damages by him sustained, and the cost of suit, including a reasonable attorney's fee." The antitrust laws to which reference is made includes, in addition to the Robinson-Patman Act, Sections 1 and 2 of the Sherman Act and Sections 3, 7, and 8 of the Clayton Act. The nature of the right to private action thus created involves a number of complex problems, the explanation of which will occupy most of the remainder of this chapter.

At the outset it should be noted that in addition to a violation of the antitrust laws, a private plaintiff must establish two things: first, that the illegal conduct charged actually caused an injury to his business or property, and second, that the injury suffered is measurable in damages. Under Section 4 of the Clayton Act, injury is a prerequisite to standing to sue, and damages are the law's cognition of injury. The courts have long recognized that there is a basic distinction between the fact of harm—legal injury—and the amount of damages incurred as a result of that injury. While proof of injury often will be interwoven with proof of damages, there is no legal requirement that the two be coextensive.

Only those damages to the *business or property* of the plaintiff caused by antitrust violations can be recompensed under Section 4. The injury to a shareholder resulting from the diminution in value of his stock brings no right to treble recovery, for stock ownership is not part of the shareholder's business or property. Similarly, one cannot recover for a violation that prevents the establishment of a new business. Because by definition no business exists until it is started, the violation that prevented a business from opening could not work an injury to the business or property of the claimant. The injury must be to actual assets and not to a mere expectancy of future assets. This distinction serves to explain a case in which recovery was allowed for antitrust violations that had prevented the plaintiff from opening a business. In that case, the injured party had contracted to distribute milk to be furnished by the other contracting party. Fearing competition, the existing milk distributors banded together to induce the milk producer to breach the contract. The court allowed recovery on the basis that the *contract* was part of the plaintiff's business or property, that the violation had rendered it valueless, and that such diminution in value was a recoverable element of damages.

An additional requirement of Section 4 is that there be *injury* to the plaintiff's business or property *caused by* the defendant's violations. A private litigant has no standing to enforce the Robinson-Patman Act unless the violation has caused actual injury to his business from the violation. Only the Attorney General has an absolute right to exact compliance with the law. The absence of any precise limitations to this causation requirement has been one of the perplexing problems in treble damage actions. In *Loeb* v. *Eastman Kodak*, for example, the Third Circuit denied standing to sue to a stockholder-creditor of a corporation forced into bankruptcy by the defendant's antitrust violations on the ground that any injury to the plaintiff was indirect; the injury was directed to the company. According to the court, a "plaintiff must show that his loss was not a consequence of injury to someone else, i.e., that he had direct relations with the wrongdoer." And yet several courts have found sufficient adverse effects upon officers, directors, and employees of injured corporations. Other decisions in which recovery has been denied because of the remoteness of the plaintiff's injury to the violation alleged have involved a franchisor of injured franchisees, a patent owner suffering royalty losses resulting from injuries to his licensee, and a landlord of an injured lessee. While recovery has generally been denied plaintiffs where their loss is "derivative," the tendency of the courts, as exemplified by the Ninth Circuit in *Karseal Corp.* v. *Richfield Oil Corp.*, has been to find actionable injury if the plaintiff "was within the target area of the illegal practices." A plaintiff has standing to sue if he was "not only hit, but was aimed at." That the "target area" theory is more flexible than the direct-indirect injury approach can be seen in the Supreme Court's recent *Perkins* decision (discussed at length in Chapter 6). The plaintiff in that case purchased gasoline from the defendant at prices higher than those paid by a competing wholesaler with the result that his retail outlets were unable to compete with the retail outlets supplied by the favored wholesaler. As a result, he went out of business. Perkins submitted some evidence tending to show that he, as an individual, had suffered financial losses because the two failing corporations owned by him (the actual operators of the business which was destroyed) were unable to pay him agreed brokerage fees for securing gasoline, rental on leases of service stations, and other indebtedness. The court of appeals concluded that Perkins as an individual was only *incidentally* injured by the defendant's violation of the antitrust laws. The Supreme Court held, however, that "Perkins was no mere innocent bystander; he was the principal victim of the price discrimination. . . . Since he was directly injured and was clearly entitled to bring this suit, he was entitled to present evidence of all of his losses to the jury." In other words, once having established his standing to sue, Perkins was permitted to recover all actual damages, direct and indirect, suffered by him as a consequence of the defendant's unlawful conduct.

Even if a plaintiff came within the "target area" of the defendant's unlawful actions, however, no recovery would be allowed if the injury resulted simply from normal competitive stresses or from mismanagement by the company's officers. So also, if the violation had no effect on the plaintiff, an action should fail. For example, if any higher prices charged to customers were passed on by them to their own customers, without thereby losing any sales, no measurable financial injury to the manufacturer's customers would appear to have occurred; therefore, no recovery would be allowed. But a recent Supreme Court decision raises the question of whether the fact that a disfavored purchaser passes on his higher prices to his customers immunizes the supplier from legal liability to that disfavored purchaser. The *Hanover Shoe* case rejected the use of the *passing on* defense in a Sherman Act context. The Court believed ". . . it is not unlikely that if the existence of the defense is generally confirmed, anti-trust defendants will frequently seek to establish its applicability. Treble damage actions would often require additional long and complicated proceedings involving massive evidence and complicated theories." In addition, the Court stated that if the defense were accepted, the effective-ness of damage actions would be "substantially reduced in effectiveness." It reasoned that ". . . if buyers are subjected to the passing on defense, those who buy from them would also have to meet the challenge that they passed on their higher price to *their* customers. These ultimate consum-ers . . . would have only a tiny stake in a lawsuit and little interest in attempting a class action."

Robinson-Patman violations are often difficult to prove. This is par-ticularly so for the private litigant, often a small businessman who is already a financial victim of an economically stronger violator and unable to bear the burden of litigating the issue of violation. Recogniz-ing the economic burden, as well as the public interest in encourag-ing private enforcement, Congress enacted a special provision—Section 5 of the Clayton Act—designed to aid private litigants in carrying this burden of proof. Section 5 provides that a final judgment or decree, resulting from any civil or criminal antitrust action (except damage suits) instituted by the United States, which affirms that the defendant has violated the antitrust laws, can be used in other actions as proof of those facts necessarily proved in the government's action. This relieves the private litigant of the task of proving the existence of a violation; all that he need prove is that the violation caused injury to his business or prop-erty. Not surprisingly, the practical result of this provision often is a host of private actions following a successful prosecution by the govern-ment for antitrust violations.

There are two major exceptions to this provision. Section 5 states that this rule will not apply to "consent judgments or decrees entered before any testimony has been taken." This exception is of tremendous practi-cal importance, and it acts as a spur to defendants to refrain from contesting actions brought by the government in order to avoid a subse-quent flood of private litigation should the case be lost. But the provision also works to the government's benefit, for it saves the time and money necessarily lost in trial—time and money therefore available for use in other enforcement activities.

Section 5(a) of the Clayton Act also requires that any final order sub-mitted to establish a prima facie case must be based on a government proceeding brought under one of the antitrust laws. It is well settled that an FTC action brought under the Clayton Act is such a proceeding, as is one brought under the Robinson-Patman Act. However, the unique problems surrounding buyer inducement of promotional allowances and services have necessitated the indirect use of Section 5 of the FTC Act. Some doubt has been voiced as to whether the FTC Act is an antitrust law for purposes of establishing a prima facie case. At least one United States District Court has indicated that it is not. In *Y & Y Popcorn Supply Co.* v. *ABC Vending Corp.*, the court refused to admit an FTC order as prima facie proof because the vagueness of the order raised the possibility that it might be based solely on a violation of Section 5 of the FTC Act.

In addition, it should be recalled from Chapter 13 that Section 3 of the Robinson-Patman Act, the criminal provision, has been held *not* to be one of the antitrust laws. Thus, a government decree based on Section 3 may *not* be used as prima facie proof that an antitrust violation has occurred.

In 1955, Congress enacted a four-year statute of limitations applicable to private antitrust (including Robinson-Patman) actions. It provides that no antitrust cause of action may be the basis of a suit more than four years after it has accrued. The first question raised, therefore, is when the cause of action accrues. The general rule is that a cause of action accrues when injury to the plaintiff occurs. This does not mean, however, that measurable economic damage must take place just then. Rather, it means that those acts have occurred that injure the plaintiff and that necessarily will result in present or future economic damage.

A slightly more complicated set of rules governs the accrual of a cause of action based on a civil violation. Again, the significant date is the date of injury to the plaintiff, not the date on which the violation takes place. Once an act by the defendant has injured the plaintiff, a cause of action has arisen, and the statute of limitations starts to run. It continues to run until it bars the suit four years later. The fact that the violation continues in no way affects the running of the statute in regard to those damages caused by any particular act of the defendant. But a new cause of action arises with each act causing injury. The plaintiff can recover for those damages that resulted from overt acts of the defendant occurring within four years of the institution of plaintiff's action. For example, suppose that a violation commences in 1955, and the defendant commits injurious acts until 1968. In 1968, an injured person files an action. Without a showing of fraudulent concealment, the plaintiff can recover only for injuries inflicted during the four-year period, 1964–1968.

A significant exception to the rules governing the statute of limitations is contained in Section 5 of the Clayton Act. It provides that the running of the statute on any private right of action arising under the antitrust laws shall be suspended during the pendency of any government action (except a damage suit) designed to prevent, restrain, or punish violations of the antitrust laws. A private litigant, to take advantage of this provision, must base his cause of action "in whole or in part" on violations alleged by the government action. The suspension of the statute of limitations is not absolute. Rather, the suspension lasts only during the pendency of the government action and for one year thereafter. Any private action must be commenced either within four years after the cause of action accrued or during the period of suspension. For example, suppose that a cause of action accrued in 1948, that the government instituted suit for the same violation in 1950, that this suit was terminated in 1954, and that a private action was commenced in 1956. The private suit would be barred, because it was instituted more than four years after the cause of action accrued and not during the period of suspension. This is so even though the statute was suspended for five of the eight years after the accrual of the cause of action.

Another important situation in which the statute of limitations is suspended has recently assumed importance because of the electrical conspiracy cases. These decisions appear to indicate that the statute of limitations will be suspended during the period in which the violator has engaged in acts designed to prevent the plaintiff from discovering the existence of a cause of action. This suspension results from a doctrine known as "tolling by fraudulent concealment." In order to take advantage of this doctrine, a plaintiff must show that the defendant affirmatively acted to conceal the facts underlying the cause of action from the plaintiff's view and, therefore, that the plaintiff could not have discovered his cause of action in the exercise of reasonable diligence. The applicability of the doctrine of fraudulent concealment to the statute of limitations has not been definitely decided. At present, however, it appears likely that the doctrine will be held to apply.

A number of defenses are available in private actions. Many of these, of course, are equally available in any lawsuit. Three defenses that are interrelated deserve special mention because of their special importance in Robinson-Patman litigation. The first of these is the defense of *in pari delicto* (equal fault). In the past, the courts were hesitant to allow treble recovery for damages caused by violations to plaintiffs who were also guilty of violations. In part, this hesitance was based on the feeling that it would be inequitable to allow one violator to point the finger of guilt at another violator and recover what amounted to punitive damages. This illustrates an important point in private litigation. Because of the drastic nature of treble relief, courts have required perhaps even a higher degree of proof by private plaintiffs than by the government, feeling that such harsh punishment should be inflicted only after a strong showing of illegality. This atitude strongly influenced the application of the *in pari delicto* defense in the past. Not only was a clear showing of illegality required, but a plaintiff also had to establish itself as a paragon of business virtue before any relief could be obtained.

This puritanical approach to private enforcement has abated in recent years. The reason is the judicial recognition that a violator should not elude punishment simply because he has injured a party who might also be engaging in violations. The injured party may be subject to other enforcement proceedings without adding the additional penalty of the loss of a justified cause of action. The Supreme Court's recent review of the *in pari delicto* doctrine in *Perma Life Mufflers* resulted in a sharp curtailment, and possibly an abolishment, of its use in an antitrust context. Confusion as to what precisely the Court held in that decision arises from the fact that there were no less than five separate opinions. Speaking for four members of the Court, Justice Black stated that the plaintiff who benefits from treble damages may be no less morally reprehensible than the defendant, "but the law encourages his suit to further the overriding public policy in favor of competition." He concluded that "the doctrine of *in pari delicto*, with its complex scope, contents and effects, is not to be recognized as a defense to an antitrust action." Justice Black added, however, that the extent to which the plaintiff may have benefited from its own violations of the antitrust laws can be taken into consideration in computing damages. The general thrust of the four concurring opinions (representing five members of the Court) was that *in pari delicto* should continue to have a significant if limited role in private antitrust law where the plaintiff and defendant *bear substantially equal responsibility for injury* resulting to one of them. The defense should be available where there is equal fault between the two parties.

A closely related defense is that of *volenti non fit injuria* (he who consents to an act is not wronged by it). The rationale of the *volenti* doctrine is that it is inequitable to allow a person to observe an arrangement voluntarily and then recover treble damages for having done so. Indeed, such an allowance would invite companies to incur damages from violations so that they could enjoy the punitive trebling of those damages.

The final defense, closely related to the other two, is that of mitigation of damages. A party being injured by Robinson-Patman violations is under an obligation to avoid as much of the resultant damage as possible. A chain of stores losing money as a result of the illegality of another's conduct would probably not be allowed to recover for additional losses caused by the opening of new stores, because it knew that such further losses were inevitable. The duty to minimize the extent of damages deserves strict enforcement in private litigation. If it is not strictly enforced, a terrible temptation will be created to increase one's damages unjustifiably in order to enjoy an even larger gratuitous recovery because of the trebling provision of Section 4 of the Clayton Act.

A brief word should be said about the proof and measure of damages in private actions. This area is probably the biggest hurdle facing a private antitrust litigant. That a plaintiff is entitled to recover for all damages proximately caused by a violation has already been noted. But the actual amount of damage suffered must be proved. A court or jury is not entitled to award damages, particularly when they will be trebled, simply by speculating how much the plaintiff *may* have lost or by compromising on what *appears* to be a just award under all the circumstances. But absolute certainty as to amount of damage is not required. In *Story Parchment Co.* v. *Paterson Parchment Paper Co.*, the Supreme Court held the following criteria applicable to a jury's assessment of damages in private antitrust actions:

> Juries are allowed to act upon probable and inferential, as well as direct and positive proof. And when, from the nature of the case, the amount of damages can not be estimated with certainty, or only a part of them can be so estimated, we can see no objection to placing before the jury all the facts and circumstances of the case having any tendency to show damages, or their probable amount; so as to enable them to make the most intelligible and probable estimate which the nature of the case will permit.

To the same effect is *Flintkote Co.* v. *Lysfjord*, where the Court ruled that the controlling rule today in seeking damages for loss of profits in antitrust cases is that the plaintiff is required to establish with reasonable probability the existence of some causal connection between defendant's wrongful act and some loss of anticipated revenue. Once that has been accomplished, "the jury will be permitted to 'make a just and reasonable estimate of the damage based on relevant data, and render its verdict accordingly.' "

Even when proof of damages looks easy, it may not be. For example, suppose that an unlawful price discrimination resulted in an additional cost of ten cents a unit to a customer. On the surface, damages would appear to be ten cents multiplied by the number of units purchased at this higher price. The courts are split, however, on whether to permit reliance upon this so-called automatic rule of damages. The two leading cases on the opposing views are *Elizabeth Arden Sales Corporation* v. *Gas Glass Co.*, and *Enterprise Industries, Inc.* v. *Texas Co. Arden* held that the amount of such a discrimination can properly be made the basis and measure of a general damage award, where the evidence does not establish a greater consequential or special injury. It took the view that, within legal and commercial realities, the nonfavored customer would at least "be injured in his business or property" to the extent of the diminution or deprivation thus occasioned to his treasury or asset position. *Enterprise* held, in an opinion written by Judge Learned Hand, that no such direct damage award is entitled to be made under the act; that the non-favored customer is required to prove consequential injury to his business in loss of customers or profits; and that only such injury can be made the basis and measure of any recovery for a discrimination. Those supporting the *Enterprise* theory maintain that many other factors enter into a determination of actual damages. For example, if the customer was able to pass the higher cost on, in whole or in part, to his customers, then he suffered no compensable injury at all, or only a limited injury. On the other hand, such action may have resulted in a loss of customers. This, in turn, created additional compensable damages. The Ninth Circuit recently cast its vote in favor of the automatic rule in *Fowler Manufacturing Co.* v. *H. H. Gorlick.* The court found that while the Supreme Court had not undertaken to resolve the question adjudicatively, it had engaged in some expression thereon in *Bruce's Juices, Inc.* v. *American Can Co.,* where it stated that the disfavored purchaser had been damaged, in the absence of extraordinary circumstances, at least in the amount of the discrimination. Thus, the Ninth Circuit concluded:

> unless the evidence established a greater consequential injury, discrimination in prices or allowances is entitled to be regarded as constituting a direct business injury and that the amount thereof thus properly can be made the basis and measure of a general damages award.

Section 16 of the Clayton Act allows private litigants to seek injunctive relief against threatened loss or damage by a violation of the antitrust laws. This partial dispensation for private parties to enforce the laws is hedged about by a number of limitations. First, and most important, the violation in question must actually threaten direct and serious loss or damage to the business or property of the plaintiff. Secondly, such relief will be limited to enjoining the violation; no attempt will be made to put the plaintiff in a preferred position. Normally, a court will not enjoin conduct that is already proscribed under a government decree. It goes without saying that a private injunction cannot run counter to the provisions of a government decree.

A special form of injunctive relief—although it does not seem to come under the provisions of Section 16 of the Clayton Act—has recently assumed great significance. The circumstances are very simple: Suppose a customer sues a supplier for treble damages. What remedy, if any, does the customer have if the supplier attempts through economic coercion to force the customer to drop the suit by threatening to refuse to sell to him in the future? In two recent cases, two federal courts of appeals reached contrary decisions on whether the customer should be entitled to a court order requiring the supplier to continue to sell to him during the pendency of the suit. An examination of some of the considerations involved in answering this question will provide a suitable conclusion to our chapter on private enforcement.

It has been antitrust dogma for years that a supplier has an absolute right, in the absence of a conspiracy or a purpose to monopolize, to deal or to refuse to deal with a customer for any reason or for no reason at all. The exercise of this right to select the customers with whom one will deal has been generally considered to be per se lawful. Requiring a supplier to continue dealing with a customer when the supplier wishes not to, of course, is simply contrary to this well-established rule. Furthermore, it may require the continuation of a customer relationship when that is particularly difficult because of the antagonistic positions in which the parties find themselves. Put another way, it may be extremely hard for companies that are sworn enemies in the courtroom to generate the mutual trust and confidence outside the courtroom that is necessary to develop and maintain an effective and satisfying supplier-customer relationship.

In the cases that have been decided so far, the defendants admitted that they stopped dealing solely to induce the plaintiffs to drop their suits. Both courts recognized that this action by the defendant had the effect of thwarting the public's interest in encouraging private suits for enforcement of law. But, the courts have diverged in their assessment of the relative importance of this public interest and the private interest in free choice of customers.

If injunctive relief is to be granted, its basis will probably not be Section 16 of the Clayton Act. As we noted, refusal to deal is not normally an antitrust violation, and such a violation is a sine qua non to the use of Section 16. Relief may be granted, however, by reference to the inherent powers of a court of equity to enjoin acts interfering with the maintenance of a lawsuit in order to maintain judicial integrity. But that a court has the power to enjoin a refusal to deal does not in itself answer the question of whether that power should be utilized.

Plainly, there is a strong public interest in private enforcement. Equally plain is the necessary thwarting of that interest by private use of economic coercion. In some industries, such as the drug industry, customers must have certain products. A pharmacist is required to follow the brand designation in a physician's prescription. If he is unable to obtain that brand, his business will end. In such circumstances a refusal to deal because of private litigation should be enjoinable.

On the other hand, many countervailing factors militate against granting injunctive relief. We have already mentioned the supplier's interest in the right to choose his customers for any reason at all and the difficulty of maintaining a supplier-customer relationship when litigation is pending between the parties. Furthermore, if forced dealing is required during the pendency of an action, this will still permit economic coercion in the form of a threatened refusal to deal after the action's completion. Of course, refusal to deal after the action serves no economic interest of the supplier, but simple vindictiveness might still lead to such a refusal. Permanent forced dealing could be required, with all its compulsory overtones, but even this might create further problems. If such a mandatory injunction were issued, it might prevent a refusal to deal based on sound business reasons. A company should not lose its business freedom in the future simply because of a past wrong.

It is apparent that serious problems are posed by the current efforts to obtain injunctive relief against coercive refusals to deal directed at ending private enforcement. It would be presumptuous to predict what the final outcome of these battles will be. The very existence of the battles, however, indicates the tremendous importance that is now attached to private enforcement.

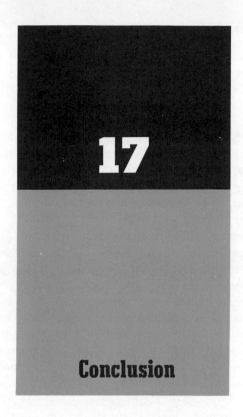

17

Conclusion

In 1936, the Robinson-Patman Act was indelibly pressed by Congress into the fabric of our federal antitrust laws. Rising, as it were, like a Phoenix from the ashes of the NRA Blue Eagle, the act sought to protect independent merchants from being placed at an unfair marketing disadvantage by having to compete with mass distributors and chains who had received the largesse of discriminatory prices and promotional allowances from suppliers.

From the moment of its conception, Robinson-Patman was pilloried and buffeted, harpooned and lambasted, condemned—and by some—consigned to the scrap heap of meaningless and unenforceable legislation. At Bar Association meeting after Bar Association meeting, speakers have delighted in kicking around Mr. Patman's "legislative dog." The act was, and remains today, the Peck's Bad Boy of antitrust.

For those who, during the years, have found the texture of this cloth too coarse or its cut unseemly, the act is confusing and inconsistent. Admittedly, the Robinson-Patman Act is not a model of legislative clarity.

However, to paraphrase Mark Twain, reports of its death are exaggerated —not one word of the statute has been changed in its thirty-four-year span of existence. Like Mount Everest, it is still very much there, very much a challenge that must be met and understood by responsible businessmen.

Many businessmen have long since learned that Robinson-Patman will not simply go away if they leave it alone. Apathy and resistance are dangerous replies by industry to this legislation. Understanding of its basic provisions is, therefore, imperative if businessmen are to compete effectively and, at the same time, to comply with the law. The stakes are high, but so are the antitrust risks.

Furthermore, despite the criticism that the act has encountered, it is clear that a price discrimination law is necessary if the American free enterprise system is to work effectively. History has demonstrated that unregulated price discrimination will destroy the small businessman. The exacting of price concessions by volume purchasers in the 1920s and 1930s, with the resulting drastic decline in the number of small retailers, was, in fact, the very impetus for the Robinson-Patman Act. And, a price discrimination law is necessary to the preservation of big business as well, because if unregulated price discrimination should force small business out of existence, it seems clear that even more drastic legislative restraints would be imposed on big business.

Free enterprise does not mean the absence of government regulation. In fact, free enterprise cannot work without laws that make competition both fair and free. The antitrust laws, of which the Robinson-Patman Act is a part, constitute a uniquely American solution to the Scylla of statism on the one hand, and the Charybdis of monopoly—the result of unfettered, uninhibited capitalism—on the other. They represent the effort of a people dedicated to capitalism to save capitalism. In the area of business regulation, America has surrendered neither to the forces of predatory combination nor to the forces of statism. We have merely developed pragmatic devices to confine the areas of conflict while preserving our system of free competition. Thus, the antitrust laws embody a principle of conservatism. They were designed to preserve competition, not to eradicate it. The laws attack those forces that would restrict the right to compete. They afford means for avoiding the concentration of power, whether in private hands, as in monopoly, or in government hands, as in a statist regime.

The antitrust laws are, of course, not self-executing. They must be effectively enforced to obtain the goal of making competition both fair and free. Historically, two principal approaches to antitrust enforcement were evolved at the Federal Trade Commission, which, it will be recalled, is the principal enforcing agency of the Robinson-Patman Act. The first of these was vigorous, all-out enforcement through compulsory procedures. The second was an appeal to industry for self-regulation, supported by a government educational program. In the course of time, these two approaches acquired labels. The first approach came to be called hard enforcement, and the second approach, soft enforcement. These positions were thought to be antithetical.

Hard enforcement came to be equated by the public with all-out prosecution engendered by suspicion, if not open hostility, toward business motives and practices. In the minds of some, the hard enforcement position required that any and every suspected violation be met with a formal complaint, without regard to the magnitude of the offense, the relative degree of public interest, the availability and proper allocation of limited funds and skilled manpower, the propriety of informal techniques, or the problems of a given industry. Justly or unjustly, this position came to be equated with a concentration on successful prosecution, rather than meaningful compliance. The important thing was to get an order—an ever-increasing number of orders—without much consideration of the effect of the order. The emphasis on new prosecutions was to be maintained even at the expense of inadequate or nonexistent policing of compliance with outstanding orders. This total emphasis on prosecution meant that no advance warnings would be given to the business community, either through general education or by careful explanation of the rationale of formal opinions, lest an advantage be surrendered to an implacable adversary.

The soft enforcement position, in the course of time, acquired equally unfortunate connotations. This position was equated with a benign willingness to allow business conduct to go unregulated. The emphasis on business education was not coupled with any overriding emphasis on thoroughgoing compliance when such compliance required resort to compulsory procedure.

It seems to me that both of these historical positions are unsatisfactory. If our goal is to ensure the operation of our nation's economy in conformity to the antitrust and trade regulation laws, neither position alone is likely to achieve it. But are the two positions mutually exclusive? I believe not. I am firmly convinced that vigorous enforcement, on the one hand, and meaningful business education in the requirements of the laws, followed by effective self-regulation, on the other hand, are not antithetical. Rather, they are complementary tools for achieving the same goal. Vigorous enforcement alone cannot do the job; the time and resources of the enforcement agency are cruelly limited. A program of business education without additional measures cannot do the job, for honest men are likely to succumb to temptation if dishonest men are not deterred.

The concept of *meaningful compliance* implies a degree of flexibility in the employment of available techniques and in the timing and emphasis of actions. Because time and resources are limited, and because the relative degree of public interest shifts as circumstances change, there must be a careful selection of the areas of greatest impact for any given action. There must be a careful adaptation of technique to situation in order to achieve a state of compliance in the cheapest and quickest way possible. The minimum effort necessary to correct any given situation must be employed in order to cover the broadest total area possible. If a situation will not yield to any of the commission's traditional techniques, then new techniques must be evolved. Most important, the focus must be firmly fixed on the goal of meaningful compliance, with no method or technique exalted at the expense of that goal.

Lax enforcement can never produce meaningful compliance. Government regulation is a mockery unless the enforcement agency and its personnel actively pursue their statutory mandates. The proper role of government in the economy is that of a referee, not of a player; but this does not mean that the referee should remain supinely idle while one player gouges another and the contest turns into chaos. There must be a vigorous enforcement of the ground rules of competition. A government agency charged with the enforcement of the antitrust and trade regulation laws and the proscription of unfair trade practices must actively use every resource available to it to insure that competition is free and fair.

Another consideration that should guide enforcement activity is a regard for fairness. An administrative agency charged with the enforcement of the antitrust and trade regulation laws must show continuous, careful regard for the procedural requirements that ensure fairness in adjudicative proceedings. The Federal Trade Commission's orders are not instruments of punishment. Rather, they are instruments designed to prevent future violations and to ensure meaningful compliance. No order issued without regard to procedural due process can create a climate of meaningful compliance. Corner-cutting by the government breeds corner-cutting conduct by others. In a government of laws, fairness must be an end in itself.

We must try to prevent the unfairness that results when one company is singled out for attention in a whole industry that is rife with violations. With the broad powers entrusted to the commission by Congress, there is no reason why the FTC should not proceed simultaneously on an industrywide front where necessary. The FTC, in recent years, has moved in this direction. However, much remains to be done, and must be done, because administration of the antitrust and trade regulation laws can never be made truly effective if this kind of fairness is lacking.

Finally, I will discuss in the context of these concluding thoughts a matter that from time to time has troubled the business community.

It has been suggested that our antitrust laws are being increasingly enforced and applied so as to stifle competition and discourage efficiency, whereas the true purpose of those laws is to preserve competition and stimulate efficiency. Indeed, the thought is that a number of those anti- trust laws—including those concerned with price discrimination—are perhaps themselves anticompetitive in effect, because they are based on unsound theoretical and empirical foundations.

The question of whether our antitrust laws are anticompetitive stems inevitably from the fact that these laws are to an extent directed at the *regulation* of competition. Antitrust philosophy, as we have conceived it in this country, is largely based on the premise that, in order to pre- serve competition in the long run, you have to place certain restraints on it in the short run. This process of saving competition by restricting it is, admittedly, a difficult and delicate operation, and perhaps one that will not succeed. But, personally, I believe that the laws on the books today have put us on the right road in terms of preserving competition over the long haul.

I do not think that those defects that may exist in antitrust methods can be attributed either to fatal flaws in the statutes themselves or to any general misenforcement or misapplication of those statutes. The answer may simply be that the problem of the application of the anti- trust statutes, and of their underlying policies, has inevitably been so difficult that bad law has been created along with good law.

The Robinson-Patman Act, as well as each of the other antitrust laws, has a firm empirical base in the economic history of this country. Hard economic facts and the fear of growing economic concentration was the basis for the adoption of the Robinson-Patman Act in 1936. The intent was to preserve competition for the long run by saddling it with certain limitations. The primary objective sought by passage of the Robinson- Patman Act was, of course, the neutralization in large measure of the sheer economic power of the retail chain stores to extract substantially lower prices from their suppliers than their single-unit competitors could obtain. There was good reason to fear that, if this economic power were left unrestrained, the smaller competitors in each industry would even- tually be driven out of business. The passage of the act plainly resulted from a value judgment by the Congress that the preservation of independ- ent local retailing was of greater importance than the temporary benefit of lower prices to consumers effected by the power of the chain retailers.

It can fairly be said, moreover, that the Robinson-Patman Act does not force the larger buyer to give up the advantages stemming from his greater efficiency—he can claim a price benefit to the extent that it is in fact cost justified. The act simply limits him in the use of his *economic power*. This, I would suggest, is not too high a price to pay to maintain the many economic benefits that our economy derives from industries that are multimember in their composition.

The spirit and design of each of the antitrust laws is essentially in favor of competition and in favor of efficiency. They are anticompetitive only in the sense that they oppose the unfettered competition that must eventually lead to the destruction of competition. They are antiefficiency only in the sense that they reject the temporary efficiency offered by the firm seeking dominance in favor of the more gradual, but more stable, efficiency offered by a fully competitive system.

I do not believe that, when fairly and effectively administered and applied, the antitrust statutes are anticompetitive in effect. The comparative youth of our antitrust statutes, their ambitious scope, and their undoubted complexity have, unfortunately, produced a number of questionable judicial decisions, as well as some law enforcement of debatable wisdom.

However, the debate over marginal questions has contributed nothing to the basic need for developing an understanding in the business community of its actual present responsibilities under the law. The businessman needs to understand the basic concepts of discrimination in price and of discriminatory promotional allowance. He needs help both to understand these basic requirements and to conform his everyday business practices so that they comply with the law. The business community to which the act is addressed should be encouraged to maintain an attitude of respect and understanding toward this difficult statute, even though we must continuously reexamine and reconsider the propriety and efficacy of this statute, as well as other antitrust legislation.

If we can achieve a greater understanding of our antitrust laws, impart more respect for them to the business community, and enforce their prohibitions swiftly and consistently, I, for one, believe that they will safeguard competition in our economy.

Appendix I

Selected Bibliography

General Works

ABA, Antitrust Section, *The Robinson-Patman Act: 1936–1966,* Vol. 30 (1966).

Attorney General, *Report of the National Committee to Study the Antitrust Laws* (1955).

Austin, *Price Discrimination,* 2nd ed. (1959).

Baum, *The Robinson-Patman Act—Summary and Comment* (1964).

Edwards, *The Price Discrimination Law* (1959).

Patman, *Complete Guide to the Robinson-Patman Act* (1963).

Rowe, *Price Discrimination Under the Robinson-Patman Act* (1962) and *Supplement* (1965).

Sawyer, *Business Aspects of Pricing Under the Robinson-Patman Act* (1963).

Stickells, *Legal Control of Business Practice* (1965).

Symposium, *The Robinson-Patman Act: Retrospect and Prospect,* 17 ABA Antitrust Sect. Rep. (1960).

Taggart, *Cost Justification* (1959).

Van Cise, *Understanding the Antitrust Laws* (1963)

Chapter 2: Historical Background of the Robinson-Patman Act

BIBLIOGRAPHY

Austin, *Price Discrimination,* 2nd ed. (1959).
Baum, *The Robinson-Patman Act—Summary and Comment* (1964).
Edwards, *The Price Discrimination Law* (1959).
Patman, *Complete Guide to the Robinson-Patman Act* (1963).
Rowe, *Price Discrimination Under the Robinson-Patman Act* (1962) and *Supplement* (1965).
Sawyer, *Business Aspects of Pricing Under the Robinson-Patman Act* (1963).

LEGISLATIVE MATERIALS

Report of the Senate Committee on the Judiciary, S. Rep. No. 1502, 74th Cong., 2nd sess. (1936).
Report of the House Committee on the Judiciary, H.R. Rep. No. 2287, 74th Cong., 2d sess. (1936).
Report of Conference Committee, S. Rep. No. 267, 74th Cong., 2d sess. (1936).
Hearings Before the House Committee on the Judiciary on Bills to Amend the Clayton Act, 74th Cong., 1st sess. (1935).
Legislative Discussion of S. 3154 and H.R. 8442 as contained in *Congressional Record,* Vols. 79 and 80 (1935–1936).
The Federal Trade Commission Final Report on the Chain Store Investigation, S. Doc. No. 4, 74th Cong., 1st sess. (1935).

CASES

Central Lumber Co. v. *South Dakota,* 226 U.S. 157 (1912).
Fairmont Creamery Co. v. *Minnesota,* 274 U.S. 1 (1927).
George Van Camp & Sons v. *American Can Co.,* 278 U.S. 245 (1929).
Schechter Poultry Corp. v. *United States,* 295 U.S. 495 (1935).

Chapter 3: A Bird's-Eye View of the Robinson-Patman Act

BIBLIOGRAPHY

Austin, *Price Discrimination,* 2nd ed. (1959).
Edwards, *The Price Discrimination Law* (1959).
Rowe, *Price Discrimination Under the Robinson-Patman Act* (1962) and *Supplement* (1965).
Sawyer, *Business Aspects of Pricing Under the Robinson-Patman Act* (1963).
Symposium, *The Robinson–Patman Act: Retrospect and Prospect,* 17 ABA Antitrust Sec. Rep. (1960).
Taggart, *Cost Justification* (1959).

CASES

A. E. Staley Manufacturing Co. v. *FTC,* 324 U.S. 746 (1945).
Alhambra Motor Parts v. *FTC,* 309 F. 2d 213 (9th Cir. 1962).

Amana Refrigeration, Inc. v. *Columbia Broadcasting System,* 295 F. 2d 375 (7th Cir. 1961).

American Motor Specialties Co. v. *FTC,* 278 F. 2d 225 (2d Cir.), *cert. denied,* 364 U.S. 884 (1960).

American News Co. v. *FTC,* 300 F. 2d 104 (2d Cir.), *cert. denied,* 371 U.S. 824 (1962).

Anheuser-Busch, Inc. v. *FTC,* 289 F. 2d 835 (7th Cir. 1961).

Atalanta Trading Corp. v. *FTC,* 258 F. 2d 365 (2d Cir. 1958).

Atlas Building Products Co. v. *Diamond Block & Gravel Co.,* 269 F. 2d 950 (10th Cir. 1959), *cert. denied,* 363 U.S. 843 (1960).

Automatic Canteen Co. v. *FTC,* 346 U.S. 61 (1953).

Baim & Blank, Inc. v. *Philco Corp.,* 148 F. Supp. 541 (E.D. N.Y. 1957).

Balian Ice Cream Co. v. *Arden Farms Co.,* 104 F. Supp. 796 (S.D. Cal. 1952), *aff'd,* 231 F. 2d 356 (9th Cir. 1955), *cert. denied,* 350 U.S. 991 (1956).

Borden Co., Dkt. 7129 (1963), *set aside,* 339 F. 2d 953 (7th Cir. 1964), *rev'd,* 383 U.S. 637 (1966).

Bruce's Juices, Inc. v. *American Can Co.,* 330 U. S. 743 (1947).

Carpel Frosted Foods, Inc., 48 FTC 581 (1951).

Central Ice Cream Co. v. *Golden Rod Ice Cream Co.,* 287 F. 2d 265 (7th Cir.), *cert. denied,* 368 U.S. 829 (1961).

Champion Spark Plug Co., 50 FTC 30 (1953).

Chicago Seating Co. v. *S. Karpen & Bros.,* 177 F. 2d 863 (7th Cir. 1949).

Corn Products Refining Co. v. *FTC,* 324 U.S. 726 (1945).

Curtiss Candy Co., 44 FTC 237 (1947).

Dantzler v. *Dictograph Products, Inc.,* 272 F. 2d 172 (4th Cir. 1959).

Day's Tailor-D Clothing, Inc., 55 FTC 1584 (1959).

Elizabeth Arden, Inc. v. *FTC,* 156 F. 2d 132 (2d Cir. 1946), *cert. denied,* 331 U.S. 806 (1947).

Elizabeth Arden Sales Corp. v. *Gus Blass Co.,* 150 F. 2d 988 (8th Cir.), *cert. denied,* 326 U.S. 773 (1945).

Enterprise Industries, Inc. v. *Texas Co.,* 240 F. 2d 457 (2d Cir.), *cert. denied,* 353 U.S. 965 (1957).

Exquisite Form Brassiere, Inc. v. *FTC,* 301 F. 2d 499 (D.C. Cir. 1961), *cert. denied,* 369 U.S. 888 (1962).

FTC v. *Anheuser-Busch, Inc.,* 363 U.S. 536 (1960).

FTC v. *Henry Broch & Co.,* 363 U.S. 166 (1960).

FTC v. *Morton Salt Co.,* 334 U.S. 37 (1948).

FTC v. *Simplicity Pattern Co.* 360 U.S. 55 (1959).

FTC v. *Standard Oil Co.,* 355 U.S. 396 (1958).

FTC v. *Sun Oil Co.,* 371 U.S. 505 (1963).

Forster Manufacturing Co., Dkt. 7207, 56 FTC 1633 (1963).

Fred Meyer, Inc., 359 F. 2d 351 (9th Cir. 1966), *rev'd,* 390 U.S. 838 (1967).

General Foods Corp., 50 FTC 885 (1954).

General Foods Corp., 52 FTC 798 (1956).

General Shale Products Co. v. *Struck Construction Co.,* 37 F. Supp. 598 (W.D. Ky. 1941), *aff'd,* 132 F. 2d 425 (6th Cir. 1942), *cert. denied,* 318 U.S. 780 (1943).

Gerber Products Co. v. *Beech-Nut Life Savers, Inc.,* 160 F. Supp. 916 (S.D. N.Y. 1958).

Giant Food, Inc. v. *FTC,* 307 F. 2d 184 (D.C. Cir. 1962), *cert. denied,* 372 U.S. 910 (1963).

Kay Windsor Frocks, Inc., 51 FTC 89 (1954).

Kraft-Phenix Cheese Corp., 25 FTC 537 (1937).

Krug v. *International Telephone & Telegraph Corp.,* 142 F. Supp. 230 (N.J. 1956).

Lever Bros. Co., 50 FTC 494 (1953).

Liggett & Myers Tobacco Co., 56 FTC 221 (1959).

Ludwig v. *American Greetings Corp.,* 264 F. 2d 286 (6th Cir. 1959).

Moog Industries, Inc. v. *FTC,* 355 U.S. 411 (1955).

Moore v. *Mead's Fine Bread Co.,* 348 U.S. 115 (1954).

Mid-South Distributors, Inc. v. *FTC,* 287 F. 2d 512 (5th Cir.), *cert. denied,* 368 U.S. 838 (1961).

Minneapolis-Honeywell Regulator Co. v. *FTC,* 191 F. 2d 786 (7th Cir. 1951), *cert. dismissed,* 344 U.S. 206 (1952).

Mueller Co. v. *FTC,* 323 F. 2d 44 (9th Cir. 1963).

Nashville Milk Co. v. *Carnation Co.,* 355 U.S. 373 (1958).

Perkins v. *Standard Oil of California,* 1969 Trade Cases ¶ 72,829 (Sup. Ct. 1969).

P. Lorillard Co. v. *FTC,* 267 F. 2d 439 (3d Cir.), *cert. denied,* 361 U.S. 923 (1959).

Purex Corp., Ltd., Dkt. 6008, 51 FTC 100 (1954).

Russellville Canning Co. v. *American Can Co.,* 191 F. 2d 38 (8th Cir. 1951).

Sano Petroleum Corp. v. *American Oil Co.,* 187 F. Supp. 345 (E.D. N.Y. 1960).

Secatore's Inc. v. *Esso Standard Oil Co.,* 171 F. Supp. 665 (D. Mass. 1959).

Shreveport Macaroni Manufacturing Co. v. *FTC,* 321 F. 2d 404 (5th Cir. 1963).

Shulton, Inc. v. *FTC,* 305 F. 2d 36 (7th Cir. 1962).

Skinner v. *United States Steel Corp.,* 233 F. 2d 762 (5th Cir. 1956).

Southgate Brokerage Co. v. *FTC,* 150 F. 2d 607 (4th Cir.), *cert. denied,* 326 U.S. 774 (1945).

Standard Oil Co. v. *FTC,* 340 U.S. 231 (1951).

State Wholesale Grocers v. *Great Atlantic & Pacific Tea Co.,* 258 F. 2d 831 (7th Cir. 1958), *cert. denied,* 358 U.S. 947 (1959).

Student Book Co. v. *Washington Law Book Co.,* 232 F. 2d 49 (D.C. Cir. 1955), *cert. denied,* 350 U.S. 988 (1956).

Sunshine Biscuits, Inc. v. *FTC,* 306 F. 2d 48 (7th Cir. 1962).

Sylvania Electric Products, Inc., 51 FTC 282 (1955).

Thomasville Chair Co. v. *FTC,* 306 F. 2d 541 (5th Cir. 1962).

Thompson Products, Inc., 55 FTC 1252 (1959).

Tri-Valley Packing Association, FTC Dkt. 7225 (1962), 55 FTC 2073, set aside, 329 F. 2d 694 (9th Cir. 1964).

United States v. *Borden Co.,* 370 U.S. 460 (1962).

United States v. *National Dairy Products Corp.,* 372 U.S. 29 (1963).

Chapter 4: Jurisdictional Requirements of Section 2(a)

BIBLIOGRAPHY

ABA Antitrust Section, *The Robinson–Patman Act: 1936–1966,* Vol. 30 (1966).

Austin, *Price Discrimination,* 2nd ed. (1959).

Baum, *The Robinson-Patman Act—Summary and Comment* (1964).

Patman, *Complete Guide to the Robinson-Patman Act* (1963).

Rowe, *Price Discrimination Under the Robinson-Patman Act.* (1962) and *Supplement* (1965).

Sawyer, *Business Aspects of Pricing Under the Robinson-Patman Act* (1963).

Stickells, *Legal Control of Business Practice* (1965).

Van Cise, *Understanding the Antitrust Laws* (1963).

CASES

Ace Book Co., Dkt. 8557 [1965–1967 CCH Transfer Binder] Trade Reg. Rep. ¶ 17,273 (1965).

A. J. Goodman & Sons, Inc. v. *United Lacquer Mfg. Corp.,* 81 F. Supp. 809 (D. Mass. 1949).

Alabama Independent Service Station Ass'n v. *Shell Petroleum Corp.,* 28 F. Supp. 386 (D. Ala. 1939).

Aluminum Co. of America v. *Tandet,* 235 F. Supp. 111 (D. Conn. 1964).

American News Co. v. *FTC,* 300 F. 2d 104 (2d Cir.), *cert. denied,* 371 U.S. 824 (1962).

Atalanta Trading Corp. v. *FTC,* 258 F. 2d 365 (2d Cir. 1958).

Baim & Blank, Inc. v. *Philco Corp.,* 148 F. Supp. 541 (E.D. N.Y. 1957).

Baum and Shulman v. *Investors Diversified Services, Inc.,* 1969 Trade Cases ¶ 72,774 (7th Cir. 1969).

Baldwin Hills Bdg. Material Co. v. *Fiberboard Paper Products Corp.,* 283 F. Supp. 202 (C.D. Calif. 1968).

Balian Ice Cream Co. v. *Arden Farms Co.,* 104 F. Supp. 796 (D. Cal. 1952), *aff'd,* 231 F. 2d 356 (9th Cir. 1955), *cert. denied,* 350 U.S. 991 (1956).

Baysoy v. *Jessop Steel Co.,* 90 F. Supp. 303 (W.D. Pa. 1950).

Bergen Drug Co. v. *Parke, Davis & Co.,* 307 F. 2d 725 (3d Cir. 1962).

Bird & Sons, Inc., 25 FTC 548 (1937).

Bowman Dairy Co. v. *Hedlin Dairy Co.,* 126 F. Supp. 749 (D. Ill. 1954).

Bruce's Juices, Inc. v. *American Can Co.,* 187 F. 2d 919 (5th Cir.), *cert. dismissed,* 342 U.S. 875 (1951).

Castlegate, Inc. v. *National Tea Co.,* 34 F. R. D. 221 (D. Colo. 1963).

Central Ice Cream Co. v. *Golden Rod Ice Cream Co.,* 287 F. 2d 265 (7th Cir.), *cert. denied,* 368 U.S. 829 (1961).

Champion Spark Plug Co., Dkt. 3977, 50 FTC 30 (1953).

Checker Motors Corp. v. *Chrysler Corp.,* 283 F. Supp. 876 (S.D. N.Y.), *affirmed,* 1969 Trade Cases ¶ 72,672 (2d Cir. 1969), *cert. denied,*—U.S.—(1969).

Clausen and Sons, Inc. v. *Theo. Hamm Brewing Co.,* 284 F. Supp. 148 (D. Minn. 1967).

Columbia Broadcasting System v. *Amana Refrigeration Inc.,* 295 F. 2d 375 (7th Cir. 1961).

Corn Products Refining Co. v. *FTC,* 324 U.S. 726 (1945).

Dan Dee Pretzel & Potato Chip Co., Dkt. 6919, 54 FTC 1844 (1958).

Danko v. *Shell Oil Co.,* 115 F. Supp. 886 (E.D. N.Y. 1953).

Dean Milk Co., Dkt. 8032 [1965–1967 CCH Transfer Binder], Trade Reg. Rep. ¶ 17,357 (1965).

Dean Milk v. *FTC*, 1968 Trade Cases ¶ 72,393 (7th Cir. 1968).

Delaware Watch Co. v. *FTC*, 332 F. 2d 745 (2d Cir. 1964).

Elizabeth Arden Inc. v. *FTC*, 156 F. 2d 132 (2d Cir. 1946).

Fleetway Inc. v. *Public Service Interstate Transportation Co.*, 72 F. 2d 761 (3d Cir. 1934).

Food Basket, Inc. v. *Albertson's, Inc.*, 383 F. 2d 785 (10th Cir. 1967).

Foremost Dairies Inc. v. *FTC*, 348 F. 2d 674 (5th Cir. 1965), *cert. denied*, 382 U.S. 959 (1965).

Fred Meyer, Inc. v. *FTC*, 359 F. 2d 351 (9th Cir. 1966), *rev'd in part*, 390 U.S. 341 (1968).

FTC v. *Borden Co.*, 383 U.S. 637 (1966).

FTC v. *Simplicity Pattern Co.*, 360 U.S. 55 (1959).

Gaylord Shops, Inc. v. *Pittsburgh Miracle Mile Town and Country Shopping Center, Inc.*, 219 F. Supp. 400 (W.D. Pa. 1963).

General Foods Corp., Dkt. 6018, 52 FTC 798 (1956).

General Shale Products Corp. v. *Struck Construction Co.*, 132 F. 2d 425 (6th Cir. 1942), *cert. denied*, 318 U.S. 780 (1943).

George W. Warner & Co. v. *Black & Decker Mfg. Corp.*, 172 F. Supp. 221 (E.D. N.Y. 1959), *rev'd on other grounds*, 277 F. 2d 787 (2d Cir. 1960).

Gummed Industries Ass'n, Dkt. 6227, 55 FTC 1409 (1959).

Hansen Innoculator, Dkt. 3624, 26 FTC 303 (1938).

Hartley & Parker, Inc. v. *Florida Beverage Co.*, 307 F. 2d 916 (5th Cir. 1962).

Hiram Walker, Inc. v. *A & S Tropical, Inc.*, 1969 Trade Cases ¶ 72,698 (5th Cir. 1969).

H. J. Heinz Co., Dkt. 5994, 52 FTC 1607 (1956), *rev'd sub nom. on other grounds, Stokeley Van Camp Corp.* v. *FTC*, 246 F. 2d 458 (7th Cir. 1957).

Hood Rubber Co., Dkt. 4971, 46 FTC 1015 (1949).

Jones v. *Metzger Dairies Inc.*, 334 F. 2d 919 (5th Cir. 1964), *cert. denied*, 379 U. S. 965 (1965).

Joseph Kaplan & Sons, Inc., Dkt. 7813 [1963–1965 CCH Transfer Binder], Trade Reg. Rep. ¶ 16,666 (1963), *aff'd*, 247 F. 2d 785 (D.C. Cir. 1965).

Kay Windsor Frocks, Inc., Dkt. 5735, 51 FTC 89 (1954).

Klein v. *The Lionel Corp.*, 237 F. 2d 13 (3d Cir. 1956).

Kraft-Phenix Cheese Corp., 25 FTC 537 (1937).

Krug v. *International Telephone & Telegraph Corp.*, 142 F. Supp. 230 (D. N.J. 1956).

K. S. Corp. v. *Chemstrand Corp. and Fabrex Corp.*, 198 F. Supp. 310 (D. N.J. 1961).

La Salle Street Press, Inc. v. *McCormick and Henderson, Inc.*, 1968 Trade Cases ¶ 72,733 (N.D. Ill. 1968).

Liggett & Myers Co., Dkt. 6642, 56 FTC 221 (1959).

Logan Lanes, Inc. v. *Brunswick Corp.*, 378 F. 2d 212 (9th Cir.), *cert. denied*, 389 U. S. 898 (1967).

Loren Specialty Mfg. Co. v. *The Clark Mfg. Co.*, 241 F. Supp. 493 (D. Ill. 1965), *aff'd*, 360 F. 2d 913 (7th Cir.), *cert. denied*, 385 U.S. 957 (1966).

Massachusetts Brewers Ass'n v. *P. Ballantine & Sons*, 129 F. Supp. 736 (D. Mass. 1955).

Moog Industries v. *FTC*, 238 F. 2d 48 (8th Cir. 1956), *aff'd*, 355 U.S. 411 (1958).

Moore v. *Mead's Fine Bread Co.,* 348 U.S. 115 (1954).

National Lead Co. v. *FTC,* 227 F. 2d 825 (7th Cir. 1955), *rev'd on other grounds,* 352 U.S. 419 (1957).

Package Closure Corp. v. *Sealright Co.,* 141 F. 2d 972 (2d Cir. 1944).

Page Dairy Co., Dkt. 5974, 50 FTC 395 (1953).

Perkins v. *Standard Oil of California,* 1969 Trade Cases ¶ 72,829 (Sup. Ct. 1969).

Perma Life Mufflers, Inc. v. *International Parts Corp.,* 1966 CCH Trade Cases ¶ 71,802 (D. Ill.), *aff'd in part; rev'd in part,* 376 F. 2d 692 (7th Cir. 1967), *rev'd,* 88 S. Ct. 1981 (1968).

Peter Satori of California v. *Studebaker-Packard Corp.,* 1964 CCH Trade Cases ¶ 71,309 (S.D. Cal. 1964).

Purolator Products, Inc., Dkt. 7850 [1963–1965 CCH Transfer Binder], Trade Reg. Rep. ¶ 16,877 (1964).

Quaker Oats Co., Dkt. 8112 [1963–1965 CCH Transfer Binder], Trade Reg. Rep. ¶ 17,134 (1964).

Rangen, Inc. v. *Sterling Nelson & Sons,* 351 F. 2d 851 (9th Cir. 1965).

Reines Distributors, Inc. v. *Admiral Corp.,* 257 F. Supp. 619 (S.D. N.Y. 1965).

Robinson v. *Stanley Home Products, Inc.,* 178 F. Supp. 230 (D. Mass.), *aff'd,* 272 F. 2d 601 (1st Cir. 1959).

Royal Crown Cola Co., Dkt. 8295, [1963–1965 CCH Transfer Binder] Trade Reg. Rep. ¶ 16,707 (1963).

Scott Publishing Co. v. *Columbia Basin Publishers,* 180 F. Supp. 754 (W.D. Wash. 1959).

Shaw's Inc. v. *Wilson-Jones Co.,* 105 F. 2d 331 (3d Cir. 1939).

Shreveport Macaroni Mfg. Co. v. *FTC,* 321 F. 2d 404 (5th Cir. 1963), *cert. denied,* 375 U. S. 971 (1964).

Simpson v. *Union Oil Co.,* 377 U.S. 13 (1964).

Sorrentino v. *Glen-Gery Shale Brick Corp.,* 46 F. Supp. 709 (D. D.C. 1942).

Southern New England Distributing Corp. v. *Admiral Corp.,* 1965 CCH Trade Cases ¶ 71,471 (D. Conn. 1965).

Standard Oil Co. v. *FTC,* 340 U.S. 231 (1949).

State Wholesale Grocers v. *Great Atlantic & Pacific Tea Co.,* 202 F. 2d 768 (N.D. Ill. 1961).

Sterling Nelson & Sons v. *Rangen, Inc.,* 235 F. Supp. 393 (D. Idaho 1964), *aff'd,* 351 F. 2d 851 (9th Cir. 1965), *cert. denied,* 383 U.S. 936 (1966).

Student Book Co. v. *Washington Law Book Co.,* 232 F. 2d 49 (D.C. Cir. 1955).

Tri-State Broadcasting Co. v. *United Press International, Inc.,* 369 F. 2d 268 (5th Cir. 1966).

United States v. *Colgate & Co.,* 250 U.S. 300 (1919).

United States v. *General Electric Co.,* 272 U.S. 476 (1926).

Universal-Rundle Corp., Dkt. 8070, [1963–1965 CCH Transfer Binder] Trade Reg. Rep. ¶ 16,948 (1964), *aff'd,* 387 U.S. 244 (1967).

U.S. Rubber Co., Dkt. 4972, 46 FTC 998 (1950).

Valley Plymouth v. *Studebaker-Packard Corp.,* 219 F. Supp. 608 (S.D. Cal. 1963).

Warren Petroleum, Dkt. 6227, 53 FTC 268 (1956).

W. F. Schrafft & Sons Corp., Dkt. 7743 [1963–1965 CCH Transfer Binder] Trade Reg. Rep. ¶ 16,882 (1964).

Whitaker Cable Corp., Dkt. 5722, 51 FTC 958 (1955).

Willard Dairy Corp. v. *National Dairy Products Corp.,* 309 F. 2d 943 (6th Cir. 1962), *cert. denied,* 373 U.S. 934 (1963).

Chapter 5: The Meaning of Competition Under Section 2(a)

BIBLIOGRAPHY

Austin, *Price Discrimination,* 2nd ed. (1959).
Patman, *Complete Guide to the Robinson-Patman Act* (1963).
Rowe, *Price Discrimination Under the Robinson-Patman Act* (1962) and *Supplement* (1965).

CASES

American Oil Co. v. *FTC,* 325 F. 2d 101 (7th Cir. 1963), *cert. denied,* 377 U.S. 954 (1964).
Borden Co. v. *FTC,* 339 F. 2d 953 (7th Cir. 1964), *rev'd,* 383 U.S. 637 (1966).
Corn Products Refining Co. v. *FTC,* 324 U.S. 726 (1945).
FTC v. *Anheuser–Busch, Inc.,* 363 U.S. 536 (1960).
FTC v. *Morton Salt Co.,* 334 U.S. 37 (1948).
FTC v. *Sun Oil Co.,* 371 U.S. 505 (1963).
George Van Camp & Sons v. *American Can Co.,* 278 U.S. 245 (1929).
Lloyd A. Fry Roofing Co. v. *FTC,* 371 F. 2d 277 (7th Cir. 1966).
Minneapolis-Honeywell Regulator Co. v. *FTC,* 191 F. 2d 786 (7th Cir. 1951), *cert. dismissed,* 344 U.S. 206 (1952).
Perkins v. *Standard Oil Co. of California,* 1969 Trade Cases ¶ 72,829 (Sup. Ct. 1969).
Purex Corp., Ltd., Dkt. 6008, 51 FTC 100 (1954).
Shore Gas & Oil Co. v. *Humble Oil & Refining Co.,* 1964 CCH Trade Cases ¶ 70,990 (D. N.J. 1963).
Standard Oil Co. v. *Perkins,* 396 F. 2d 809 (9th Cir. 1967).
Utah Pie Co. v. *Continental Baking Co.,* 386 U.S. 685 (1967).
Whitaker Cable Corp. v. *FTC,* 239 F. 2d 253 (7th Cir. 1956), *cert. denied,* 353 U.S. 938 (1957).

Chapter 6: Competitive Injury Under Section 2(a)

BIBLIOGRAPHY

Austin, *Price Discrimination,* (2nd ed. 1959).
Lifland, *Responding to Local Competition—The Utah Pie Case,* 14 Antitrust Bull. 805 (1967).
Massell, *Competition and Monopoly* (1962).
Patman, *Complete Guide to the Robinson-Patman Act* (1963).
Rowe, *Price Discrimination Under the Robinson-Patman Act* (1962) and *Supplement* (1965).
Sawyer, *Business Aspects of Pricing Under the Robinson-Patman Act* (1963).
Schniderman, *"The Tyranny of Labels"—A Study of Functional Discounts Under the Robinson-Patman Act,* 60 *Harv. L. Rev.* 571 (1947).

CASES

American Oil Co. v. *FTC,* 325 F. 2d 101 (7th Cir. 1963), *cert. denied,* 377 U.S. 944 (1964).

Atlas Building Products Co. v. *Diamond Block & Gravel Co.,* 269 F. 2d 950 (10th Cir. 1959), *cert. denied,* 363 U.S. 843 (1960).

Automotive Parts Cases, 265 F. 2d 674 (2d Cir.), *cert. denied,* 361 U.S. 826 (1959).

Balian Ice Cream Co. v. *Arden Farms Co.,* 231 F. 2d 356 (9th Cir. 1955), *cert. denied,* 350 U.S. 991 (1956).

Bolick-Gillman Co. v. *Continental Baking Co.,* 206 F. Supp. 151 (D. Nev. 1961).

Borden Co. v. *FTC,* 381 F. 2d 175 (5th Cir. 1967).

Callaway Mills Co. v. *FTC,* 362 F. 2d 435 (5th Cir. 1966).

Chicago Board of Trade v. *United States,* 246 U.S. 231 (1918).

Dean Milk Co. [1965–1967 CCH Transfer Binder] Trade Reg. Rep. ¶ 17,357 (1965), *aff'd in part and rev'd in part,* 1968 CCH Trade Cases ¶ 72,393 (7th Cir. 1968).

Doubleday & Co., 52 FTC 169 (1955).

E. B. Muller & Co. v. *FTC,* 142 F. 2d 511 (6th Cir. 1944).

Enterprise Industries, Inc. v. *Texas Co.,* 240 F. 2d 457 (2d Cir. 1957).

Forster Mfg. Co., Dkt. 7207 (1958), *set aside,* 335 F. 2d 47 (1st Cir. 1964), *cert. denied,* 380 U.S. 906 (1965).

FTC v. *Anheuser-Busch, Inc.,* 363 U.S. 536 (1960).

FTC v. *Morton Salt Co.,* 334 U.S. 37 (1948).

FTC v. *Ruberoid Co.,* 343 U.S. 470 (1952).

H. J. Heinz v. *Beech-Nut Life Savers, Inc.,* 181 F. Supp. 452 (S.D. N.Y. 1960).

Hruby Distributing Co., Dkt. 8068, 61 FTC 1437 (1962).

Ingram v. *Phillips Petroleum Co.,* 259 F. Supp. (D. N.M. 1966).

Krug v. *International Telephone & Telegraph Corp.,* 142 F. Supp. 230 (D. N.J. 1956).

Lloyd A. Fry Roofing Co. v. *FTC,* 371 F. 2d 277 (7th Cir. 1966).

McWhirter v. *Monroe Calculating Machine Co.,* 76 F. Supp. 456 (W.D. Mo. 1948).

Mennen Co. v. *FTC,* 288 Fed. 774 (2d Cir.), *cert. denied,* 262 U. S. 759 (1923).

Minneapolis-Honeywell Regulator Co. v. *FTC,* 191 F. 2d 786 (7th Cir. 1951), *cert. denied,* 344 U.S. 206 (1952).

Moore v. *Mead's Fine Bread Co.,* 348 U.S. 115 (1954).

National Dairy Products Corp. v. *FTC,* 1969 Trade Cases ¶ 72,829 (7th Cir. 1969).

Perkins v. *Standard Oil Co. of California,* 1969 Trade Cases ¶ 72,829 (Sup. Ct. 1969).

Porto Rican-American Tobacco Co. v. *American Tobacco Co.,* 30 F. 2d 234 (2d Cir. 1929).

Quaker Oats Co., Dkt. 8112 [1963–1965 CCH Transfer Binder], Trade Reg. Rep. ¶ 17,134 (1964).

Shore Gas & Oil Co. v. *Humble Oil & Refining Co.,* 1964 CCH Trade Cases ¶ 70,990 (D. N.J. 1963).

Standard Oil Co. v. *Perkins,* 396 F. 2d 809 (9th Cir. 1967).

United Biscuit Co. v. *FTC,* 325 F. 2d 101 (7th Cir. 1963), *cert. denied,* 377 U.S. 944 (1964).

Utah Pie Co. v. *Continental Baking Co.*, 386 U.S. 685 (1967).
William H. Rorer, Inc. v. *FTC*, 374 F. 2d 622 (2d Cir. 1967).

Chapter 7: Cost Justification Defense

BIBLIOGRAPHY

Copeland, *Significance of the Cost Defense*, 11 Antitrust Bull. 925 (1966).
Hampton, *Defenses Under Robinson-Patman*, 37 A.B.A. Antitrust L. J. 57 (1968).
Taggart, *1956 Report, FTC Advisory Committee on Cost Justification* (Supp. I, 1964, Supp. II, 1967).
Taylor, *Cost Accounting Under the Robinson-Patman Act*, 3 Antitrust Bull. 188 (1958).

CASES

American Can Co. v. *Russellville Canning Co.*, 191 F. 2d 38 (8th Cir. 1951).
American Motors Corp. v. *FTC*, 384 F. 2d 247 (6th Cir. 1967), *cert. denied*, 390 U.S. 1012 (1968).
Automatic Canteen Co. of America v. *FTC*, 346 U.S. 61 (1953).
B. F. Goodrich Co., 50 FTC 622 (1954).
Bruce's Juices, Inc. v. *American Can Co.*, 187 F. 2d 919 (5th Cir.) *cert. dismissed*, 342 U.S. 875 (1951).
Champion Spark Plug Co., Dkt. 3977, 50 FTC 30 (1953).
Eleanor G. Morton v. *National Dairy Products Corp.*, 1969 Trade Cases ¶ 72,845 (3d Cir. 1969).
FTC v. *Henry Broch & Co.*, 363 U.S. 166 (1960).
FTC v. *Morton Salt Co.*, 334 U.S. 37 (1948).
FTC v. *Simplicity Pattern Co.*, 360 U.S. 55 (1959).
FTC v. *Standard Motor Products, Inc.*, 371 F. 2d 613 (2d Cir. 1967).
Minneapolis-Honeywell Regulator Co. v. *FTC*, 191 F. 2d 786 (7th Cir. 1951), *cert. dismissed*, 344 U. S. 206 (1952).
Mueller Co. v. *FTC*, 323 F. 2d 44 (7th Cir. 1963).
National Dairy Products v. *FTC*, 395 F. 2d 517 (7th Cir. 1968).
Standard Oil Co., 41 FTC 263 (1945).
Suburban Propane Gas Corp. v. *FTC*, F. Supp. (S.D. N.Y. 1968).
Sylvania Electric Products, Inc., 51 FTC 282 (1955).
Thomasville Chair Co. v. *FTC*, 306 F. 2d 541 (5th Cir. 1962).
Thompson Products Co., 55 FTC 1252 (1959).
United States v. *Borden Co.*, 370 U.S. 460 (1962).
United States Rubber Co., 46 FTC 998 (1950).

Chapter 8: The Meeting Competition Defense

BIBLIOGRAPHY

Austin, *Price Discrimination*, 2nd ed. (1959).
Edwards, *The Price Discrimination Law* (1959).

FTC, *Gasoline Marketing Report,* CCH Trade Reg. Rep. ¶ 50,177 (1967).
Note, *The Good Faith Defense of the Robinson-Patman Act: A New Restriction Appraised,* 66 Yale L. J. 935 (1957).
Note, *Pricing Systems and the Meeting Competition Defense,* 49 Va. L. Rev. 1325 (1963).
Patman, *Complete Guide to the Robinson-Patman Act* (1963).
Rowe, *Price Discrimination Under the Robinson-Patman Act* (1962) and *Supplement* (1965).
38 ABA Antitrust L. J.—(1969).

CASES

Beatrice Foods Co. v. *United States,* 312 F. 2d 29 (8th Cir.), *cert. denied,* 373 U.S. 904 (1963).
Callaway Mills Co. v. *FTC,* 362 F. 2d 435 (5th Cir. 1966).
Continental Baking Co., Dkt. 7630, [1963–1965 CCH Transfer Binder] Trade Reg. Rep. ¶ 16,720 (1963).
Exquisite Form Brassiere, Inc. v. *FTC,* 301 F. 2d 499 (D.C. Cir. 1961), *cert. denied,* 369 U. S. 888 (1962).
FTC v. *A. E. Staley,* 324 U.S. 746 (1945).
FTC v. *Sun Oil Co.,* 371 U.S. 505 (1963).
Ingram v. *Phillips Petroleum Co.,* 259 F. Supp. 176 (D. N.M. 1966).
Knoll Associates, Inc. [1965–1967 CCH Transfer Binder], Trade Reg. Rep. ¶ 17,668 (1966).
National Dairy Products Corp. v. *FTC,* 395 F. 2d 517 (7th Cir. 1968).
Standard Oil Co. v. *FTC,* 340 U.S. 231 (1951).
Standard Oil Co. v. *Perkins,* 396 F. 2d 809 (9th Cir. 1967).
Sunshine Biscuits, Inc. v. *FTC,* 306 F. 2d 48 (7th Cir. 1962).
Surprise Brassiere Co. v. *FTC,* 1969 Trade Cases ¶ 72,692 (5th Cir. 1969).
Viviano Macaroni Co. v. *FTC,* 1969 Trade Cases ¶ 72,810 (3d Cir. 1969).

Chapter 9: Miscellaneous Defenses and Exemptions

BIBLIOGRAPHY

Austern, *Presumption and Precipience About Competitive Effect Under Section 2 of the Clayton Act,* 81 Harv. L. Rev. 773 (1968).
Austin, *Price Discrimination,* (2nd ed. 1959).
Millstein, *The Status of "Availability" Under Section 2(a) of the Robinson-Patman Act.* 42 NYU L. Rev. 416 (1967).
Patman, *Complete Guide to the Robinson-Patman Act* (1963).
Rowe, *Price Discrimination Under the Robinson-Patman Act* (1962) and *Supplement* (1965).

CASES

Balian Ice Cream Co. v. *Arden Farms Co.,* 231 F. 2d 356 (9th Cir. 1955).
Dayco Corp., Dkt. 7604 [1963–1965 CCH Transfer Binder], Trade Reg. Rep. ¶ 17,029 (1964).
Fruitvale Canning Co., 52 FTC 1504 (1956).

FTC v. *Anheuser-Busch, Inc.*, 363 U.S. 536 (1960).

FTC v. *Borden Co.*, 383 U.S. 637 (1966).

FTC v. *Morton Salt Co.*, 334 U.S. 37 (1948).

Logan Lanes, Inc. v. *Brunswick Corp.*, 378 F. 2d 212 (9th Cir.), *cert. denied*, 389 U.S. 898 (1967).

Moore v. *Mead Service Co.*, 190 F. 2d 540 (10th Cir. 1951).

Student Book Co. v. *Washington Law Book Co.*, 232 F. 2d 49 (D.C. Cir. 1955).

Tri-Valley Packing Ass'n v. *FTC*, 329 F. 2d 694 (9th Cir. 1964).

Valley Plymouth v. *Studebaker-Packard Corp.*, 219 F. Supp. 608 (S.D. Cal. 1963).

Chapter 10: Brokerage and Payments in Lieu Thereof Under Section 2(c)

BIBLIOGRAPHY

Austin, *Price Discrimination*, 2nd ed. (1959).

Edwards, *The Price Discrimination Law* (1959).

Mezines, *Brokerage—When Is It Permitted Under the Robinson-Patman Act?*, 4 B.C. Ind. & Comm. L. Rev. 821 (1966).

Oppenheim, *Administration of the Brokerage Provision of the Robinson-Patman Act*, 8 Geo. Wash. L. Rev. 511 (1940).

Patman, *Complete Guide to the Robinson-Patman Act* (1963).

Rowe, *Price Discrimination Under the Robinson-Patman Act* (1962) and *Supplement* (1965).

Stickells, *Legal Control of Business Practice* (1965).

CASES

Albert W. Sisk & Sons, 31 FTC 1543 (1940).

Biddle Purchasing Co. v. *FTC*, 96 F. 2d 687 (2d Cir.), *cert. denied*, 305 U.S. 634 (1938).

Empire Rayon Yarn Co. v. *American Viscose Corp.*, 160 F. Supp. 334 (S.D. N.Y. 1958).

Fitch v. *Kentucky-Tennessee Light & Power Co.*, 136 F. 2d 12 (6th Cir. 1943).

Flotill Products, Inc., Dkt. 7226 [1963–1965 CCH Transfer Binder], Trade Reg. Rep. ¶ 16,970 (1964).

Freedman v. *Philadelphia Terminals Auction Co.*, 145 F. Supp. 820 (E.D. Pa. 1956).

FTC v. Henry Broch & Co., 363 U.S. 166 (1960).

FTC v. *Washington Fish & Oyster Co.*, 271 F. 2d 39 (9th Cir. 1959).

Garrett-Holmes & Co., Dkt. 8564, [1963–1965 CCH Transfer Binder] Trade Reg. Rep. ¶ 17,209 (1964).

Great Atlantic & Pacific Tea Co. v. *FTC*, 106 F. 2d 667 (3d Cir. 1939).

Hruby Distributing Co., Dkt. 8068, 61 FTC 1437 (1962).

Independent Grocers Alliance Distributing Co. v. *FTC*, 203 F. 2d 941 (7th Cir. 1953).

In re Whitney & Co., 273 F. 2d 211 (9th Cir. 1959).

Jarrett v. *Pittsburgh Plate Glass Co.*, 131 F. 2d 674 (5th Cir. 1942).

Main Fish Co., 53 FTC 88 (1956).

National Retailer-Owned Grocers, Inc., Dkt. 7121, 60 FTC 1208 (1962), *rev'd sub nom., Central Retailer-Owned Grocers, Inc.* v. *FTC,* 319 F. 2d 410 (7th Cir. 1963).

Oliver Bros., Inc. v. *FTC,* 102 F. 2d 763 (4th Cir. 1939).

Quality Bakers of America v. *FTC,* 114 F. 2d 393 (1st Cir. 1940).

Robinson v. *Stanley Home Products, Inc.,* 272 F. 2d 601 (1st Cir. 1959).

Southgate Brokerage Co. v. *FTC,* 150 F. 2d 607 (4th Cir. 1945).

Thomasville Chair Co. v. *FTC,* 306 F. 2d 541 (5th Cir. 1962).

Webb-Crawford Co. v. *FTC,* 109 F. 2d 268 (5th Cir. 1940).

Western Fruit Growers Sales Co. v. *FTC,* 322 F. 2d 67 (9th Cir. 1963).

Chapter 11: Promotional Allowances and Services Under Sections 2(d) and 2(e)

BIBLIOGRAPHY

ABA Antitrust Section, *The Robinson-Patman Act: 1936–1966,* Vol. 30 (1966).

Austin, *Price Discrimination,* 2nd ed. (1959).

Edwards, *The Price Discrimination Law* (1959).

Miller, *Section 2(d) and 2(e) of the Robinson-Patman Act: Seller in a Quandary,* 45 Marq. L. Rev. 511 (1962).

Patman, *Complete Guide to the Robinson-Patman Act* (1963).

Rowe, *Price Discrimination Under the Robinson-Patman Act* (1962) and *Supplement* (1965).

Stickells, *Legal Control of Business Practice* (1965).

CASES

Advisory Opinion Digest No. 94, [CCH Transfer Binder] Trade Reg. Rep. ¶ 17,720 (1967).

American Can Co. v. *Russellville Canning Co.,* 191 F. 2d 38 (8th Cir. 1951).

Atlantic Products Corp., Dkt. 8513, [1963–1965 CCH Transfer Binder] Trade Reg. Rep. ¶ 16,676 (1963).

Automatic Canteeen Co. of America v. *FTC,* 346 U.S. 61 (1953).

Chain Lightning Cases, 267 F. 2d 439 (3d Cir.), *cert. denied,* 361 U.S. 923 (1959).

Chicago Seating Co. v. *Karpen & Bros.,* 177 F. 2d 863 (7th Cir. 1949).

Corn Products Refining Co. v. *FTC,* 324 U.S. 726 (1945).

Dantzler v. *Dictograph Products, Inc.,* 272 F. 2d 172 (4th Cir. 1959).

Elizabeth Arden, Inc., 39 FTC 288 (1944), *aff'd,* 156 F. 2d 132 (2d Cir. 1946), *cert. denied,* 331 U.S. 806 (1947).

Exquisite Form Brassiere, Inc. v. *FTC,* 301 F. 2d 499 (D.C. Cir. 1961), *cert. denied,* 369 U.S. 888 (1962).

Fred Meyer, Inc. v. *FTC,* 390 U.S. 341 (1968).

FTC v. *Simplicity Pattern Co.,* 360 U.S. 55 (1959).

General Foods Co., 52 FTC 798 (1956).

Liggett & Myers Co., 60 FTC 1881 (1959).

NuArc Co. v. *FTC,* 316 F. 2d 576 (7th Cir. 1963).

Skinner v. *United States Steel Corp.,* 233 F. 2d 762 (5th Cir. 1956).

Soap Cases, 50 FTC 494 (1953).

State Wholesale Grocers v. *Great Atlantic & Pacific Tea Co.*, 258 F. 2d 831 (7th Cir. 1958), *cert. denied*, 358 U.S. 947 (1959).

United Banana Co. v. *United Fruit Co.*, 362 F. 2d 849 (2d Cir. 1966).

United States v. *Colgate & Co.*, 250 U.S. 300 (1919).

Vanity Fair Paper Mills, Inc. v. *FTC*, 311 F. 2d 480 (2d Cir. 1962).

Yakima Fruit & Cold Storage Co., Dkt. 7718, 59 FTC 693 (1960).

Chapter 12: Buyer Inducement or Receipt of Discriminations

BIBLIOGRAPHY

Austin, *Price Discrimination*, 2nd ed. (1959).

Barnes, *The Robinson-Patman Act Challenge to Buyers' Competition*, 9 Antitrust Bull. 415 (1964).

Frey, *The Evidentiary Burden on Affirmative Defenses Under Section 2(f) of the Robinson-Patman Act: Automatic Canteen Revisited*, 36 Geo. Wash. L. Rev. 347 (1967).

Handler & Rahl, *Does Section 5 of the F.T.C. Act Extend to the Clayton Act?*, 5 Antitrust Bull. 533 (1960).

Keck, *Lawful Price Discrimination*, 8 Antitrust Bull. 381 (1963).

Kintner, *Automotive Parts Distribution and The Federal Trade Commission*, 17 Bus. Law. 272 (1962).

Medow, *Bargaining for Lower Prices*, 45 Chi. B. Rec. 178 (1964).

Mezines, *Group Buying*, 12 Antitrust Bull 535 (1967).

Note, *Buyers' Responsibility Under the Robinson-Patman Act*, 49 NW. U. L. Rev. 273 (1954).

Note, *Buyers' Liability for Price Discrimination Under Robinson-Patman Act*, 63 Yale L. J. 264–65 (1953).

Palmer, *Buying Groups Under the Robinson-Patman Act*, 42 Chi-Kent L. Rev. 143 (1966).

Patman, *Complete Guide to the Robinson-Patman Act* (1963).

Rowe, *Price Discrimination Under the Robinson-Patman Act* (1962) and *Supplement* (1965).

Steel & Coughlin, *Buyers' Responsibility Before the Federal Trade Commission*, 2 B. C. Ind. & Comm. L. Rev. 257 (1961).

Steele, *Caveat Emptor Under the Robinson-Patman Act—A Reappraisal of Current Developments in Buyers' Liability*, 27 Ohio St. L. J. 19 (1966).

CASES

Alhambra Motor Parts v. *FTC*, 309 F. 2d 213 (9th Cir. 1962).

American Motors Specialties Co. v. *FTC*, 278 F. 2d 225 (2d Cir.), *cert. denied*, 364 U.S. 884 (1960).

Atlas Supply Co., 48 FTC 53 (1951).

Automatic Canteen Co. of America v. *FTC*, 346 U.S. 61 (1953).

Corn Products Refining Co. v. *FTC*, 324 U.S. 726 (1940).

Fred Meyer, Inc. v. *FTC*, 359 F. 2d 351 (9th Cir. 1966), *rev'd on other grounds*, 390 U.S. 341 (1968).

Grand Union Co. v. *FTC*, 300 F. 2d 92 (2d Cir. 1962).

Great Atlantic & Pacific Tea Co. v. *FTC,* 106 F. 2d 667 (3d Cir. 1939), *cert. denied,* 308 U.S. 625 (1940).

Mid-South Distributors v. *FTC,* 287 F. 2d 512 (5th Cir.), *cert. denied,* 368 U.S. 838 (1961).

R. H. Macy & Co. v. *FTC,* 326 F. 2d 445 (2d Cir. 1964).

Chapter 13: Criminal Sanctions Under Section 3

BIBLIOGRAPHY

Baum, *The Robinson-Patman Act—Summary and Comment* (1964).

Edwards, *The Price Discrimination Law* (1959).

Note, *The Meaning and Judicial Development of Section 3 of the Robinson-Patman Act,* 49 Nw. U. L. Rev. 285 (1954).

Patman, *Complete Guide to the Robinson-Patman Act* (1963).

Rose, *The Right of a Businessman to Lower the Price of His Goods,* 4 Vand. L. Rev. 221 (1951).

Rowe, *Price Discrimination Under the Robinson-Patman Act* (1962) and *Supplement* (1965).

CASES

F & A Ice Cream Co. v. *Arden Farms Co.,* 98 F. Supp. 180 (S.D. Cal. 1951).

Fred Meyer, Inc. v. *FTC,* 390 U.S. 341 (1968).

Klein v. *Lionel Corp.,* 237 F. 2d 13 (3d Cir. 1956).

Moore v. *Mead's Fine Bread Co.,* 348 U.S. 115 (1954).

Nashville Milk Co. v. *Carnation Co.,* 355 U.S. 373 (1958).

United States v. *Bowman Dairy Co.,* 89 F. Supp. 112 (N.D. Ill. 1949).

United States v. *National Dairy Products Corp.,* 372 U.S. 29 (1963).

Chapter 14: Enforcement by the Federal Trade Commission

BIBLIOGRAPHY

Baker & Baum, *Enforcement, Voluntary Compliance, and the Federal Trade Commission,* 38 Ind. L. J. 322 (1963).

Burrus & Savarese, *Institutional Decision Making and the Problem of Fairness in FTC Antitrust Enforcement,* 53 Geo. L. J. 655 (1965).

Burrus & Teter, *Antitrust: Rulemaking* v. *Adjudication in the FTC,* 54 Geo. L. J. 1106 (1966).

Dixon, "The Federal Trade Commission and the Antitrust Laws," in Van Cise, *Understanding the Antitrust Laws* (1963).

Chapter 15: Enforcement by the Department of Justice

BIBLIOGRAPHY

Congress Enacts Antitrust Civil Process Act, 111 U. Pa. L. Rev. 1021 (1963).

Dabney, *Consent Decrees Without Consent,* 63 Colum. L. Rev. 1053 (1963).

Decker, *The Civil Investigative Demand,* 21 ABA Antitrust Sect. Rep. 370 (1962).

Emmerglick, *Proposals for Balancing All Public Interests in Fashioning Antitrust Remedies,* 21 ABA Antitrust Sect. Rep. 387 (1962).

Kadish, *Some Observations on the Use of Criminal Sanctions in Enforcing Economic Regulations,* 30 U. Chi. L. Rev. 423 (1963).

Loevinger, "The Department of Justice and the Antitrust Laws," in Van Cise, *Understanding the Antitrust Laws* (1963).

CASES

Ford Motor Co. v. *United States,* 335 U.S. 303 (1948).
In re Gold Bond Stamp Co., 221 F. Supp. 391 (D. Minn. 1963).
Hughes v. *United States,* 342 U.S. 353 (1952).
United States v. *Swift & Co.,* 286 U.S. 106 (1932).
United States v. *Swift & Co.,* 189 F. Supp. (N.D. Ill. 1960), *aff'd,* 367 U.S. 909 (1961) (per curiam).

Chapter 16: Private Enforcement

BIBLIOGRAPHY

Note, *The Admissibility and Scope of Guilty Pleas in Antitrust Treble Damage Actions,* 71 Yale L. J. 684 (1962).
Note, *Clayton Act Statute of Limitations and Tolling by Fraudulent Concealment,* 72 Yale L. J. 600 (1963).
Note, *Discouragement of Private Treble Damage Suits Through a Simple Refusal to Deal,* 71 Yale L. J. 1565 (1962).
Note, *The Role of State Law in Federal Antitrust Treble Damage Actions,* 75 Harv. L. Rev. 1395 (1962).
Pollock, *The "Injury" and "Causation" Elements of a Treble Damage Antitrust Action,* 57 Nw. U. L. Rev. 691 (1963).
Symposium, *The Trial of an Antitrust Action,* 18 ABA Antitrust Sec. Rep. (1961).
Timberlake, *Federal Treble Damage Antitrust Action* (1965).

CASES

Atlantic City Electric Co. v. *General Electric Co.,* 312 F. 2d 236 (2d Cir. 1962), *cert. denied,* 373 U.S. 909 (1963).
Bergen Drug Co. v. *Parke, Davis & Co.,* 307 F. 2d 725 (3d Cir. 1962).
Bruce's Juices, Inc. v. *American Can Co.,* 330 U.S. 743 (1947).
Commonwealth Edison Co. v. *Allis-Chalmers Manufacturing Co.,* 1963 CCH Trade Cases ¶ 70,884 (7th Cir. 1963).
Dailey v. *Quality School Plan, Inc.,* 380 F. 2d 484 (5th Cir. 1967).
Data Digests, Inc. v. *Standard & Poor's Corp.,* 1967 Trade Cases ¶ 72,323 (S.D. N.Y. 1967).
Eastman Kodak Co. v. *Southern Photo Materials Co.,* 273 U.S. 359 (1927).
Elizabeth Arden Sales Corporation v. *Gas Glass Co.,* 150 F. 2d 988 (8th Cir. 1946).
Enterprise Industries, Inc. v. *Texas Co.,* 240 F. 2d 457 (2nd Cir. 1959).

Erone Corp. v. *Skouras Theaters Corp.*, 166 F. Supp. 621 (S.D. N.Y. 1957).

Flintkote Co. v. *Lysfjord,* 246 F. 2d 368 (9th Cir. 1957).

Fowler Manufacturing Co., v. *H. H. Gorlick,* 427 ATRR x-4 (9th Cir. 1969).

Hanover Shoe, Inc. v. *United Shoe Machinery Corp.,* 392 U.S. 481 (1968).

Harrison v. *Paramount Pictures, Inc.,* 115 F. Supp. 312 (E.D. Pa.), affirmed *per curiam,* 211 F. 2d 405 (3rd Cir. 1954), *cert. denied,* 348 U.S. 828 (1955).

House of Materials, Inc. v. *Simplicity Pattern Co.,* 298 F. 2d 867 (2d Cir. 1962).

Karseal Corp. v. *Richfield Oil Corp.,* 221 F. 2d 358 (9th Cir. 1955).

Keogh v. *Chicago & Northwestern Railway,* 260 U.S. 156 (1922).

Kiefer-Stewart Co. v. *Joseph E. Seagram & Sons,* 340 U.S. 211 (1951).

Loeb v. *Eastman Kodak,* 133 Fed. 704 (3rd Cir. 1910).

Momand v. *Universal Film Exchange, Inc.,* 43 F. Supp. 996 (D. Mass. 1942).

Nationwide Auto Appraiser Service, Inc. v. *Association of Casualty & Surety Cos.,* 382 F. 2d 925 (10th Cir. 1967).

New Sanitary Towel Supply, Inc. v. *Consolidated Laundries Corp.,* 211 F. Supp. 276 (S.D. N.Y. 1962).

Nichols v. *Spencer International Press, Inc.,* 371 F. 2d (7th Cir. 1967).

North Texas Milk Producer's Association v. *Young,* 308 F. 2d 235 (5th Cir. 1962), *cert. denied,* 372 U.S. 929 (1963).

Pennsylvania Water & Power Co. v. *Consolidated Gas, Electric Light & Power Co.,* 209 F. 2d 131 (4th Cir. 1953), *cert. denied,* 347 U.S. 960 (1954).

Perkins v. *Standard Oil Co. of California,* 1969 Trade Cases ¶ 72,829 (Sup. Ct. 1969).

Perma Life Mufflers, Inc. v. *International Parts Corp.,* 392 U.S. 135 (1968).

Productive Inventions, Inc. v. *Trico Products Corp.,* 244 F. 2d 678 (2nd Cir. 1955).

Rogers v. *American Can Co.,* 305 F. 2d 297 (3d Cir. 1962).

Simpson v. *Union Oil Co.,* 311 F. 2d 764 (9th Cir.), *cert. granted,* 373 U.S. 901 (1963).

Story Parchment Co. v. *Paterson Parchment Paper Co.,* 282 U.S. 555 (1931).

Union Carbide & Carbon Corp. v. *Nisley,* 300 F. 2d 561 (10th Cir. 1961).

Appendix II

Original Section 2
of the
Clayton Act of 1914

It shall be unlawful for any person engaged in commerce, in the course of such commerce either directly or indirectly to discriminate in price between different purchasers of commodities, which commodities are sold for use, consumption, or resale within the United States or any territory thereof or the District of Columbia or any insular possession or other place under the jurisdiction of the United States, where the effect of such discrimination may be to substantially lessen competition or tend to create a monopoly in any line of commerce: *Provided,* That nothing herein contained shall prevent discrimination in price between purchasers of commodities on account of differences in the grade, quality, or quantity of the commodity sold, or that makes only due allowance for difference in the cost of selling or transportation, or discrimination in price in the same or different communities made in good faith to meet competition: *And provided further,* That nothing herein contained shall prevent persons engaged in selling goods, wares, or merchandise in commerce from selecting their own customers in bona fide transactions and not in restraint of trade.

Appendix III

The Robinson-Patman Act

[Public-No. 692-74th Congress]
[H. R. 8442]
AN ACT

To amend section 2 of the Act entitled "An Act to supplement existing laws against unlawful restraints and monopolies, and for other purposes," approved October 15, 1914, as amended (U. S. C., title 15, sec. 13), and for other purposes.

Be it enacted by the Senate and House of Representatives of the United States of America in Congress assembled, That section 2 of the Act entitled "An Act to supplement existing laws against unlawful restraints and monopolies, and for other purposes," approved October 15, 1914, as amended (U. S. C., title 15, sec. 13), is amended to read as follows:

SEC. 2. (a) That it shall be unlawful for any person engaged in commerce, in the course of such commerce, either directly or indirectly, to discriminate in price between different purchasers of commodities of like grade and quality, where either or any of the purchases involved in such discrimination are in

333

commerce, where such commodities are sold for use, consumption, or resale within the United States or any Territory thereof or the District of Columbia or any insular possession or other place under the jurisdiction of the United States, and where the effect of such discrimination may be substantially to lessen competition or tend to create a monopoly in any line of commerce, or to injure, destroy, or prevent competition with any person who either grants or knowingly receives the benefit of such discrimination, or with customers of either of them: *Provided,* That nothing herein contained shall prevent differentials which make only due allowance for differences in the cost of manufacture, sale, or delivery resulting from the differing methods or quantities in which such commodities are to such purchasers sold or delivered: *Provided, however,* That the Federal Trade Commission may, after due investigation and hearing to all interested parties, fix and establish quantity limits, and revise the same as it finds necessary, as to particular commodities or classes of commodities, where it finds that available purchasers in greater quantities are so few as to render differentials on account thereof unjustly discriminatory or promotive of monopoly in any line of commerce; and the foregoing shall then not be construed to permit differentials based on differences in quantities greater than those so fixed and established: *And provided further,* That nothing herein contained shall prevent price changes from time to time where in response to changed conditions affecting the market for or the marketability of the goods concerned, such as but not limited to actual or imminent deterioration of perishable goods, obsolescence of seasonal goods, distress sales under court process, or sales in good faith in discontinuance of business in the goods concerned.

(b) Upon proof being made, at any hearing on a complaint under this section, that there has been discrimination in price or services or facilities furnished, the burden of rebutting the prima-facie case thus made by showing justification shall be upon the person charged with a violation of this section, and unless justification shall be affirmatively shown, the Commission is authorized to issue an order terminating the discrimination: *Provided, however,* That nothing herein contained shall prevent a seller rebutting the prima-facie case thus made by showing that his lower price or the furnishing of services or facilities to any purchaser or purchasers was made in good faith to meet an equally low price of a competitor, or the services or facilities furnished by a competitor.

(c) That it shall be unlawful for any person engaged in commerce, in the course of such commerce, to pay or grant, or to receive or accept, anything of value as a commission, brokerage, or other compensation, or any allowance or discount in lieu thereof, except for services rendered in connection with the sale or purchase of goods, wares, or merchandise, either to the other party to such transaction or to an agent, representative, or other intermediary therein where such intermediary is acting in fact for or in behalf, or is subject to the direct or indirect control, of any party to such transaction other than the person by whom such compensation is so granted or paid.

(d) That it shall be unlawful for any person engaged in commerce to pay or contract for the payment of anything of value to or for the benefit of a customer of such person in the course of such commerce as compensation or in consideration for any services or facilities furnished by or through such customer in connection with the processing, handling, sale, or offering for sale of any products or commodities manufactured, sold, or offered for sale by such person, unless such payment or consideration is available on proportionally equal terms to all other customers competing in the distribution of such products or commodities.

(e) That it shall be unlawful for any person to discriminate in favor of one purchaser against another purchaser or purchasers of a commodity bought for resale, with or without processing, by contracting to furnish or furnishing, or by contributing to the furnishing of, any services or facilities connected with the processing, handling, sale, or offering for sale of such commodity so purchased upon terms not accorded to all purchasers on proportionally equal terms.

(f) That it shall be unlawful for any person engaged in commerce, in the course of such commerce, knowingly to induce or receive a discrimination in price which is prohibited by this section.

SEC. 2. That nothing herein contained shall affect rights of action arising, or litigation pending, or orders of the Federal Trade Commission issued and in effect or pending on review, based on section 2 of said Act of October 15, 1914, prior to the effective date of this amendatory Act: *Provided,* That where, prior to the effective date of this amendatory Act, the Federal Trade Commission has issued an order requiring any person to cease and desist from a violation of section 2 of said Act of October 15, 1914, and such order is pending on review or is in effect, either as issued or as affirmed or modified by a court of competent jurisdiction, and the Commission shall have reason to believe that such person has committed, used or carried on, since the effective date of this amendatory Act, or is committing, using or carrying on, any act, practice or method in violation of any of the provisions of said section 2 as amended by this Act, it may reopen such original proceeding and may issue and serve upon such person its complaint, supplementary to the original complaint, stating its charges in that respect. Thereupon the same proceedings shall be had upon such supplementary complaint as provided in section 11 of said Act of October 15, 1914. If upon such hearing the Commission shall be of the opinion that any act, practice, or method charged in said supplementary complaint has been committed, used, or carried on since the effective date of this amendatory Act, or is being committed, used or carried on, in violation of said section 2 as amended by this Act, it shall make a report in writing in which it shall state its findings as to the facts and shall issue and serve upon such person its order modifying or amending its original order to include any additional violations of law so found. Thereafter the provisions of section 11 of said Act of October 15, 1914, as to review and enforcement of orders of the Commission shall in all things apply to such modified or amended order. If upon review as provided in said section 11 the court shall set aside such modified or amended order, the original order shall not be affected thereby, but it shall be and remain in force and effect as fully and to the same extent as if such supplementary proceedings had not been taken.

SEC. 3. It shall be unlawful for any person engaged in commerce, in the course of such commerce, to be a party to, or assist in, any transaction of sale, or contract to sell, which discriminates to his knowledge against competitors of the purchaser, in that, any discount, allowance, or advertising service charge is granted to the purchaser over and above any discount, rebate, allowance, or advertising service charge available at the time of such transaction to said competitors in respect of a sale of goods of like grade, quality, and quantity; to sell, or contract to sell, goods in any part of the United States at prices lower than those exacted by said person elsewhere in the United States for the purpose of destroying competition, or eliminating a competitor in such part of the United States; or, to sell, or contract to sell, goods at unreasonably low prices for the purpose of destroying competition or eliminating a competitor.

Any person violating any of the provisions of this section shall, upon conviction thereof, be fined not more than $5,000 or imprisoned not more than one year, or both.

SEC. 4. Nothing in this Act shall prevent a cooperative association from returning to its members, producers, or consumers the whole, or any part of, the net earnings or surplus resulting from its trading operations, in proportion to their purchases or sales from, to, or through the association.

Approved, June 19, 1936.

Appendix IV

The Federal Trade
Commission Act

[Public–No. 203–63d Congress, as amended by Public–No. 447–75th Congress, as amended by Public–No. 459–81st Congress, as amended by Public–No. 542–82d Congress, as amended by Public–No. 85–791–85th Congress, as amended by the Public–No. 85–909 85th Congress] [1]

[H.R. 15613, S. 1077, H.R. 2023, H.R. 5767, H.R. 6788 and H.R. 9020]
An Act To create a Federal Trade Commission, to define its powers and duties, and for other purposes.

Be it enacted by the Senate and House of Representatives of the United States of America in Congress assembled, That a commission is hereby created and established, to be known as the Federal Trade Commission (hereinafter referred to as the commission), which shall be composed of five commissioners,

---

[1] The Act is published as also amended by Public No. 706, 75th Congress and by Public No. 542, 82d Congress (see Footnote 7), and as further amended, as above noted, by Public No. 459, 81st Congress, Ch. 61, 2d Sess., H.R. 2023 (An Act to regulate oleomargarine, etc.), approved March 16, 1950, and effective July 1, 1950 (see footnotes 9, 12, and 13).

who shall be appointed by the President, by and with the advice and consent of the Senate. Not more than three of the commissioners shall be members of the same political party. The first commissioners appointed shall continue in office for terms of three, four, five, six, and seven years, respectively, from the date of the taking effect of this Act, the term of each to be designated by the President, but their successors shall be appointed for terms of seven years, except that any person chosen to fill a vacancy shall be appointed only for the unexpired term of the commissioner whom he shall succeed: *Provided, however,* That upon the expiration of his term of office a Commissioner shall continue to serve until his successor shall have been appointed and shall have qualified. The commission shall choose a chairman from its own membership.[2]

No commissioner shall engage in any other business, vocation, or employment. Any commissioner may be removed by the President for inefficiency, neglect of duty, or malfeasance in office. A vacancy in the commission shall not impair the right of the remaining commissioners to exercise all the powers of the commission.

The commission shall have an official seal, which shall be judicially noticed.

SEC. 2. That each commissioner shall receive a salary of $10,000 a year, payable in the same manner as the salaries of the judges of the courts of the United States.[3] The commission shall appoint a secretary, who shall receive a salary of $5,000 a year,[4] payable in like manner, and it shall have authority to employ and fix the compensation of such attorneys, special experts, examiners, clerks and other employees as it may from time to time find necessary for the proper performance of its duties and as may be from time to time appropriated for by Congress.[5]

[2] Under the provisions of Section 3 of Reorganization Plan No. 8 of 1950, effective May 24, 1950 (as published in the Federal Register for May 25, 1950, at page 3175) the functions of the Commission with respect to choosing a chairman from among the membership of the Commission was transferred to the President. Under said plan, prepared by the President and transmitted to the Senate and House on March 13, 1950, pursuant to the provisions of the Reorganization Act of 1949, approved June 20, 1949, there were also transferred to the Chairman of the Commission, subject to certain limitations, "the executive and administrative functions of the Commission, including functions of the Commission with respect to (1) the appointment and supervision of personnel employed under the Commission, (2) the distribution of business among such personnel and among administrative units of the Commission, and (3) the use and expenditure of funds."

[3] The salary of the Chairman was fixed at $20,500 and the salaries of the other four Commissioners at $20,000 by Sec. 105 (9) and Sec. 106 (a) (45), respectively, of Public Law 854, 84th Congress, Chapter 804, 2d Sess. H.R. 7619 (An Act to adjust the rates of compensation of the heads of the executive departments and of certain other officials of the Federal Government, and for other purposes), approved July 31, 1956. (The salaries of the commissioners have since been raised again.)

[4] The salary of the Secretary is controlled by the provisions of the Classification Act of 1923, approved March 4, 1923, 42 Stat. 1488, as amended, which likewise generally controls the compensation of the employees.

[5] See preceding footnote.

With the exception of the secretary, a clerk to each commissioner, the attorneys, and such special experts and examiners as the commission may from time to time find necessary for the conduct of its work, all employees of the commission shall be a part of the classified civil service, and shall enter the service under such rules and regulations as may be prescribed by the commission and by the Civil Service Commission.

All of the expenses of the commission, including all necessary expenses for transportation incurred by the commissioners or by their employees under their orders, in making any investigation, or upon official business in any other places than in the city of Washington, shall be allowed and paid on the presentation of itemized vouchers therefor approved by the commission.

Until otherwise provided by law, the commission may rent suitable offices for its use.

The Auditor for the State and Other Departments shall receive and examine all accounts of expenditures of the commission.[6]

SEC. 3. That upon the organization of the commission and election of its chairman, the Bureau of Corporations and the offices of Commissioner and Deputy Commissioner of Corporations shall cease to exist; and all pending investigations and proceedings of the Bureau of Corporations shall be continued by the commission.

All clerks and employees of the said bureau shall be transferred to and become clerks and employees of the commission at their present grades and salaries. All records, papers, and property of the said bureau shall become records, papers, and property of the commission, and all unexpended funds and appropriations for the use and maintenance of the said bureau, including any allotment already made to it by the Secretary of Commerce from the contingent appropriation for the Department of Commerce for the fiscal year nineteen hundred and fifteen, or from the departmental printing fund for the fiscal year nineteen hundred and fifteen, shall become funds and appropriations available to be expended by the commission in the exercise of the powers, authority, and duties conferred on it by this Act.

The principal office of the commission shall be in the city of Washington, but it may meet and exercise all its powers at any other place. The Commission may, by one or more of its members, or by such examiners as it may designate, prosecute any inquiry necessary to its duties in any part of the United States.

SEC. 4. The words defined in this section shall have the following meaning when found in this Act, to wit:

"Commerce," means commerce among the several States or with foreign

[6] Auditing of accounts was made a duty of the General Office by the Act of June 10, 1921, 42 Stat. 24.

nations, or in any Territory of the United States or in the District of Columbia, or between any such Territory and another, or between any such Territory and any States or foreign nation, or between the District of Columbia and any State or Territory or foreign nation.

"Corporation" shall be deemed to include any company, trust, so-called Massachusetts trust, or association, incorporated or unincorporated, which is organized to carry on business for its own profit or that of its members, and has shares of capital or capital stock or certificates of interest, and any company, trust, so-called Massachusetts trust, or association, incorporated or unincorporated, without shares of capital or capital stock or certificates of interest, except partnerships, which is organized to carry on business for its own profit or that of its members.

"Documentary evidence" includes all documents, papers, correspondence, book of account, and financial and corporate records.

"Acts to regulate commerce" means the Act entitled "An Act to regulate commerce," approved February 14, 1887, and all Acts amendatory thereof and supplementary thereto and the Communications Act of 1934 and all Acts amendatory thereof and supplementary thereto.

"Antitrust Acts," means the Act entitled "An Act to protect trade and commerce against unlawful restraints and monopolies," approved July 2, 1890; also sections 73 to 77, inclusive, of an Act entitled "An Act to reduce taxation, to provide revenue for the Government, and for other purposes," approved August 27, 1894; also the Act entitled "An Act to amend section 73 and 76 of the Act of August 27, 1894, entitled 'An Act to reduce taxation, to provide revenue for the Government, and for other purposes,'" approved February 12, 1913; and also the Act entitled "An Act to supplement existing laws against unlawful restraints and monopolies, and for other purposes," approved October 15, 1914.

SEC. 5. (a) (1) Unfair methods of competition in commerce, and unfair or deceptive acts or practices in commerce, are hereby declared unlawful.

(2) Nothing contained in this Act or in any of the Antitrust Acts shall render unlawful any contracts or agreements prescribing minimum or stipulated prices, for the resale of a commodity which bears, or the label or container of which bears, the trade-mark, brand, or name of the producer or distributor of such commodity and which is in free and open competition with commodities of the same general class produced or distributed by others, when contracts or agreements of that description are lawful as applied to intrastate transactions under any statute, law, or public policy now or hereafter in effect in any State, Territory, or the District of Columbia in which such resale is to be made, or to which the commodity is to be transported for such resale.

(3) Nothing contained in this Act or in any of the Antitrust Acts shall render unlawful the exercise or the enforcement of any right or right of action created by any statute, law, or public policy now or hereafter in effect in any State, Territory, or the District of Columbia, which in substance provides that will-

fully and knowingly advertising, offering for sale, or selling any commodity at less than the price or prices prescribed in such contracts or agreements whether the person so advertising, offering for sale, or selling is or is not a party to such a contract or agreement, is unfair competition and is actionable at the suit of any person damaged thereby.

(4) Neither the making of contracts or agreements as described in paragraph (2) of this subsection, nor the exercise or enforcement of any right or right of action as described in paragraph (3) of this subsection shall constitute an unlawful burden or restraint upon, or interference with, commerce.

(5) Nothing contained in paragraph (2) of this subsection shall make lawful contracts or agreements providing for the establishment or maintenance of minimum or stipulated resale prices on any commodity referred to in paragraph (2) of this subsection, between manufacturers, or between producers, or between wholesalers, or between brokers, or between factors, or between retailers, or between persons, firms, or corporations in competition with each other.

(6) The Commission is hereby empowered and directed to prevent persons, partnerships, or corporations, except banks, common carriers subject to the Acts to regulate commerce, air carriers, and foreign air carriers subject to the Civil Aeronautics Act of 1938, and persons, partnerships, or corporations insofar as they are subject to the Packers and Stockyards Act, 1921, as amended, except as provided in section 406 (b) of said Act, from using unfair methods of competition in commerce and unfair or deceptive acts or practices in commerce.[7]

[7] Public No. 542, 82d Cong., Ch. 745, 2d Sess. H. R. 5767, approved July 14, 1952 (the McGuire Act, 15 U. S. C. 45, 66 Stat. 631), amended Sec. 5(a) of this Act, by inserting in lieu thereof Sec. 5 (a) (1) through (6).

Therefore, by subsection (f) of Section 1107, of the "Civil Aeronautics Act of 1938," approved June 23, 1938, Public No. 706, 75th Cong., Ch. 601, 3d Sess., S. 3845, 52 Stat. 1028, the language of former Sec. 5(a) was amended by inserting immediately following the words "to regulate commerce," the words "air carriers and foreign air carriers subject to the Civil Aeronautics Act of 1938," as above set out in Sec. 5(a) (6).

Public No. 85–909, 85th Cong., H. R. 9020, approved September 2, 1958, amended the Packers and Stockyards Act, 1921, as amended (7 U. S. C. 226, 227 and 72 Stat. 1749, 1750) by striking out subsection (b) of Section 406 and inserting in lieu thereof the following:

"(b) The Federal Trade Commission shall have power and jurisdiction over any matter involving meat, meat food products, livestock products in unmanufactured form, or poultry products, which by this Act is made subject to the power or jurisdiction of the Secretary, as follows:

"(1) When the Secretary in the exercise of his duties requests of the Commission that it make investigations and reports in any case.

"(2) In any investigation of, or proceeding for the prevention of, an alleged violation of any act administered by the Commission, arising out of acts or transactions involving meat, meat products, livestock products in unmanufactured form, or poultry products, if the Commission determines that effective exercise of its power or jurisdiction with respect to retail sales of any such commodities is or will be impaired by the absence of power or jurisdiction over all acts or transactions involving such commodities in such investigation or proceeding. In order to avoid unnecessary duplication of effort by the Government and burdens upon the industry, the Commissioner shall notify the Secretary of such determination, the reasons therefor,

(b) Whenever the Commission shall have reason to believe that any such person, partnership, or corporation has been or is using any unfair method of competition or unfair or deceptive act or practice in commerce, and if it shall appear to the Commission that a proceeding by it in respect thereof would be in the interest of the public, it shall issue and serve upon such person, partnership, or corporation a complaint stating its charges in that respect and containing a notice of a hearing upon a day and at a place therein fixed at least thirty days after the service of said complaint. The person, partnership, or corporation so complained of shall have the right to appear at the place and time so fixed and show cause why an order should not be entered by the Commission requiring such person, partnership, or corporation to cease and desist from the violation of the law so charged in said complaint. Any person, partnership or corporation may make application, and upon good cause shown may be allowed by the Commission to intervene and appear in said proceeding by counsel or in person. The testimony in any such proceeding shall be reduced to writing and filed in the office of the Commission. If upon such hearing the Commission shall be of the opinion that the method of competition or the act or practice in question is prohibited by this Act, it shall make a report in writing in which it shall state its findings as to the facts and shall issue and cause to be served on such person, partnership, or corporation an order requiring such person, partnership, or corporation to cease and desist from using such method of competition or such act or practice. Until the expiration of the time allowed for filing a petition for review, if no such petition has been duly filed within such time, or, if a petition for review has been filed within such time then until the record in the proceeding has been filed in a court of appeals of the United States, as hereinafter provided, the Commission may at any time, upon such notice and in such manner as it shall deem proper, modify or set aside, in whole or in part, any report or any order made or issued by it under this section.[8] After the expiration of the time allowed for filing a petition for review, if no such peti-

---

and the acts or transactions involved, and shall not exercise power or jurisdiction with regard to acts or transactions (other than retail sales) involving such commodities if the Secretary within ten days from the date of receipt of the notice notifies the Commission that there is pending in his Department an investigation of, or proceeding for the prevention of, an alleged violation of this Act involving the same subject matter.

"(3) Over all transactions in commerce in margarine or oleomargarine and over retail sales of meat, meat food products, livestock products in unmanufactured form, and poultry products.

"(c) The Federal Trade Commission shall have no power or jurisdiction over any matter which by this Act is made subject to the jurisdiction of the Secretary, except as provided in subsection (b) of this section."

The same Public Law also amended Subsection 6 of section 5(a) of the Federal Trade Commission Act (15 U. S. C. 45(a) (6) and 38 Stat. 719) by substituting "persons, partnerships, or corporations insofar as they are subject to the Packers and Stockyards Act, 1921, as amended, except as provided in Section 406(b) of said Act" for "persons, partnerships, or corporations subject to the Packers and Stockyards Act, 1921, except as provided in section 406(b) of said Act."

[8] This sentence was amended by Public Law 85-791, 85th Cong., H. R. 6788, approved August 28, 1958, 72 Stat. 942.

tion has been duly filed within such time, the Commission may at any time, after notice and opportunity for hearing, reopen and alter, modify, or set aside, in whole or in part, any report or order made or issued by it under this section, whenever in the opinion of the Commission conditions of fact or of law have so changed as to require such action or if the public interest shall so require: *Provided, however,* That the said person, partnership, or corporation may, within sixty days after service upon him or it of said report or order entered after such a reopening, obtain a review thereof in the appropriate circuit court of appeals of the United States, in the manner provided in subsection (c) of this section.

(c) Any person, partnership, or corporation required by an order of the Commission to cease and desist from using any method of competition or act or practice may obtain a review of such order in the circuit court of appeals of the United States, within any circuit where the method of competition or the act or practice in question was used or where such person, partnership, or corporation resides or carries on business, by filing in the court, within sixty days [9] from the date of the service of such order, a written petition praying that the order of the Commission be set aside. A copy of such petition shall be forthwith transmitted by the clerk of the court of the Commission, and thereupon the Commission shall file in the court the record in the proceeding, as provided in section 2112 of title 28, United States Code. Upon such filing of the petition the court shall have jurisdiction of the proceeding and of the question determined therein concurrently with the Commission until the filing of the record and shall have power to make and enter a decree affirming, modifying, or setting aside the order of the Commission, and enforcing the same to the extent that such order is affirmed and to issue such writs as are ancillary to its jurisdiction or are necessary in its judgment to prevent injury to the public or to competitors pendente lite.[10] The findings of the Commission as to the facts, if supported by evidence, shall be conclusive. To the extent that the order of the Commission is affirmed, the court shall thereupon issue its own order commanding obedience to the terms of such order of the Commission. If either party shall apply to the court for leave to adduce additional evidence, and shall show to the satisfaction of the court that such additional evidence is material and that there were reasonable grounds for the failure to adduce such evidence in the proceeding before the Commission, the court may order such additional evidence to be taken before the Commission and to be adduced upon the hearing in such manner and upon such terms and conditions as to the court may seem proper. The Commission may modify its findings as to the facts, or make new findings as to the facts, or make new findings, by reason of the additional evidence so taken, and it shall file such modified or new findings, which, if supported by evidence, shall be conclusive, and its recommendation, if any, for the modification or setting aside of its original order, with the return

[9] Section 5(a) of the amended Act of 1938 provides: Sec. 5(a) In case of an oder by the Federal Trade Commission to cease and desist, served on or before the date of the enactment of this Act, the sixty-day period referred to in section 5(c) of the Federal Trade Commission Act, as amended by this Act, shall begin on the date of the enactment of this Act.

[10] The above two sentences were also amended by Public Law 85–791.

of such additional evidence. The judgment and decree of the court shall be final, except that the same shall be subject to review by the Supreme Court upon certiorari, as provided in section 240 of the Judicial Code.

(d) Upon the filing of the record with it the jurisdiction of the court of appeals of the United States to affirm, enforce, modify, or set aside orders of the Commission shall be exclusive.[11]

(e) Such proceedings in the circuit court of appeals shall be given precedence over other cases pending therein, and shall be in every way expedited. No order of the Commission or judgment of court to enforce the same shall in anywise relieve or absolve any person, partnership, or corporation from any liability under the Antitrust Acts.

(f) Complaints, orders, and other processes of the Commission under this section may be served by anyone duly authorized by the Commission, either (a) by delivering a copy thereof to the person to be served, or to a member of the partnership to be served, or the president, secretary, or other executive officer or a director of the corporation to be served; or (b) by leaving a copy thereof at the residence or principal office or place of business of such person, partnership, or corporation; or (c) by registering and mailing a copy thereof addressed to such person, partnership, or corporation at his or its residence or principal office or place of business. The verified return by the person so serving said complaint, order, or other process setting forth the manner of said service shall be proof of the same, and the return post office receipt for said complaint, order, or other process registered and mailed as aforesaid shall be proof of the service of the same.

(g) An order of the Commission to cease and desist shall become final

(1) Upon the expiration of the time allowed for filing a petition for review, if no such petition has been duly filed within such time; but the Commission may thereafter modify or set aside its order to the extent provided in the last sentence of subsection (b); or

(2) Upon the expiration of the time allowed for filing a petition for certiorari, if the order of the Commission has been affirmed, or the petition for review dismissed by the circuit court of appeals, and no petition for certiorari has been duly filed; or

(3) Upon the denial of a petition for certiorari, if the order of the Commission has been affirmed or the petition for review dismissed by the circuit court of appeals; or

(4) Upon the expiration of thirty days from the date of issuance of the mandate of the Supreme Court, if such Court directs that the order of the Commission be affirmed or the petition for review dismissed.

(h) If the Supreme Court directs that the order of the Commission be modified or set aside, the order of the Commission rendered in accordance with the mandate of the Supreme Court shall become final upon the expiration of thirty days from the time it was rendered, unless within such thirty days either party has instituted proceedings to have such order corrected to accord with the mandate, in which event the order of the Commission shall become final when so corrected.

(i) If the order of the Commission is modified or set aside by the circuit

[11] The above section was also amended by Public Law 85–791.

court of appeals, and if (1) the time allowed for filing a petition for certiorari has expired and no such petition has been duly filed, or (2) the petition for certiorari has been denied, or (3) the decision of the court has been affirmed by the Supreme Court, then the order of the Commission rendered in accordance with the mandate of the circuit court of appeals shall become final on the expiration of thirty days from the time such order of the Commission was rendered, unless within such thirty days either party has instituted proceedings to have such order corrected so that it will accord with the mandate, in which event the order of the Commission shall become final when so corrected.

(j) If the Supreme Court orders a rehearing; or if the case is remanded by the circuit court of appeals to the Commission for a rehearing, and if (1) the time allowed for filing a petition for certiorari has expired, and no such petition has been duly filed, or (2) the petition for certiorari has been denied, or (3) the decision of the court has been affirmed by the Supreme Court, then the order of the Commission rendered upon such rehearing shall become final in the same manner as though no prior order of the Commission had been rendered.

(k) As used in this section the term "mandate," in case a mandate has been recalled prior to the expiration of thirty days from the date of issuance thereof, means the final mandate.

(l) Any person, partnership, or corporation who violates an order of the Commission to cease and desist after it has become final, and while such order is in effect, shall forfeit and pay to the United States a civil penalty of not more than $5,000 for each violation, which shall accrue to the United States and may be recovered in a civil action brought by the United States. Each separate violation of such an order shall be a separate offense, except that in the case of a violation through continuing failure or neglect to obey a final order of the Commission each day of continuance of such failure or neglect shall be deemed a separate offense.[12]

SEC. 6. That the commission shall also have power [13]—

(a) To gather and compile information concerning, and to investigate from time to time the organization, business, conduct, practices, and management of any corporation engaged in commerce, excepting banks and common carriers subject to the Act to regulate commerce, and its relation to other corporations and to individuals, associations, and partnerships.

(b) To require, by general or special orders, corporations engaged in commerce, excepting banks, and common carriers subject to the Act to regulate commerce, or any class of them, or any of them, respectively, to file with the commission in such form as the commission may prescribe annual or special, or both annual and special, reports or answers in writing to specific questions, furnishing to the commission such information as it may require as to the

[12] Foregoing sentence added by subsection (c) of Sec. 4, Public No. 459, 81st Congress. (See Footnote 1)

[13] Public No. 78, 73d Cong., approved June 16, 1933, making appropriations for the fiscal year ending June 30, 1934, for the "Executive Office and sundry independent bureaus, boards, commissions," etc., made the Commission contingent upon the provision (48 Stat. 291; 15 U. S. C., sec. 46a) that "hereafter no new investigations shall be initiated by the Commission as the result of a legislative resolution, except the same be a concurrent resolution of the two Houses of Congress."

organization, business, conduct, practices, management, and relation to other corporations, partnerships, and individuals of the respective corporations filing such reports or answers in writing. Such reports and answers shall be made under oath, or otherwise, as the commission may prescribe, and shall be filed with the commission within such reasonable period as the commission may prescribe, unless additional time be granted in any case by the commission.

(c) Whenever a final decree has been entered against any defendant corporation in any suit brought by the United States to prevent and restrain any violation of the antitrust Acts, to make investigation, upon its own initiative, of the manner in which the decree has been or is being carried out, and upon the application of the Attorney General it shall be its duty to make such investigation. It shall transmit to the Attorney General a report embodying its findings and recommendations as a result of any such investigation, and the report shall be made public in the discretion of the commission.

(d) Upon the direction of the President or either House of Congress to investigate and report the facts relating to any alleged violations of the antitrust Acts by any corporation.

(e) Upon the application of the Attorney General to investigate and make recommendations for the readjustment of the business of any corporation alleged to be violating the antitrust Acts in order that the corporation may thereafter maintain its organization, management, and conduct of business in accordance with law.

(f) To make public from time to time such portions of the information obtained by it hereunder, except trade secrets and names of customers, as it shall deem expedient in the public interest; and to make annual and special reports to the Congress and to submit therewith recommendations for additional legislation; and to provide for the publication of its reports and decisions in such form and manner as may be best adapted for public information and use.

(g) From time to time to classify corporations and to make rules and regulations for the purpose of carrying out the provisions of this Act.

(h) To investigate, from time to time, trade conditions in and with foreign countries where associations, combinations, or practices of manufacturers, merchants, or traders, or other conditions, may affect the foreign trade of the United States, and to report to Congress thereon, with such recommendations as it deems advisable.

SEC. 7. That in any suit in equity brought by or under the direction of the Attorney General as provided in the antitrust Acts, the court may, upon the conclusion of the testimony therein, if it shall be then of opinion that the complainant is entitled to relief, refer said suit to the commission, as a master in chancery, to ascertain and report an appropriate form of decree therein. The commission shall proceed upon such notice to the parties and under such rules of procedure as the court may prescribe, and upon the coming in of such report such exceptions may be filed and such proceedings had in relation thereto as upon the report of a master in other equity causes, but the court may adopt or reject such report, in whole or in part, and enter such decree as the nature of the case may in its judgment require.

SEC. 8. That the several departments and bureaus of the Government when directed by the President shall furnish the commission, upon its request, all records, papers, and information in their possession relating to any corporation subject to any of the provisions of this Act, and shall detail from time to time such officials and employees to the commission as he may direct.

SEC. 9. That for the purposes of this Act the commission, or its duly authorized agent or agents, shall at all reasonable times have access to, for the purpose of examination, and the right to copy any documentary evidence of any corporation being investigated or proceeded against; and the commission shall have power to require by subpoena the attendance and testimony of witnesses and the production of all such documentary evidence relating to any matter under investigation. Any member of the commission may sign subpoenas, and members and examiners of the commission may administer oaths and affirmations, examine witnesses, and receive evidence.

Such attendance of witnesses, and the production of such documentary evidence, may be required from any place in the United States, at any designated place of hearing. And in case of disobedience to a subpoena the commission may invoke the aid of any court of the United States in requiring the attendance and testimony of witnesses and the production of documentary evidence.

Any of the district courts of the United States within the jurisdiction of which such inquiry is carried on may, in case of contumacy or refusal to obey a subpoena issued to any corporation or other person, issue an order requiring such corporation or other person to appear before the commission, or to produce documentary evidence if so ordered, or to give evidence touching the matter in question; and any failure to obey such order of the court may be punished by such court as a contempt thereof.

Upon the application of the Attorney General of the United States, at the request of the commission, the district courts of the United States shall have jurisdiction to issue writs of mandamus commanding any person or corporation to comply with the provisions of this Act or any order of the commission made in pursuance thereof.

The commission may order testimony to be taken by deposition in any proceeding or investigation pending under this Act at any stage of such proceeding or investigation. Such depositions may be taken before any person designated by the commission and having power to administer oaths. Such testimony shall be reduced to writing by the person taking the deposition, or under his direction, and shall then be subscribed by the deponent. Any person may be compelled to appear and depose and to produce documentary evidence in the same manner as witnesses may be compelled to appear and testify and produce documentary evidence before the commission as hereinbefore provided.

Witnesses summoned before the commission shall be paid the same fees and mileage that are paid witnesses in the courts of the United States, and witnesses whose depositions are taken, and the persons taking the same shall severally be entitled to the same fees as are paid for like services in the courts of the United States.

No person shall be excused from attending and testifying or from producing documentary evidence before the commission or in obedience to the subpoena of the commission on the ground or for the reason that the testimony or evidence, documentary or otherwise, required of him may tend to incriminate him or subject him to a penalty or forfeiture. But no natural person shall be prosecuted or subjected to any penalty or forfeiture for or on account of any transaction, matter, or thing concerning which he may testify, or produce evidence, documentary or otherwise, before the commission in obedience to a subpoena issued by it: *Provided,* That no natural person so testifying shall be exempt from prosecution and · punishment for perjury committed in so testifying.

SEC. 10. That any person who shall neglect or refuse to attend and testify, or to answer any lawful inquiry, or to produce documentary evidence, if in his power to do so, in obedience to the subpoena or lawful requirement of the commission, shall be guilty of an offense and upon conviction thereof by a court of competent jurisdiction shall be punished by a fine of not less than $1,000 nor more than $5,000, or by imprisonment for not more than one year, or by both such fine and imprisonment.

Any person who shall willfully make, or cause to be made, any false entry or statement of fact in any report required to be made under this Act, or who shall willfully make, or cause to be made, any false entry in any account, record, or memorandum kept by any corporation subject to this Act, or who shall willfully neglect or fail to make, or cause to be made, full, true, and correct entries in such accounts, records, or memoranda of all facts and transactions appertaining to the business of such corporation, or who shall willfully remove out of the jurisdiction of the United States, or willfully mutilate, alter, or by any other means falsify any documentary evidence of such corporation, or who shall willfully refuse to submit to the commission or to any of its authorized agents, for the purpose of inspection and taking copies, any documentary evidence of such corporation in his possession or within his control, shall be deemed guilty of an offense against the United States, and shall be subject, upon conviction in any court of the United States of competent jurisdiction, to a fine of not less than $1,000 nor more than $5,000 or to imprisonment for a term of not more than three years, or to both such fine and imprisonment.

If any corporation required by this Act to file any annual or special report shall fail so to do within the time fixed by the commission for filing the same, and such failure shall continue for thirty days after notice of such default, the corporation shall forfeit to the United States the sum of $100 for each and every day of the continuance of such failure which forfeiture shall be payable into the Treasury of the United States, and shall be recoverable in a civil suit in the name of the United States brought in the district where the corporation has its principal office or in any district in which it shall do business. It shall be the duty of the various district attorneys, under the direction of the Attorney General of the United States, to prosecute for the recovery of forfeitures. The costs and expenses of such prosecution shall be paid out of the appropriation for the expenses of the courts of the United States.

Any officer or employee of the commission who shall make public any information obtained by the commission without its authority, unless directed by a court, shall be deemed guilty of a misdemeanor, and, upon conviction thereof, shall be punished by a fine not exceeding $5,000, or by imprisonment not exceeding one year, or by fine and imprisonment, in the discretion of the court.

SEC. 11. Nothing contained in this Act shall be construed to prevent or interfere with the enforcement of the provisions of the antitrust Acts or the Acts to regulate commerce, nor shall anything contained in the Act be constructed to alter, modify, or repeal the said antitrust Acts or the Acts to regulate commerce or any part or parts thereof.

SEC. 12. (a) It shall be unlawful for any person, partnership, or corporation to disseminate, or cause to be disseminated, any false advertisement—(1) By United States mails, or in commerce by any means, for the purpose of inducing, or which is likely to induce, directly or indirectly the purchase of food, drugs, devices or cosmetics; or (2) By any means, for the purpose of inducing, or which is likely to induce, directly or indirectly, the purchase in commerce of food, drugs, devices, or cosmetics.

(b) The dissemination or the causing to be disseminated of any false advertisement within the provisions of subsection (a) of this section shall be an unfair or deceptive act or practice in commerce within the meaning of section 5.

SEC. 13. (a) Whenever the commission has reason to believe—(1) that any person, partnership, or corporation is engaged in, or is about to engage in, the dissemination or the causing of the dissemination of any advertisement in violation of section 12, and (2) that the enjoining thereof pending the issuance of a complaint by the Commission under section 5, and until such complaint is dismissed by the Commission or set aside by the court on review, or the order of the Commission to cease and desist made thereon has become final within the meaning of section 5, would be to the interest of the public, the Commission by any of its attorneys designated by it for such purpose may bring suit in a district court of the United States or in the United States court of any Territory, to enjoin the dissemination or the causing of the dissemination of such advertisement. Upon proper showing a temporary injunction or restraining order shall be granted without bond. Any such suit shall be brought in the district in which such person, partnership, or corporation resides or transacts business.

(b) Whenever it appears to the satisfaction of the court in the case of a newspaper, magazine, periodical, or other publication, published at regular intervals—(1) that restraining the dissemination of a false advertisement in any particular issue of such publication would delay the delivery of such issues after the regular time therefor, and (2) that such delay would be due to the method by which the manufacture and distribution of such publication is customarily conducted by the publisher in accordance with sound business practice, and not to any method or device adopted for the evasion of this section or to prevent or delay the issuance of an injunction or restraining order with respect to such false advertisement or any other advertisement, the court shall exclude such issue from the operation of the restraining order or injunction.

SEC. 14. (a) Any person, partnership, or corporation who violates any provision of section 12(a) shall, if the use of the commodity advertised may be injurious to health because of results from such use under the conditions prescribed in the advertisement thereof, or under such conditions as are customary or usual, or if such violation is with intent to defraud or mislead, be guilty of a misdemeanor, and upon conviction shall be punished by a fine of not more than $5,000 or by imprisonment for not more than six months, or by both such fine or imprisonment; except that if the conviction is for a violation committed after a first conviction of such person, partnership, or corporation, for any violation of such section, punishment shall be by a fine of not more than $10,000 or by imprisonment: *Provided,* That for the purposes of this section meats and meat food products duly inspected, marked, and labeled in accordance with rules and regulations issued under the Meat Inspection Act approved March 4, 1907, as amended, shall be conclusively presumed not injurious to health at the time the same leave official "establishments." [14]

(b) No publisher, radio-broadcast licensee, or agency or medium for the dissemination of advertising, except the manufacturer, packer, distributor, or seller of the commodity to which the false advertisement relates, shall be liable under this section by reason of the dissemination by him of false advertisement, unless he has refused, on the request of the Commission, to furnish the Commission the name and post-office address of the manufacturer, packer, distributor, or advertising agency, residing in the United States, who caused him to disseminate such advertisement. No advertising agency shall be liable under this section by reason of the causing by it of the dissemination of any false advertisement, unless it has refused, on the request of the Commission, to furnish the Commission the name and post-office address of the manufacturer, packer, distributor, or seller, residing in the United States, who caused it to cause the dissemination of such advertisement.

SEC. 15. For the purposes of sections 12, 13, and 14—
(a) (1) The term "false advertisement" means an advertisement, other than labeling, which is misleading in a material respect; and in determining whether any advertisement is misleading, there shall be taken into account (among other things) not only representations made or suggested by statement, word, design, device, sound, or any combination thereof, but also the extent to which the advertisement fails to reveal facts material in the light of such representations or material with respect to consequences which may result from the use of the commodity to which the advertisement relates under the conditions prescribed in said advertisement, or under such conditions as are customary or usual. No advertisement of a drug shall be deemed to be false if it is disseminated only to members of the medical profession, contains no false representation of a material fact, and includes, or is accompanied in each instance by

[14] Section 5 (b) of the amending Act of 1938 provides: Section 14 of the Federal Trade Commission Act, added to such Act by section 4 of this Act, shall take effect on the expiration of sixty days after the date of the enactment of this Act.

truthful disclosure of, the formula showing quantitatively each ingredient of such drug.

(2) In the case of oleomargarine or margarine an advertisement shall be deemed misleading in a material respect if in such advertisement representations are made or suggested by statement, word, grade designation, design, device, symbol, sound, or any combination thereof, that such oleomargarine or margarine is a dairy product, except that nothing contained herein shall prevent a truthful, accurate, and full statement in any such advertisement of all the ingredients contained in such oleomargarine or margarine.[15]

(b) The term "food" means (1) articles used for food or drink for man or other animals, (2) chewing gum, and (3) articles used for components of any such article.

(c) The term "drug" means (1) articles recognized in the official United States Pharmacopoeia, official Homoeopathic Pharmacopoeia of the United States, or official National Formulary, or any supplement to any of them: and (2) articles intended for use in the diagnosis, cure, mitigation, treatment, or prevention of disease in man or other animals; and (3) articles (other than food) intended to affect the structure or any function of the body of man or other animals; and (4) articles intended for use as a component of any article specified in clause (1), (2), or (3); but does not include devices or their components, parts, or accessories.

(d) The term "device" (except when used in subsection (a) of this section) means instruments, apparatus, and contrivances, including their parts and accessories, intended (1) for use in the diagnosis, cure, mitigation, treatment, or prevention of disease in man or other animals; or (2) to affect the structure or any function of the body of man or other animals.

(e) The term "cosmetic" means (1) articles to be rubbed, poured, sprinkled, or sprayed on, introduced into, or otherwise applied to the human body or any part thereof intended for cleansing, beautifying, promoting attractiveness, or altering the appearance, and (2) articles intended for use as a component of any such article; except that such term shall not include soap.

(f) For the purposes of this section and section 407 of the Federal Food, Drug, and Cosmetic Act, as amended, the term "oleomargarine" or "margarine" includes—

(1) all substances, mixtures, and compounds known as oleomargarine or margarine;

(2) all substances, mixtures, and compounds which have a consistence similar to that of butter and which contain any edible oils or fats other than milk fat if made in imitation or semblance of butter.[16]

---

[15] Subsection (a) of Sec. 4 of Public No. 459, 81st Congress (see Footnote 1), amended sec. 15 of this Act by inserting "(1)" after the letter "(a)" in subsection (a) above, and by adding the end of such subsection new paragraph (2), above set out.

[16] Subsection (b) of Sec. 4, of Public No. 495, 81st Congress (see Footnote 1) further amended sec. 15 of this Act, by adding at the end thereof the new subsection (f) as above set out.

SEC. 16. Whenever the Federal Trade Commission has reason to believe that any person, partnership, or corporation is liable to a penalty under section 14 or under subsection (1) of section 5, it shall certify the facts to the Attorney General, whose duty it shall be to cause appropriate proceedings to be brought for the enforcement of the provisions of such section or subsection.

SEC. 17. If any provision of this Act, or the application thereof to any person, partnership, corporation, or circumstance, is held invalid, the remainder of the Act and the application of such provision to any other person, partnership, corporation, or circumstance, shall not be affected thereby.

SEC. 18. This Act may be cited as the "Federal Trade Commission Act."
Original approved September 26, 1914.
Amended and approved March 21, 1938.[17]

---

[17] See Footnote 1.

Appendix V

Suggestions for Compliance with the Brokerage Provisions of the Robinson-Patman Act (Section 2 [c] of the Amended Clayton Act)*

1. *As a general rule, a seller may not pay brokerage or other compensation to the buyer in connection with the sale of goods in interstate commerce.*

This is true whether the payment is made directly or indirectly or whether it is made in the form of a payment or in the form of a reduction on price in lieu of the payment. The law is also violated by the buyer in receiving the payment or discount.

2. *The seller may not pay directly to the buyer brokerage or other compensation in connection with a sale.*

There have been two principal situations in which direct payments have been questioned.

(a) When a broker or other sales representative or intermediary purchases goods for his own account rather than acting as an agent for the seller in the sale of the goods, he is clearly the buyer and the seller may not pay a commission to him on these purchases. If the broker also in other transactions is making sales for the seller as a broker, the seller may pay commissions on such other sales.

* Suggestions made by the author to the National Food Brokers Association, December 10, 1960.

353

(b) In some cases, payments alleged to have been made for services performed by the buyer have been declared unlawful payments of brokerage because the services, such as warehousing or reselling, were of a kind that the buyer would ordinarily perform for himself. These holdings do not preclude the use of legitimate cooperative merchandising plans.

3. *The seller may not pay brokerage or other commissions in connection with the sale of goods to an intermediary who represents or is controlled by the buyer.*

The problem here has been whether the intermediary represents or is controlled by the buyer. Several examples where the intermediary has been held to represent or be controlled by the buyer follow:

(a) The broker as a partnership whose partners owned virtually all of the stock of the buyer corporation. Brokerage fees were not paid over to the buyer corporation but were distributed to the partners or individuals. Nevertheless, it was held that the seller's payments of brokerage to the brokerage partnership were illegal.

(b) A broker acted as the agent for several buyers although he received no fees from them in connection with purchases made for them. Nevertheless, he could not lawfully receive a commission from the sellers on these purchases.

(c) A broker under contract with buyers supplied them with market information and purchases for them for a small monthly fee. He placed orders with sellers for goods and obtained brokerage fees from the seller that were credited to the buyers' account. The seller was prohibited from paying the fees.

(d) In a situation similar to the last one, all of the buyers advertised a common trademark. The broker obtained fees from the seller for advertising the trademark and passed the fees on to the buyers. Here again, the seller could not lawfully make the payments.

(e) All of the stock of a brokerage concern was owned by the buyers. All of the fees obtained by the brokerage concern were required to pay expenses. The seller was prohibited from paying fees because the brokerage concern represented the buyers.

(f) A broker represented both the buyer and the seller and divided its charges equally between the two so that in effect the buyer and seller each paid half of the brokerage fee. The payments by each were prohibited because they were payments to a representative of the other party to the transaction.

4. *A seller's broker may not pay all or part of the brokerage to the buyer either directly or through a reduction in price by the seller.*

This point was settled in a case where the buyer demanded a lower price than the seller was willing to accept.

A seller's broker was charging a 5 per cent commission for handling the seller's product; in order to make a sale of significant quantities of the product to a particular buyer who would not pay the seller's going price, the seller agreed to lower the price if the broker would lower the commission; the broker agreed and a series of sales to the particular buyer were made on this basis.

It was held that the broker violated the law.

5. *A seller may not reduce his price on the grounds that he has not paid brokerage or other commission on the sale.*

Generally, the fact that the reduction in price was based on a savings in sales commission has been proved by the fact that the price was reduced by the amount of the commission, but the rule would apply also where the price was reduced by only part of the commission or reduced more than the amount of the commission if this were actual basis of the reduction. But a seller is not required to use brokers at all or to pay any given percentage at a brokerage fee.

6. *Is cost justification a defense?*

No. It is no defense to violation of 2(c) for a seller to show that a reduction in price in lieu of brokerage or the payment of brokerage to the buyer could be justified through savings in cost of manufacture, sale, or delivery.

7. *Is meeting competition in good faith a defense?*

No. A seller charged with a violation of Section 2(c) may not defend his actions by showing that the alleged reduction in price in lieu of brokerage or the payment of brokerage to the buyer was made in good faith to meet an equivalent reduction or payment made by a competitor.

8. *Can a broker or other representative of either the buyer or seller be held for violating this law?*

Yes. The buyer's or seller's broker or other intermediary in the sale of goods who receives or passes on the brokerage fee or other commission from one party to the sale to the other violated the law in so doing.

For example: B, acting as the seller's broker, passes on part of his brokerage fee to the purchaser. B violates the law. The buyer in receiving brokerage and the seller in paying a brokerage fee to the buyer also violate the law.

Appendix VI

FTC Guides

Guides for Advertising Allowances and Other Merchandising Payments and Services

16 CFR Part 240

INTRODUCTION

These Guides are designed to highlight legal problems that may be encountered by businessmen who want to utilize promotional or advertising allowances and similar merchandising payments or services to stimulate the sale of their products. The Guides are not intended to serve as a comprehensive statement of the law or as a legal treatise, but are instead intended to serve as a practical manual—in the form of basic rules of thumb, specific examples, and carefully considered suggestions—for the honest businessman who wants to conform his conduct to the requirements of the law without giving up the benefits that can be derived from this form of promotional activity. The Guides are designed to furnish guidance and assistance for the businessman seeking to comply with the law and to avoid even inadvertent violations.

Simply stated, what the law requires, in essence, is that those who grant promotional and advertising allowances treat their customers fairly and without discrimination, and not use such allowances to disguise discriminatory price discounts. In interpreting and enforcing the law, the Commission will recognize the practicalities of business while preventing the kind of discriminatory practices at which the law was aimed. Realistic and reasonable enforcement of the law will enable the Commission to enlist the aid of businessmen in eliminating undesirable practices and abuses without interfering with legitimate promotional and merchandising activities.

[Upon issuance of the guides, the FTC announced its intention to re-examine them after they have been in effect 18 months and to solicit formal comments thereon from interested parties at that time.]

WHAT THE GUIDES ARE MEANT TO DO

These Guides can be of great value to businessmen who want to avoid violating the laws against giving or receiving improper promotional allowances, including advertising or special services, for promoting products. The Guides will make possible a better understanding of the obligations of sellers and their customers in joint promotional activities.

The Commission's responsibility is to obtain compliance with these laws. It has a duty to move against violators.[1] However, as an administrative agency, the Commission believes the more knowledge businessmen have with respect to the laws enforced by the Commission, the greater the likelihood that voluntary compliance with the laws will be obtained.

For the Commission to perform its responsibilities properly, and for business to avoid violation of the law, it is necessary that every effort be made to furnish individual businessmen a better understanding of these laws. It will help businessmen—and the Commission's law enforcement efforts—if they have a good general knowledge of what they can and cannot do in the field of promotional allowances and services.

WHAT THE GUIDES ARE NOT MEANT TO DO

It should be made clear too that the Guides are not meant to do several things:

(1) They are not meant to cover every situation. Decided cases dealing with unusual situations are not covered.

(2) They are not a substitute for sound legal advice.

(3) They are not intended to be a legal treatise. They should be read as a nontechnical explanation of what the law means.

(4) They do not make it mandatory (nor does the law itself) that sellers provide promotional allowances, services, or facilities to any customer. They only come into play when the seller determines to employ such promotional practices.

WHAT THE LAW COVERS GENERALLY

The Robinson–Patman Act is an amendment to the Clayton Act. It is directed at preventing competitive inequalities that come from certain types of discrimination by sellers in interstate commerce. Sections 2(d) and (e) of the Act deal with discriminations in the field of promotional payments and services made available to customers who buy for resale. Where the seller pays the buyer to perform the service, Section 2(d) applies. Where the seller furnishes the service itself to the buyer, Section 2(e) applies. Both sections require a seller to treat competing customers on proportionally equal terms in connection with the resale of the seller's products of like grade and quality.

OTHER LAW INVOLVED

In several places, the Guides are concerned with laws other than Sections 2(d) and (e):

[1] The Commission has issued many orders to cease and desist which include proscriptions under Section 2(d) and/or 2(e) of the amended Clayton Act, that antedate the Supreme Court's decision in the matter of *Federal Trade Commission* v. *Fred Meyer, Inc., et al.* [1968 Trade Cases ¶ 72,383], 390 U.S. 341 (1968). In this regard, it should be noted that future obligations of those companies and individuals under those orders shall be measured against said decision, as supplemented by these Guides.

(1) A seller who pays a customer for services that are not rendered, or who overpays for services which have been rendered, may thereby violate Section 2(a) of the Clayton Act, as amended. (See § 240.11.)

(2) A customer who receives discriminatory or other improper payments, services, or facilities may thereby violate Section 2(f) of the Clayton Act, as amended by the Robinson–Patman Act, or Section 5 of the Federal Trade Commission Act. (See §§ 240.11 and 240.14.)

(3) A third party who helps a customer claim reimbursement greater than that to which he is entitled under a seller's program (by furnishing the customer with a false invoice or other statement, for instance), may thereby violate Section 5 of the Federal Trade Commission Act. (See § 240.13.)

(4) A third party who devises and/or administers a promotional assistance program on behalf of one or more sellers may violate Section 5 of the Federal Trade Commission Act if the use, administration, or operation of the program results in violation of law. (See § 240.13.)

(5) The examples are not intended to be all-inclusive. The Guides do not purport to set forth all the legal rules governing a seller's promotional practices or other vertical arrangements, but are directed primarily to the seller's obligation in making promotional offers to notify, and offer proportionally equal terms to his competing customers. Related practices, not directly involving notification or proportionalization, are not necessarily covered by these Guides.

Authority: The provisions of this Part 240 issued under Secs. 5, 6, 38 Stat. 719, as amended, 721; 15 U.S.C. 45, 46; 49 Stat. 1526; 15 U.S.C. 13, as amended. [Guide 1]

§ 240.1 When does the law apply?

Sections 2(d) and (e) apply to a seller of products in interstate commerce, if he either directly or through an intermediary (a) pays for services or facilities furnished by a customer in connection with the distribution of his products [Section 2(d)], or (b) furnishes such services or facilities to a customer [Section 2(e)] who competes with any other customer in the resale of the seller's products of like grade and quality.

[Guide 2]

§ 240.2 Who is a seller?

"Seller" includes anyone (manufacturer, wholesaler, distributor, etc.) who sells products for resale, with or without further processing. Selling candy to a retailer is a sale for resale without processing. Selling corn syrup to a candy manufacturer is an example of a sale for resale with processing.

[Guide 3]

§ 240.3 Who is a customer?

A "customer" is someone who buys for resale directly from the seller, the seller's agent or broker; and, in addition, a "customer" is any buyer of the seller's product for resale who purchases from or through a wholesaler or other intermediate reseller. In this part, the word "customer" which is used in Section 2(d) of the Act includes "purchaser" which is used in Section 2(e).

[Note: In determining whether a seller has fulfilled his obligations toward his customers, the Commission will recognize that there may be some exceptions to this general definition of "customer." For example, the purchaser of distress merchandise would not be considered a "customer" simply on the basis of such purchase. Similarly, those retailers who purchase from other retailers, those who make only sporadic purchases, and those who do not regularly sell the seller's product or who are a type of retail outlet not usually selling such products (e.g., a hardware store stocking a few isolated food items) will not be considered "customers" of the seller unless the seller has been put on notice that such retailers are selling his product.]

"Competing customers" are all businesses that compete in the resale of the seller's products of like grade and quality at the same functional level of distribution regardless of whether they purchase direct from the supplier or through some intermediary.

Example 1: A manufacturer sells to some retailers directly and to others through wholesalers. Retailer "X" purchases the manufacturer's product from a wholesaler and resells some of it to retailer "Y." Retailer "X" is a customer of the manufacturer. Retailer "Y" is not a customer unless the fact that he purchases the manufacturer's product is known to the manufacturer.

Example 2: A manufacturer sells directly to some independent retailers, sells to the headquarters of chains and cooperative stores, and also sells to wholesalers. The direct buying independent retailers and the wholesaler's independent retailer customers are customers of the manufacturer. Individual retail outlets which are part of the chains or members of the cooperatives are not customers of the manufacturer.

[Guide 4]

§ 240.4 What is interstate commerce?

This term has not been precisely defined in the statute. In general, if there is any part of a business which is not wholly within one state (for example, sales or deliveries of products, their subsequent distribution or purchase, or delivery of supplies or raw materials), the business may be subject to the Robinson–

Patman Act. Sales in the District of Columbia are also covered by the Act. [Guide 5]

§ 240.5 What are services or facilities?

These terms have not been exactly defined by the statute or in decisions. The following are merely examples—the Act covers many other services and facilities.

(a) The following are some of the services or facilities covered by the Act where the seller pays the buyer for furnishing them:

> Any kind of advertising, including cooperative advertising.
> Handbills.
> Window and floor displays.
> Special sales or promotional efforts for which "push money" is paid to clerks, salesmen, and other employees of the customers.
> Demonstrators and demonstrations.

(b) Here are some examples of services or facilities covered by the Act when the seller furnishes them to a customer:

> Any kind of advertising.
> Catalogs.
> Demonstrators.
> Display and storage cabinets.
> Display materials.
> Special packaging, or package sizes.
> Acepting returns for credit.
> Prizes or merchandise for conducting promotional contests.

[Note: In these Guides, the term "services" is used to encompass both "services and facilities."]
[Guide 6]

§ 240.6 Need for a Plan.

If a seller makes payments or furnishes services that come under Section 2(d) or (e) of the Clayton Act, as amended, he should do it under a plan that meets several requirements. In addition, if there are many competing customers to be considered, or if the plan is at all complex, the seller would be well advised to put his plan in writing. Briefly, the requirements are:

(a) The payments or services under the plan should be available on proportionally equal terms to all competing customers. (See § 240.7.)

(b) The seller should take action designed to inform all of his competing customers of the existence of and essential features of the promotion plan in ample time for them to take full advantage of it. (See § 240.8.)

(c) If the basic plan is not functionally available to (i.e., suitable for and usable by) some customers competing in the resale of the seller's products of like grade and quality with those being furnished payments or services, alternatives that are functionally available should be offered to such customers. (See § 240.9.)

(d) In informing customers of the details of a plan, the seller should provide them sufficient information to give a clear understanding of the exact terms of the offer, including all alternatives, and the conditions upon which payment will be made or services furnished. (See § 240.10.)

(e) The seller should take reasonable precautions to see that the services are actually performed and that he is not overpaying for them. (See § 240.11.)

[Guide 7]

§ 240.7 Proportionally equal terms.

The payment or services under the plan should be made available to all competing customers on proportionally equal terms. This means that payments or services should be proportionalized on some basis that is fair to all customers who compete in the resale of the seller's products. No single way to proportionalize is prescribed by law. Any method that treats competing customers on proportionally equal terms may be used. Generally, this can best be done by basing the payments made or the services furnished on the dollar volume or on the quantity of goods purchased during a specified period. Other methods which are fair to all competing customers are also acceptable.

Example 1: A seller may properly offer to pay a specified part (say 50%) of the cost of local advertising up to an amount equal to a set percentage (such as 5%)of the dollar volume of purchases during a specified time.

Example 2: A seller may properly place in reserve for each customer a specified amount of money for each unit purchased, and use it to reimburse those customers for the actual cost of their advertising of the seller's product.

Example 3: A seller should not select one or a few customers to receive special allowances (e.g., 5% of purchases) to promote his product, while making allowances available on some lesser basis (e.g., 2% of purchases) to customers who compete with them.

Example 4: A seller's plan should not provide an allowance on a basis that has rates graduated with the amount of goods purchased, as, for instance, 1% of the first $1,000 purchases per month, 2% of second $1,000 per month, and 3% of all over that.

Example 5: A seller should not identify or feature one or a few customers in his own advertising without making the same service available on proportionally equal terms to customers competing with the identified customer or customers.

Example 6: A seller who makes his employees available or arranges with a third party to furnish personnel for purposes of performing work for a customer should make the same offer available on proportionally equal terms to all other competing customers. In addition the seller should offer usable and suitable alternatives of equivalent measurable cost to those competing customers to whom such services are not usable and suitable.

[Guide 8]

§ 240.8 Seller's duty to inform.

(a) The seller should take reasonable action, in good faith, to inform all his competing customers of the availability of his promotional program. Such notification should include all the relevant details of the offer in time to enable customers to make an informed judgment whether to participate. In the alternative, such notification should include a summary of the essential features and a specific source to contact for further details on a specific promotion. Where such one-step notification is impracticable, the seller may, in lieu thereof, maintain a continuing program of first notifying all competing customers of the types of promotions offered by the seller and a specific source for the customer to contact in order to receive full and timely notice of all relevant details of the supplier's promotions. Such notice should also inform all competing customers that the seller offers advertising allowances and/or other promotional assistance that are usable in a practical business sense by all retailers regardless of size. When a customer indicates his desire to be put on the notification list, the seller should keep that customer advised of all promotions available in his area as long as the customer so desires. The seller can make this notification by any means he chooses, but if he wants to be able to show later that he gave notice to a certain customer, he is in a better position to do so if it was given in writing.

If more direct methods of notification are impracticable, a seller may employ one or more of the following methods, the sufficiency of which will depend upon the nature of the industry and the complexity of his own distribution system. Different sellers may find that different notification methods are most effective for them.

(1) The seller may enter into contracts with his wholesalers, distributors, or other third parties which conform to the requirements of § 240.13.

(2) The seller may place appropriate announcements on product containers or inside thereof with conspicuous notice of such enclosure on the outside. Where this notification procedure is utilized, however, the seller should take whatever steps are necessary to help insure that the notice will come to the attention of the customer's managerial personnel.

(3) The seller may publish notice of the availability and essential features of the plan in a publication of general distribution in the trade.

[*Note:* Whatever procedure is used to give notice to the customer it should prove to be effective in practice. In many instances where customers of wholesalers or other intermediaries are involved and it is necessary to coordinate buying for a promotion such as a one-time buy promotion, a minimum lead time for notification may be 60 days more.]

Example 1: A seller has a plan for the retail promotion of his products in Philadelphia. Some of his retailing customers purchase directly, and he offers the plan to them. Some other Philadelphia retailers purchase his products through wholesalers. The seller may use the wholesalers to reach the retailing customers who buy through them, either by having the wholesalers notify those retailers in accordance with § 240.13, or by using the wholesalers' customer lists for direct notification by the seller.

Example 2: A seller has a plan for the retail promotion of his products in Kansas City. Some of his retailing customers purchase directly and he offers the plan to them. Others purchase his products through wholesalers. The seller may satisfy his notification obligations to them by undertaking, in good faith, one or more of the following measures:

A. Placing on a shipping container or a product package that can reasonably be expected to come to the attention of the managerial personnel of all retailing customers handling the promoted product in time to enable them to participate in the program a conspicuous notice of the availability and essential features of his proposal, identifying a specific source for further particulars and details. In lieu of identifying a source for further particulars, brochures describing the details of the offer may be included in the shipping containers. If it is impractical to include the essential features of the proposal on or in the shipping container, the seller may substitute in the notice, as stated above, a summary of the types of promotions offered (e.g., allowances for advertising in newspapers, hand bills, or envelope stuffers; allowances for radio or television advertising; short-term display allowances, etc.) and a statement that such promotions are usable in a practical business sense by all retailers regardless of size. In order to insure that such notices will come to the attention of the appropriate personnel it may well be necessary for the seller to supplement notices on shipping containers, especially during the initial stages of such a procedure, with additional notices, such as trade journal publications, invoice notices, envelope stuffers for use by wholesalers, etc.

B. If a promotional plan simply consists of providing retailers with display materials, including the materials within the product container.

C. Advising customers from accurate and reasonably complete mailing lists. If the product may be sold lawfully only under Government license (alcoholic beverages, etc.), informing all license holders would be sufficient.

D. Placing an announcement of the availability and essential features of promotional programs, and identifying a specific source for further particulars and details, at reasonable intervals in publications which have general and widespread distribution in the trade, and which are recognized in the trade as means by which sellers announce the availability of such programs.

Example 3: The seller has a wholesaler-oriented plan whereby he pays wholesalers to advertise the seller's product in the wholesalers' order books, or in the wholesalers' price lists directed to retailers purchasing from the wholesalers. He should notify all competing wholesalers of the availability of this plan, but the seller is not required to notify retailing customers.

Example 4: A seller who sells on a direct basis to some retailers in an area, and to other retailers in the area through wholesalers, has a plan for the promotion of his products at the retail level. If the seller directly notifies not only all competing direct purchasing retailers, but also all competing retailers purchasing through the wholesaler, as to the availability, terms, and conditions of the plan, the seller is not required to notify his wholesalers.

Example 5: A seller regularly promotes his products at the retail level, and during the year he has various special promotional offers. His competing customers include large direct-purchasing retailing customers and smaller customers who purchase through wholesalers. Many of the promotions he offers can best be used by his smaller customers if the funds to which the smaller customers are entitled are pooled and used by the wholesalers in their behalf (newspaper advertisements, for example). The seller may encourage, but not coerce, the retailer purchasing through a wholesaler to designate a wholesaler as his agent for receiving notice of collecting and using promotional allowances for him. If a wholesaler by agreement with a retailer is actually authorized to perform for the retailer the promotional services as to which a promotional offer is made, the seller may assume that notice of, and payment under, a promotional plan to the wholesaler constitutes notice and payment to the retailer.

A seller who follows any procedure reasonably designed to inform all his competing customers of his promotional programs, including any of the procedures illustrated under Example 2 above, will be considered by the Commission to have fulfilled his "good faith" obligation under this section if he accompanies such procedure with the following supplementary measures: At regular intervals (of at least every 90 days) during the year, a seller who conducts promotional programs takes affirmative steps to verify the effectiveness of his notification procedure by making spot checks designed to reach a representative cross section of his indirect-buying customers. Whenever such spot checks indicate that the notification procedure is deficient, in that some indirect customers are not receiving actual notice of the promotion, the seller takes immediate steps to expand or to supplement his notification procedure in a manner reasonably designed to eliminate the repetition or continuation of any such deficiency in the future.

[Guide 9]

§ 240.9 Availability to all competing customers.

The plan should be such that all types of competing customers may participate. It should not be tailored unfairly to favor or discriminate against a particular class of customers. This may require offering all such customers more than one way to participate in the plan or offering alternative terms and conditions to customers for whom the basic plan is not usable and suitable. The seller should not either expressly, or by the way the plan operates, eliminate some competing customers, although he may offer alternative plans designed for different customer classes. If he offers alternative plans, all of the plans offered should provide the same proportionate equality and the seller should inform competing customers of the various alternative plans.

With respect to promotional plans offered to retailers, the seller should ensure that his plans or alternatives do not bar any competing retailer customers from participation whether they purchase directly from him or through a wholesaler or other intermediary.

When a seller, in good faith, offers a basic plan, including alternatives, which is reasonably fair and nondiscriminatory, and refrains from taking any steps which would prevent any customer, or class of customers, from participating in his program, he shall be deemed to have satisfied his obligation to make his plan "functionally available" to all customers, and the failure of any customer or customers to participate in the program shall not be deemed to place the seller in violation of the Act.

Example 1: A manufacturer offers a plan for construction of store displays of varying sizes, including some small enough so that all his competing customers are reasonably able to satisfy the requirement. The plan also calls for certification of performance by the retailer. Because they are reluctant to process any paperwork, many small retailers do not participate. This fact is not deemed to place the manufacturer in violation of § 240.9 and he is under no obligation to provide additional alternatives.

Example 2: A manufacturer offers a plan for cooperative advertising on radio, television, or in newspapers of general circulation. The purchases by some of his customers are too small to permit effective use of this offer in promoting the manufacturer's product. The manufacturer may offer them a "functionally available" alternative on proportionally equal terms, such as envelope stuffers, handbills, or other usable services furnished by the manufacturer.

Example 3: The seller's plan provides for furnishing demonstrators to large department store customers. He should provide usable and suitable alternatives on proportionally equal terms to those competing customers who cannot use demonstrators. The alternatives may be usable and suitable services furnished by the seller, or payments by the seller to customers for their advertising or promotion of the seller's product.

[Guide 10]
§ 240.10 Need to understand terms.

In informing customers of the details of a plan, the seller should provide them sufficient information to give a clear understanding of the exact terms of the offer, including all alternatives, and the conditions upon which payment will be made or services furnished.

[Guide 11]
§ 240.11 Checking customer's use of payments.

The seller should take reasonable precautions to see that services he is paying for are furnished and also that he is not overpaying for them. Moreover, the customer must expend an allowance solely for the purpose for which it was given. If the seller knows or should know that what he pays or furnishes is not being properly used by some customers, the improper payments or services should be discontinued.

A seller who, in good faith, takes reasonable and prudent measures to verify the performance of his competing customers will be deemed to have satisfied his obligations under the Act. Also, a seller who, in good faith, concludes a promotional agreement with wholesalers or other intermediaries and who otherwise conforms to the standards of § 240.13 shall be deemed to have satisfied this obligation. If a seller has taken such steps, the fact that a particular customer has retained an allowance in excess of the cost or value of services performed by him shall not alone be deemed to place a seller in violation of the Act.

Example 1: A manufacturer gives "functionally available" promotional allowances for cooperative advertising which require placing advertisements in whatever medium the customer normally utilizes—e.g., radio, newspaper, magazines, handbills, etc. The manufacturer requires that each customer's request for payment be signed and attest that the required performance was rendered. Further, whenever evidence of the advertising—such as a tear sheet or a copy of the invoice from the radio station—is readily available to the customer, the manufacturer requires that such evidence accompany the request for payment. In cases in which such verification is not readily available, the manufacturer spot checks in a manner designed to reach a representative cross section of participating retailer customers to ascertain proof of performance. The manufacturer has satisfied his obligations of verification under the Act.

[Guide 12]

§ 240.12 Competing customers.

The seller is required to provide in his plan only for those customers who compete with each other in the resale of the seller's products of like grade and quality. Therefore, a seller should make available to all competing wholesalers any plan providing promotional payments or services to wholesalers and, similarly, should make available to all competing retailers any plan providing promotional payments or services to retailers. With these requirements met, a seller can limit the area of his promotion. However, this section is not intended to deal with the question of a seller's liability for use of an area promotion where the effect may be to injure the seller's competition.

Example 1: Manufacturer A, located in Wisconsin and distributes shoes nationally, sells shoes to three retailers who compete with each other and sell only in the Roanoke, Virginia, area. He has no other customers selling in Roanoke or its vicinity. If he offers his promotion to one Roanoke customer, he must include all three, but he can limit it to them. The trade area selected must be a natural one and not drawn arbitrarily so as to exclude competing retailers.

Example 2: A national seller has direct-buying retailing customers reselling exclusively within the Baltimore city trade area, and other customers within that area purchasing through wholesalers. The seller may lawfully engage in a promotional campaign confined to the Baltimore area, provided he affords all of his retailing customers within the area the opportunity to participate, including those who purchase through wholesalers.

Example 3: A seller manufactures and sells men's suits and sport jackets (of one quality level) to retail stores nationally. He may restrict allowances to Philadelphia area retailers for their promotion of sport jackets during a particular season. He may not restrict allowances in the Philadelphia area for the promotion of certain styles of sport jackets unless all retailers of his sport jackets in the area are offered the opportunity to purchase the promoted styles and participate in the promotion.

[Note: The seller should be careful here not to discriminate against customers located on the fringes but outside the area selected for the special promotion, since they may be actually competing with those participating.]

[Guide 13]

§ 240.13 Wholesaler or third-party performance of seller's obligations.

(a) A seller may, in good faith, enter into written agreements with intermediaries, such as wholesalers, distributors, or other third parties, including promoters of tripartite promotional plans which provide that such intermediaries will perform all or part of the seller's obligations under this part. However, the interposition of intermediaries between the seller and his customers does not relieve the seller of his ultimate responsibility of compliance with the law. The seller, in order to demonstrate his good faith effort to discharge his obligations under this part, should include in any such agreement provisions that the intermediary will:

(1) Give notice to the seller's customers in conformity with the standards set forth in § 240.8.

(2) Check customer performance in conformity with the standards set forth in § 240.11.

(3) Implement the plan in a manner which will ensure its functional availability to the seller's customers in conformity with the standards set forth in § 240.9. (This must be done whether the plan is one devised by the seller himself or by the intermediary for use by the seller's customers.)

(4) Provide certification in writing and at reasonable intervals that the seller's customers have been and are being treated in conformity with the agreement.

(b) A seller who negotiates such agreements with his wholesalers, distributors, or third-party promoters will be considered by the Commission to have justified his "good faith" obligations under this section if he accompanies such agreements with the following supplementary measures:

At regular intervals (of at least every 90 days) during the year, the seller takes affirmative steps to verify that his customers are receiving the proportionally equal treatment to which they are entitled by making spot checks designed to reach a representative cross section of his indirect buying customers. Whenever such spot checks indicate that the agreements are not being implemented in such a way that the indirect customers are receiving such proportionally equal treatment, the seller takes immediate steps to expand or to supplement such agreements in a manner reasonably designed to eliminate the repetition or continuation of any such discriminations in the future.

Example 1: A seller should not buy advertising time from a radio station and have the station furnish free radio time only to certain favored customers of the seller.

Example 2: A seller should not participate in a tripartite promotional plan providing for in-store promotion of his products unless all his competing customers are given an opportunity to participate in the intermediary's basic plan and, in the event some cannot use the basic plan, a suitable and usable alternative is made available on proportionally equal terms. A seller may demonstrate his good faith effort to discharge his obligations, in the event the intermediary operates a nondiscriminatory program in a discriminatory manner, by establishing that he has an agreement with the intermediary as described above and has fulfilled his duty to conduct periodic checks of the intermediary's performance.

Example 3: A seller should not participate in a tripartite plan involving many sellers if the customers to whom the plan is offered must purchase the products of the other participating sellers before they are eligible to receive the benefits of the promotional program. The customer of any one seller should not be required to purchase or promote other sellers' products as a condition to receiving promotional payments or services from the seller, even though a tripartite program is involved.

(c) Intermediaries administering promotional assistance programs on behalf of a seller may violate Section 5 of the Federal Trade Commission Act if they have agreed to perform the seller's obligations under the law with respect to a program which they have represented to be usable and suitable for all the seller's competing customers if it should later develop that the program was not offered to all or, if offered, was not usable or suitable, or was otherwise administered in a discriminatory manner.

Example: Promoter A devises a program for in-store advertising of grocery products on shopping carts. No alternative means of participation are provided. Seller B enters into a contract with A for participation in the program. In fact, some of Seller B's competing customers do not have shopping carts. Assuming that Seller B is in violation of Section 2(d) of the Clayton Act, as amended, Promoter A may be in violation of Section 5 of the Federal Trade Commission Act for his participation in the program which resulted in B's violation. [Guide 14]

§ 240.14 Customer's liability.

Sections 2(d) and (e) apply only to sellers and not to customers. However, a customer who knows, or should know, that he is receiving payments or services which are not available on proportionally equal terms to his competitors engaged in the resale of the same seller's products, may be proceeded against by the Commission under Section 5 of the Federal Trade Commission Act, which prohibits unfair methods of competition.

Example 1: A customer should not receive advertising allowances for special promotion of the seller's products in connection with the customer's anniversary sale or new store opening, unless he has taken such affirmative steps as would satisfy a reasonable and prudent businessman that such allowances are affirmatively offered and otherwise made available by such seller on proportionally equal terms to all of its other customers competing with the customer in the distribution of the seller's products and that usable and suitable alternatives are offered them.

Example 2: A customer should not receive seller contributions to the cost of his institutional advertising, unless he has taken such affirmative steps as would satisfy a reasonable and prudent businessman that such allowances are affirmatively offered and otherwise made available by such seller on proportionally equal terms to all of its other customers competing with the customer in this distribution of the seller's products and that usable and suitable alternatives are offered them.

Example 3: A customer, an experienced buyer, is offered an allowance of 25% of his purchase volume by a seller for cooperative advertising to be paid for 100% by the seller. The customer knows, or should know, that most co-operative advertising programs in the industry allow payments of from 3 to 7% of purchases, and require 50–50 sharing by the seller and the customer. He would be on notice to inquire of the seller and to take such other affirmative steps as would satisfy a reasonable and prudent businessman that such allowances are affirmatively offered and otherwise made available by such seller on proportionally equal terms to all of its other customers competing with the customer in the distribution of the seller's products.

Example 4: A customer should not receive from a seller or intermediary services, such as those services performed in connection with a store opening, re-modeling or special sales promotion, etc., unless he has taken such affirmative steps as would satisfy a reasonable and prudent businessman that such services are affirmatively offered and otherwise made available by such seller on pro-portionally equal terms to all of its other customers competing with the cus-tomer in the distribution of the seller's products and that usable and suitable alternatives are offered them if the basic offer is not suitable for and usable by them.

Example 5: Frequently the employees of sellers or third parties such as brokers perform in-store services for their grocery retailer customers such as stocking of shelves, building of displays, and checking or rotating inventory. A customer operating a retail grocery business may not induce or receive such services when the customer knows or should know that such services are not available on proportionally equal terms to all of the other customers of the seller competing with him in the distribution of the seller's products.

Example 6: Where a customer has entered into a contract, understanding, or arrangement for the purchase of advertising with a newspaper or other advertising media which provides for a deferred rebate or other reduction in the price thereof, he should advise any seller from whom he claims reimbursement for such advertising that the claimed rate of reimbursement is subject to a deferred rebate or other reduction in price. In the event that any rebate or adjustment in the price is received, the customer should refund to the seller the amount of excess payment or allowance.

[Guide 15]

§ 240.15 Third party liability for double billing.

An advertising medium (newspaper, broadcast station, printer of catalogs, etc.) which (1) publishes a rate schedule containing fictitious rates or rates which are not reasonably expected to be applicable to a representative number of advertisers, or (2) furnishes a customer or his representative with an invoice that does not reflect the customer's actual net advertising cost, or that does not clearly state the discounts, rebates, earned rebates, etc., to which the invoice amount may be subject, or to which the invoiced party may be entitled, may violate Section 5 of the Federal Trade Commission Act if the customer uses such deceptive schedule or invoice for a claim for an advertising allowance, payment or credit greater than that to which he is entitled under the terms of the supplier's promotional program.

Example 1: Newspaper A has a "national" rate of $1.50 per inch and a "local" rate of $1.00 per inch. Retailer B places an advertisement with Newspaper A for a product sold to him by Supplier C, from whom he is later to seek reimbursement under Supplier C's cooperative advertising plan. Newspaper A should not furnish two bills to Retailer B, one at the "national" rate of $1.50 per inch, the other at the "local" rate of $1.00 per inch actually charged Retailer B.

Example 2: Newspaper A has various published rates. Retailer B is a large advertiser who in the past has earned the lowest rate. Newspaper A should not submit monthly invoices to Retailer B at a high rate agreed to by the parties unless the invoice discloses that Retailer B may receive a rebate.

Example 3: Radio Station A has a flat rate of $10 for 30-second spot announcements, subject to volume discounts ranging up to fifty per cent. Retailer B buys enough spots to qualify for the fifty per cent discount. Radio Station A should not furnish Retailer B with an invoice that does not show either the $5 net cost to Retailer B or the fifty per cent discount to which the $10 amount is subject.

Example 4: Advertising Agent A purchases a large volume of newspaper advertising space at a low, unpublished negotiated rate. Agent A subsequently sells such space to various retailers at a rate lower than each could purchase the space from the newspaper. Agent A should not furnish the retailers invoices showing a rate charge higher than that actually paid him by the retailers.

[Guide 16]

§ 240.16 Meeting competition.

A seller charged with discrimination in violation of Section 2(d) or Section 2(e) may defend his actions by showing that the payments were made or the services were furnished in good faith to meet equally high payments made by a competing seller to the particular customer, or to meet equivalent services furnished by a competing seller to the particular customer. This defense, however, is subject to important limitations. For instance, it is insufficient to defend a charge of violating either Section 2(d) or 2(e) solely on the basis that competition in a particular industry is very keen, requiring that special allowances must be given to some customers if a seller is "to be competitive."

[Guide 17]

§ 240.17 Cost justification.

It is no defense to a charge of unlawful discrimination in the payment of an allowance or the furnishing of a service for a seller to show that such payment, service, or facility could be justified through savings in the cost of manufacture, sale, or delivery.

[Effective date of the Guides: June 1, 1969, subject to further revision.]

DISSENTING STATEMENT OF COMMISSIONER ELMAN

The Commission's final Guides are complicated and confusing, and fail to provide reasonable and realistic guidelines for the business community. None of the serious deficiencies pointed out in my earlier statement dissenting from the proposed Guides has been corrected. The effect of the changes that have been made is unclear, and these changes may render the final Guides even more restrictive than the previous version.

For example, what is the statutory basis for distinguishing in Example 2 of Guide 3 between the retail members of retailer-owned cooperatives and the retailers affiliated with voluntary wholesale buying groups? What are the Commission's reasons for drawing this seemingly irrelevant distinction?

Similarly, how is a manufacturer to comply with the provision of revised Guide 8 requiring him to place on shipping containers or packages "that can reasonably be expected to come to the attention of the mangerial personnel of all retailing customers handling the promoted products" a description of the "essential features" of his offer? What is the statutory justification for imposing this requirement, which as a practical matter—as all segments of the grocery industry, large and small, have informed the Commission—simply cannot be complied with? The Grocery Manufacturers of America, National Association of Food Chains, National Association of Retail Grocers, and National Food Brokers Association, have filed a joint statement in which they explain that a manufacturer "cannot effectively control the flow of an individual product container between the time it leaves his plant or warehouse and the time . . . [it arrives at] its ultimate destination in the hands of some retailer somewhere in the United States." Grocery products promotions are of numerous, diverse types, have to be changed frequently in response to competitive conditions, and vary in duration and in the geographical area covered. Thus, "the 'essential features' of each such promotional arrangement cannot be memorialized on a shipping container or a product package in any practical manner that can insure that they are not misleading, inaccurate, or obsolete, by the time they reach the customer. . . ."

Instead of forthrightly admitting that it was wrong and that its proposed Guide 8 might "destroy the utility of the most economical and practical direct customer notification method in the grocery industry," the Commission has now encrusted Guide 8 with additional requirements and created new ambiguities. Whether the revisions are intended to make the Guide more or less flexible than before and what the practical effect of the revisions will be are unclear. To be sure the revised Guide seems to sanction as a third alternative in its complex hierarchial structure a less burdensome form of notice to be used only when "it is impractical to include the essential features." But what the Guide apparently gives, it immediately takes away. This theoretically less burdensome form of notice, which must include an enumeration of all the types of promotions offered and a statement warranting their practical utility to all retailers regardless of size, will not alone suffice but will almost always have to be supplemented with additional notices, including "trade journal publications, invoice notices, envelope stuffers for use by wholesalers, etc." The manufacturer acts at his peril—and the Commission offers him no guidance—in trying to design a notification procedure that will not only meet these requirements but will also be sure to receive the personal attention of each retailer's managerial personnel. The short of it is that the Commission apparently believes that a promotional allowance is not made available unless each retailer receives a hand-delivered engraved invitation (or continuing series of invitations) to accept promotional assistance from the manufacturer. It insults the framers of the Robinson-Patman Act to suggest that anything in the law as enacted by Congress requires such silliness.

The Commission has disregarded the Supreme Court's mandate to develop practical, realistic, and workable Guides implementing the decision in *Federal Trade Commission* v. *Fred Meyer, Inc.,* 390 U. S. 341 (1968). It is no service to the business community for the Commission to issue Guides which (a) do not provide reasonable guidance, (b) do not conform to the provisions of the statute, and (c) the Commission lacks the capacity to enforce.

SEPARATE STATEMENT OF COMMISSIONER MACINTYRE

In general, I agree with the Guides as finally revised. My position on the following points, however, should be clarified:

(1) The Guides could have been improved by remedying the Commission's previous failure to rule on the legality of advertising allowances conditioned on an agreement to feature certain prices. The Commission's dismissal without findings in the *General Electric* case [1] of charges involving precisely that issue have left this issue in a legal limbo, confusing to Commission staff and businessmen alike. Guide 9, relating to "Availability," would have been an appropriate vehicle to deal with that problem.

(2) Conflicting comments were filed on the issue of whether individual retail

---

[1] F.T.C. Docket No. 8487 (order dismissing complaint), Trade Reg. Rep. (1963–65 Transfer Binder), ¶ 16,817.

outlets belonging to cooperatives should be considered "customers" within the scope of Sections 2(d) and 2(e). There is merit to the suggestion that the Guides as previously drafted deprived many independent food retailers and others of the protection of those sections. Example 2, Guide 3, entitled "Who is a customer," laid down the general rule that "members of [a] cooperative are not customers of the manufacturer." This may deny such retailers the benefits of the Act and of the *Fred Meyer* decision. Consider, for example, the case where a cooperative warehouse management rejects a promotional program on the ground that it does not have sufficient value in terms of its general operations. Nevertheless, although a small-volume product in terms of the warehouse operation, it may be of considerable importance to some of the cooperative's members. Under Example 2, retailer members of a cooperative in that situation would not be entitled to such promotional assistance however desirous they were of participation and despite the fact that direct-buying competitors were securing benefits thereunder.

The redraft of Example 2 under Guide 3 has not cured this situation, and I would have eliminated the example entirely. At this time a general rule holding that members of retailer-owned cooperatives are not customers is neither necessary nor appropriate. The facts now available to the Commission do not justify such an all-inclusive holding. The determination of whether members of cooperatives are "customers" is a difficult problem involving complex legal and factual questions. In view of the wide diversity of cooperative organizations, the issue should be resolved on the pertinent facts bearing on the specific cooperative under consideration. It is not a question which readily lends itself to rulemaking.

(3) Finally, I wish to make it clear that I view the Guides as an expression of the Commission's attempt to provide guidance through practical methods to facilitate compliance with the law. That objective I have supported and it will continue to receive my full support. However, it should be pointed out that in thus assisting businessmen in their efforts to comply with the law the Commission has not undertaken to rewrite the law, as some apparently would have had the Commission do. For example, the law requires that advertising allowances or the furnishing of promotional services, if offered, shall be made available on proportionally equal terms to competing customers. No deviation from that standard is provided for in the law. In other words, Congress did not provide for the Commission to interpret that provision of the law under or in accordance with a "rule of reason." [2] As I have noted, it has gone to great lengths to advise businessmen concerning the utilization of practical methods by which they may comply with the law's requirements. This is what we seek, and what I support.

CONCURRING STATEMENT OF COMMISSIONER NICHOLSON

I previously filed a dissenting statement in connection with the issuance of the proposed Guides in which I noted my disagreement with the definition of a "customer" as set forth in Guide 3, but in which I also noted my general feeling that the Guides represented a constructive step forward in the reasonable

[2] See *Simplicity Pattern Co.* v. *Federal Trade Commission*, 360 U.S. 55 (1959).

interpretation of a difficult and complex statute. I remain much of the same mind as I here elect to file a concurring statement to the issuance of the final Guides.

I note that concurrence here because I believe the procedure we have followed is adapted to and has resulted in very nearly as informative set of Guides as could be evolved under the circumstances. On my motion, the proposed Guides were not made final at the time but were issued in proposed form in order to give all interested parties another opportunity to comment and make suggestions. The number and content of the comments received have resulted in several significant changes in the final Guides here issued, resulting, in the main, in a compilation of guidelines which are reasonable, pragmatic and, we hope, workable.

This is not to say that I cast my vote wholly free of reservations. All along I have entertained some doubts as to the detailed coverage which some of these provisions have given to practices perhaps best left to the individual judgment of the sellers concerned acting pursuant to more general guidance as to the results which they were expected to achieve. It is not entirely clear to me, for example, why we need spell out with such specificity how a seller is to get notice to his customers once we clearly inform him that such notice must be given. For my part, I care little whether he writes each of them a personal letter or shouts the glad tidings from his office window so long as they get the message. Thus I have some sympathy for some of the views expressed by the dissenter, though I cannot subscribe to his conclusions which fail to acknowledge the progress here made.

If we have erred too much on the side of detail, however, I would note that the procedure being followed contains another safeguard in the undertaking by the Commission to review the effectiveness and the adequacy of these Guides eighteen months after they become effective. It is my hope that when that re-examination takes place the Commission will have the benefit of the comments of those who have been governed by these Guides as well as the benefit of our own experience in enforcing them over that span of time. Commission Guides should at all costs avoid the deadening effect of rigidity and keep pace with changing market conditions and new distributional practices.

Appendix VII

Digests of
Selected FTC
Advisory Opinions

No. 10 Cooperative Advertising Allowances

A Federal Trade Commission advisory opinion informed a manufacturer that the requirements of Section 2(d) of the amended Clayton Act will be satisfied where the proposed advertising allowance program reflects that alternative methods of promotion are available to customers unable to use the preferred method of advertising in the regular course of their business.

As explained by the manufacturer, all of its customers will be offered advertising allowances equal to 1 per cent of net purchases to defray up to a maximum of 50 per cent of the actual cost of advertising its branded, first-quality products in any Advertising Checking Bureau, Inc. (ACB) daily and Sunday newspaper. Where a retailer is unable in a practical business sense to advertise in such newspaper, the program will provide him with adequate alternative methods of sales promotion such as, but not limited to, other newspapers, letter stuffers, or handbills as will enable him to earn the allowances specified. A retailer may use up to 30 per cent of his allowance in Christmas catalog advertising where the brand name or label is prominently mentioned, payment for which is based on catalog circulation. New accounts and those with which the manufacturer has had less than one year's experience will be offered the same allowance, payment for which will be computed on the basis of purchases for the first full quarter year. All accounts will be notified of the program by first-class mail, by the manufacturer's sales representatives, and by notices accompanying invoices.

December 9, 1965

374

No. 13 Discount Buying Membership Organization

A Federal Trade Commission advisory opinion informed a promoter that there were no actionable trade restraints inherent in his proposed plan.

As explained by the promoter, the plan involved the formation of a membership organization. Membership, available at an annual fee to the general public without restriction, confers the right to purchase at a stated discount from the prevailing prices of retail merchants. Local retailers can participate in the plan without restriction.

The commission pointed out that its approval was limited to the proposed plan itself and no views were expressed as to the plan's implementation. Without imputing any lack of good faith to the requesting party, the commission noted that if, for example, members of the purchasing public were misled or deceived, or could be misled or deceived, as to benefits available under the plan, such result might be actionable.

February 1, 1966

No. 23 Establishment of Buying Corporation by Broker

An advisory opinion rendered by the FTC notified a broker-distributor of fresh fruits and vegetables that either of his proposed alternative plans to establish a buying corporation would involve grave risk of illegality.

The businessman had inquired whether or not under the Perishable Agricultural Commodities Act and FTC law he might lawfully (1) establish a corporation as an exclusive buying company for a purchaser for resale, this corporation to buy and be billed in its own name. The purchaser for resale would own one or more shares of the common stock of the buying company and would participate in the brokerage received by that company, or (2) establish a corporation as described for the purposes described here, the difference being that shippers would directly invoice and be paid by the purchaser for resale rather than the proposed corporation.

The Commission advised him that it had no comment on the Perishable Agricultural Commodities Act because it does not administer this law. The advisory opinion continued:

> The immediately applicable statute is, as you know, Section 2(c) of the Clayton Act, as amended by the Robinson-Patman Act, which makes unlawful the payment or receipt of brokerage or allowances in lieu thereof in certain commercial contexts.
>
> In the Commission's view, either of the plans you propose, if adopted, would carry with them grave risk that the statute will be violated.
>
> Absent any indication to the contrary, they appear to amount merely to a means whereby both the letter and the spirit of the statute are to be avoided.

April 1, 1966

No. 24 Tripartite Promotional Assistance Program

An advisory opinion by the FTC informed a company of the "very serious possibility" that a proposed promotional plan would subject participating food-supplier advertisers to a charge of law violation.

The plan involved the distribution of reprints of advertisements to the public through retail food stores, the cost of the reprints to be shared by participating suppliers. No mention would be made of any specific retailer in the advertising and ten million reprints would be offered at no cost. Each retailer would receive the number requested provided the total ordered did not exceed this available supply. If the orders exceeded ten million, this number would be divided by the total number of checkstands in stores requesting copies to determine how many each store would receive.

> It appears, the FTC's advisory opinion stated: . . . that no problem would arise under the laws administered by this Commission unless and until the requests for reprints exceed the available supply of 10,000,000. In such event, it is doubtful that the basis chosen for distribution of the reprints among competing retailers would result in the proportional equality required by the law [Section 2(e) of the Robinson-Patman Act]. While the Act does not specify any single standard for proportionalizing merchandising services and facilities, it does not appear that the required result will be achieved when the standard selected is the number of checkstands in the stores requesting copies. This standard bears no ascertainable relation to the volume of business which any of the retailers involved might conduct with any of the participating suppliers. In fact, it could result in a situation in which retailers who have a small volume with the participating suppliers would receive more reprints than competing retailers with a much larger volume solely because of a greater number of checkstands. We cannot conclude then that the plan as it is presently proposed would necessarily result in the proportionally equal treatment of all competing customers that the law requires. Consequently, there is a very serious possibility that it would subject the participating suppliers to a charge of violation of Section 2(e) of the Robinson-Patman Act.

April 1, 1966

(NOTE: The commission subsequently modified this opinion to require the promoter to make it clear to each supplier and each retailer that even though an intermediary is employed in the plan, it remains the supplier's responsibility to take all reasonable steps so that each of the supplier's customers, who compete with one another in reselling his products, is offered either an opportunity to participate in the promotional assistance plan on proportionally equal terms, or a suitable alternative if the customer is unable as a practical matter to participate in the plan. If not, the supplier, the retailer, and the promoter participating in the plan may be acting in violation of Section 2(d) or (e) of the Clayton Act and/or Section 5 of the Federal Trade Commission Act.)

July 11, 1968

No. 62 Tripartite Promotional Assistance Program

The landlord of an exhibition building has been advised by the FTC that a proposed promotional plan in which suppliers and a grocery chain would lease exhibition display space with the chain also providing in-store promotion of suppliers' displayed products would probably result in violation of commission-administered statutes.

According to the proposed plan, part of the exhibit in the building would be displays provided and maintained by manufacturers, processors, and distributors of food products and grocery store items. These exhibitors—the suppliers—may give away samples, take orders for off-premise delivery, and sell at retail. The grocery chain's contract with the landlord would provide that the chain would conduct one-week, chain-wide, in-store promotions of the exhibitors' products; that exhibitors may be required to furnish the chain with materials for the promotion; that the landlord and the chain would cooperate in setting up the exhibitors' displays; and that the chain would have the right to approve only exhibitors whose products are sold in its stores.

The commission advised the landlord that implementation of the plan probably would result in violation of Sections 2(d) and (e) of the Robinson-Patman amendment to the Clayton Act and Section 5 of the FTC Act unless promotional payments or services were made available to the exhibitor-suppliers' competing customers on proportionally equal terms.

The 2(d) and (e) aspects, the commission said, stem from the fact that exhibitor-suppliers would be vulnerable to a charge that they were illegally discriminating between their customers in according promotional benefits. The Section 5 aspects involve questions as to whether the chain and the landlord would be inducing a violation of Section 2(d) by participating exhibitor-suppliers.

June 21, 1966

No. 94 Tripartite Promotional Assistance Program

The commission issued an advisory opinion regarding the obligations of a supplier in offering alternatives to his basic plan for providing promotional assistance to his competing retailer-customers by placing advertisements on shopping carts.

The requesting party, a promoter, had a basic promotional assistance plan that some competing retailer-customers of suppliers participating in the plan were functionally unable to use because the retailer-customers did not have or use shopping carts. The plan provided that such competing retailer-customers were to be offered a reasonably usable alternative way of obtaining the proportionally equal assistance to which they are entitled under the provisions of Sections 2(d) and (e) of the Robinson-Patman amendment to the Clayton Act.

The question presented was whether a retailer-customer, whose business operation was such that he was functionally able to use and benefit from the basic (shopping cart) plan could demand the alternative form of assistance, if he so desired.

In its opinion, the commission stated that whether a supplier's promotional assistance plans are reasonable and nondiscriminatory in their application is essentially a question of fact. The commission held that if the retailer-customer was able, in fact, to use and benefit from the basic plan offered, but rejected same, the supplier need not offer such retailer-customer the alternative plan. The commission pointed out that the burden of proof on this issue of fact as it may arise in particular cases will rest upon the supplier. The commission added that if a competing retailer-customer is unable to use the basic plan, because of the nature of his business operation, he must be offered an alternative plan. However, if he rejects the alternative plan for reasons of his own and said plan could be reasonably used to his benefit, then, the supplier would incur no liability for declining to offer another alternative.

October 18, 1966

(NOTE: This advisory opinion is subject to the same modification reported previously under Advisory Opinion Digest No. 24.)

No. 106 Tripartite Promotional Assistance Program

The commission announced it could not give its approval to a three-party promotional plan, which involved the placing of a film projector in grocery stores to advertise certain food products, because it contained two provisions that would probably be in violation of the law.

According to the terms of the proposed plan, which were submitted by a third-party promoter, the entire cost of the plan would be borne by participating food suppliers. Each retailer who participates in the plan will be paid on a sliding scale for the space occupied by the film projector, depending on the amount of floor space in the entire store. The reason advanced for the basing of payments on floor space is that, over all, larger stores will attract more customers and hence more viewers of the projected ads.

In order to induce customers to look at the projected ads, each person entering the store will be given a card containing a number that, if it turns out to be a lucky number, entitles the holder to a prize regardless of whether the holder makes a purchase in the store. However, if the holder of the lucky number has in his shopping cart one or more of the products advertised on the film projector, he will receive a bonus prize on occasion in addition to the regular prize.

In its opinion the commission said that Sections 2(d) and (e) of the Robinson-Patman Act

> require a supplier to treat all of his competing customers on a nondiscriminatory basis, which means that if the supplier furnishes promotional assistance to one customer he must make that assistance available on proportionately equal terms to all competing customers. The courts have also held that the supplier must comply with these provisions of the law irrespective of whether the promotional assistance is furnished to the retailer directly or through an intermediary.

Commenting on specific features of the plan, the commission said that it contained two features that would probably violate the law.

First, the Commission is of the opinion that the standard of payment to retailers, which you contemplate basing upon floor space, does not meet the statutory standard of "proportionally equal terms" as required by Sections 2(d) and (e) of the Robinson-Patman Act. The proposed standard bears no ascertainable relation to the volume of business which any of the retailers involved might conduct with any of the participating suppliers. Moreover, the proposed standard could result in a situation in which retailers who have a small volume with the participating suppliers would receive more than competing retailers with a much larger volume solely because of larger floor space.

Second, the Commission is of the opinion that the feature of the plan which induces customers to view the projected ads constitutes the sale of merchandise by means of a lottery or by means of a chance or gaming device contrary to public policy and the provisions of Sec. 5 of the FTC Act.

The Commission's opinion also pointed out that, if the plan is revised so as to eliminate the two foregoing objections, it would still be necessary for the following four conditions to be met: First, all competing retailers must be notified of their right to participate in the plan on a nondiscriminatory basis. Secondly, it must be made available to all competing retailers within a given marketing area and to those who, geographically, are on the periphery of that area if they in fact compete with the favored retailers. Thirdly, it must be made available to all retailers who compete in the resale of the supplier's product, irrespective of their functional classification. Therefore, if the items involved in the plan are also sold by nongrocery stores, they must be accorded the same opportunity to participate in any promotional assistance given by the suppliers to competing grocery outlets. Fourthly, an alternative plan on proportionally equal terms must be offered to those retailers who, for practical business reasons, find the film projector not to be usable and suitable.

January 7, 1967

(NOTE: Modified as per Advisory Opinion Digest No. 24.)

No. 111 Functional Discounts

The Commission advised that the 14 per cent discount that would be offered under the proposed plan probably would result in violation of commission-administered law.

At present, the manufacturer sells his product to manufacturers of a complementary product exclusively. The purchasing manufacturers resell the product to independent distributors and to ultimate consumers.

The selling manufacturer proposes to sell to independent distributors directly, charging them approximately 14 per cent more than the purchasing manufacturers would be charged on shipments to the warehouses of the latter. On drop-shipments to purchasers buying through the purchasing manufacturers, the manufacturers would be charged the independent distributors' price. On drop shipments to consumers of the product, the independent distributors' price would be charged. Drop-shipments could be ordered by any customer and would be openly available to all on the same terms.

There would be no agreement between purchasing manufacturers or distributors and the manufacturers as to prices the former would charge; however, the manufacturer does now suggest and would continue to suggest prices to be charged consumers. No other form of control over resale of the product is now or would be exercised by the manufacturer.

The commission pointed out that the price difference that would result from the proposed discount is within the purview of Section 2(a) of the Robinson-Patman amendment to the Clayton Act. Section 2(a) provides, in essence, that it is unlawful for a seller in commerce to discriminate between different purchasers of goods of like grade and quality where the effect may be substantially to lessen competition or to tend to create a monopoly.

The commission added that the 14 per cent discount to be offered to purchasing manufacturers is a functional discount. Such discounts, furthermore, are not prohibited by the applicable law or judicial interpretations thereof unless the discounts result in the adverse competitive effects the law proscribes. The commission was of the view that such adverse effects were likely to result from the fact that purchasing manufacturers would compete against distributors in selling to ultimate consumers and the manufacturers would enjoy a 14 per cent price advantage on such sales. The commission pointed out that unless the 14 per cent only made due allowance for differences in the cost of manufacture, sale, or delivery, resulting from the differing methods or quantities in which the tile cement would be sold or delivered to the manufacturers—substantial anticompetitive effects probably would result from implementation of the plan. Such a result would be violative of Section 2(a) of the Robinson-Patman amendment to the Clayton Act.

February 2, 1967

No. 132 Giving of Free Merchandise to Obtain New Customers

The commission was requested to render an advisory opinion with respect to the legality of a proposal by a seller to give free merchandise in order to obtain new customers among retail food outlets not presently selling the products of the seller. According to information supplied by the requesting party, such offers are often introductory in nature, and are used by manufacturers to acquire new customers or to introduce new products. Only one free case of goods is given and the offers are generally not repeated.

Under the proposal, for each such outlet, which has from one to six check-outs—both inclusive—the seller will give one free case of each product that is purchased by or for sale through such an outlet. The requisite purchase must be in case lots. For each such outlet that has seven or more check-outs, the seller will give two free cases of each product that is purchased by or for sale through such an outlet and the requisite purchase again must be in case lots. For the purpose of this offer, the term *check-outs* means cash registers or other places in the outlet at which customers regularly pay for food purchases made in said outlet.

The commission advised that it was of the opinion that where a seller gives his customers free merchandise without expecting any promotional performance in return, he has in effect and in law granted a reduction in price to the extent of the value of the free merchandise. This being so, the practice would be governed by the provisions of Section 2(a) of the Clayton Act, as amended by the Robinson-Patman Act, which, in brief, provides that it shall be unlawful for a seller to discriminate in price between different purchasers of goods of like grade and quality where the effect may be to substantially lessen competition and where none of the defenses afforded by the act are present. Thus, the seller was advised that it could give free merchandise under these circumstances to the same extent and in the same amounts as it could grant lower prices to the recipients thereof.

Considering the nature of the statute involved, the commission went on to advise that it was difficult to rule categorically with respect to any particular proposal in the context of an advisory opinion. This is especially true when it comes to measuring in a prospective manner the competitive effects of a proposal that has not yet been placed into effect. Despite the presence of these unknown factors, the commission did feel that it could offer certain comments of a cautionary nature that might prove helpful to the seller in determining whether or not to embark upon this program.

Under the formula that the seller proposed to use for determining the amount of free goods to be given each customer—namely, one free case for each outlet with up to six check-outs and two free cases for each outlet with more than six—it appeared unlikely to the commission that any of the defenses made available by the act could be established. The only ones that would seem to have any possible application to this situation would be good faith meeting of competition and cost justification. The very statement of facts seemed to negate any question of meeting competition, for the seller obviously would not be reacting to any competitive situation, but would instead be motivated solely by its own marketing purposes.

Additionally, it was difficult for the commission to visualize how these offers could be cost justified, because cost factors obviously do not enter into the determination of the amount of free goods to be given. Quite the contrary, the amount is to be determined solely by the number of check-outs per outlet that the purchasers operate, without regard to quantities ordered or differences in the cost of manufacture, sale, or delivery.

If the offer is made to obtain new customers, the commission felt that price discriminations could result as between new customers who would receive varying amounts of free goods depending on the number of outlets they operate, or between any given new customers and competing old customers who would receive nothing under the proposal. Even if the offers were made to all customers for the purpose of introducing a new product, price discriminations could result because of the varying amounts of free goods depending on the number of outlets they operate. The question of whether such price differentials would have the probability of anticompetitive effect requisite to a finding of illegality under the statute would depend on the specific circumstances of the individual case. This determination cannot be made with certainty at this time. In view of the possibility of a violation of Section 2(a) of the Clayton Act as amended by the Robinson-Patman Act, the commission is unable to give its approval to this plan.

June 27, 1967

No. 143 Promotional Allowances

In an advisory opinion, the commission ruled that a fabric supplier who makes advertising allowances available to one or more resellers of a finished product, irrespective of the fact that an intermediary performs work on the raw material that transforms it into the finished product, thereby adopts those resellers of the finished product as his customers and must comply with Section 2(d) of the Robinson-Patman Act.

Commenting further on the customer relationship, the commission said:

> We think Congress clearly intended to ban discriminations in the form of advertising allowances, regardless of the fact that intermediaries might be interposed, where the grantor deliberately contacts hundreds of retailers directly with the purpose of expending thousands of dollars for advertising purposes. Thus where a supplier initiates such a promotional plan with retailers and has primary, if not the sole, responsibility over the control and administration of the plan, we think the customer relationship has been established and the plan must be tested in the light of the requirements of Sec. 2(d) of the Act.

Under the terms of the proposed plan, the fabric supplier would pay 50 per cent of retailers' advertising costs if the retailer sells and advertises wearing apparel manufactured from a certain line of fabric, up to a total cost of 1,200 lines published in ACB newspapers. Retailers who use non-ACB-rated newspapers, radio, television, handbills, or mail stuffers will be paid an equivalent measurable cost. The plan will be made available to all retailers located in selected trading areas of all wearing apparel manufacturers who purchase and produce the finished product from the fabric in question. Only dealers who purchase apparel at regular wholesale prices will be eligible to participate.

In its opinion, the commission concluded that the plan complies with Section 2(d) of the Robinson-Patman Act with two reservations. In commenting on the first reservation, the commission said:

> The statute requires one who gives advertising allowances to make those payments available to all competing customers. Availability means that the grantor of the allowance must notify all competing customers of their right to participate in the plan. Thus the provision of the plan which requires a retailer located just outside one of the selected areas to show that he competes with one or more of the favored retailers in order to have the offer made available to him would appear to shift the responsibility of notification required under the statute. For this reason, the Commission cannot approve this particular provision of the plan should it result in discrimination against retailers located on the periphery of the selected trading areas.

With respect to its second reservation, the commission said that its opinion should not be construed as implying approval of the phrase "at regular wholesale prices" if the practical effect of that language is to procure resale price maintenance.

September 12, 1967

No. 145 Aggregation of Purchases for Discount Purposes

The commission rendered an advisory opinion in which it concluded that it would not be permissible under Section 2(a) of the amended Clayton Act to aggregate the purchases of three centrally owned retail grocery stores for the purpose of cost justifying a lower price to those stores.

"The reason for this," the commission said, "is that discounts to multi-unit purchasers must be cost justified on a store-by-store basis where, as here, each store orders separately, receives separate delivery and is invoiced separately."

Concluding its opinion, the commission said:

> Since independent and singly owned retail stores are served in identically the same manner, it would confer an advantage on the multi-unit store, not by virtue of any savings in cost to the store but solely by reason of its membership in the centrally owned organization. Combining or aggregating purchases, therefore, for the purpose of determining costs of a multi-unit organization is not related to the realities of the market since the independent or singly owned store competes with the individual stores of the chain organization.

The particular facts in the advisory opinion involved three centrally owned retail grocery stores. Each store placed separate orders with the wholesaler, had its goods delivered separately, and was invoiced separately. In addition, some singly owned stores bought in larger volume than the smallest store belonging to the centrally owned organization.

October 17, 1967

No. 147 "Back-Haul" Allowances

The commission rendered an advisory opinion advising a manufacturer of food products that it would probably be illegal to grant so-called back-haul allowances to customers who pick up their own purchases at the manufacturer's warehouses.

The manufacturer in question presently sells its products on a delivered-price basis with bracket pricing and does not permit customers to pick up products at warehouses or plants. Customers with trucks returning empty to their warehouses along routes near the manufacturer's warehouses and plants are now demanding the opportunity to pick up products and to earn an allowance by so doing. Consequently, the manufacturer proposed to institute a program whereunder customers would be permitted to pick up products and be paid an allowance equal to the amount the manufacturer would otherwise have to pay a common carrier to deliver to the customer.

The commission advised that the proposal was governed by the provisions of Section 2(a) of the Clayton Act, as amended by the Robinson-Patman Act, which, in brief, provides that it shall be unlawful for a seller to discriminate in price between different purchasers of goods of like grade and quality where the effect may be substantially to lessen competition or to create a monopoly and where none of the defenses afforded by the act is present. Considered in the light of this statute, the commission concluded that, assuming the presence of all other elements necessary to a determination of a violation of the statute, the implementation of this proposal would probably result in a violation of the law. This result seemed to the commission necessarily to flow from the use of a delivered-price system, for in such a case the freight factor included within the price is not the actual freight to any given point, but an average of the freight costs for all customers within the zone wherein the delivered price is quoted, or, at least, a figure determined by some formula apart from actual costs. If one customer is then given a back-haul allowance for the actual freight saved, the opinion advised that a serious possibility of discrimination would exist in any delivered-price system; it is highly doubtful that the defense of cost justification, at least, would be available.

Although this conclusion may seem unreasonable from one point of view —because the allowance would be for no more than the actual freight saved— it seemed to the commission to be a necessary result of using a delivered-price system. Whenever such a seller departs from his delivered prices for the benefit of one customer, he leaves himself open to a charge of discriminating against his other competing customers who order in the same quantities and hence fall within the same pricing bracket because he failed to make allowances for the individual cost factors present in their situations. The law does not require that a seller pass on his cost savings to his customers, the commission stated, but where he elects to do so in one instance, it does require that he not discriminate between his purchasers where such discrimination has the proscribed adverse effect on competition.

Commissioner Elman did not concur.

October 24, 1967

No. 155 Varying Discount Pricing Schedule—Distributor Recruitment Through Grant of Override Bonuses

The FTC advised a manufacturer of household products that his proposed varying discount price schedule and his proposed granting of bonus payments to recruiting distributors on the business of distributors whom they recruit would, under the facts presented, in all probability result in violation of both Section 2(a) of the amended Clayton Act and Section 5 of the Federal Trade Commission Act.

The manufacturer proposed to appoint as independent distributors such persons as would buy the requisite amount of inventory. Initial sales to such distributors would be at 33⅓ per cent off the manufacturer's suggested price for his products. Incentive bonuses, computed at from 5 to 60 per cent of the value of their purchases, increasing as the value of purchases increased, would be paid from time to time to the distributors. Distributors would be encouraged to recruit additional distributors who would also make a capital investment in inventory. A recruiting distributor would be given a 10 to 12 per cent override on the dollar volume of purchases of any distributor whom he had recruited.

The commission noted that because of the nature of the plan it was almost inevitable that very wide differences in prices would be charged customers, some of whom would, by reasonable assumption, be competitive with others. These differences would be so great that the anticompetitive effects made unlawful by the amended Clayton Act would almost certainly follow.

In addition, it is clear from the facts presented that the requesting party contemplates that the so-called independent distributors would be for the most part selling at retail. The marketing plan is not primarily designed as an offer to knowledgeable businessmen, competent to weigh and evaluate commercial risks. It is designed, rather, to appeal to uninformed members of the general public, unaware of and unadvised of the true nature of the risks run—persons with limited capital who are led to part with that capital by promise and hopes that are seldom, if ever, fulfilled. A particular vice of the plan is that part providing override bonuses for recruited distributors. Implicit in such an arrangement is the promise, rarely if ever kept, that the recruiting distributor can, without himself working, profit greatly from the work of others.

December 29, 1967

No. 157 Advertising Allowance to Customers in Selected Trade Area

The commission rendered an advisory opinion in which it advised a manufacturer of a household product that it would be permissible to pay advertising allowances to all customers in a limited trading area without offering the allowance to all of its customers.

In its opinion, the commission said that it was a well-settled principle of law that if a supplier offers advertising allowances to one customer, he is required by Section 2(d) of the Robinson-Patman Act to make those allowances available to those customers who compete in the distribution of the product for which an allowance is being paid. Under these circumstances, it follows that the supplier can limit the area in which the promotional allowance will be paid, as long as the allowance is made available on proportionally equal terms to all customers who compete in the distribution of the product being promoted.

"This means," the commission concluded, "that if there are customers located on the periphery of the selected trade area who in fact compete with the favored customers, they must also have the opportunity of participating in the promotional program on proportionally equal terms." Concluding its opinion, the Commission said, "Assuming that you selected a reasonable trading area, even though limited, and assuming that you confine the duration of the program within the strict time limits absolutely necessary for you to determine the efficacy or feasibility of the program, we do not believe that your action will run afoul of any law administered by this Commission."

January 4, 1968

No. 194 Uniform Pricing System Effected by Deducting Freight Allowances

The commission advised a West Coast manufacturer of industrial parts that it would not be illegal to use either a conventional, uniform delivered-price system based on average cost factors or a uniform delivered-price system that would be effected by granting so-called freight allowances to be deducted from the manufacturer's f.o.b. factory price.

The facts with respect to the second alternative were that the manufacturer proposed to establish an f.o.b. factory price of, for purposes of illustration, $99.50. Actual freight to West Coast customers may be 50 cents, and such customers would receive no allowance. Thus, they would pay the manufacturer $99.50 and the carrier 50 cents making a total of $100. Then, again using hypothetical figures for purposes of illustration, actual freight to a Denver customer may be $1. The manufacturer would grant such a customer a 50-cent freight allowance to be deducted from the f.o.b. price, thus leaving the customer paying the manufacturer a price of $99 and the carrier $1, making a total of $100. Continuing east, actual freight to a Kansas City customer may be $1.50. The freight allowance would be $1, leaving the customer paying the manufacturer $98.50 and the carrier $1.50, for a total again of $100. This would continue in graduated steps across the country to where an East Coast customer with actual freight costs of $3 would receive an allowance of $2.50 leaving him also paying a total of $100. The manufacturer advised that it was considering this alternative for administrative reasons, because it wished to pass title to the customers on delivery to the carrier and have the customers handle all freight bills.

With respect to the first question, the commission advised that it was of the view that there could be no question of the manufacturer's right to unilaterally employ a uniform delivered-price system, because if each buyer pays the same delivered price no question under the Clayton Act, as amended by the Robinson-Patman Act, would arise. Although the factual situation under the second alternative is somewhat more complicated, the commission was, furthermore, of the view that it also would not result in a violation of law if implemented exactly as outlined here. In the commission's view, the difference between the two systems is one of form rather than of substance. That it would make no legal difference whether the manufacturer computes its factory price and adds to it an amount equal to the average freight costs for delivering to all customers, as is done in the usual uniform delivered-price system, or whether it accomplishes the same result by deducting an amount from the factory price, which would have the effect of leaving each buyer paying an amount roughly equal to the same freight factor. In either event, it would seem that the manufacturer would have made freight a part of the price, so that each buyer's out-of-pocket costs would be exactly the same.

The commission further cautioned, however, that because this opinion deals in a projected manner with hypothetical figures chosen for illustrative purposes, the computations later to be made based on actual cost factors must in practice achieve the result claimed in that each buyer will pay exactly the same net price including the freight. Any other result, the commission stated, would be outside the scope of this opinion.

February 24, 1968

No. 261 Promotional Allowances

The commission was requested to render an advisory opinion with respect to the legality of a supplier's proposed promotional program under an outstanding Commission order that, in pertinent part, prohibits the supplier from making promotional payments to its customers in a discriminatory manner. According to information provided by the supplier, all its sales are made to retailer customers—distributors or other intermediaries are not utilized in the distribution of the supplier's products.

Under the proposed program as set forth and explained by the supplier, promotional allowances would be made available to all customers of the supplier. They could be applied by the customers to the costs incurred by them in three categories of advertising and promotional activity: point-of-sale materials; cooperative advertising in daily and Sunday newspapers listed in Standard Rate and Data; and so-called other store promotions, including advertising in newspapers not listed in Standard Rate and Data, catalog and local radio and TV advertising, envelope stuffers, and sales incentive programs and contests.

Furthermore, the amounts of such allowances would be determined at the rate of 7 per cent of each participating customer's net purchases from the supplier in a six-month period, although this figure could be adjusted within any given trading area (defined by Management Survey of Metropolitan County Areas) as operating experience requires. In the case of Standard Rate and Data newspapers, the allowances could be applied to two thirds the cost of such advertising, and for all other forms of eligible advertising and promotional activity, allowances could be applied to the full cost of the activity. In all cases, and whether any customer chooses to participate in any or all of said categories of advertising and promotional activity, the supplier's total contribution to the customer's costs would be subject to the 7 per cent of purchases limit. Allowances earned but not used by any customer in a six-month period could not be carried forward to the following such period.

Regarding the point-of-sale materials, the supplier would mail or deliver quantities of these materials to all customers, and each customer would be advised in advance that such point-of-sale materials would be charged against his available promotional and advertising allowances, unless returned to the supplier within ten days of receipt by mail or delivery to the supplier's salesman.

The supplier was advised that the proposed promotional program if implemented, in a nondiscriminatory manner, would not be in violation of the commission's order or Section 2(d) of the Clayton Act.

The commission cautioned that its opinion was predicated upon the supplier's assurance that all provisions of the proposed program, particularly that concerning the availability of cooperative advertising allowances for advertising in non-Standard Rate and Data newspapers—providing only that such newspapers have verifiable costs and circulation, and that concerning the return privilege regarding point-of-sale materials that would be mailed or delivered to the supplier's customers—would be effectively communicated to all customers of the supplier.

The commission further cautioned that a customer who is located on the periphery of a particular trading area, and who competes in fact with a customer located within such trading area, should be offered the particular promotional plan available to the customer within the trading area so as to preclude discrimination between customers competing in the resale of the supplier's products.

July 2, 1968

No. 263 Lower Price to "Stocking" Dealers

The commission rendered an advisory opinion in which it said that it could not give its approval to a plan whereby manufacturers would give a lower price to stocking dealers who compete with nonstocking dealers. The opinion was given to a trade association that represents manufacturers of a household product.

As justification for the variance in the proposed pricing schedules, the association pointed out that stocking dealers experience a higher cost of doing business and therefore must sell at higher prices than their competing nonstocking dealers. It was also contended that such a price differential would stimulate the purchase of the product in question for inventory.

Expressing the view that it could not give its approval to such two-price schedules if the stocking and nonstocking dealers compete and if the pricing differentials are of sufficient magnitude to adversely affect competition, the commission concluded that the proposed plan could result in illegal price discrimination under Section 2(a) of the Clayton Act, as amended. In its opinion, the commission went on to point out that such price differences would be illegal unless they could be justified on the basis of one of the specific defenses provided in Sections 2(a) and (b) of the statute.

The Commission said:

> For example, the law permits price differences which can be justified by provable cost differences in the manufacture, sale or delivery of such products resulting from the differing methods or quantities in which the products are sold or delivered. Accordingly, Section 2(a) does not preclude prices reflecting less costly and, therefore, more efficient methods of distribution provided that the standards inherent in the statute's cost justification proviso are met.

Although the party seeking the advisory opinion did not raise the question, the commission's opinion touched on another point of interest in this type of a situation. Specifically, the Commission said:

> it is conceivable that certain members may wish to compensate their customers for services which the customers may render for them in connection with the handling or resale of products manufactured by such members. The law provides a means by which this may be done, but if it is done, the manufacturer must comply with the requirements of Section 2(d) of the Act. This requirement is simply that compensation for such services, if made by a manufacturer to one customer, must be made available on proportionally equal terms to other customers of that manufacturer who compete with the favored customer in the sale of the manufacturer's products. This means, among other things, that any plan or program, under which the payments are made must, if necessary, provide for alternative services or facilities which, as a practical matter, can be provided by all competing customers.

Concluding its opinion, the commission cautioned as follows:

It should be noted, however, that payments by manufacturers to their customers "to stimulate the purchase of their goods for inventory," are not payments of the type contemplated by Section 2(d). Such a payment would merely be a reduction in price to induce the purchase of the manufacturer's goods and, if given to some but not all of the manufacturer's customers, might be unlawful price discrimination within the meaning of Section 2(a).

Commissioners Elman and Nicholson dissented from that part of the advisory opinion relating to discounts for stocking dealers.

July 9, 1968

No. 269 Pooling of Allowances for Purposes of Joint Advertising

The commission was requested to render an advisory opinion concerning the legality of a proposal by a group of independent retailers to pool the advertising allowances due the members for purposes of joint advertising.

Under the proposal, all money earned by the members under the suppliers' cooperative advertising programs would be assigned to the group in a collective advertising effort for the suppliers. Each supplier would receive, on the cases of the amount of money earned from him by all members of the group, radio advertising through the medium of three-minute programs, each of which would have one minute of time available for the suppliers' commercial messages. The content of the one-minute commercial would be governed by the suppliers themselves and would not be connected in any way with the retailers' advertising.

As part of the proposal, for each program a supplier receives, the retailers would receive broadcast time on the same stations for their message. That would be institutional in nature and would extol the advantages of dealing with independent retailers. Under this type of advertising program, it would not be possible to mention individual dealers, nor would prices be mentioned in such advertising.

The opinion advised that the commission could see no objection to the proposal on the understanding that the fund used by or on behalf of the participating group to purchase advertising space will consist only of the aggregate of advertising allowances properly available to the members individually under the terms of Section 2(d) of the Clayton Act, as amended by the Robinson-Patman Act. In brief, that section prohibits the payment by sellers of allowances to some customers that are not made available on proportionally equal terms to all competing customers. In this connection, the opinion further advised that it would be unlawful if the combined power of the group was used to induce from the suppliers allowances greater than those to which the individual members were entitled under this section.

July 17, 1968

Index